THE ARCTIC
p 139

GERMANY &
THE ALPINE STATES
pp 76-77

THE LOW
COUNTRIES
pp 68-69

land
67

NORTHERN EUROPE
pp 66-67

RUSSIA & KAZAKHSTAN
pp 94-95

HE BRITISH
ISLES
pp 70-71

CENTRAL
EUROPE
pp 80-81

EUROPEAN RUSSIA
pp 86-87

EUROPE
pp 62-89

ASIA
pp 90-109

FRANCE
pp 72-73

EASTERN
EUROPE
pp 84-85

ITALY
pp 78-79

SOUTHEAST
EUROPE
pp 82-83

TURKEY &
THE CAUCASUS
pp 96-97

CENTRAL
ASIA
pp 100-101

EAST
ASIA
pp 104-105

JAPAN &
KOREA
pp 102-103

SPAIN &
PORTUGAL
pp 74-75

Malta
p 88

THE
MEDITERRANEAN
pp 88-89

Cyprus
p 88

Israel
p 99

SOUTHWEST
ASIA
pp 98-99

Ryukyu
Islands
p 105

PACIFIC

OCEAN

NORTH AFRICA
pp 122-123

SOUTH
ASIA
pp 106-107

WEST AFRICA
pp 124-125

EAST
AFRICA
pp 126-127

Andaman
& Nicobar
Islands
p 107

SOUTHEAST
ASIA
pp 108-109

AFRICA
pp 118-129

SOUTHWEST
PACIFIC
pp 136-137

AUSTRALASIA
& OCEANIA
pp 130-137

Samoa
p 136

SOUTHERN
AFRICA
pp 128-129

INDIAN

OCEAN

AUSTRALIA
pp 132-133

NEW ZEALAND
pp 134-135

ANTARCTICA
p 138

# student
# ATLAS

DK PUBLISHING, INC.
LONDON • NEW YORK • MUNICH • MELBOURNE • DELHI
www.dk.com

A DORLING KINDERSLEY BOOK
www.dk.com

EDUCATIONAL CONSULTANTS
Dr. David Lambert, Institute of Education, University of London, David R Wright, BA MA

TEACHER REVIEWERS
US: Ramani DeAlwis; UK: Kevin Ball, Pat Barber, Stewart Marson

DORLING KINDERSLEY CARTOGRAPHY

MANAGING EDITOR
Lisa Thomas

MANAGING ART EDITOR
Philip Lord

PROJECT EDITORS
Debra Clapson, Wim Jenkins, Jill Hamilton (US)

PROJECT DESIGNERS
Rhonda Fisher, Karen Gregory

EDITORIAL CONTRIBUTORS
Thomas Heath, Kevin McRae, Constance Novis,
Iris Rossoff (US), Siobhan Ryan

DESIGNERS
Carol Ann Davis, David Douglas,
Nicola Liddiard

MANAGING CARTOGRAPHER
David Roberts

SENIOR CARTOGRAPHIC EDITOR
Roger Bullen

CARTOGRAPHERS
Pamela Alford, James Anderson, Chris Atkinson, Dale Buckton, Tony Chambers, Ian Clark,
Martin Darlison, Damien Demaj, Paul Eames, Sally Gable, Jeremy Hepworth, Michael Martin,
Ed Merritt, Simon Mumford, John Plumer, Gail Townsley, Julie Turner,
Sarah Vaughan, Jane Voss, Peter Winfield

DATABASE MANAGER
Simon Lewis

DIGITAL MAPS CREATED IN DK CARTOPIA BY
Phil Rowles, Rob Stokes

PLACENAMES DATABASE TEAM
Natalie Clarkson, Julia Lynch,

EDITORIAL DIRECTION
Andrew Heritage

PICTURE RESEARCH
Louise Thomas

PRODUCTION
Heather Hughes

First American Edition, 1998.
Reprinted with Revisions, 1999.
Second Edition (revised) 2002, Reprinted 2003, Third Edition (revised) 2004,
Fourth Edition (revised) 2006

Published in the United States by DK Publishing Inc.
375 Hudson Street, New York, New York, 10014

A Penguin Company

Copyright © 1998, 1999, 2002, 2003, 2004, 2006 Dorling Kindersley Limited, London.

Student Atlas.
    p.    cm.
    Summary: Maps, illustrations and text describe various aspects of
countries of the world including physical features, population,
standards of living, natural resources, industries, environmental
issues and climate.
        ISBN-13: 978-0-75661-875-9
        ISBN-10: 0-7566-1875-4
        1. Children's atlases.   [1. Atlases.] I. DK Publishing, Inc.
    G1021 .S78 1998   <G&M>
    912--DC21                                    97-45730
                                                 CIP
                                                 MAPS

Printed and bound in China by Toppan Printing Co. (Shenzen) Ltd.

ACKNOWLEDGMENTS
The publishers are grateful for permission to reproduce the following photographs:
t=top, b=bottom, a=above, l=left, r=right, c=center
**Axiom**: Jiri Rezac 64br; J Spaull 92br. **Bridgeman Art Library**: Hereford Cathedral, Trustees of the Hereford Mappa Mundi 8tr.
**J Allan Cash**: 120cr. **Bruce Coleman Ltd**: C Ott 28cr (below); Dr E Pott 4bc; H Reinhard 19cr; J Murray 130bl; Peter Terry 19crr. **Colourific**:
Black Star/R Rogers 113br; Frank Herrmann 119bc. **Comstock**: 17tc. **James Davis Travel Photography**: 44tr, 119tr. **Robert Harding Picture
Library**: 6tr (below); 21c, 21cr, 22br, 92c (above), 28bl, 30cr, 30br, 31bl, 38tr, 118bl; A Tovy 120br; Adam Woolfitt 62br; C Bowman 112tr;
Charcrit Boonson 90cr (below); David Lomax 20tr; Franz Joseph Land 19tr; G Boutin 120cl (below); G Renner 17c, 118cr(above); Gavin
Hellier 31tr; Geoff Renner 39cr (above); H P Merten 23tl; Jane Sweeney 23bl; Louise Murray 93tr; Peter Scholey 91tr; Robert Francis 23cr;
Schuster/Keine 62cr (above); Simon Westcott 90br. **Hutchison Library**: A Zvoznikov 19cl; J Nowell 93bl; R Ian Lloyd 10cl. **Image Bank**:
Carlos Navajas 17bl; M Isy-Schwart 17bc; P Grumann 64cr (below); Steve Proehl 30cr (below); Terje Rakke 17br. **Images Colour Library**:
19c, 62cr (below), 118br. **Impact**: Jeremy Nicholl 121cl (below); Mark Henley 20bl; Paul O'Driscoll 63cr; Robin Lubbock 118br. **Frank Lane
Picture Agency**: D Smith 19bc; W Wisniewsli 17cr. **Magnum**: Chris Steele Perking 120tr (below); Jean Gaumy 65cl. **N.A.S.A**: 9tc. **N.H.P.A**:
M Wendler 4cl, 110bl. **Oxford Scientific Films**: Konrad Wothe 19tc; L Gould 4tr; Nobert Rosing 28cl. **Panos Pictures**: Alain le Garsheur
92cr; Alain le Garsmeur 31cl (below); Alberto Arzoz 63tr; Bruce Paton 121bl; Jeremy Hartley 120bl; Maria Luiza M Cavalho 112cl (below);
Paul Smith 111cr; Rhodri Jones 113bl; Ron Gilling 119cr; Trygve Bolstad 22bl. **Edward Parker**: 17cr (above). **Pictor International**: 4tc, 10bc,
18tr, 20br, 36bc, 38br. **Planet Earth Pictures**: J Waters 113bc. **South American Pictures**: Robert Francis 29cr; Tony Morrison 110cr, 111cl.
**Spectrum Colour Library**: 29br. **Frank Spooner Pictures**: Gamma/E Baitel 91cl. **Still Pictures**: J Frebet 113cr; R Seitre 90cr (above). **Tony
Stone Images**: 17tr, 112cl; A Sacks 28cr; Alan Levenson 92cr; Charles Thatcher 39tr; D Austen 131cr; D Hanson 17cl; Donald Johnson 62bc;
Earth Imaging 6tr (above); G Johnson 90bl; H Strand 113tr; Hans Schlapfer 38bc; J Jangoux 19bcr; J Warden 110bc; John Garrett 121br; L
Resnick 121tr; Larry Ulrich 37br; P Chesley 130tr; Paul Chesley 36br; Randy Wells 19br; Robert Frerck 65tr; Tom Walker 36bl; Tony Craddock
65cr. **Telegraph Colour Library**: 29tr. **Travel Ink**: Colin Marshall 22bc. **Trip**: A Kuznetsov 92bc; H Rogers 90cr; M Barlow 12bl; N Ray 10tr;
Robert Belbin 92bl; V Kolpakov 93cr (below); V Sidoropolev 64cr; W Jacobs 130c. **World Pictures**: 131tr. **ZEFA Picture Library**: 19bcl, 19cll,
63bc; Bramaz 30bl; Damm 19cl; Heilman 110cr (below); K Siewert 110cl; Kitchen 19bll; Sunak 91cr; Surpress 111tr. **JACKET IMAGES**:
Front: **Corbis**: Richard Berenholtz br; Bob Krist tc, bl; JamesRandklev tr, bl; Keren Su tl.; **Science Photo Library/NOAA**. Back: **Corbis**:
Robert Y. Ono bc; James Randklevbl; Paul A. Souders br; Royalty Free Images: Cobis tc; Corbis tr. Spine: **Corbis**: Robert Y. Ono

# CONTENTS

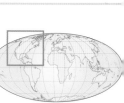

☐ **KEY TO MAP SYMBOLS ON FRONT ENDPAPER**

☐ **FLAGS ON BACK ENDPAPER**

# AMAZING EARTH

**Earth is unique** among the nine planets that circle the Sun. It is the only one that can support life, because it has enough oxygen in its atmosphere and plentiful water. In fact, seen from space, the Earth looks almost entirely blue. This is because about 70% of its surface is under water, submerged beneath four huge oceans: the Pacific, Atlantic, Indian and Arctic oceans. Land makes up about 30% of the Earth's surface. It is divided into seven landmasses of varying shapes and sizes called continents. These are, from largest to smallest: Asia, Africa, North America, South America, Antarctica, Europe, and Australia.

## THE SHAPE OF THE EARTH

**Photographs taken from space** by astronauts in the 1960s, and more recently from orbiting satellites, have proven beyond doubt what humans had worked out long ago – that the Earth is shaped like a ball. But it is not perfectly round. The force of the Earth's rotation makes the world bulge very slightly at the Equator and go a little flat at the North and South Poles. So the Earth is actually a flattened sphere, or a "geoid."

### WET EARTH

Tropical rain forests grow in areas close to the Equator, where it is wet and warm all year round. Although they cover just 7% of the Earth's land, these thick, damp forests form the richest ecosystems on the planet. More plant and animal species are found here than anywhere else on Earth.

### DRY EARTH

Deserts are among the most inhospitable places on the planet. Some deserts are scorching hot, others are freezing cold, but they have one thing in common – they are all dry. Very few plant and animal species can survive in these harsh conditions. The world's coldest and driest continent, Antarctica (*left*), is a cold desert.

### WATERY WORLD

The Earth's oceans and seas cover more than 142 million sq miles – that is twice the surface of Mars and nine times the surface of the moon.

Beneath the ocean waves lies the biggest and most unexplored landscape on Earth. Here are coral reefs, enormous, open plains, deep canyons, and the longest mountain range on Earth – the Mid-Atlantic Ridge – which stretches almost from pole to pole.

### HEIGHTS AND DEPTHS

The Pacific Ocean contains the deepest places on the Earth's surface – the ocean trenches. The very deepest is Challenger Deep in the Mariana Trench which plunges 36,201 ft into the Earth's crust. If Mount Everest, the highest point on land at 29,035 ft, was dropped into the trench, its peak wouldn't even reach the surface of the Pacific.

### WATER

Over 97% of the Earth's water is salt water. The total amount of salt in the world's oceans and seas would cover all of Europe to a depth of three miles. Less than 3% of the Earth's water is fresh. Of this, 2.24% is frozen in ice sheets and about 0.6% is stored underground as groundwater. The remainder is in lakes and rivers.

### COASTS

The total length of the Earth's coastlines is more than 300,000 miles – that is the equivalent of 12 times around the globe. A high percentage of the world's people live in coastal zones: of the ten most populated cities on Earth, seven are situated on estuaries or the coast.

### BIODIVERSITY

Today, almost 6,500,000,000 humans, approximately one million animal species, and 355,000 known plant species depend on the air, water, and land of planet Earth.

### VANISHING FORESTS

10,000 years ago, thick forests covered about half of the Earth's land surface. Today, 33% of those forests no longer exist, and more than half of what remains has been dramatically altered. During the 20th century, more than 50% of the Earth's rain forests have been felled.

# DIFFERENT WORLD VIEWS

Because the Earth is round, we can only see half of it at any one time. This half is called a hemisphere, which means "half a sphere." There are always two hemispheres – the half that you see and the other half that you don't see. Two hemispheres placed together will always make a complete sphere.

# PLANET WATER, PLANET LAND

The Earth can also be divided into land and water hemispheres. The land hemisphere shows most of the land on the Earth's surface. The water hemisphere is dominated by the vast Pacific Ocean – from this view, the Earth appears to be almost entirely covered by water.

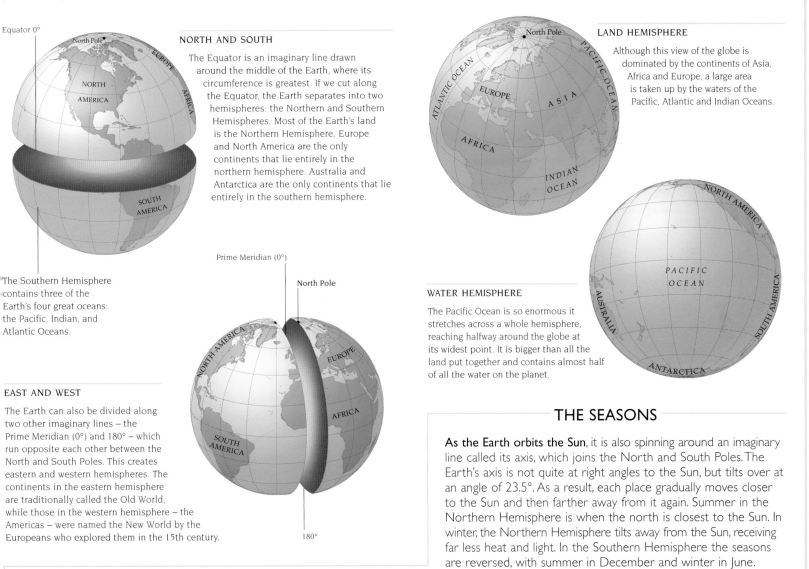

### NORTH AND SOUTH

The Equator is an imaginary line drawn around the middle of the Earth, where its circumference is greatest. If we cut along the Equator, the Earth separates into two hemispheres: the Northern and Southern Hemispheres. Most of the Earth's land is the Northern Hemisphere. Europe and North America are the only continents that lie entirely in the northern hemisphere. Australia and Antarctica are the only continents that lie entirely in the southern hemisphere.

The Southern Hemisphere contains three of the Earth's four great oceans: the Pacific, Indian, and Atlantic Oceans.

### EAST AND WEST

The Earth can also be divided along two other imaginary lines – the Prime Meridian (0°) and 180° – which run opposite each other between the North and South Poles. This creates eastern and western hemispheres. The continents in the eastern hemisphere are traditionally called the Old World, while those in the western hemisphere – the Americas – were named the New World by the Europeans who explored them in the 15th century.

### LAND HEMISPHERE

Although this view of the globe is dominated by the continents of Asia, Africa and Europe, a large area is taken up by the waters of the Pacific, Atlantic and Indian Oceans.

### WATER HEMISPHERE

The Pacific Ocean is so enormous it stretches across a whole hemisphere, reaching halfway around the globe at its widest point. It is bigger than all the land put together and contains almost half of all the water on the planet.

## THE SEASONS

As the Earth orbits the Sun, it is also spinning around an imaginary line called its axis, which joins the North and South Poles. The Earth's axis is not quite at right angles to the Sun, but tilts over at an angle of 23.5°. As a result, each place gradually moves closer to the Sun and then farther away from it again. Summer in the Northern Hemisphere is when the north is closest to the Sun. In winter, the Northern Hemisphere tilts away from the Sun, receiving far less heat and light. In the Southern Hemisphere the seasons are reversed, with summer in December and winter in June.

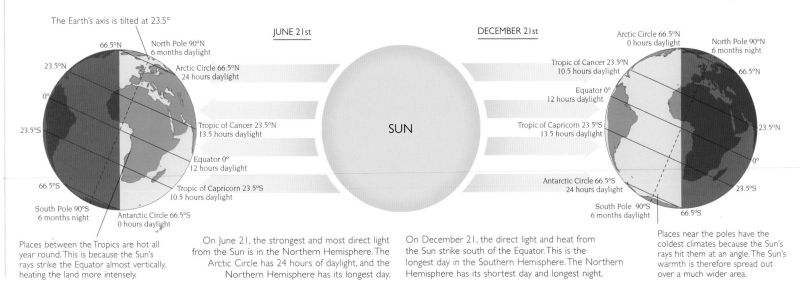

Places between the Tropics are hot all year round. This is because the Sun's rays strike the Equator almost vertically, heating the land more intensely.

On June 21, the strongest and most direct light from the Sun is in the Northern Hemisphere. The Arctic Circle has 24 hours of daylight, and the Northern Hemisphere has its longest day.

On December 21, the direct light and heat from the Sun strike south of the Equator. This is the longest day in the Southern Hemisphere. The Northern Hemisphere has its shortest day and longest night.

Places near the poles have the coldest climates because the Sun's rays hit them at an angle. The Sun's warmth is therefore spread out over a much wider area.

# MAPPING THE WORLD

The main purpose of a map is to show, or locate, where things are. The only truly accurate map of the whole world is a globe – a round model of the Earth. But a globe is impractical to carry around, so mapmakers (cartographers) produce flat paper maps instead. Changing the globe into a flat map is not simple. Imagine cutting a globe in half and trying to flatten the two hemispheres. They would be stretched in some places, and squashed in others. In fact, it is impossible to make a map of the round Earth on flat paper without some distortion of area, distance, or direction.

MODELS OF THE WORLD

Satellite images can show the whole world as it appears from space. However, this image shows only one half of the world, and is distorted at the edges.

A globe (*right*) is the only way to illustrate the shape of the Earth accurately. A globe also shows the correct positions of the continents and oceans and how large they are in relation to one another.

## LATITUDE

We can find out exactly how far north or south, east or west any place is on Earth by drawing two sets of imaginary lines around the world to make a grid. The horizontal lines on the globe below are called lines of latitude. They run from east to west. The most important is the Equator, which is given the value 0°. All other lines of latitude run parallel to the Equator. and are numbered in degrees either north or south of the Equator.

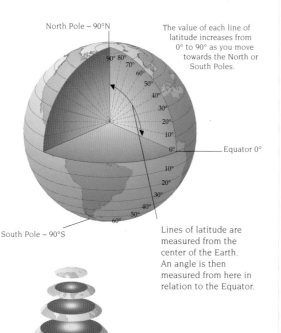

North Pole – 90°N

The value of each line of latitude increases from 0° to 90° as you move towards the North or South Poles.

90° 80° 70° 60° 50° 40° 30° 20° 10° 0°

Equator 0°

South Pole – 90°S

Lines of latitude are measured from the center of the Earth. An angle is then measured from here in relation to the Equator.

One degree of latitude is approximately 70 miles.

Lines of latitude divide the world into "slices" of equal thickness on either side of the Equator.

## LONGITUDE

The vertical lines on the globe below run from north to south between the poles. They are called lines of longitude. The most important passes through Greenwich, England, and is numbered 0°. It is called the Prime Meridian. All other lines of longitude are numbered in degrees either east or west of the Prime Meridian. The line directly opposite the Prime Meridian is numbered 180°.

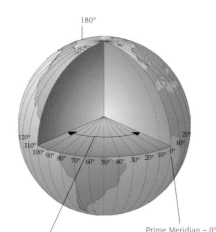

180°

120° 110° 100° 90° 80° 70° 60° 50° 40° 30° 20° 10° 0°

20° 10°

Prime Meridian – 0°

Lines of longitude are also measured from the center of the Earth. This time, the angle is taken in relation to the Prime Meridian.

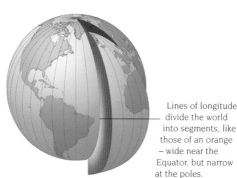

Lines of longitude divide the world into segments, like those of an orange – wide near the Equator, but narrow at the poles.

## WHERE ON EARTH?

When lines of latitude and longitude are combined on a globe, or as here, on a flat map, they form a grid. Using this grid, we can locate any place on land, or at sea, by referring to the point where its line of latitude intersects with its line of longitude. Even when a place is not located exactly where the lines cross, you can still find its approximate position.

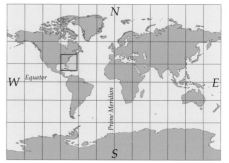

N

W  *Equator*  E

*Prime Meridian*

S

85° 80° 75° 70°

40°  New York  40°
Baltimore
Washington DC

35°  35°

*Atlantic Ocean*

30°  30°

25°  Miami  25°

Havana

85° 80° 75° 70°

The map above is of the eastern US. It is too small to show all the lines of latitude and longitude, so they are given at intervals of 5°. Miami is located at about 26° north of the Equator and 80° west of the Prime Meridian. We write its location 26°N 80°W.

# MAKING A FLAT MAP FROM A GLOBE

**Cartographers use a technique** called projection to show the Earth's curved surface on a flat map. Many different map projections have been designed. The distortion of one feature – either area, distance, or direction – can be minimized, while other features become more distorted. Cartographers must choose which of these things it is most important to show correctly for each map that they make. Three major families of projections can be used to solve these questions.

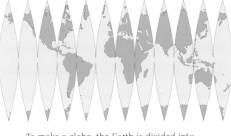

To make a globe, the Earth is divided into segments or 'gores' along lines of longitude.

## 1 CYLINDRICAL PROJECTIONS

These projections are "cylindrical" because the surface of the globe is transferred onto a surrounding cylinder. This cylinder is then cut from top to bottom and "rolled out" to give a flat map. These maps are very useful for showing the whole world.

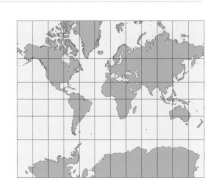

The cylinder touches the globe at the Equator. Here, the scale on the map will be exactly the same as it is on the globe. At the northern and southern edges of the cylinder, which are farthest away from the surface of the globe, the map is most distorted. The Mercator projection (*above*), created in the 16th century, is a good example of a cylindrical projection.

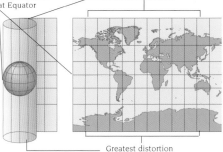

Scale accurate at Equator

Greatest distortion

Greatest distortion

## 2 AZIMUTHAL PROJECTIONS

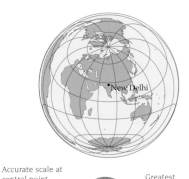

North Pole

New Delhi

Azimuthal projections put the surface of the globe onto a flat circle. "Azimuthal" means that the direction or "azimuth" of any line coming from the center point of that circle is correct. Azimuthal maps are useful for viewing hemispheres, continents, and the polar regions. Mapping any area larger than a hemisphere gives great distortion at the outer edges of the map.

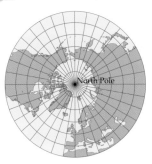

Accurate scale at central point

Greatest distortion

The circle only touches the globe's surface at one central point. The scale is only accurate at this point and becomes less and less accurate the farther away the circle is from the globe. This kind of projection is good for maps centering on a major city or on one of the poles.

## 3 CONIC PROJECTIONS

Conic projections are best used for smaller areas of the world, such as country maps. The surface of the globe is projected onto a cone which rests on top of it. After cutting from the point to the bottom of the cone, a flat map in the shape of a fan is left behind.

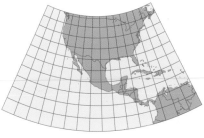

The conic projection touches the globe's surface at one latitude. This is where the scale of the map will be most accurate. The parts of the cone farthest from the globe will be the most distorted and are usually omitted from the map itself.

Greatest distortion

Most accurate scale

# PROJECTIONS USED IN THIS ATLAS

The projections that are appropriate for showing maps at a world, continental, or country scale are quite different. The projections for this atlas have been carefully chosen. They are ones that show areas as familiar shapes that are distorted as little as possible.

## 1 World Maps

**The Wagner VII** projection is used for our world maps as it shows all the countries at their correct sizes relative to one another.

## 2 Continents

**The Lambert Azimuthal Equal Area** is used for continental maps. The shape distortion is relatively small and countries retain their correct sizes relative to one another.

## 3 Countries

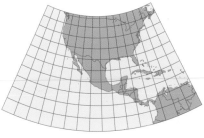

**The Lambert Conformal Conic** shows countries with as little distortion as possible. The angles from any point on the map are the same as they would be on the surface of the globe.

# HOW MAPS ARE MADE

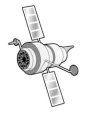

**New technologies** have revolutionized mapmaking. Computers and information from satellites have replaced drawing boards and drafting pens, and the process of creating new maps is now far easier. But mapmaking is still a skilled and often time-consuming process. Information about the world must be gathered, sorted, and checked. The cartographer must make decisions about the function of the map and what information to select in order to make it as clear as possible.

Maps have been made for thousands of years. The 13th-century Mappa Mundi, meaning "known world" shows the Mediterranean Sea and the Don and Nile rivers. Asia is at the top, with Europe on the left, and Africa to the right. The oceans are shown as a ring surrounding the land. The map reflects a number of biblical stories.

## HISTORICAL MAP MAKING

This detailed hand-drawn map of the southern coast of Spain was made in about 1750. The mountains are illustrated as small hills and the labels have been hand lettered.

For centuries, maps were drawn by hand. Very early maps were no more than a pictorial representation of what the surface of the ground looked like. Where there were hills, pictures were drawn to represent them. Later maps were drawn using information gathered by survey teams. They would carefully mark out and calculate the height of the land, the positions of towns, and other geographical features. As knowledge and techniques improved, maps became more accurate.

## NEW TECHNIQUES

Computers make it easier to change map information and styles quickly. This map of the southern coast of Spain, made in 1997 has been made using digital terrain modeling (see below) and traditional cartography.

Today, cartographers have access to far more data about the Earth than in the past. Satellites collect and process information about its surface. This is called remote-sensed data. Further information may be drafted in the traditional way. Locations can be verified by GPS (Global Positioning Systems) linked to satellites. Computers are now widely used to combine different kinds of map information. Any computerized map is produced using a GIS (Geographical Information System).

## MODERN MAP MAKING

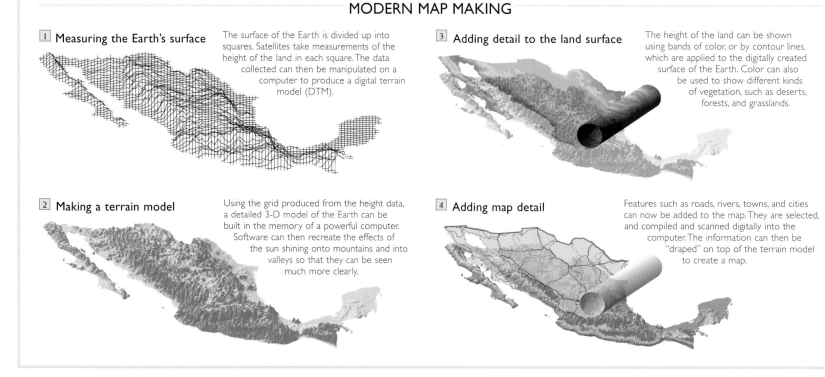

**1 Measuring the Earth's surface**
The surface of the Earth is divided up into squares. Satellites take measurements of the height of the land in each square. The data collected can then be manipulated on a computer to produce a digital terrain model (DTM).

**3 Adding detail to the land surface**
The height of the land can be shown using bands of color, or by contour lines, which are applied to the digitally created surface of the Earth. Color can also be used to show different kinds of vegetation, such as deserts, forests, and grasslands.

**2 Making a terrain model**
Using the grid produced from the height data, a detailed 3-D model of the Earth can be built in the memory of a powerful computer. Software can then recreate the effects of the sun shining onto mountains and into valleys so that they can be seen much more clearly.

**4 Adding map detail**
Features such as roads, rivers, towns, and cities can now be added to the map. They are selected, and compiled and scanned digitally into the computer. The information can then be "draped" on top of the terrain model to create a map.

# SHOWING INFORMATION ON A MAP

A map is a selective diagram of a place. It is the cartographer's job to decide what kind of information to show on a map. They can choose to highlight certain kinds of features – such as roads, rivers, and land height. They can also show other features such as sea depth, place names, and borders that would be impossible to see either on the ground or from a photograph. The information that can be shown on a map is influenced by a number of factors, most notably by its scale.

This is a satellite photograph of the harbor area of Rio de Janeiro in Brazil. Although you can see the bay and where most of the housing is, it is impossible to see roads or get any sense of the position of places relative to one another.

This is a map of the same area as you can see in the photograph. Much of the detail has been greatly simplified. Towns are named and marked; contours indicate the height of the land; and roads, railways and borders between districts have been added.

# SCALE

To make a map of an area it needs to be greatly reduced in size. This is known as drawing to scale. The scale of the map shows us by how much the area has been reduced. The smaller the scale, the greater the area of land that can be shown on the map. There will be far less detail and the map will not be as accurate. The maps below show the different kinds of information that can be shown on maps of varying scales.

When using a map to work out what areas or distances are in reality, we need to refer to the scale of that particular map. Map scales can be shown in several ways.

## WAYS TO SHOW SCALE

**1** **Representative fraction**
One unit on the map would be equal to 1,000,000 units on the ground.

**1:1,000,000**

**2** **Linear scale**
The line is marked off in units which represent the real distances of the map, given in both miles and kilometers.

SCALE BAR

0 km   10   20

0 miles   10   20

**3** **Statement of scale**
It means that 1 inch on the map represents 1 mile on the ground.

**1 inch represents 1 mile**

---

LONDON 1:21,000,000

This small-scale map shows the position of London in relation to Europe. Very little detail can be seen at this scale – only the names of countries and the largest towns.

LONDON 1:5,500,000

At a scale of 1 to 5,500,000 you can see the major road network in the southeast of the UK. Many towns are named and you can see the difference in size and status.

LONDON 1:900,000

This map is at a much larger scale. You can see the major roads that lead out from London and the names of many suburbs, places of interest, and airports.

LONDON 1:12,500

This is a street map of central London. The streets are named, as are places of interest, train and subway stations. The scale is large enough to show plenty of detail.

# READING MAPS

Maps use a unique visual language to convey a great deal of detailed information in a relatively simple form. Different features are marked out using special symbols and styles of print. These symbols are explained in the key to the map and you should always read a map alongside its key or legend. This page explains how to look for different features on the map and how to unravel the different layers of information that you can find on it.

## PHYSICAL FEATURES

All the regional and country maps in this atlas are based on a model of the Earth's surface. The computer-generated relief gives an accurate picture of the surface of the land. Colors are used to show the relative heights of the land; green is for low-lying land, and yellows, browns, and grays are for higher land. Water features like streams, rivers, and lakes are also shown.

### 1 WATER FEATURES

On this map extract, the blue lines show a number of rivers, including the Salween and the Irrawaddy. The Irrawaddy forms a huge delta, splitting into many streams as it reaches the sea.

### 2 RELIEF

These mountains are in the north of Southeast Asia. The underlying relief on the map and the colored bands help you to see the height of the land.

## HUMAN FEATURES

Maps also reveal a great deal about the human geography of an area. In addition to showing the location of towns and roads, different symbols can tell you more about the size of towns and the importance of a road. Borders between countries or regions can only be seen on a map.

## 3 BORDERS

Borders on the map are marked by a thick purple line. The boundary between Laos and Vietnam is in sparsely populated mountainous terrain, with the border generally running along a mountain range.

### KEY TO MAP SYMBOLS

**BOUNDARIES**

| | |
|---|---|
| | Full international border |
| | Disputed border |

**COMMUNICATION FEATURES**

| | |
|---|---|
| | Major road |
| | Minor road |
| | Railway |
| ✈ | International airport |

**DRAINAGE FEATURES**

| | |
|---|---|
| | Major river |
| | Minor river |
| | Lake |
| | Wetland |

**LANDSCAPE FEATURES**

| | |
|---|---|
| △ | Mountain |

**POPULATED PLACES**

| | |
|---|---|
| ○ | Less than 50,000 |
| ⊙ | 50,000–100,000 |
| ⊙ | 100,000–500,000 |
| ▣ | Greater than 500,000 |
| ● | Capital city |

**NAMES**

| | |
|---|---|
| **MYANMAR** | Country |
| **PARACEL ISLANDS** (disputed by China, Taiwan & Vietnam) | Dependent territory |
| **JAKARTA** | Capital city |
| **Sarawak** | Cultural region |
| *Chin Hills* | Landscape feature |
| *Puncak Jaya 16,535ft* | Mountain/pass |
| *Red River* | River/lake |
| *Java Sea* | Sea feature |

## 4 SETTLEMENTS

The symbol for a settlement can tell you its position, population, and political status. Most towns are shown by a circle or a square. These represent the size of their population. Where the dot for a town is colored red, this shows that it is a capital city such as Kuala Lumpur in Malaysia.

## FINDING PLACES

### Alphanumeric grid references

All the maps in this book are indexed using their alphanumeric grid reference – for example, G4. To find a place you must first look up its page number and then its grid reference. Read the letters and numbers off the bottom and side of the grid. Using rulers held at right angles to one another you will find the point where the lines meet. The place will be located within this square.

### Latitude and longitude references

The lines of latitude and longitude are known as graticules. They are shown on the map as thin blue lines with the value of their latitude or longitude given as a blue number at the edge of the map.

**LAND HEIGHT**

| | |
|---|---|
| | Above 13,120ft |
| | 6,560–13,120ft |
| | 3,280–6,560ft |
| | 1,640–3,280ft |
| | 820–1,640ft |
| | 330–820ft |
| | 0–330ft |

**SEA DEPTH**

| | |
|---|---|
| | 0–820ft |
| | 820–1,640ft |
| | 1,640–3,280ft |
| | 3280–6,560ft |
| | 6,560–9,840ft |
| | 9,840–13,120ft |
| | Below 13,120ft |

**CITIES AND TOWNS**

| | |
|---|---|
| ▣ | Over 500,000 people |
| ⊙ | 100,000–500,000 |
| ○ | 50,000–100,000 |
| ○ | Less than 50,000 |

## 5 ROADS AND RAILROADS

**a** The major road and railroad links between Hue and Nha Trang hug the Vietnamese coast. A string of coastal towns is often connected by road and rail in this manner.

Chiang Mai, in northern **b** Thailand, is linked to the capital Bangkok to the south by railroad and road. At Chiang Mai, the mountains are too high for the railroad to continue, and only roads go north into Myanmar.

# USING THE ATLAS

This Atlas has been designed to develop map-reading skills and to introduce readers to a wide range of different maps. It also provides a wealth of detailed geographic information about the world today. The Atlas is divided into four sections: Learning Map Skills; The World About Us, covering global geographic patterns; the World Atlas, dealing with the world's regions and an Index.

## LEARNING MAP SKILLS

Maps show the Earth – which is three-dimensional – in just two dimensions. This section shows how maps are made; how different kinds of information are shown on maps; how to choose what to put on a map and the best way to show it. It also explains how to read the maps in this Atlas.

## THE WORLD ABOUT US

These pages contain a series of world maps that show important themes, such as physical features, climate, life zones, population, and the world economy, on a global scale. They give a worldwide picture of concepts that are explored in more detail later in the book.

Text introduces themes and concepts in each spread.

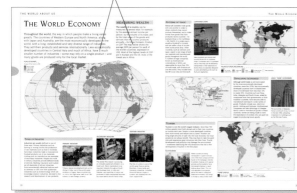

Photographs illustrate examples of places or topics shown on the main map.

World maps show geographic patterns on a global scale.

Introduction to projections: different projections and how they work.

Choosing the best projections: the map projections used in this book.

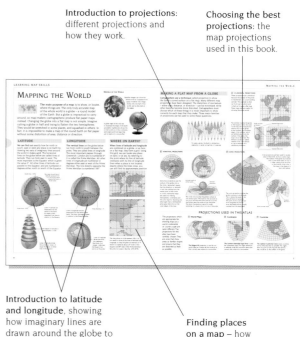

Introduction to latitude and longitude, showing how imaginary lines are drawn around the globe to create a reference grid.

Finding places on a map – how to locate a place.

## CONTINENTAL MAPS

A cross section through the continent shows the relative height of certain features.

A detailed physical map of the continent shows major natural geographic features, including mountains, lakes and rivers.

Photographs and locator maps illustrate the main geographic regions and show you where they are.

The industry map shows the main industrial towns and cities and the main industries in each continent. It also shows the wealth of each country relative to the rest of the world.

### CONTINENTAL GEOGRAPHY PAGES

Humans have colonized and changed all the continents except Antarctica. These pages show the factors which have affected this process: climate, the availability of resources such as coal, oil, and minerals, and varying patterns of land use. Mineral resources are directly linked to many industries, and most agriculture is governed both by the quality of the land and the climate

### CONTINENTAL PAGES

These pages show the physical shape of each continent and the impact that humans have made on the natural landscape – building towns and roads and creating borders between countries. They show where natural features such as mountain ranges and rivers have created physical boundaries, and where humans have created their own political boundaries between states.

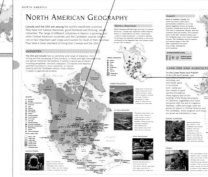

The political map of the continent shows country boundaries and country names.

The climate map shows the main types of climate across the continent and where the hottest and coldest, wettest and driest places are.

The mineral resources map shows where the most important reserves of minerals, including coal and precious metals, are found.

The land use map shows different types of land and the main kinds of farming that take place in each area.

# REGIONAL MAPS

**The main part of the Atlas** contains detailed maps of countries and regions. Each of these is accompanied by a series of small thematic maps, models, and charts, which give information about the climate, where people live, how they use the land, the different kinds of industry, and important environmental issues.

## TERRAIN MODEL

A computer-generated landscape model shows what the land really looks like. There are no roads or towns to mask the physical geography of the country or region. Mountain ranges, plains, and river basins can be easily seen.

## COLOURED THUMB TAGS

Each section has its own colour code.

Learning Map Skills

The World About Us

Europe

Asia

North America

South America

Africa

Australasia and Oceania

Antarctica and the Arctic

## CLIMATE MAPS

These maps show the temperature and rainfall patterns in January and July. Colored bands indicate temperatures: blue for low temperatures, orange for high ones. Rainfall is represented by black lines with a number giving the average amount of rain. These are called isohyets.

Isohyets show the rainfall patterns in inches per year. The areas between the lines are either over or under the figures shown on the isohyets.

The hottest areas are colored orange.

Here the rainfall is between 2 and 4 inches per year.

## LOCATOR GLOBE

This shows the location of the country or region both within its continent and in relation to the rest of the world.

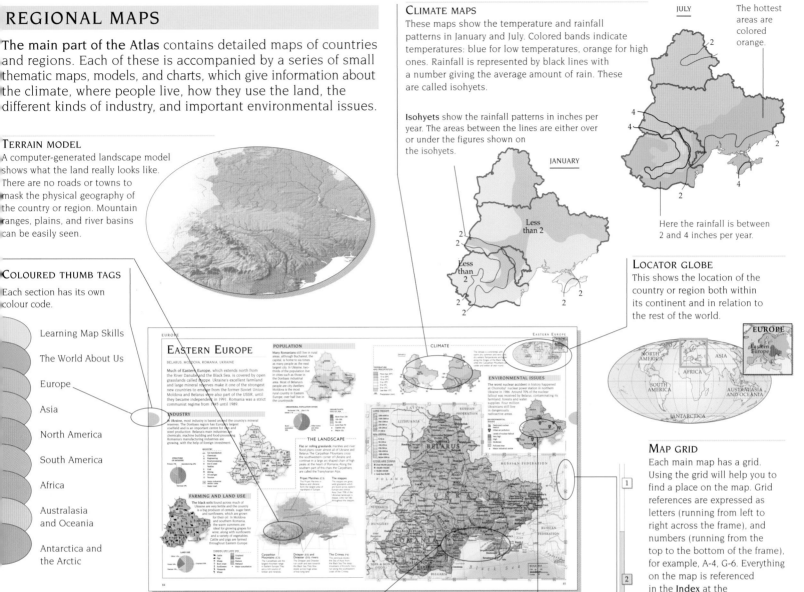

## MAP GRID

Each main map has a grid. Using the grid will help you to find a place on the map. Grid references are expressed as letters (running from left to right across the frame), and numbers (running from the top to the bottom of the frame), for example, A-4, G-6. Everything on the map is referenced in the **Index** at the back of the book.

## REGIONAL MAPS

The main map on each regional page shows the main topographical features of the area: the height of the land, the major roads, the rivers and lakes. It also shows the main cities and towns in the region – represented by different symbols.

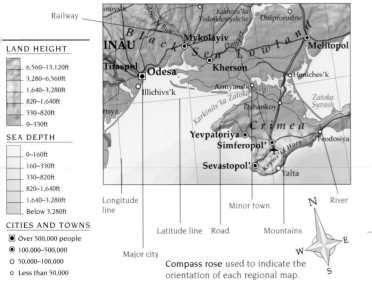

Railway

**LAND HEIGHT**

- 6,560–13,120ft
- 3,280–6,560ft
- 1,640–3,280ft
- 820–1,640ft
- 330–820ft
- 0–330ft

**SEA DEPTH**

- 0–160ft
- 160–330ft
- 330–820ft
- 820–1,640ft
- 1,640–3,280ft
- Below 3,280ft

**CITIES AND TOWNS**

- Over 500,000 people
- 100,000–500,000
- 50,000–100,000
- Less than 50,000

Longitude line

Latitude line

Road

Mountains

River

Major city

Minor town

Compass rose used to indicate the orientation of each regional map.

## THEMATIC MAPS

These small maps show various aspects of the geography of the country or region. The environment maps cover topics such as the effects of pollution. Industry, land use, and population maps locate the major industries, types of agriculture, and the distribution of population.

Diagrams are used to show the geographic information on the map statistically.

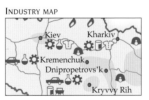

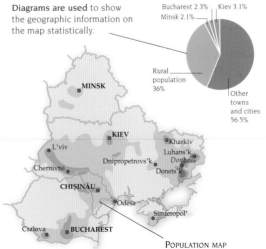

POPULATION MAP

INDUSTRY MAP

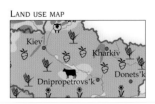

LAND USE MAP

ENVIRONMENT MAP

# THE PHYSICAL WORLD

**This map shows** the main physical features of the world: the mountain ranges, the great rivers and lakes, deserts, grassland plains, seas, and oceans. No human settlements are named on this map – only the physical or landscape features.

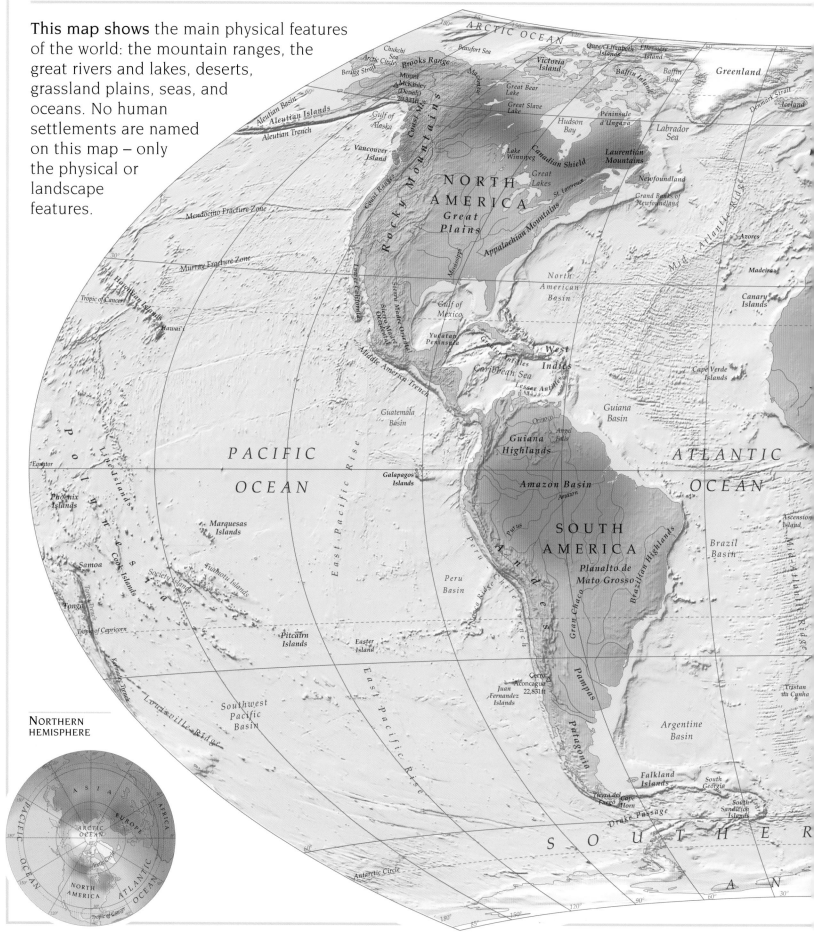

ARCTIC OCEAN

Queen Elizabeth Islands · Ellesmere Island

Chukchi Sea · Beaufort Sea · Victoria Island · Baffin Island · Baffin Bay · Greenland

Arctic Circle · Bering Strait · Brooks Range · Mackenzie · Great Bear Lake · Great Slave Lake · Hudson Bay · Péninsule d'Ungava · Labrador Sea · Denmark Strait · Iceland

Aleutian Basin · Aleutian Islands · Aleutian Trench · Gulf of Alaska · Mount McKinley (Denali) 20,321ft · Lake Winnipeg · Canadian Shield · Laurentian Mountains · Newfoundland

Vancouver Island · Coast Range · Rocky Mountains · NORTH AMERICA · Great Lakes · St. Lawrence · Grand Banks of Newfoundland · Mid-Atlantic Ridge

Mendocino Fracture Zone · Great Plains · Appalachian Mountains · Mississippi · Azores

Hawaiian Islands · Tropic of Cancer · Murray Fracture Zone · Lower California · Sierra Nevada · Sierra Madre Occidental · Sierra Madre Oriental · Gulf of Mexico · North American Basin · Madeira · Canary Islands

Hawai'i · Yucatan Peninsula · Greater Antilles · West Indies · Caribbean Sea · Lesser Antilles · Cape Verde Islands

Equator · Phoenix Islands · Polynesia · Line Islands · PACIFIC OCEAN · Middle America Trench · Guatemala Basin · Galapagos Islands · Orinoco · Guiana Highlands · Angel Falls · Guiana Basin · ATLANTIC OCEAN

Marquesas Islands · East Pacific Rise · Amazon Basin · Amazon · SOUTH AMERICA · Brazil Basin · Ascension Island

Samoa · Cook Islands · Society Islands · Tuamotu Islands · Peru Basin · Andes · Purus · Planalto de Mato Grosso · Brazilian Highlands

Tonga · Tonga Trench · Tropic of Capricorn · Pitcairn Islands · Easter Island · Peru-Chile Trench · Nazca Ridge · Gran Chaco · Pampas

Kermadec Trench · Louisville Ridge · Southwest Pacific Basin · East Pacific Rise · Cerro Aconcagua 22,831ft · Juan Fernandez Islands · Patagonia · Argentine Basin · Tristan da Cunha

Falkland Islands · South Georgia

Tierra del Fuego · Cape Horn · Drake Passage · South Sandwich Islands

Antarctic Circle · SOUTHERN OCEAN

NORTHERN HEMISPHERE

ASIA · EUROPE · AFRICA · PACIFIC OCEAN · ARCTIC OCEAN · ATLANTIC OCEAN · Arctic Circle · NORTH AMERICA · Tropic of Cancer

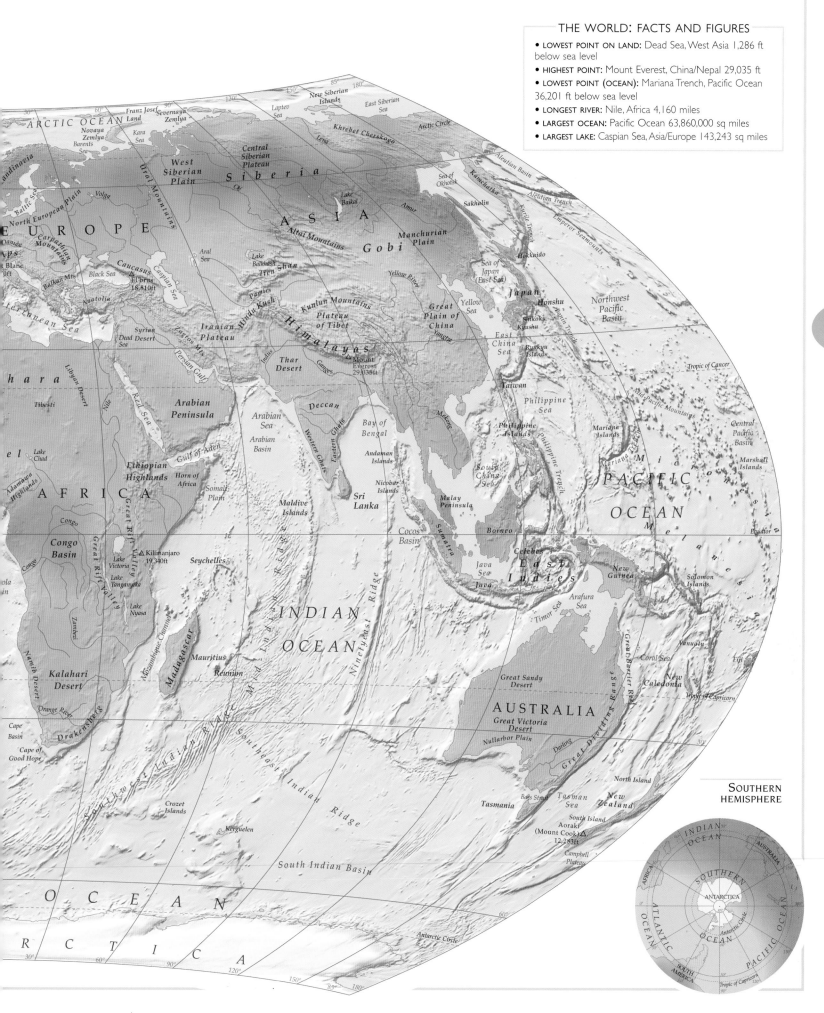

- **LOWEST POINT ON LAND:** Dead Sea, West Asia 1,286 ft below sea level
- **HIGHEST POINT:** Mount Everest, China/Nepal 29,035 ft
- **LOWEST POINT (OCEAN):** Mariana Trench, Pacific Ocean 36,201 ft below sea level
- **LONGEST RIVER:** Nile, Africa 4,160 miles
- **LARGEST OCEAN:** Pacific Ocean 63,860,000 sq miles
- **LARGEST LAKE:** Caspian Sea, Asia/Europe 143,243 sq miles

ARCTIC OCEAN

Franz Josef Land
Severnaya Zemlya
Novaya Zemlya
Kara Sea
Barents Sea
Laptev Sea
New Siberian Islands
East Siberian Sea
Arctic Circle
Khrebet Cherskogo

Scandinavia
Baltic Sea
North European Plain
Volga
Ural Mountains
West Siberian Plain
Central Siberian Plateau
Siberia
Ob
Lena

EUROPE
Carpathian Mountains
Danube
Alps
Mont Blanc
Balkan Mts
Black Sea
Anatolia
Caucasus
El'brus 18,510ft
Caspian Sea
Aral Sea
Lake Balkhash
Altai Mountains
ASIA
Gobi
Manchurian Plain
Amur
Sakhalin
Sea of Okhotsk
Kamchatka
Aleutian Trench
Aleutian Basin

Mediterranean Sea
Syrian Desert
Dead Sea
Zagros Mts
Iranian Plateau
Hindu Kush
Pamirs
Tien Shan
Kunlun Mountains
Plateau of Tibet
Himalayas
Mount Everest 29,035ft
Great Plain of China
Yangtze
Yellow River
Yellow Sea
Hokkaido
Japan
Honshu
Sea of Japan (East Sea)
Shikoku
Kyushu
East China Sea
Ryukyu Islands
Kurile Trench
Emperor Seamounts
Northwest Pacific Basin
Japan Trench

Sahara
Libyan Desert
Nile
Red Sea
Tibesti
Arabian Peninsula
Persian Gulf
Thar Desert
Indus
Ganges
Deccan
Taiwan
Philippine Sea
Philippine Islands
Philippine Trench
Mariana Islands
Mariana Trench
Mid-Pacific Mountains
Tropic of Cancer
Central Pacific Basin
Marshall Islands
Micronesia

Gulf of Aden
Ethiopian Highlands
Horn of Africa
Somali Plain
Arabian Sea
Arabian Basin
Western Ghats
Eastern Ghats
Bay of Bengal
Andaman Islands
South China Sea
Malay Peninsula
PACIFIC OCEAN
Melanesia

Lake Chad
Adamawa Highlands
AFRICA
Maldive Islands
Sri Lanka
Nicobar Islands
Sumatra
Cocos Basin
Borneo
Celebes
East Indies
New Guinea
Solomon Islands
Equator

Congo
Congo Basin
Great Rift Valley
Lake Victoria
Kilimanjaro 19,340ft
Seychelles
Java Sea
Java
Arafura Sea
Vanuatu

Angola
Lake Tanganyika
Lake Nyasa
Zambezi
Mozambique Channel
Madagascar
Mauritius
Réunion
Mid-Indian Ridge
Ninetyeast Ridge
Timor Sea
Coral Sea
New Caledonia
Fiji
Great Barrier Reef

Namib Desert
Kalahari Desert
INDIAN OCEAN
Great Sandy Desert
AUSTRALIA
Great Victoria Desert
Tropic of Capricorn

Orange River
Cape Basin
Cape of Good Hope
Drakensberg
Southwest Indian Ridge
Southeast Indian Ridge
Crozet Islands
Kerguelen
Nullarbor Plain
Darling
Great Dividing Range
North Island
Tasman Sea
Bass Strait
Tasmania
South Island
New Zealand
Aoraki (Mount Cook) 12,283ft
Campbell Plateau

South Indian Basin

OCEAN
ARCTICA
Antarctic Circle

SOUTHERN HEMISPHERE

INDIAN OCEAN
AUSTRALIA
AFRICA
SOUTHERN
OCEAN
ANTARCTICA
ATLANTIC OCEAN
Antarctic Circle
PACIFIC OCEAN
SOUTH AMERICA
Tropic of Capricorn

# THE EARTH'S STRUCTURE

**The shape and position** of the Earth's oceans and continents make a familiar pattern. This is just the latest in a series of forms that the Earth has taken in the hundreds of millions of years since its creation. Massive forces inside the Earth cause the continents and oceans to move apart and together again, forming larger landmasses and then breaking them apart – a process known as plate tectonics. The movement is very slow – but over millions of years, the changes can be enormous.

## DYNAMIC EARTH

**The heart of the Earth** is a solid core of iron surrounded by several layers of very hot – sometimes liquid – rock. The crust is relatively thin and is made up of a series of "plates" that fit closely together. Movement of the molten rock deep within the mantle of the Earth causes the plates to move, creating changes in the surface features of the Earth.

### THE EARTH'S PLATES

Continental plate

Oceanic plate

Plate boundary or margin

Continental and oceanic plates are tectonic plates are made from crustal rock

### INSIDE THE EARTH

Rocky crust

Outer core – liquid iron and nickel

Inner core – made of iron

Mantle – r from solid molten

### TECTONIC PLATES, VOLCANOES AND EARTHQUAKES

▲    Volcanic zone

   Earthquake zone on land

⇨    Direction of plate movement

ᐯᐯᐯᐯ    Rift valley

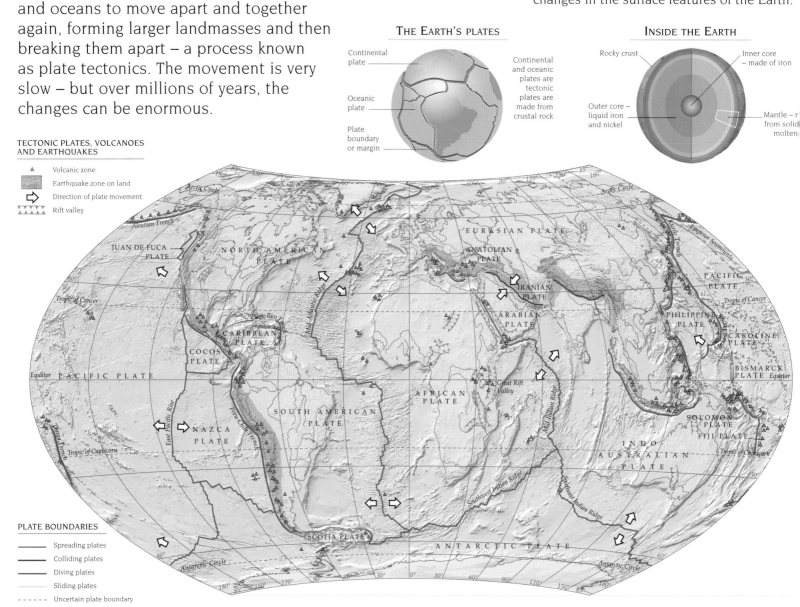

### PLATE BOUNDARIES

——— Spreading plates

——— Colliding plates

——— Diving plates

——— Sliding plates

– – – – – Uncertain plate boundary

## PLATE BOUNDARIES

**The point** where two plates meet is known as a plate boundary. As the Earth's plates move together or apart or slide alongside one another, the great forces that result cause great changes in the landscape. Mountains can be created, earthquakes occur, and there may be frequent volcanic eruptions.

## SPREADING PLATES

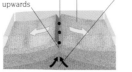

Earthquake zone    Ocean floor

Magma pushed upwards    Solid mantle

As plates move apart, magma rises through the outer mantle. When it cools, it forms new crust. The Mid-Atlantic Ridge is caused by spreading plates.

## COLLIDING PLATES

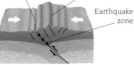

Colliding plate    Mountains thrust upwards

Earthquake zone

When two plates bearing landmasses collide with one another, the land is crumpled upward into high mountain peaks such as the Alps and the Himalayas.

## DIVING PLATES

Earthquake zone    Mountains

Ocean plate    Continental plate

When an ocean-bearing plate collides with a continental plate it is forced downward under the other plate and into the mantle. Volcanoes occur along these boundaries.

## SLIDING PLATES

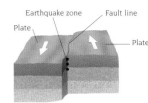

Earthquake zone    Fault line

Plate      Plate

As two plates slide past each other, great friction is set up along the fault line that lies between them. This can lead to powerful earthquakes.

## SHAPING THE LANDSCAPE

**The Earth's surface** is made from solid rock or water. The land is constantly reshaped by external forces. Water flowing as rivers or in the oceans erodes and deposits material to create valleys and lakes and to shape coastlines. When water is built up and compressed into solid sheets of ice, it can erode more deeply, creating deeper, wider valleys. Wind also has a powerful effect: stripping away vegetation and transporting rock particles vast distances.

### RIVERS

Most rivers have their sources in mountain areas. They flow fast through the mountains, eroding deep V-shaped valleys. As they reach flatter areas they begin to meander in great loops, both eroding and then depositing rock particles as they slow down.

### GLACIERS

In cold areas, close to the poles or on mountaintops, snow is built up into rivers of ice called glaciers. They move slowly, eroding deep U-shaped valleys. When the glacier melts, ridges of eroded rock called moraines are left at the sides and end of the glacier.

### SEA ACTION

The oceans change the landscape in two major ways. They batter cliffs, causing rock to break away and the land to retreat, and they carry eroded material along the coast, to make beaches and sandbars.

### WIND

Wind can erode and break down rock into smaller boulders and stones and eventually into sand. Desert sand dunes are shaped by the force of the wind and vary from ripples to hills 650 ft high.

### LANDSLIDES

Heavy rain can loosen soil and rock beneath the surface of slopes. As this moves, the top layers slip, forming heaps of rubble at the base of the slope.

## THE WORLD'S OCEANS

**Just over two-thirds of the Earth's surface** is covered by water and more than 97% of this water is contained in the oceans. Movements within the Earth shape the ocean floor in the same way they do the land surface, creating mountain ranges, trenches, and plateaus, and changing the shape and size of the oceans. The difference between an ocean and a sea is simply its size; oceans are much bigger.

### POLAR OCEANS

The Southern and Arctic Oceans contain large icebergs that have broken away from the ice shelf.

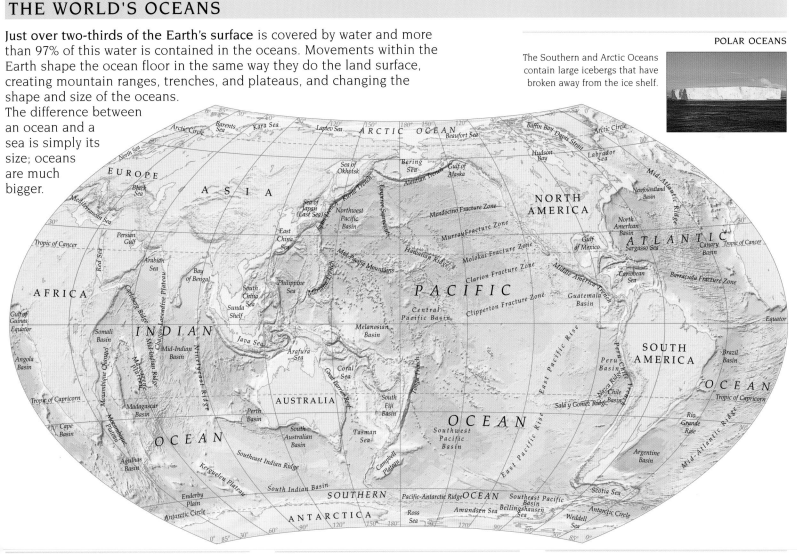

### INDIAN OCEAN

The Indian Ocean covers about 20% of the world's surface. Ocean swells, starting deep in the Southern Ocean, often cause flooding in Sri Lanka and the Maldives.

### PACIFIC OCEAN

The Pacific is the largest and deepest ocean in the world. It is surrounded by an arc of volcanoes, including Japan, Indonesia, and the Andes, known as the "Ring of Fire."

### ATLANTIC OCEAN

The Atlantic Ocean was formed about 180 million years ago. The land that now forms Europe and Africa pulled apart from the Americas to create an ocean 1,900 miles wide.

# CLIMATE AND LIFE ZONES

This map shows the different climates found around the world. Climates are particular combinations of temperature and humidity. Climates are affected by latitude, the height of the land, winds, and ocean currents. Climates can change, but not overnight. Weather is local and consists of short-term events such as thunderstorms, hurricanes, and blizzards.

Hurricanes are violent cyclonic windstorms, driven by heat energy gathered from tropical seas. The Caribbean islands and the east coast of the US are particularly prone to hurricanes.

**WORLD CLIMATE**

- Ice cap
- Subarctic
- Tundra
- Continental
- Temperate
- Warm temperate

(continued)
**WORLD CLIMATE**

- Mediterranean
- Semiarid
- Arid
- Hot humid
- Humid equatorial
- Tropical

## WINDS

All over the Earth there are a series of large-scale wind patterns called prevailing winds that have a direct effect on weather and climate. The direction of the wind depends on global air pressure. Winds travel from areas of high pressure to areas of low pressure. The westerlies, polar easterlies, and northeast and southeast trade winds are all prevailing winds. The Equator is known for its light winds – referred to as the Doldrums. Changes in the direction of the prevailing winds can have a serious impact on the weather all over the planet.

**WINDS**

- Cool wind
- Warm wind

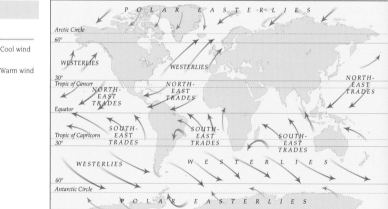

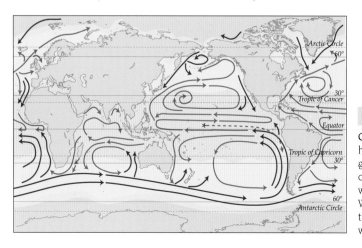

## OCEAN CURRENTS

Ocean currents help distribute heat around the Earth and have a great influence on climate. Convection currents circulate massive amounts of warm and cold water around the oceans. Warm water is moved away from the tropics to higher latitudes and cold water is moved toward the tropics.

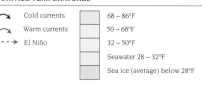

**OCEAN CURRENTS AND SURFACE TEMPERATURES**

- Cold currents
- Warm currents
- El Niño

- 68 – 86°F
- 50 – 68°F
- 32 – 50°F
- Seawater 28 – 32°F
- Sea ice (average) below 28°F

# LIFE ZONES

The map below shows the Earth divided into different biomes – also called biogeographical regions. The combination of climate, the type of landscape, and the plants and animals that live there are used to classify a region. Similar biomes are found in very different places around the world.

## POLAR REGIONS

The North and South Poles are permanently covered by ice. Only a few plants and animals can live here.

## TUNDRA

Tundra is flat, cold, and dry, with few trees. Plants such as mosses and lichens grow close to the ground.

## DESERTS
Very little rain falls in desert areas, whether they are hot deserts such as the Sahara or cold deserts like the Gobi.

## CONIFEROUS FORESTS
Tall coniferous trees such as pine and spruce, with spines or needles instead of leaves, grow in the far north of Scandinavia, Canada, and the Russian Federation.

## BROADLEAF FORESTS
Broadleaf or deciduous forests once covered temperate regions over most of the Northern Hemisphere. They contain trees of many varieties – all of which shed their leaves every year.

## TEMPERATE RAINFORESTS
Evergreen, broadleaved trees need a warmer, wetter climate than deciduous trees. They are known as temperate rainforests.

## MEDITERRANEAN
Close to the shores of the Mediterranean Sea, the vegetation consists mainly of herbs, shrubs, and drought-resistant trees.

### BIOME TYPES

- Mountains
- Polar regions
- Tundra
- Tropical rainforests
- Dry woodlands
- Savannah
- Temperate grasslands

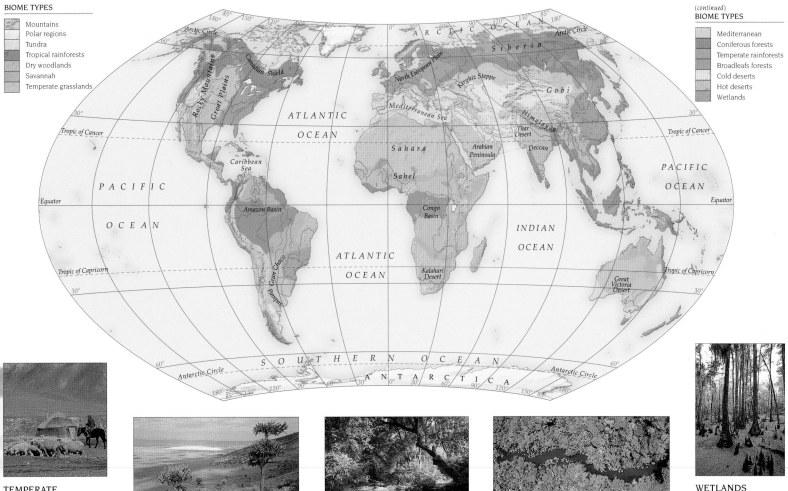

### (continued) BIOME TYPES

- Mediterranean
- Coniferous forests
- Temperate rainforests
- Broadleafs forests
- Cold deserts
- Hot deserts
- Wetlands

## TEMPERATE GRASSLANDS
Grasslands cover the central areas of the continents. They are known in the middle latitudes as prairies, steppe, and pampas.

## SAVANNA
The savanna consists of woodland interspersed with grassland. These regions lie between the tropical rain-forest and hot desert regions.

## DRY WOODLANDS
Dry woodlands are found at the edge of grasslands. They contain small trees and shrubs adapted to dry conditions.

## TROPICAL RAINFORESTS
Around the Equator, where temperatures are high and there is plenty of rain, tropical rainforests flourish. Trees grow continuously and are tall with huge, broad leaves.

## WETLANDS
Low-lying swamps and marshes are known as wetlands. They are often home to a rich variety of animal, plant, and bird species.

# WORLD POPULATION

There are now nearly 6,500,000,000 people on Earth. The population has increased to nearly four times that of 1900. Before that date, the number of people increased slowly because people were born and died at similar rates. With improved living conditions, better medical care, and more efficient food production, more people survived to adulthood, and the population began to grow much faster. If growth continues at the present rate, the world's population is likely to reach 7.5 billion by the year 2020.

*Favelas* – or shanty towns – have grown up around many South American cities because of overcrowding.

## POPULATION STRUCTURES

**Measuring the numbers** of old and young people gives the age structure of a country or continent. If there are large numbers of young people and a high birthrate, the population is said to be youthful – as is the case in many African, Asian, and South American countries. If the birthrate is low but many people survive into old age, the population distribution is said to be aging – this is true of much of Europe, Japan, Canada, and the US. Extreme events like wars can distort the population, leading to a loss of population in certain age groups.

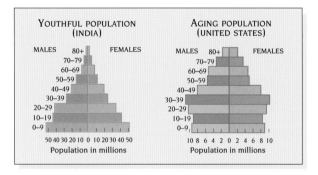

YOUTHFUL POPULATION (INDIA)

MALES    80+    FEMALES
         70–79
         60–69
         50–59
         40–49
         30–39
         20–29
         10–19
         0–9

50 40 30 20 10  0  10 20 30 40 50
Population in millions

AGING POPULATION (UNITED STATES)

MALES    80+    FEMALES
         70–79
         60–69
         50–59
         40–49
         30–39
         20–29
         10–19
         0–9

10 8 6 4 2 0 2 4 6 8 10
Population in millions

## POPULATION DENSITY

**The main map** (*center*) and the map below both show population density – the number of people who live in a given area. The map below shows the average population density per country. You can see that European countries and parts of Asia are very densely populated. The large map shows where people actually live. While the average population density in Brazil and Egypt is quite low, the coasts of Brazil and the areas close to the Nile River in Egypt are very densely populated.

### DENSE POPULATION

Huge crowds near the Haora Bridge in Kolkata (Calcutta), India – one of the world's most densely populated cities.

POPULATION DENSITY

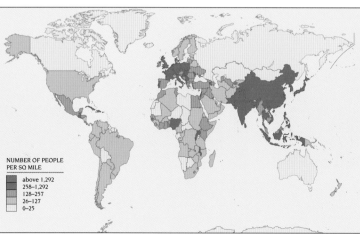

NUMBER OF PEOPLE PER SQ MILE

above 1,292
258–1,292
128–257
26–127
0–25

### SPARSE POPULATION

The cold north of Canada has one of the lowest population densities in the world. Some people live in extreme isolation, separated from others by lakes and forests.

*(map labels: Arctic Circle, 180°, 85°, 150°, 120°, 90°, 60°, 30°, 30°, Tropic of Cancer, Equator, Tropic of Capricorn, 30°, 60°, Antarctic Circle, 180°, 85°, 150°, 120°, 90°, 60°, 30°)*

## URBAN GROWTH

The 20th century saw a huge increase in the number of people living in urban areas. This has led to more large cities and the development of some "super cities" such as Mexico City and Tokyo, each with more than 20 million people. In 1900, only about 10% of the population lived in cities. Now it is closer to 50% and soon the figure may be nearer two in three people. Some continents are far more "urbanized" than others: in South America nearly 80% of people live in cities, whereas in Africa the figure is only about 30%.

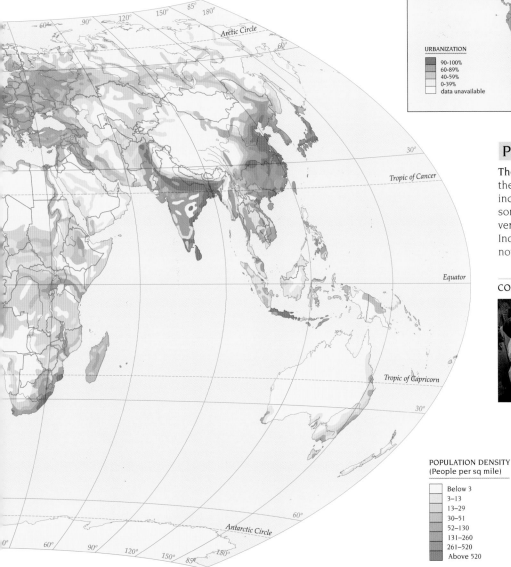

POPULATION DENSITY
(People per sq mile)

- Below 3
- 3–13
- 13–29
- 30–51
- 52–130
- 131–260
- 261–520
- Above 520

## LEVELS OF URBANIZATION

URBANIZATION

- 90-100%
- 60-89%
- 40-59%
- 0-39%
- data unavailable

## POPULATION GROWTH

The rate of population growth varies dramatically between the continents. Europe has a large population but it is increasing slowly. Africa is still sparsely populated, but in some countries such as Kenya, the population is growing very rapidly, increasing pressure on the land. China and India have the world's largest populations. Both countries now have laws designed to curb the birthrate.

### CONTROLLING GROWTH

In 1980, fewer than 25% of women in less-developed countries used birth control. Education programs and more widely available contraceptives are thought to have doubled this figure. But many families still have no access to contraception.

### AN AGING POPULATION

In some countries, a low birthrate and an increasingly long-lived elderly population have greatly increased the ratio of old people to younger people, putting a strain on health and social services. For example, in Japan, most people can now expect to live to at least 80 years of age.

## BIRTHRATE

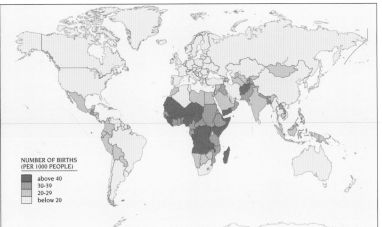

NUMBER OF BIRTHS
(PER 1000 PEOPLE)

- above 40
- 30-39
- 20-29
- below 20

## LIFE EXPECTANCY

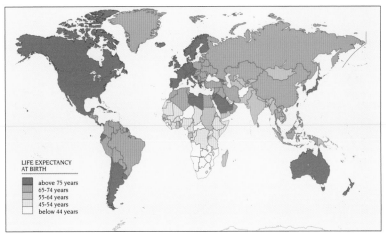

LIFE EXPECTANCY
AT BIRTH

- above 75 years
- 65-74 years
- 55-64 years
- 45-54 years
- below 44 years

# THE WORLD ECONOMY

Throughout the world, the way in which people make a living varies greatly. The countries of Western Europe and North America, along with Japan and Australia, are the most economically developed in the world, with a long- established and very diverse range of industries. They sell their products and services internationally. Less economically developed countries in Central Asia and much of Africa have a much smaller number of industries – some may rely on a single product – and many goods are produced only for the local market.

## MEASURING WEALTH

The wealth of a country can be measured in several ways: for example, by the average annual income per person; by the volume of its trade; and by the total value of the goods and services that the country produces annually – its Gross Domestic Product or GDP. The map below shows the average GDP per person for each of the world's countries, expressed in US$. Most of the highest levels of GDP are in Europe and the US; most of the lowest are in Africa.

### WORLD ECONOMIES

Average GDP per capita (in US$)

- Above 20,000
- 5,000–20,000
- 2,000–5,000
- Below 2,000
- Data unavailable

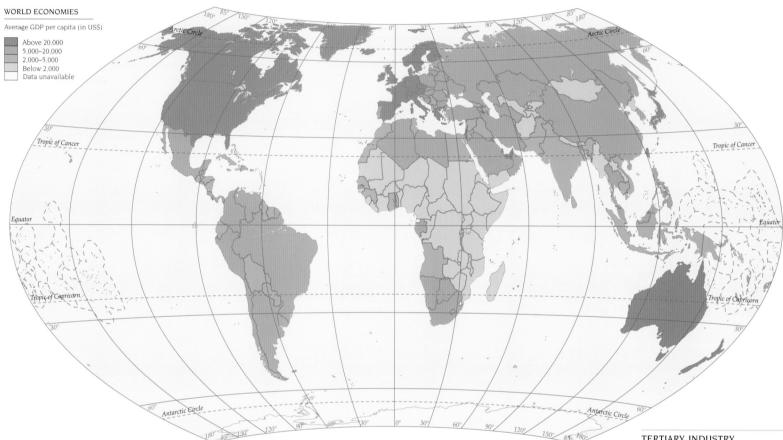

## TYPES OF INDUSTRY

Industries are usually defined in one of three ways. Primary industries such as farming or mining involve the production of raw materials such as food or minerals. Secondary industries make or manufacture finished products out of raw materials: clothing and car manufacture are examples of secondary industries. People who work in tertiary industries provide different kinds of services. Banking, insurance, and tourism are all examples of tertiary industries. Some economically advanced nations such as Germany and the US now have quaternary industries, such as biotechnology which are knowledge-creation industries, devoted to the research and development of new products.

### PRIMARY INDUSTRY

Tobacco leaves are picked and laid out for drying in Cuba, one of the world's great producers of cigars. Many countries rely on one or two high-value "cash crops" like tobacco to earn foreign currency.

### SECONDARY INDUSTRY

This skilled Thai weaver is producing an intricately patterned silk fabric on a hand loom. Fabric manufacture is an important industry throughout South and Southeast Asia. In India and Pakistan, vast quantities of cotton are produced in highly mechanized factories, but many fabrics are still hand woven.

### TERTIARY INDUSTRY

The City of London is one of the world's great finance centers. Branches of many banks and insurance companies, including the world-famous Lloyds of London, are clustered into the City's "square mile."

## PATTERNS OF TRADE

Almost all countries trade goods with one another in order to obtain products they cannot produce themselves, and to make money from goods they have produced. Some countries – for example those in the Caribbean – rely mainly on a single export, usually a food or mineral, and can suffer a loss of income when world prices drop. Other countries, such as Germany and Japan, export a vast range of both raw materials and manufactured goods throughout the world. A number of huge companies, known as multinational corporations, are responsible for more than 70% of world trade, with divisions all over the world. They include firms like Exxon, Coca Cola, and Microsoft.

### CONTAINER SHIPS

Many products are transported around the world on container ships. Containers are of a standard size so that they can be efficiently transported to their destinations. Some ships are specially designed to carry perishable goods such as fruit and vegetables.

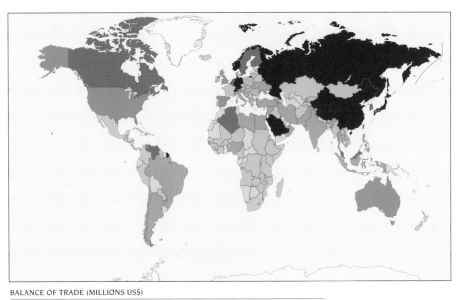
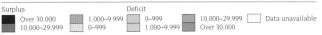

BALANCE OF TRADE (MILLIONS US$)

Surplus
- Over 30,000
- 10,000–29,999
- 1,000–9,999
- 0–999

Deficit
- 0–999
- 1,000–9,999
- 10,000–29,999
- Over 30,000
- Data unavailable

IRELAND
LUXEMBOURG
CYPRUS
CHINA
SOUTH KOREA
TAIWAN
INDIA
THAILAND
MALAYSIA
SINGAPORE
BOTSWANA
MAURITIUS

## DEVELOPING ECONOMIES

Although world trade is still dominated by the more economically developed countries, since the 1970s, less economically developed countries have increased their share of world trade from less than 10% to nearly 30%. Countries such as China, India, Malaysia, and South Korea, aided by investment from their governments or from wealthier countries, have become able to manufacture and export a wide variety of goods. These products include cars, electronics, clothing, and footwear. Multinational companies can take advantage of cheaper labor costs to manufacture goods in these countries. Moves are being made to limit the exploitation of workers who are paid very low wages for producing luxury goods.

### ASIAN 'TIGER' ECONOMIES

The economies of Malaysia, Taiwan, and South Korea boomed in the late 1980s, attracting investment for buildings such as the Petronas Towers (*above*).

## TOURISM

Tourism is now the world's largest industry. More than 700 million people travel both abroad and in their own countries as tourists each year. People in more developed countries have more money and leisure time to travel. Tourism can bring large amounts of cash into the local economy, but local people do not always benefit. They may have to take low-paid jobs and experience great intrusions into their lives. Tourist development and pollution may damage the environment – sometimes destroying the very attractions that led to the development of tourism in the first place.

### ECOTOURISM

These tourists are being introduced to a giant tortoise, one of the many unique animals found in the Galapagos Islands. A number of places with special animals and ecosystems have introduced programs to teach visitors about them. This not only educates people about the need to safeguard these environments, but brings in money to help protect them.

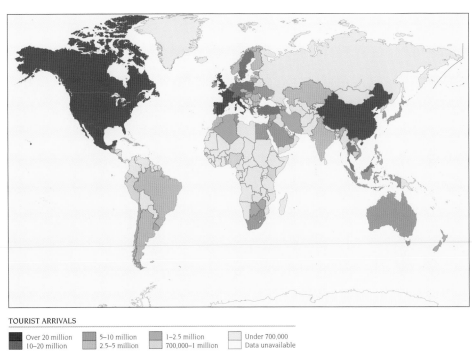

TOURIST ARRIVALS
- Over 20 million
- 10–20 million
- 5–10 million
- 2.5–5 million
- 1–2.5 million
- 700,000–1 million
- Under 700,000
- Data unavailable

# BORDERS AND BOUNDARIES

**There are more countries in the world today** than ever before – over 190 – whereas in 1950, there were only 82. Since then, many former European colonies and Soviet states have become independent. The establishment of borders for each of these countries has often been the subject of disagreement.

## Military borders
At the end of wars, new borders are often drawn up between the countries – frequently along cease-fire lines. They may remain there for many years. At the end of the Korean War in 1953, North and South Korea were divided close to the 38° line of latitude. This border has remained heavily fortified.

## Enclaves
If part of a country's territory has become separated from the rest of the country, and is surrounded by foreign territory, it is called an enclave. Kaliningrad is part of the Russian Federation, but is cut off from it by Lithuania and Belarus.

## River borders
Over one-sixth of the world's national borders are formed by rivers. Long stretches of the Danube form natural borders in southeastern Europe.

## Long borders
The border between the USA and Canada is the second longest continuous border in the world. It cuts through the center of the Great Lakes. To the west of the Great Lakes, the border runs along the 49° line of latitude.

## Mountain borders
Mountain ranges such as the Pyrenees, Alps and Himalayas form natural borders between many countries. In the Andes, border disputes between Chile and Argentina centered on finding the highest point in the mountain range that divided them.

## Straight line borders
The borders of many countries in Africa and other former colonial territories are straight lines. This was the simplest solution for colonial administrators, who often knew little of the country's geography or population.

## Lake boundaries
Countries which lie next to lakes usually fix their borders in the middle of the lake. Complicated agreements between colonial powers led to the awkward division of Lake Nyasa in Africa.

## Territorial disputes
There are still many disputed territories and borders. One of the most serious territorial disputes is between India and Pakistan over Jammu and Kashmir, which has led to three wars since 1947.

# THE ATLAS
## OF THE
# WORLD

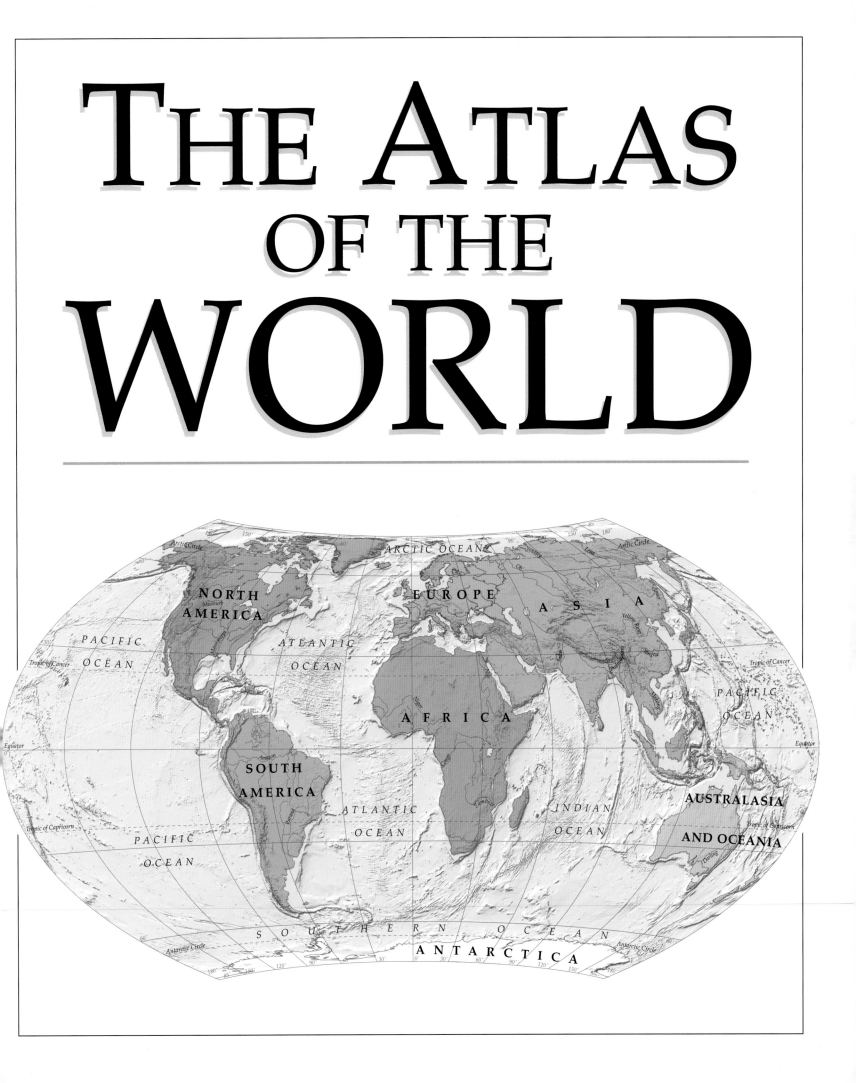

ARCTIC OCEAN

NORTH
AMERICA

EUROPE

A S I A

PACIFIC
OCEAN

ATLANTIC

OCEAN

Tropic of Cancer

AFRICA

PACIFIC
OCEAN

Tropic of Cancer

Equator

SOUTH
AMERICA

Equator

AUSTRALASIA

ATLANTIC
OCEAN

INDIAN
OCEAN

Tropic of Capricorn

Tropic of Capricorn

AND OCEANIA

PACIFIC
OCEAN

S O U T H E R N   O C E A N

Antarctic Circle

Antarctic Circle

ANTARCTICA

# THE NATIONS OF THE WORLD

**The world is divided** into 193 independent countries, and about 60 overseas territories or dependencies. The largest country is the Russian Federation covering 6,592,735 sq miles; the smallest is Vatican City in Rome, with an area of 0.17 sq miles.

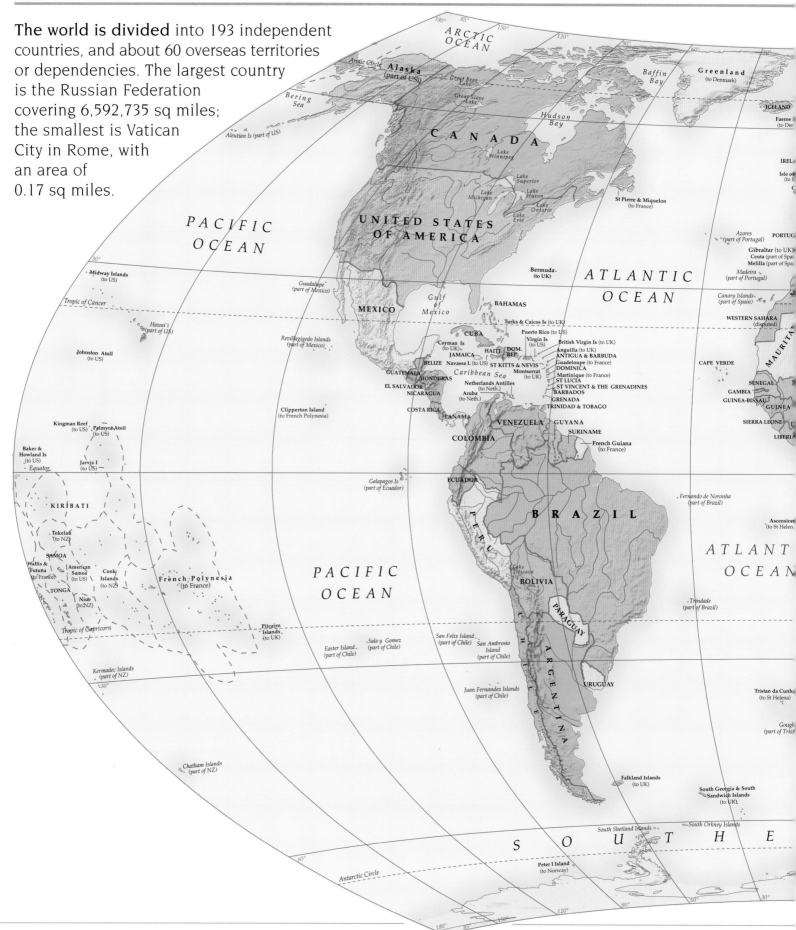

ARCTIC OCEAN

Arctic Circle
Alaska (part of US)
Great Bear Lake
Baffin Bay
Greenland (to Denmark)
Bering Sea
Great Slave Lake
Hudson Bay
ICELAND
Aleutian Is (part of US)
Faeroe Is (to Der
C A N A D A
Lake Winnipeg
IRELA
Lake Superior
Lake Michigan
Lake Huron
Lake Ontario
Lake Erie
Isle of (to U
PACIFIC OCEAN
UNITED STATES OF AMERICA
St Pierre & Miquelon (to France)
Azores (part of Portugal)
PORTUG
Midway Islands (to US)
Bermuda (to UK)
ATLANTIC OCEAN
Gibraltar (to UK)
Ceuta (part of Spai
Melilla (part of Spa
Tropic of Cancer
Guadalupe (part of Mexico)
Gulf of Mexico
BAHAMAS
Canary Islands (part of Spain)
Hawai'i (part of US)
Revillagigedo Islands (part of Mexico)
MEXICO
CUBA
Turks & Caicos Is (to UK)
Puerto Rico (to US)
WESTERN SAHARA (disputed)
Madeira (part of Portugal)
Johnston Atoll (to US)
Cayman Is (to UK)
JAMAICA
HAITI
DOM. REP.
Virgin Is (to US)
British Virgin Is (to UK)
Anguilla (to UK)
ANTIGUA & BARBUDA
Guadeloupe (to France)
DOMINICA
Martinique (to France)
ST LUCIA
ST VINCENT & THE GRENADINES
BARBADOS
GRENADA
TRINIDAD & TOBAGO
CAPE VERDE
MAURITA
BELIZE
Navassa I. (to US)
ST KITTS & NEVIS
Montserrat (to UK)
GUATEMALA
HONDURAS
Caribbean Sea
EL SALVADOR
NICARAGUA
Netherlands Antilles (to Neth.)
Aruba (to Neth.)
SENEGAL
GAMBIA
GUINEA-BISSAU
GUINEA
Clipperton Island (to French Polynesia)
COSTA RICA
PANAMA
VENEZUELA
GUYANA
SURINAME
SIERRA LEONE
LIBERIA
Kingman Reef (to US)
Palmyra Atoll (to US)
COLOMBIA
French Guiana (to France)
Baker & Howland Is (to US)
Jarvis I (to US)
Equator
Galapagos Is (part of Ecuador)
ECUADOR
Fernando de Noronha (part of Brazil)
KIRIBATI
PERU
B R A Z I L
Ascension (to St Helen
Tokelau (to NZ)
ATLANT OCEA
SAMOA
Wallis & Futuna (to France)
American Samoa (to US)
Cook Islands (to NZ)
French Polynesia (to France)
Lake Titicaca
BOLIVIA
TONGA
Niue (to NZ)
PACIFIC OCEAN
Trindade (part of Brazil)
PARAGUAY
Tropic of Capricorn
Pitcairn Islands (to UK)
Sala y Gomez (part of Chile)
San Felix Island (part of Chile)
San Ambrosio Island (part of Chile)
CHILE
ARGENTINA
URUGUAY
Trinidad (part of Brazil)
Kermadec Islands (part of NZ)
Easter Island (part of Chile)
Tristan da Cunha (to St Helena)
Juan Fernandez Islands (part of Chile)
Gough (part of Trist
Chatham Islands (part of NZ)
Falkland Islands (to UK)
South Georgia & South Sandwich Islands (to UK)
South Shetland Islands
South Orkney Islands
S O U T H E
Antarctic Circle
Peter I Island (to Norway)

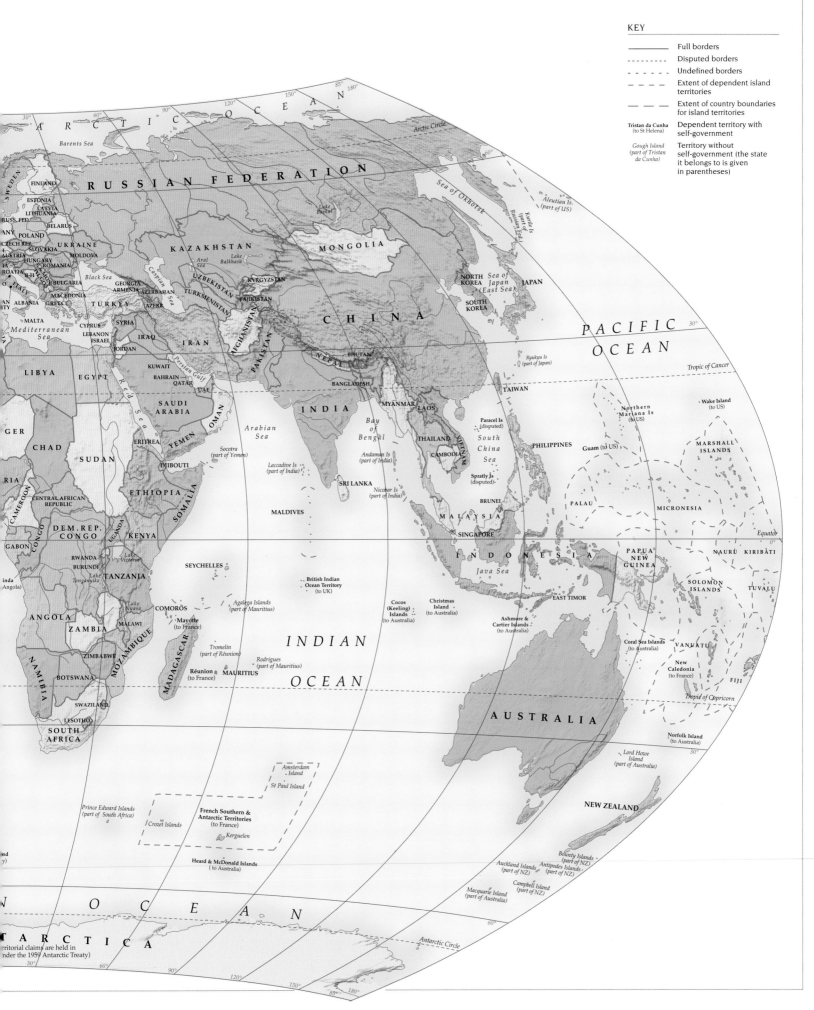

KEY

———————— Full borders

············ Disputed borders

— — — — Undefined borders

– – – – – Extent of dependent island
territories

— – — – Extent of country boundaries
for island territories

**Tristan da Cunha**
*(to St Helena)*    Dependent territory with
self-government

*Gough Island*
*(part of Tristan*
*da Cunha)*    Territory without
self-government (the state
it belongs to is given
in parentheses)

ARCTIC OCEAN

*Barents Sea*

SWEDEN
FINLAND

RUSSIAN FEDERATION

*Arctic Circle*

ESTONIA
LATVIA
LITHUANIA
RUSS. FED.
ANY
POLAND
BELARUS

CZECH REP.
SLOVAKIA
AUSTRIA
HUNGARY
MOLDOVA
UKRAINE

KAZAKHSTAN

MONGOLIA

*Lake Baikal*

*Sea of Okhotsk*

*Kurile Is*
*(part of*
*Russian Fed.)*

*Aleutian Is.*
*(part of US)*

CROATIA
ROMANIA
BULGARIA

*Black Sea*

GEORGIA
ARMENIA
AZERBAIJAN

*Aral Sea*

*Lake Balkhash*

UZBEKISTAN

KYRGYZSTAN

NORTH
KOREA

*Sea of*
*Japan*
*(East Sea)*

JAPAN

ITALY
MACEDONIA
ALBANIA
GREECE
MALTA

TURKEY

*Caspian Sea*

TURKMENISTAN

AZERB.

TAJIKISTAN

AFGHANISTAN

CHINA

SOUTH
KOREA

PACIFIC
OCEAN

*Mediterranean*
*Sea*

CYPRUS
LEBANON
ISRAEL
SYRIA

IRAQ

JORDAN

IRAN

PAKISTAN

NEPAL

BHUTAN

*Ryukyu Is*
*(part of Japan)*

*Tropic of Cancer*

LIBYA

EGYPT

*Red Sea*

KUWAIT
BAHRAIN
QATAR
UAE

SAUDI
ARABIA

OMAN

BANGLADESH

INDIA

MYANMAR
LAOS

TAIWAN

*Paracel Is*
*(disputed)*

*Northern*
*Mariana Is*
*(to US)*

*Wake Island*
*(to US)*

GER
CHAD
SUDAN

ERITREA

YEMEN

*Arabian*
*Sea*

*Bay*
*of*
*Bengal*

THAILAND

*South*
*China*
*Sea*

PHILIPPINES

*Guam (to US)*

MARSHALL
ISLANDS

RIA
CAMEROON
CENTRAL AFRICAN
REPUBLIC

DJIBOUTI

ETHIOPIA

SOMALIA

*Socotra*
*(part of Yemen)*

*Laccadive Is*
*(part of India)*

*Andaman Is*
*(part of India)*

CAMBODIA

VIETNAM

*Spratly Is*
*(disputed)*

BRUNEI

PALAU

MICRONESIA

GABON
CONGO
DEM. REP.
CONGO

UGANDA

KENYA

SRI LANKA

*Nicobar Is*
*(part of India)*

MALAYSIA

nda
(Angola)

RWANDA
BURUNDI
TANZANIA

*Lake*
*Victoria*

MALDIVES

SINGAPORE

INDONESIA

*Java Sea*

PAPUA
NEW
GUINEA

*Nauru* KIRIBATI

*Equator*

SEYCHELLES

*Lake*
*Tanganyika*

*British Indian*
*Ocean Territory*
*(to UK)*

SOLOMON
ISLANDS

TUVALU

ANGOLA
ZAMBIA
MALAWI

*Lake*
*Nyasa*

COMOROS

*Agalega Islands*
*(part of Mauritius)*

*Cocos*
*(Keeling)*
*Islands*
*(to Australia)*

*Christmas*
*Island*
*(to Australia)*

EAST TIMOR

*Ashmore &*
*Cartier Islands*
*(to Australia)*

*Coral Sea Islands*
*(to Australia)*

VANUATU

NAMIBIA
ZIMBABWE
MOZAMBIQUE
MADAGASCAR

*Mayotte*
*(to France)*

INDIAN

*Tromelin*
*(part of Réunion)*

*Rodrigues*
*(part of Mauritius)*

OCEAN

*New*
*Caledonia*
*(to France)*

FIJI

BOTSWANA

*Réunion*
*(to France)*

MAURITIUS

*Tropic of Capricorn*

SWAZILAND

SOUTH
AFRICA

LESOTHO

AUSTRALIA

*Norfolk Island*
*(to Australia)*

*Amsterdam*
*Island*

*St Paul Island*

*Lord Howe*
*Island*
*(part of Australia)*

NEW ZEALAND

*Prince Edward Islands*
*(part of South Africa)*

*Crozet Islands*

**French Southern &**
**Antarctic Territories**
**(to France)**

*Kerguelen*

**Heard & McDonald Islands**
**(to Australia)**

*Bounty Islands*
*(part of NZ)*

*Auckland Islands*
*(part of NZ)*

*Antipodes Islands*
*(part of NZ)*

*Macquarie Island*
*(part of Australia)*

*Campbell Island*
*(part of NZ)*

OCEAN

N OCEAN

ARCTICA

*Antarctic Circle*

(territorial claims are held in
under the 1959 Antarctic Treaty)

30°  60°  85° 180°

60°

120°

150°

85° 180°

# CONTINENTAL NORTH AMERICA

**North America is the world's** third largest continent, stretching from icy Greenland to the tropical Caribbean. The first people came from Asia more than 20,000 years ago. Their descendants spread across the continent, ate fish, meat, and wild and cultivated plants, and developed a wide variety of cultures and languages. About 500 years ago, immigrants from Europe, Africa, and Asia began to arrive in North America, bringing their own languages and cultures to the "New World."

4,600 miles
3,540 miles

## CROSS-SECTION THROUGH NORTH AMERICA

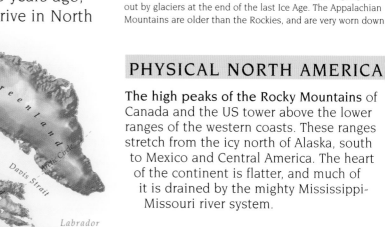

Rocky Mountains    Great Plains    Great Lakes    Appalachian Mountains

W      3,200 miles      E

In the west the land rises from the Pacific Ocean to the coastal ranges and the Rocky Mountains. Farther east, the continent flattens into the Great Plains and the Great Lakes – gouged out by glaciers at the end of the last Ice Age. The Appalachian Mountains are older than the Rockies, and are very worn down.

## PHYSICAL NORTH AMERICA

**The high peaks of the Rocky Mountains** of Canada and the US tower above the lower ranges of the western coasts. These ranges stretch from the icy north of Alaska, south to Mexico and Central America. The heart of the continent is flatter, and much of it is drained by the mighty Mississippi-Missouri river system.

### ARCTIC OCEAN

ASIA
Bering Strait
Beaufort Sea
Bering Sea
Aleutian Islands
Aleutian Range
Brooks Range
Arctic Circle
△ Highest point Mount McKinley 20,321ft
Gulf of Alaska
Coast Mountains
Mackenzie Mountains
Mackenzie
Great Bear Lake
Victoria Island
Greenland
Baffin Bay
Baffin Island
Arctic Circle
Davis Strait
Labrador Sea

Great Slave Lake
Rocky Mountains
Hudson Bay
Canadian Shield
Laurentian Mountains
Newfoundland
Labrador
Nova Scotia

Mount Rainier 20,321ft
△ Mount St. Helens 8,362ft
Great Basin
Great Salt Lake
Sierra Nevada
▽ Lowest point Death Valley 282ft
Sonoran Desert
Baja California
Lake Winnipeg
Lake Manitoba
Great Plains
Colorado
Missouri
Ohio
Mississippi
Arkansas
Lake Superior
Lake Michigan
Lake Huron
Lake Erie
Lake Ontario
Great Lakes
St. Lawrence
Appalachian Mountains
△ Brasstown Bald 4,783ft

ATLANTIC OCEAN

PACIFIC OCEAN
Sierra Madre Occidental
Sierra Madre Oriental
Rio Grande
Mississippi Delta
Gulf of Mexico
Tropic of Cancer
Tropic of Cancer
West Indies
Cuba
Greater Antilles
Lesser Antilles
Caribbean Sea
△ Citlaltépetl 18,700ft
Yucatan Peninsula
Sierra Madre del Sur
Lake Nicaragua
SOUTH AMERICA

### ① THE FAR NORTH

Much of Canada's far north is covered by ice and snow. Only in summer, when the ice thaws, can hardy lichens grow. Great pine forests are found farther south.

### ② THE MOUNTAINOUS WEST

A long mountain chain runs down the western side of the continent. These mountains are young, and are still being formed.

### ③ THE GREAT PLAINS

The fertile soils of much of the Great Plains – at the heart of the continent – allow cereal crops like wheat and corn to be grown.

### THE DESERT REGIONS ④

The Sonoran Desert in southern US and northern Mexico is typical of North America's desert regions.

### ⑤ THE TROPICAL SOUTH

The Yucatan Peninsula, in Mexico, is full of caves and sinkholes because the humid tropical climate accelerates erosion.

### ELEVATION

| | |
|---|---|
| | 19,690ft |
| | 16,400ft |
| | 13,120ft |
| | 9,840ft |
| | 6,560ft |
| | 3,280ft |
| | 1,640ft |
| | 820ft |
| | 330ft |
| | sea level |
| | below sea level |
| ►◄ | cross section |

SCALE 1:52,000,000
0 km   500   1000
0 miles 250   500   750   1000

# POLITICAL NORTH AMERICA

The US, Canada, and Mexico are all federal countries. This means that political power is shared between the national government and the state or provincial governments. Canada and the US are democracies with a long history of freedom and equal rights. Governments in the countries south of the US have been less stable, often ruled by dictators or harsh regimes. Many people have suffered for their political beliefs. During the 1960s and 70s many of the Caribbean islands gained independence from their European colonial rulers.

## POPULATION

The most densely populated parts of North America are the east and west coasts of the US, central Mexico, the countries of Central America, and the Caribbean islands. The far north of Canada, covered by ice, lakes, and forests, has a very small and scattered population.

Largest city
NEW YORK
21.7 million people

**POPULATION DENSITY**
People per sq mile

- Below 26
- 26–127
- 128–257
- 258–645
- 648–1,292
- Above 1,292

## STANDARDS OF LIVING

The US and Canada are two of the world's wealthiest countries, although pockets of poverty remain. In Central America and the Caribbean, people are less well off. Many in Mexico City live in overcrowded and inadequate housing.

STANDARD OF LIVING
(UN Human Development Index)

low          high

### THE SPACE RACE

The US has pioneered some of the great achievements of 20th century technology, including mass production of the automobile and the development of spacecraft.

**STATE ABBREVIATIONS**

AL Alabama
CT Connecticut
IN Indiana
MA Massachusetts
MS Mississippi
NH New Hampshire
PA Pennsylvania
RI Rhode Island
VT Vermont
WV West Virginia

### GREAT DISTANCES

Most people in the US and Canada rely on automobiles to transport them from place to place. Since the 1930s, extensive highway systems have been built to link all parts of the continent.

**POPULATION**

- ◉ Above 500,000
- ◎ 100,000 to 500,000
- ● 50,000 to 100,000
- • Below 50,000

SCALE 1:47,500,000

0 km    500    1000
0 miles 250  500  750  1000

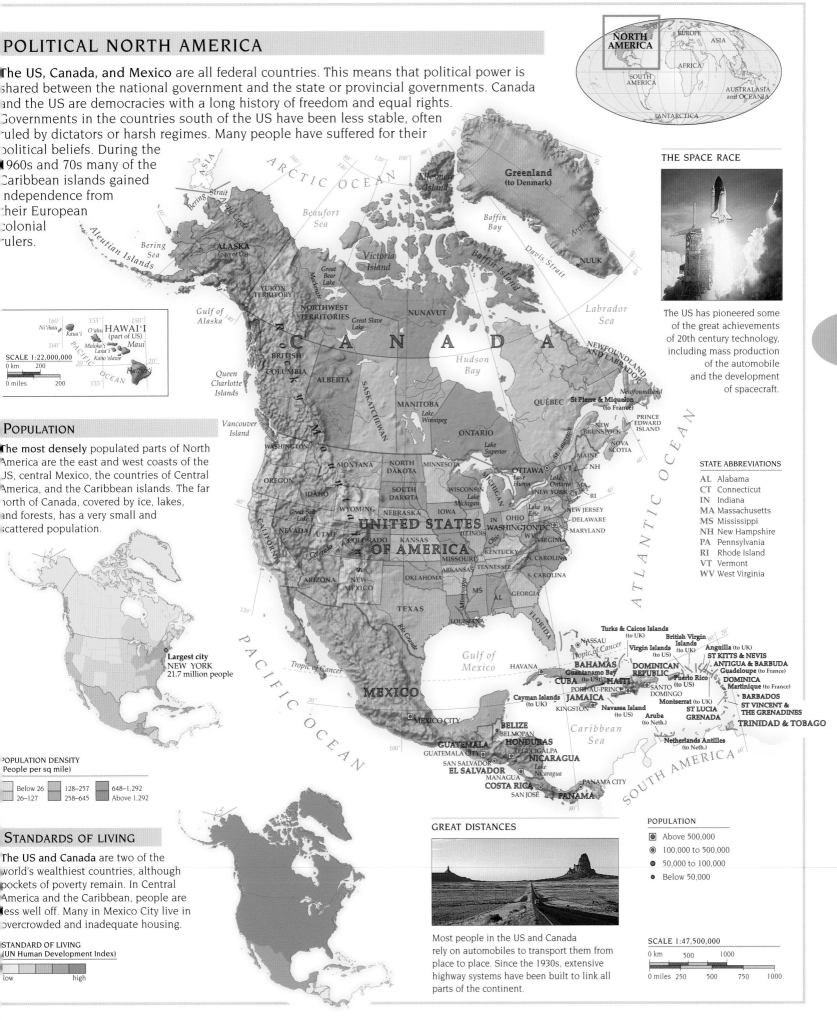

HAWAI'I (part of US)
SCALE 1:22,000,000

# NORTH AMERICAN GEOGRAPHY

**Canada and the US are among** the world's wealthiest countries. They have rich natural resources, good farmland, and thriving, varied industries. The range of different industries in Mexico is growing, but other Central American countries and the Caribbean islands rely on one or two important cash crops and tourism for most of their incomes. They have a lower standard of living than the US and Canada.

## MINERAL RESOURCES

North America still has large amounts of mineral resources. Canada has important nickel reserves, Mexico is renowned for its silver, and bauxite – used to make aluminum – is found in Jamaica. Oil and gas are plentiful, particularly in the Arctic northwest by the Beaufort Sea, and farther south by the Gulf of Mexico.

## INDUSTRY

**The US and Canada** have an extremely wide range of industries, from mining and the processing of farm produce, to heavy and light manufacturing and service industries like banking. A variety of goods are produced, including airplanes, cars, and computers. Oil exports and machine assembly are Mexico's main industries. In Central America and the Caribbean nations, most industry is based on agricultural produce.

**MINERAL RESOURCES**

- Bauxite
- Copper
- Iron
- Nickel
- Phosphates
- Silver
- Uranium
- Oil/gas field
- Coal field

### TIMBER PROCESSING

Huge tracts of forest are found toward the north of the continent; nearly 30% of Canada is covered by forest. Timber is processed to make paper in cities such as Portland and Vancouver.

### HIGH-TECH INDUSTRY

The Santa Clara Valley, just south of San Francisco, is also known as Silicon Valley because of the number of firms producing computer hardware and software and microelectronics that have set up in the area.

### FOOD PROCESSING

Jamaica has been famous for its rum since the 16th century. Syrup is extracted from sugarcane, which then fermented to make rum

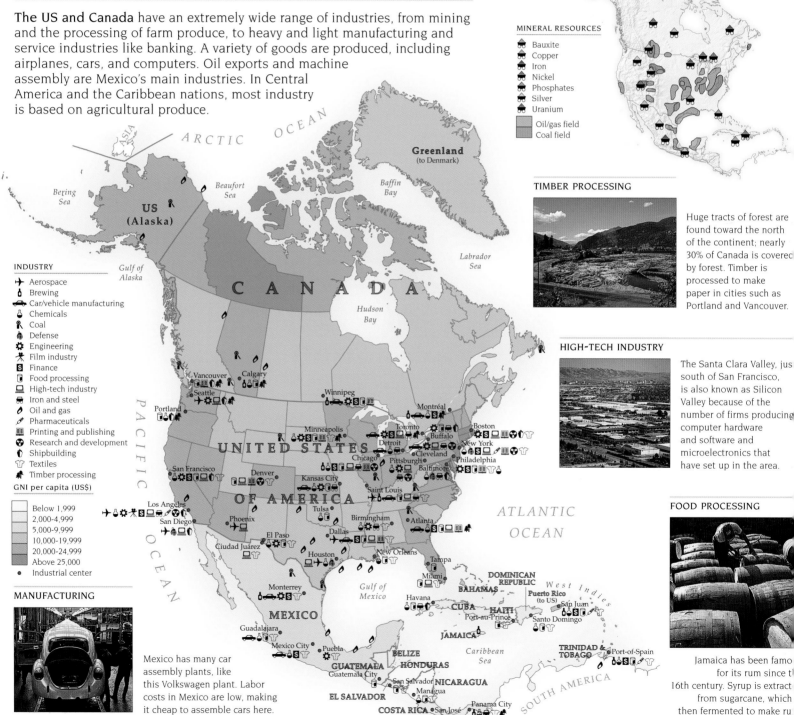

**INDUSTRY**

- ✈ Aerospace
- ♦ Brewing
- 🚗 Car/vehicle manufacturing
- 🝊 Chemicals
- ℞ Coal
- ♠ Defense
- ✿ Engineering
- ✷ Film industry
- S Finance
- Food processing
- 💻 High-tech industry
- Iron and steel
- ♦ Oil and gas
- Pharmaceuticals
- Printing and publishing
- Research and development
- Shipbuilding
- Textiles
- 🌲 Timber processing

GNI per capita (US$)

- Below 1,999
- 2,000–4,999
- 5,000–9,999
- 10,000–19,999
- 20,000–24,999
- Above 25,000
- Industrial center

### MANUFACTURING

Mexico has many car assembly plants, like this Volkswagen plant. Labor costs in Mexico are low, making it cheap to assemble cars here.

## CLIMATE

Much of northern Canada lies within the Arctic Circle and is permanently covered by ice or the sparse vegetation known as tundra. Southern Canada and much of central US have a continental climate, with hot summers and cold winters. The southern parts of the US, Central America, and the Caribbean have a hot, humid tropical climate. The Caribbean and the eastern and central states of the US often experience hurricane-force winds, waterspouts, and tornadoes.

### EXTREME WEATHER EVENTS

Symbols indicate climatic extremes

**Coldest place**
NORTHICE (Greenland)
Temp. -87°F

**Wettest place**
HENDERSON LAKE (BC, Canada)
Annual rainfall 262 in

**Hottest place**
DEATH VALLEY (CA, USA)
Temp. 135°F

**Driest place**
BATAQUES (Mexico)
Annual rainfall 1.2 in

### CLIMATE

- Ice cap
- Tundra
- Subarctic
- Cool continental
- Warm temperate
- Mediterranean
- Semiarid
- Arid
- Humid equatorial
- Tropical
- Hot humid

### NORTH AMERICA'S HOTTEST PLACE

Death Valley in California is the hottest and driest place in the US. Strong, dry winds sweep through the valley, constantly reshaping the sand and salt deposits that cover its floor.

## LAND USE AND AGRICULTURE

On the Great Plains and prairies of the US and Canada, vast quantities of cereal crops, including corn and wheat, grow in the fertile soils. Cattle are also raised on great ranches throughout these regions and on the foothills of the Rocky Mountains. In California, vegetables and fruits are grown with the aid of irrigation. Bananas, coffee, and sugarcane are grown for export in Central America and the Caribbean, while sorghum and corn are grown as subsistence crops.

### BANANA PLANTATION

Banana plantations are common in the Caribbean and Central America. The fruit is grown for local consumption and for export to the US and Europe, where they are valued for their flavor and nutritional qualities.

### FISHING

The Grand Banks off the eastern coast of Canada were once home to almost limitless fish stocks. Overfishing has reduced the number of fish to very low levels. Quotas limiting the numbers of fish caught help the numbers to rise.

### LAND USE AND AGRICULTURE

- Cattle
- Poultry
- Pigs
- Reindeer
- Sheep
- Bananas
- Cereals
- Citrus fruits
- Coffee
- Corn
- Cotton
- Fishing
- Fruit
- Peanuts
- Rice
- Shellfish
- Soybeans
- Sugarcane
- Timber
- Tobacco
- Vineyards

- Cropland
- Desert
- Forest
- Ice cap
- Mountain region
- Pasture
- Tundra
- Wetland
- Major conurbation

# WESTERN CANADA

ALBERTA, BRITISH COLUMBIA, MANITOBA, NORTHWEST
TERRITORIES, NUNAVUT, SASKATCHEWAN, YUKON TERRITORY

**The first inhabitants** of Canada's western provinces
were Native Americans. By the late 1800s, the Canadian
Pacific Railroad was completed and European settlers
moved west, turning most of the prairie into huge grain
farms. North of the prairies lie the vast, empty territories
that have significant Native American populations.
In 1999, part of the Northwest Territories, known as
Nunavut, became a self-governing Inuit homeland.

## INDUSTRY

**The major industries** in the prairie provinces
are related to agriculture, such as
meat-processing in Manitoba. Alberta
has huge reserves of fossil fuels,
and the other provinces are rich in
minerals, including zinc, nickel,
silver, and uranium. British
Columbia's economy depends
on manufacturing, especially
automobiles, chemicals, and
machinery, along
with paper and
timber industries.

**STRUCTURE OF
INDUSTRY**

Primary 6%
Services 64%
Manufacturing 30%

### INDUSTRY

- 🚗 Car manufacturing
- ⚗ Chemicals
- ⚙ Engineering
- 🍴 Food processing
- △ Metal refining
- ◊ Oil and gas
- ⛏ Mining
- 🪵 Timber processing
- ① Tourism
- ▣ Major industrial center / area
- — Major road

## ENVIRONMENTAL ISSUES

**Across the north of the region,** the ground is permanently
frozen. This is called permafrost. Building on this frozen
surface is very difficult, because the heat from houses or
roads can cause the ground to melt, and subside.
Many of the extensive forests in
British Columbia are used for
commercial lumbering. The
province produces more than
half of Canada's timber.

**ENVIRONMENTAL
ISSUES**

- 🎿 Lumbering activity
- ▦ Permafrost zone
- ● Major industrial center

## FARMING AND LAND USE

**More than 20%** of the world's wheat is
grown in Canada's prairie provinces:
Manitoba, Alberta, and
Saskatchewan. Beef cattle graze
on the ranches of Alberta and
British Columbia. Fruits,
especially apples, flourish
in the sheltered southern
valleys of British Columbia,
and Pacific salmon, and
herring are caught off
the west coast.

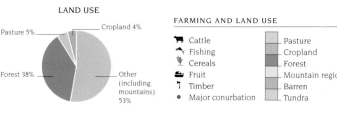

**LAND USE**

Pasture 5%
Cropland 4%
Forest 38%
Other (including mountains) 53%

**FARMING AND LAND USE**

- 🐄 Cattle
- 🎣 Fishing
- 🌾 Cereals
- 🦞 Fruit
- 🌲 Timber
- ● Major conurbation
- ▢ Pasture
- ▢ Cropland
- ▢ Forest
- ▢ Mountain regio
- ▢ Barren
- ▢ Tundra

## THE LANDSCAPE

**The prairie provinces** are mostly flat. Occasionally,
the level plains are broken up by river valleys such
as that of the Qu'Appelle in Saskatchewan. In the
west, the jagged peaks and steep passes of the Rocky
Mountains and the Coast Mountains, are covered
in snow for months on end. West of the Rockies,
the land descends sharply toward the coast of
British Columbia. The far north is covered by dense
forests and many glacial lakes.

**The Arctic**
Most of Canada's northern
islands are within of the
Arctic Circle. They are
covered by ice year-round.

**Mount Logan (B5)**
Mount Logan is Canada's
tallest peak. It rises 19,551 ft.

**Glacial lakes**
The plains are
covered by
thousands of
lakes, many of
which are vast.
They are the
remains of great
glacial lakes left
after the last
Ice Age.

**Islands and inlets (C6, C7)**
The British Columbia coast is peppered
with islands and fjordlike inlets, created
by the force of the Pacific Ocean.

**River valleys**
Prairie river valleys such as the Qu'Appelle (F7
(French for "who calls") were cut by glacial
meltwater thousands of years ago.

NORTH
AMERICA

Western
Canada

## POPULATION

**Most of the people** in western
Canada live near the Canada/
US border, taking advantage
of the warmer climate
and convenient
transportation routes.
In the cold, forested
north, the population
is sparse, with only a
few people per 100 sq
miles – many of them
Native Americans such
as the Inuit.

Edmonton
Vancouver  Calgary  Saskatoon  Winnipeg
Regina

URBAN/RURAL POPULATION DIVISION

Vancouver 22.7%
Other towns
and cities 38%
Calgary
10.8%
Edmonton
10.5%
Rural population 18%

## CLIMATE

Parts of northern Canada are frozen all
year round. The prairie provinces have
warm summers and cold winters. Coastal
British Columbia is mild and wet.

January                                July

EUROPE
ASIA
AFRICA
SOUTH
AMERICA
AUSTRALASIA
AND OCEANIA
ANTARCTICA

3/8
2
2
4
2
8
12
4
4
2
12
2
8 4 2
4
2
2

TEMPERATURE AND PRECIPITATION

More than 68°F        23 to 32°F
59 to 68°F            14 to 23°F
50 to 59°F            5 to 14°F
41 to 50°F            Less than 5°F
32 to 41°F        4   Precipitation
                         (in)

INHABITANTS
PER SQ MILE

More than 30
3–30
Less than 3
• Major city

LAND HEIGHT | SEA DEPTH
--- | ---
Above 13,120ft | 0–820ft
6,560–13,120ft | 820–1,640ft
3,280–6,560ft | 1,640–3,280ft
1,640–3,280ft | 3,280–6,560ft
820–1,640ft | 6,560–9,840ft
330–820ft | 9,840–13,120ft
0–330ft | Below 13,120ft

CITIES AND TOWNS

▣ Over 500,000 people
◉ 100,000–500,000
○ 50,000–100,000
○ Less than 50,000

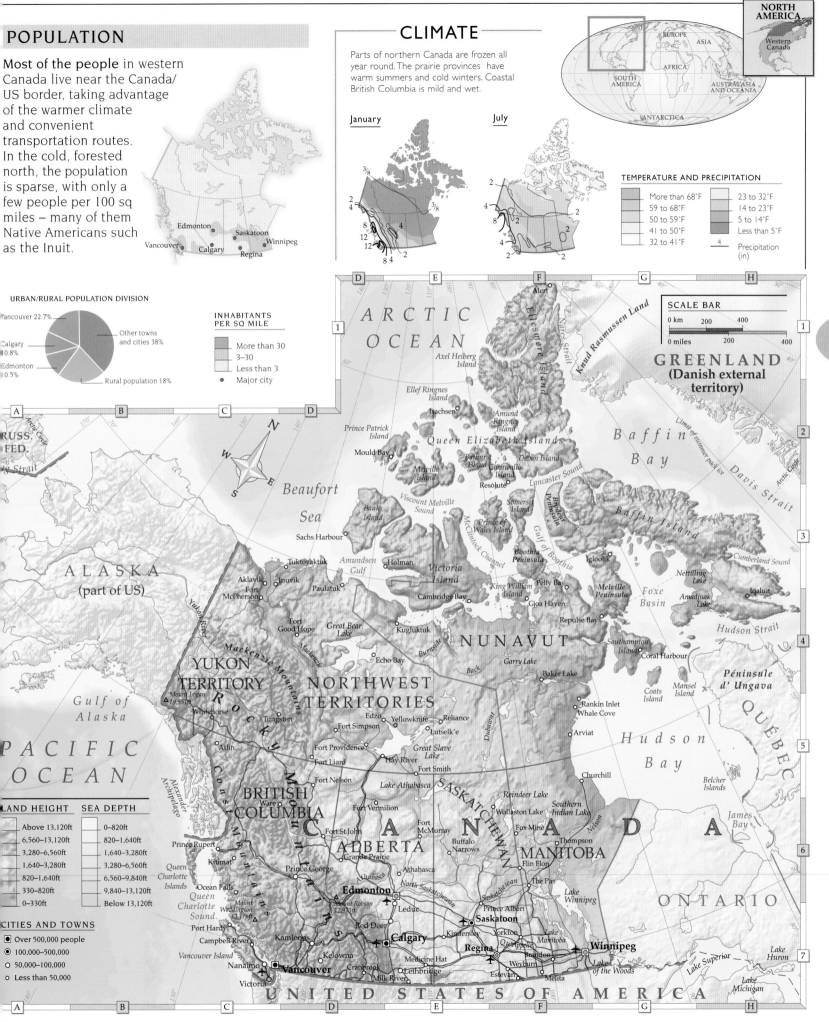

SCALE BAR

0 km    200    400

0 miles    200    400

GREENLAND
(Danish external
territory)

ARCTIC
OCEAN

Alert
Ellesmere Island
Axel Heiberg
Island
Knud Rasmussen Land
Nares Strait
Baffin
Bay
Davis Strait
Arctic Circle

Ellef Ringnes
Island
Amund
Ringnes
Island
Queen Elizabeth Islands
Bathurst
Island
Cornwallis
Island
Devon Island
Lancaster Sound
Cumberland Sound
Nettilling
Lake
Iqaluit
Amadjuak
Lake

Isachsen
Prince Patrick
Island
Mould Bay
Melville
Island
Resolute
Viscount Melville
Sound
Somerset
Island
Boothia
Peninsula
Gulf of Boothia
Baffin Island
Foxe
Basin

RUSS.
FED.

Bering Strait

ALASKA
(part of US)

Beaufort
Sea

Banks
Island
Sachs Harbour
Amundsen
Gulf
Holman
Prince of
Wales Island
McClintock Channel
Victoria
Island
King William
Island
Pelly Bay
Igloolik
Melville
Peninsula
Southampton
Island
Coral Harbour
Coats
Island
Mansel
Island
Péninsule
d' Ungava

Tuktoyaktuk
Aklavik
Inuvik
Fort
McPherson
Paulatuk
Cambridge Bay
Gjoa Haven
Repulse Bay
Hudson Strait

Yukon River
Fort
Good Hope
Great Bear
Lake
Kugluktuk
NUNAVUT
Rankin Inlet
Whale Cove
Hudson
Bay

Mackenzie Mountains
Echo Bay
Burnside
Garry Lake
Baker Lake

YUKON
TERRITORY
NORTHWEST
TERRITORIES
Back
Arviat

Mount Logan
19,551ft
Whitehorse
Tungsten
Edzo
Yellowknife
Reliance
Rankin Inlet
QUÉBEC

Gulf of
Alaska
Fort Simpson
Lutselk'e
Dubawnt
Churchill
Belcher
Islands
James
Bay

PACIFIC
OCEAN

Atlin
Fort Providence
Great Slave
Lake
Hay River
Fort Smith
SASKATCHEWAN
Reindeer Lake
Southern
Indian Lake
Nelson
ONTARIO

Fort Liard
Fort Nelson
Lake Athabasca
Wollaston Lake
Fox Mine

Alexander
Archipelago
BRITISH
COLUMBIA
Ware
Fort Vermilion
Fort
McMurray
Buffalo
Narrows
Thompson
Flin Flon

Prince Rupert
Fort St. John
Grande Prairie
ALBERTA
MANITOBA
The Pas
Lake
Winnipeg

Kitimat
Prince George
Athabasca
Athabasca
North Saskatchewan
Saskatchewan
Lake
Winnipegosis

Queen
Charlotte
Islands
Ocean Falls
Edmonton
Leduc
Prince Albert
Lake
Manitoba

Queen
Charlotte
Sound
Mount
Waddington
13,176ft
Mount Robson
12,973ft
Red Deer
Saskatoon

Port Hardy
Kamloops
Calgary
Kindersley
Yorkton
Winnipeg

Campbell River
Kelowna
Cranbrook
Medicine Hat
Qu'Appelle
Lake Manitoba
Lake
Winnipeg

Vancouver Island
Nanaimo
Vancouver
Milk River
Lethbridge
Regina
Weyburn
Estevan
Melita
Lake
of the Woods
Lake Superior
Lake
Huron

Victoria
UNITED STATES OF AMERICA
Lake
Michigan

C A N A D A

Coast Mountains
Rocky Mountains
Mackenzie

# EASTERN CANADA

NEW BRUNSWICK, NEWFOUNDLAND AND LABRADOR,
NOVA SCOTIA, ONTARIO, PRINCE EDWARD ISLAND, QUÉBEC

**The first European settlements** grew up in the Atlantic provinces, and along the St. Lawrence River, where Québec City and Montréal were founded. People gradually migrated farther west along the St. Lawrence River and the Great Lakes, establishing other cities including Toronto. Although the majority of Canadians speak English, people in Québec speak mainly French, and both English and French are official languages in Canada.

## INDUSTRY

**In the Atlantic provinces** the traditional fishing industry has declined, causing unemployment. However, Newfoundland has a thriving food processing industry. Ontario and Québec have a wide range of industries, including the generation of hydroelectricity, mining, and chemicals, car manufacturing and fruit canning in the great cities. Large amounts of wood pulp and paper are also produced.

### STRUCTURE OF INDUSTRY

Primary 7%
Services 64%
Manufacturing 29%

### INDUSTRY

- 🚗 Car manufacturing
- ⚗ Chemicals
- 🔀 Fish processing
- ▤ Food processing
- ⊹ Hydroelectric power
- △ Metal refining
- ⛏ Mining
- 🌲 Timber processing
- 🖳 High-tech industry
- 🏛 Tourism
- ⊙ Major industrial center / area
- — Major road

## FARMING AND LAND USE

**The best farmland lies** on the flat, fertile plains close to the St. Lawrence River and on the strip of land between Lake Erie and Lake Ontario. It is used to grow fruits such as grapes, cherries, and peaches, and to raise cattle. Nova Scotia has fruit farms, and the rich red soils of Prince Edward Island produce a big potato crop. The vast forests that grow across the north are a major source of timber.

### LAND USE

Pasture 2%   Cropland 2%
Other (including mountains) 32%
Forest 64%

### FARMING AND LAND USE

- 🐄 Cattle
- ⚓ Fishing
- 🦪 Fruit
- 🥔 Potatoes
- ⚑ Timber
- ▢ Pasture
- ▢ Cropland
- ▢ Forest
- ▢ Tundra
- ● Major conurbation

## ENVIRONMENTAL ISSUES

**Acid rain** caused by emissions from factories in the US and along the St. Lawrence River destroys forests and kills marine life. Massive hydro-electric power projects in James Bay on Hudson Bay have flooded huge areas of land, affecting the environment and the local Cree people. Overfishing in the Atlantic has led to limits being set on the number of fish that can be caught.

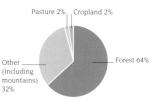

### ENVIRONMENTAL ISSUES

- 🐟 Depleted fish stocks
- 〰 Major dam
- 😷 Urban air pollution
- ▦ Affected by acid rain
- ● Major industrial center

## THE LANDSCAPE

**A huge, ancient mass of rock** called the Canadian Shield lies beneath much of eastern Canada. It is covered by low hills, rocky outcrops, thousands of lakes, and huge areas of forest. Much of the Canadian Shield is permanently frozen. The St. Lawrence River flows out of Lake Ontario and into the Atlantic Ocean. It is surrounded by rolling hills and flat areas of very fertile farmland.

### Scoured by ice

About 20,000 years ago, Labrador and northern Québec were completely covered by ice. The glaciers scraped hollows in the rock beneath. When the ice melted, lakes were left in the hollows that remained.

### Lake Superior (B5)

Lake Superior is the largest freshwater lake in the world. It covers an area of 32,150 sq miles and lies between Canada and the USA.

### St. Lawrence River (E5)

The St. Lawrence River is 2,350 miles long. Parts of it have become silted up, causing it to be braided into many different channels. Between December and mid-April the river freezes over.

### Highlands

The highlands of New Brunswick, Nova Scotia, and Newfoundland are the most northerly part of the Appalachian mountain chain.

### The Bay of Fundy (F5)

This bay has the world's highest tides. It is shaped like a funnel, and as the Atlantic flows into it, the ever narrowing shores cause the water level to rise 20–50 ft at every high tide.

# POPULATION

Colonists from both France and Britain settled in Canada from the early 1600s onward. Ontario and the Atlantic provinces are mainly English speaking. Québec is the center of French settlement; 80% of the people there have French as a first language. Most people in eastern Canada now live in large towns and cities close to the St. Lawrence River.

NORTH AMERICA
Eastern Canada

### CLIMATE

Winters are very cold, but warm winds from the Gulf of Mexico can bring hot summers to southern Ontario and the areas bordering the St. Lawrence River.

January

July

**TEMPERATURE AND PRECIPITATION**

- More than 68°F
- 59 to 68°F
- 50 to 59°F
- 41 to 50°F
- 32 to 41°F
- 23 to 32°F
- 5 to 23°F
- -13 to 5°F
- Less than -13°F

4 — Precipitation (in)

**URBAN/RURAL POPULATION DIVISION**

- Toronto 19.7%
- Montréal 14.5%
- Ottawa 3.7%
- Other towns and cities 46.1%
- Rural population 16%

**INHABITANTS PER SQ MILE**

- More than 260
- 130–260
- 3–130
- Less than 3

- ■ Capital city
- ● Major city

**CITIES AND TOWNS**

- ■ Over 500,000 people
- ◉ 100,000–500,000
- ◎ 50,000–100,000
- ○ Less than 50,000

**LAND HEIGHT**

- 1,640–3,280ft
- 820–1,640ft
- 330–820ft
- 0–330ft

**SEA DEPTH**

- 0–820ft
- 820–1,640ft
- 1,640–3,280ft
- 3,280–6,560ft
- 6,560–9,840ft
- 9,840–13,120ft
- Below 13,120ft

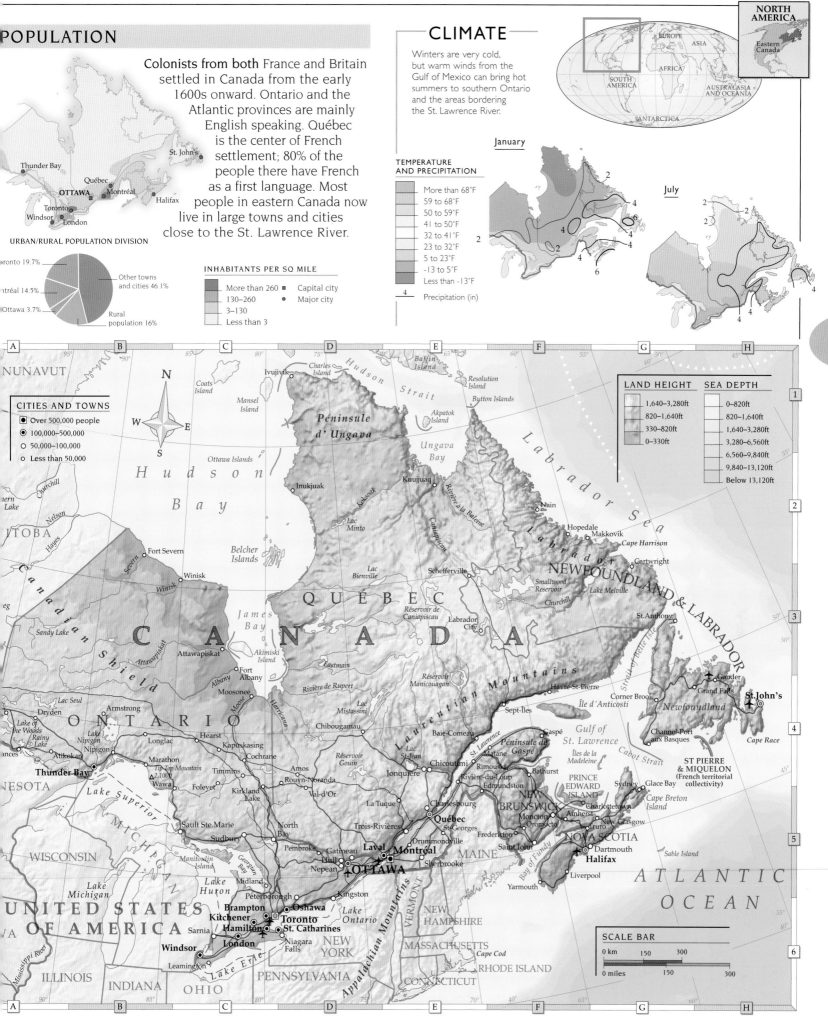

**SCALE BAR**

0 km — 150 — 300

0 miles — 150 — 300

# THE PHYSICAL US

2,807 miles

1,548 miles

**The United States of America** covers the broad central portion of North America, from the northern border with Canada to Mexico in the dry desert south, and includes the mountainous northwestern state of Alaska and the distant volcanic islands of Hawai'i. The US has large areas of fertile land at its heart, flanked by the high Rocky Mountains in the west and the ancient Appalachians in the east.

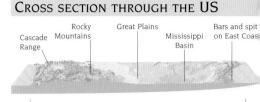
The highest points in the US are found in the wide belt of mountains in the west. Rising from the sea are the coastal ranges of the Cascades and Sierra Nevada, while the Rocky Mountains are farther inland. The terrain drops away to the east, down across the Great Plains and Mississippi Basin, toward the Appalachians and the East Coast.

## THE LANDSCAPE OF THE US

**Coastal mountains** rise from the Pacific coast, dropping inland to the deserts and salt lakes of the Great Basin. The high Rocky Mountains are new mountains, formed by the collision of two of Earth's tectonic plates. Much of the central US is flat, consisting of a series of undulating, often virtually featureless plains known as the Great Plains. The Appalachian Mountains in the East are much older, lower, and more eroded than the Rockies. The Great Lakes, the world's largest freshwater lakes, lie on the US–Canada border.

HAWAI'I

Ni'ihau · Kaua'i
O'ahu · Moloka'i
Lana'i · Maui
Kaho'olawe · Pu'u 'Ula'ula 10,023ft
Hawai'i
Mauna Kea 13,797ft
Mauna Loa 13,678ft

PACIFIC OCEAN

0 km 200
0 miles 200

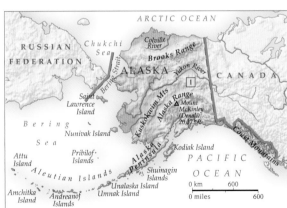

ARCTIC OCEAN

RUSSIAN FEDERATION
Chukchi Sea
Colville River
Brooks Range
Saint Lawrence Island
Bering Strait
ALASKA
Yukon River
CANADA
Kuskokwim Mts
Alaska Range
Mount McKinley (Denali) 20,323ft
Nunivak Island
Bering Sea
Attu Island
Pribilof Islands
Alaska Peninsula
Kodiak Island
PACIFIC OCEAN
Shumagin Islands
Amchitka Island
Andreanof Islands
Aleutian Islands
Unalaska Island
Umnak Island
Coast Mountains

0 km 600
0 miles 600

**LAND HEIGHT**

| | |
|---|---|
| | Above 13,120ft |
| | 6,560–13,120ft |
| | 3,280–6,560ft |
| | 1,640–3,280ft |
| | 820–1,640ft |
| | 330–820ft |
| | 0–330ft |
| | Below sea level |

CANADA

Cape Flattery
Mount Olympus 7,965ft
Glacier Peak 10,541ft
Columbia River
Mount Rainier 14,409ft
Franklin D. Roosevelt Lake
Cabinet Mountains
Lewis Range
Flathead Lake
Missouri River
Columbia Basin
Snake River
Bitterroot Range
Clearwater Mountains
Cape Blanco
Mount Hood 11,235ft
Blue Mountains
Hells Canyon
Salmon River
Musselshell River
Mount Jefferson 10,495ft
Salmon River Mountains
Borah Peak 12,660ft
Yellowstone River
Upper Klamath Lake
Harney Basin
Malheur Lake
Yellowstone Lake
Absaroka Range
Hyndman Peak 12,076ft
Grand Teton 13,769ft
Gannett Peak 13,802ft
Bighorn Mtns
Mount Shasta 14,159ft
Goose Lake
Columbia Plateau
Snake River Plain
Fremont Peak 13,743ft
Cape Mendocino
Honey Lake
Great
Humboldt River
Great Salt Lake
Bear Lake
Great Divide Basin
Point Arena
Pyramid Lake
Basin
Great Salt Lake Desert
Kings Peak 13,526ft
Uinta Mountains
Flaming Gorge Reservoir
Lake Tahoe
Utah Lake
Walker Lake
Wasatch Range
Wheeler Peak 13,060ft
White River
Mono Lake
Boundary Peak 13,139ft
Sevier Lake
Delano Peak 12,171ft
Roan Plateau
North Palisade 14,241ft
Mount Whitney 14,495ft
Death Valley
Lake Mead
Virgin River
Colorado Lake Powell
Green River
Mount Peale 12,719ft
Colorado River
Uncompahgre 14,307ft
San Juan Mountains
Owens Lake
Grand Canyon
Plateau
Blanca Peak 14,345ft
Mojave Desert
Humphreys Peak 12,634ft
Painted Desert
Little Colorado River
Channel Islands
Little Colorado River
Verde River
Salton Sea
Colorado River
Baldy Peak 11,404ft
Sonoran Desert
Gila River
Sierra Blanca Peak 11,972ft
Chiricahua Peak 9,796ft

MEXICO

Rio Grande

**1  ALASKA**

Alaska's far north is frozen solid for most of the year. Rivers can flow only during the short summer, when heat from the weak sun melts the surface ice.

**2  DESERTS**

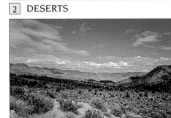

The Great Basin in the Rocky Mountains is made up of many shallow, salty lakes, deserts, and scrubby vegetation like tumbleweed.

**3  MOUNTAINS**

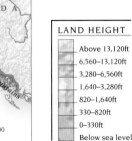

The Rocky Mountains form a spine running up the western side of the US. The mountains continue north through Canada, into Alaska.

**SCALE BAR**

0 km 100 200
0 miles 100 200

# CLIMATE

The climate of the US is generally temperate and continental – with warm summers and cold winters. Humid, subtropical climates occur only in Hawai'i and the Florida keys. In contrast, much of Alaska has a freezing arctic climate. On the Pacific Coast, warm, moist air from the ocean creates a milder climate, but the coastal mountains prevent this air from reaching the interior – making most of the central US very dry. Extreme weather events are common in the central US, including sudden tornadoes, blizzards, and hailstorms.

**NORTH AMERICA**

**CLIMATE**
- Subarctic
- Cool continental
- Temperate
- Warm temperate
- Semiarid
- Arid
- Tropical

**Wettest place**
Waialeale, Kaua'i, Hawai'i
Annual rainfall 460in

**Coldest place**
Prospect Creek, Alaska
Temperature -80°F

**Hottest and driest place**
Death Valley (California, USA)
Temperature 134F
Annual rainfall 1.63in

**EXTREME WEATHER EVENTS**
Symbols indicate climatic extremes

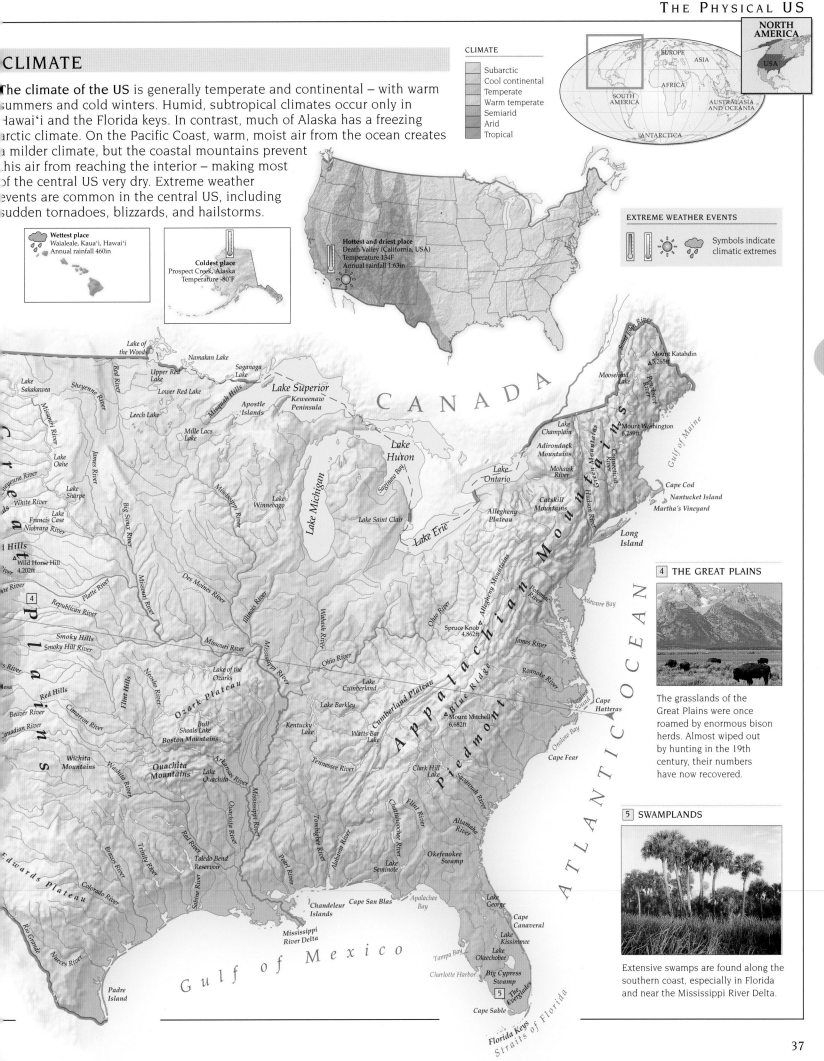

**4 THE GREAT PLAINS**

The grasslands of the Great Plains were once roamed by enormous bison herds. Almost wiped out by hunting in the 19th century, their numbers have now recovered.

**5 SWAMPLANDS**

Extensive swamps are found along the southern coast, especially in Florida and near the Mississippi River Delta.

# UNITED STATES OF AMERICA

**From a sparsely populated** "unknown" territory in the 16th century, the US has built on its natural strengths – immense tracts of fertile land and great mineral resources – to become the world's most powerful nation. Its global success was fueled by a hardworking immigrant population, exploiting their land of opportunity and sustained by the ideals of liberty and democracy that continue to bind the American people.

### WASHINGTON DC

Washington DC is the administrative capital of the US. All national government is based here, centered on the White House, an 18th-century building on Pennsylvania Avenue that is the official residence of the US president. Congress, composed of the Senate and the House of Representative meets in the Capitol.

## THE FIFTY STATES

**The US is a federation** of 50 states. Following the 1776 Revolutionary War, 13 former colonies formed the core of the new nation. Expansion continued southward and westward, aided by the Louisiana Purchase in 1803, which added former French lands to the Union. By 1867, with the purchase of Alaska, the modern shape of the US was nearly complete. Alaska and Hawai'i were admitted as states in 1959.

SCALE 1:54,000,000
0 km        600
0 miles          600

SCALE 1:22,000,000
0 km     200
0 miles        200

### NEW YORK

The first skyscrapers in New York were built at the beginning of the 20th century. The intricate Manhattan skyline has become a symbol of US urban culture throughout the world.

### STARS AND STRIPES

The 13 stripes of the US flag represent the 13 colonies that formed the first states of the Union. Each star symbolizes one of the current states; as states are admitted to the union, the number of stars increases.

### ANCIENT CIVILIZATIONS

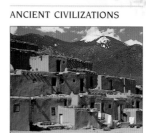

Evidence of some of the oldest cultures in the US can still be found in the Southwest. Peoples such as the Hopi and Hohokam farmed and built settlements (pueblos) here.

NORTH
AMERICA

USA

# POPULATION

The US has the most varied population in the world. The original native population has been swollen by peoples from all corners of Europe, many seeking a new life away from poverty and persecution; by Africans whose ancestors were brought to the US as slaves; and during the later half of the 20th century, by people from South America, the Caribbean, and many parts of Asia – particularly the countries on the edge of the Pacific Ocean.

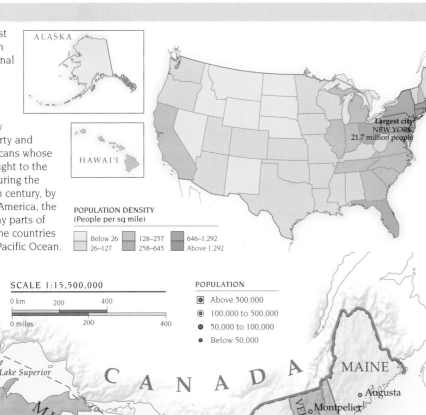

ALASKA

HAWAI'I

Largest city
NEW YORK
21.7 million people

**POPULATION DENSITY**
(People per sq mile)

Below 26
26–127
128–257
258–645
646–1,292
Above 1,292

SCALE 1:15,500,000

0 km   200   400
0 miles   200   400

**POPULATION**

◉ Above 500,000
◎ 100,000 to 500,000
● 50,000 to 100,000
• Below 50,000

## ALL AMERICANS

These children are all American citizens, regardless of their race, culture, or their parents' nationality. They show the diversity of the US, whose many different peoples came to North America for a variety of reasons.

## THE GOOD LIFE

Since the beginning of the 1980s many people have moved to the northwest Pacific states, Oregon and Washington, drawn by a more leisurely lifestyle and proximity to the magnificent countryside.

## URBAN DECAY

As industry and middle-class people have moved out of city centers into suburban areas, many inner cities have become run down, with restricted health services and delapidated amenities.

## STANDARDS OF LIVING

**Cheap and abundant food,** spacious homes equipped with labor-saving devices, and easy access to beautiful scenery for leisure activities enable many people in the US to enjoy the highest standard of living in the world. In some inner-city areas, however, unemployment has led to poverty and homelessness with related social problems. Illegal immigrants, members of minority ethnic groups, and certain isolated rural dwellers are among the less privileged people in the US.

CANADA

MAINE

Lake Superior

MICHIGAN

Lake Michigan

Lake Huron

Saint Paul

WISCONSIN

Minneapolis

Madison   Lansing

Milwaukee

Chicago

IOWA

Des Moines

Davenport   INDIANA

Detroit

Cleveland   Lake Erie

Toledo

OHIO

Columbus

Indianapolis

Springfield

Cincinnati

AMERICA

ILLINOIS

Kansas City

Jefferson City

Saint Louis

Louisville

Evansville   Frankfort

MISSOURI

Springfield

KENTUCKY

Nashville

TENNESSEE

ARKANSAS

Memphis

Little Rock

MISSISSIPPI

Shreveport

Jackson

ALABAMA

LOUISIANA

Baton Rouge

New Orleans

Mobile

Houston

Gulf of Mexico

VERMONT

Montpelier

NEW HAMPSHIRE

Concord

Boston

Albany

Lake Ontario

NEW YORK   Hartford

Buffalo

MASSACHUSETTS

Providence

RHODE ISLAND

CONNECTICUT

Newark

New York

Trenton

PENNSYLVANIA

NEW JERSEY

Pittsburgh

Harrisburg   Philadelphia

Baltimore   Dover

DELAWARE

Annapolis

Columbus

WEST VIRGINIA

WASHINGTON, DC

MARYLAND

Charleston

Richmond

VIRGINIA

Norfolk

Raleigh

NORTH CAROLINA

Charlotte

Columbia

SOUTH CAROLINA

GEORGIA

Atlanta

Birmingham

Columbus

Montgomery

Savannah

Jacksonville

Tallahassee

FLORIDA

Orlando

Tampa

Saint Petersburg

Fort Lauderdale

Miami

Appalachian Mountains

ATLANTIC OCEAN

ALASKA

HAWAI'I

**STANDARD OF LIVING**
(UN Human Development Index)

lower                    higher

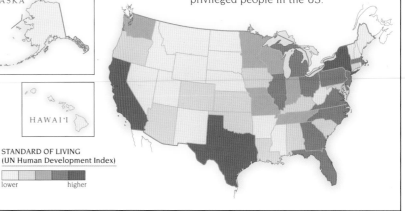

# US: THE NORTHEASTERN STATES

CONNECTICUT, DELAWARE, MAINE, MASSACHUSETTS, NEW-HAMPSHIRE, NEW JERSEY, NEW YORK, PENNSYLVANIA, RHODE ISLAND, VERMONT

**The dynamic 200-year boom** of the northeastern states has been the result of a combination of factors. Between 1855 and 1924, over 20 million people poured into the region from all over the world, hoping to build a new life. Natural resources, including coal and iron, fueled new industries and fertile farmland provided food for the region's growing population. The "gateway" cities of the Atlantic seaboard, New York and Boston, enabled manufacturers to export their goods worldwide.

## INDUSTRY

**Boston, New York, and Philadelphia** are international centers of industry and commerce. Electronics and communications are growing throughout the Northeast alongside traditional industries such as fishing and wood products. Tourism is vital for the northeastern states, particularly along the Atlantic coast.

STRUCTURE OF INDUSTRY

Manufacturing 16.5%
Primary 0.5%
Services 83%

INDUSTRY

- 🜕 Chemicals
- ✲ Engineering
- 🗋 Food processing
- ⚙ Iron and steel
- ⚗ Pharmaceuticals
- 👕 Textiles
- 🪵 Timber processing
- ⚓ Defense
- Ⓢ Finance
- ▭ High-tech
- ⊕ Research and development
- 🛳 Tourism
- [▪] Major industrial center / area
- — Major road

## ENVIRONMENTAL ISSUES

**The high level of industry** and the large population puts great pressure on the environment. Air pollution from automobiles and industry led to poor air quality in many cities and caused acid rain. The problem is worse toward the Great Lakes, where severe lake pollution has occurred.

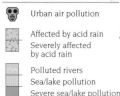

ENVIRONMENTAL ISSUES

- 💀 Urban air pollution
- Affected by acid rain
- Severely affected by acid rain
- Polluted rivers
- Sea/lake pollution
- Severe sea/lake pollution
- ● Major industrial center

## FARMING AND LAND USE

**The varied landscape** of the northeastern states supports a great range of farming. Livestock, including cattle, horses, poultry, and pigs, are raised throughout the region. The main crops are fruits and vegetables. Fishing is important, especially off the Atlantic coast of Maine.

FARMING AND LAND USE

- 🐂 Cattle
- 🐖 Pigs
- ⌄ Poultry
- ⅄ Fishing
- 🌾 Cereals
- ⁂ Cranberries
- 🍇 Fruit
- ♦ Maple syrup
- 🌲 Timber
- Cropland
- Forest
- Pasture
- ● Major conurbation

LAND USE

Pasture 6%
Cropland 14%
Other 16%
Forest 64%

## THE LANDSCAPE

**The Appalachian and Adirondack Mountains** form a barrier between the marshy lowlands of the Atlantic coast and the lowlands farther west. The interior consists of rolling hills, fertile valleys, and thousands of lakes created by the movement of glaciers.

**Appalachians (E3)**
The Appalachian Mountains, which run through most of this region, are the eroded remnants of peaks that were once much higher.

**Rocky coastline (G3)**
The coast of Maine is made up of rocky bays, islands, and inlets. If the shoreline were stretched out, it would be 2,500 miles long.

**Adirondacks (E3)**
The Adirondacks are a broad, wide mountain range, formed when older rocks were forced into a "dome" shape by movements in the Earth's crust many millions of years ago.

**Long Island Sound (F5)**
Long Island Sound is a river valley that was drowned by rising sea levels.

**Finger Lakes (D3)**
The long, narrow Finger Lakes lie in upper New York state. They were cut by glaciers.

**Delaware Bay (D6)**
Deep bays such as Delaware Bay are often surrounded by salt marshes and barrier beaches that create ideal breeding conditions for a wide variety of birds and animals.

# POPULATION

The areas along the eastern seaboard were settled by some of the earliest European colonists. The Northeast is now one of the most densely populated parts of the US. A few of the largest cities in the US, such as New York and Philadelphia, are in this region, but in the six states known as New-England many towns and cities have populations of less than 30,000 inhabitants.

## CLIMATE

Although the climate is mild during the spring and fall, summers can be hot and extremely humid, while winters are often very cold with heavy snowfall.

NORTH AMERICA

US: The Northeastern States

EUROPE
ASIA
AFRICA
SOUTH AMERICA
AUSTRALASIA AND OCEANIA
ANTARCTICA

January

July

### INHABITANTS PER SQ MILE

- More than 520
- 260–520
- 130–260
- 65–130
- Less than 65
- Major city

### URBAN/RURAL POPULATION DIVISION

New York 14.6%
Philadelphia 2.7%
Boston 1.1%
Rural population 17%
Other towns and cities 64.6%

### TEMPERATURE AND PRECIPITATION

- More than 68°F
- 59 to 68°F
- 32 to 41°F
- 23 to 32°F
- 14 to 23°F
- Less than 14°F
- 4 Precipitation (in)

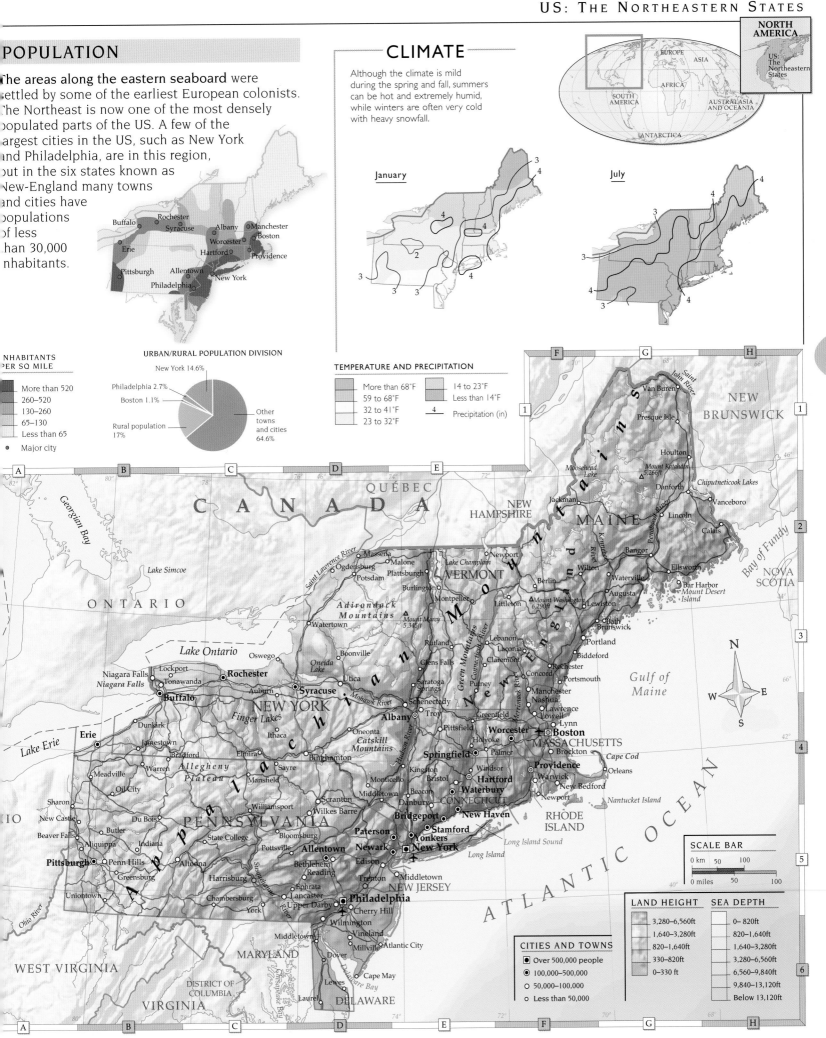

Buffalo, Rochester, Syracuse, Albany, Manchester, Worcester, Boston, Erie, Hartford, Providence, Pittsburgh, Allentown, Philadelphia, New York

CANADA
QUÉBEC
NEW HAMPSHIRE
MAINE
NEW BRUNSWICK
Van Buren
Saint John River
Presque Isle
Houlton
Moosehead Lake
Mount Katahdin 5,266ft
Danforth
Chiputneticook Lakes
Jackman
Vanceboro
Lincoln
Calais
Bay of Fundy
NOVA SCOTIA

Georgian Bay
Lake Simcoe
ONTARIO
Massena
Malone
Ogdensburg
Potsdam
Plattsburgh
Burlington
VERMONT
Newport
Berlin
Wilton
Waterville
Ellsworth
Bar Harbor
Mount Desert Island
Montpelier
Mount Washington 6,290ft
Littleton
Lewiston
Augusta
Bath
Brunswick

Adirondack Mountains
Mount Marcy 5,345ft
Watertown
Lake Ontario
Oswego
Boonville
Oneida Lake
Utica
Rutland
Green Mountains
Connecticut River
Lebanon
Claremont
Concord
Rochester
Portland
Biddeford
Gulf of Maine

Niagara Falls
Niagara Falls
Lockport
Tonawanda
Rochester
Auburn
Syracuse
Saratoga Springs
Glens Falls
Putney
Merrimack River
Manchester
Portsmouth

Buffalo
NEW YORK
Finger Lakes
Ithaca
Schenectady
Albany
Troy
Greenfield
New England Mountains
Nashua
Lawrence
Lowell
Lynn

Erie
Lake Erie
Dunkirk
Jamestown
Bradford
Elmira
Binghamton
Oneonta
Catskill Mountains
Hudson River
Pittsfield
Worcester
Boston
MASSACHUSETTS
Brockton
Cape Cod

Meadville
Warren
Allegheny Plateau
Sayre
Mansfield
Kingston
Springfield
Holyoke
Palmer
Providence
Orleans
New Bedford
Newport
Nantucket Island

Sharon
Oil City
Williamsport
Scranton
Wilkes Barre
Monticello
Middletown
Bristol
Windsor
Hartford
Waterbury
Warwick
CONNECTICUT

New Castle
Butler
Du Bois
PENNSYLVANIA
Bloomsburg
Beacon
Danbury
Bridgeport
New Haven
RHODE ISLAND
Long Island Sound

Beaver Falls
Aliquippa
Indiana
State College
Pottsville
Paterson
Yonkers
New York
Long Island

Pittsburgh
Penn Hills
Altoona
Allentown
Newark
Stamford

Greensburg
Harrisburg
Bethlehem
Reading
Edison
ATLANTIC OCEAN

Uniontown
Chambersburg
Susquehanna River
Ephrata
Lancaster
Upper Darby
Trenton
Middletown
NEW JERSEY

Ohio River
York
Philadelphia
Cherry Hill
Wilmington
Vineland
Atlantic City

WEST VIRGINIA
Middletown
Millville
MARYLAND
Dover
Delaware Bay
Cape May
Chesapeake Bay
Lewes
Cape May
DISTRICT OF COLUMBIA
VIRGINIA
Laurel
DELAWARE

N
W E
S

### SCALE BAR

0 km 50 100
0 miles 50 100

### CITIES AND TOWNS

- Over 500,000 people
- 100,000–500,000
- 50,000–100,000
- Less than 50,000

### LAND HEIGHT

- 3,280–6,560ft
- 1,640–3,280ft
- 820–1,640ft
- 330–820ft
- 0–330 ft

### SEA DEPTH

- 0– 820ft
- 820–1,640ft
- 1,640–3,280ft
- 3,280–6,560ft
- 6,560–9,840ft
- 9,840–13,120ft
- Below 13,120ft

# US: THE SOUTHERN STATES

ALABAMA, ARKANSAS, DISTRICT OF COLUMBIA, FLORIDA, GEORGIA, KENTUCKY, LOUISIANA, MARYLAND, MISSISSIPPI, NORTH CAROLINA, SOUTH CAROLINA, TENNESSEE, VIRGINIA, WEST VIRGINIA

**The southern states** suffered great devastation and poverty as a result of the Civil War (1861–65). Recovery has come with the discovery and exploitation of resources and the development of major commercial and industrial centers. Yet these states retain the vibrant mix of cultures that reflect their French, Spanish, English, and African heritage.

## INDUSTRY

**Tourism is a major industry** in the "sunbelt" states, especially Florida, and many people move to the area when they retire to enjoy the climate. Oil and gas are extracted along the coast of the Gulf of Mexico, and there are many related chemical industries. Textiles are still produced in North and South Carolina, but aerospace and other high-tech industries have been established as well.

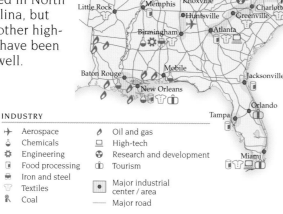

**STRUCTURE OF INDUSTRY**

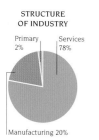

Primary 2%
Services 78%
Manufacturing 20%

**INDUSTRY**

- ✈ Aerospace
- ♨ Chemicals
- ⚙ Engineering
- 🥫 Food processing
- ⚒ Iron and steel
- ⚓ Textiles
- ⚒ Coal
- ⬟ Oil and gas
- ⌨ High-tech
- ⊗ Research and development
- ⛩ Tourism
- ● Major industrial center / area
- — Major road

## POPULATION

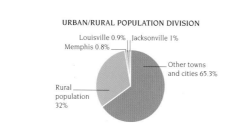

**INHABITANTS PER SQ MILE**

- More than 520
- 260–520
- 130–260
- 65–130
- Less than 65
- ■ Capital city
- ● Major city

**Creoles, descended from** Spanish and French colonizers, and Cajuns, of French-Canadian ancestry, live in the south of this region. Florida has a large Hispanic population, increased by migration from the Caribbean. In the early 20th century, five million black people, the descendants of slaves, left the South for cities in the North.

**URBAN/RURAL POPULATION DIVISION**

Louisville 0.9% | Jacksonville 1%
Memphis 0.8%
Other towns and cities 65.3%
Rural population 32%

## FARMING AND LAND USE

**Cotton is still the South's main crop,** but many old cottonfields are now pastures where all types of livestock are raised. Florida is famous for citrus fruits, while Georgia is renowned for peanuts. Sugarcane, soybeans, tobacco, corn, fruits, and rice are grown in other areas.

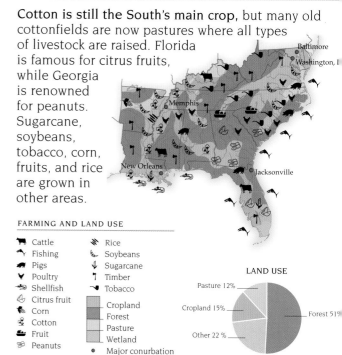

**FARMING AND LAND USE**

- 🐂 Cattle
- 🐟 Fishing
- 🐖 Pigs
- 🦃 Poultry
- 🦪 Shellfish
- 🍊 Citrus fruit
- 🌽 Corn
- ☘ Cotton
- 🍓 Fruit
- 🥜 Peanuts
- ◊ Rice
- ◊ Soybeans
- ↓ Sugarcane
- ⊺ Timber
- ↘ Tobacco

- Cropland
- Forest
- Pasture
- Wetland
- ● Major conurbation

**LAND USE**

- Pasture 12%
- Cropland 15%
- Other 22%
- Forest 51%

## THE LANDSCAPE

**The South is a land of contrasts,** the uplands of the Appalachians, the foothills of the Piedmont, and low-lying coastal regions are all featured. The interior lowlands are drained by the Mississippi. Florida is dotted with thousands of lakes and is home to The Everglades, a giant sawgrass swamp.

**Mississippi River (C4)**
A major transportation artery, the Mississippi was an essential route in opening up the interior region. With its main tributary, the Missouri, it is nearly 3,800 miles long, making it the world's fourth-longest river.

**Kentucky Bluegrass (E2)**
The gently rolling bluegrass landscape of northern Kentucky is ideal horse- and livestock-raising country.

**Barrier beaches (I3)**
Sandy barrier beaches and islands line the eastern and southern coasts, along with sheltered lagoons and salt marshes.

**The Everglades (G8)**
The Everglades cover 5,000 sq miles and support abundant wild animals and plants, many unique to the area.

**Thermal springs (B4)**
Hot Springs National Park in Arkansas has 47 thermal springs and is a popular tourist and health resort. Visitors relax here in the hot water that trickles from the hillsides.

**Tennessee River (D4)**
The Tennessee River is 625 miles long. Dams along the river generate hydro-electricity to provide most of the region's energy needs.

**Limestone caves (E4)**
Cathedral Caverns in Alabama is a collection of enormous limestone caves. The main entrance is more than 1,000 ft high and 150 ft wide.

NORTH
AMERICA

US:
The Southern
States

# ENVIRONMENTAL ISSUES

Factories in the Great Lakes region have contributed to the large blanket of acid rain across the northern part. Toward the south, hurricanes sweep in from the Atlantic Ocean and Gulf of Mexico during the hurricane season, which lasts from May to October each year.

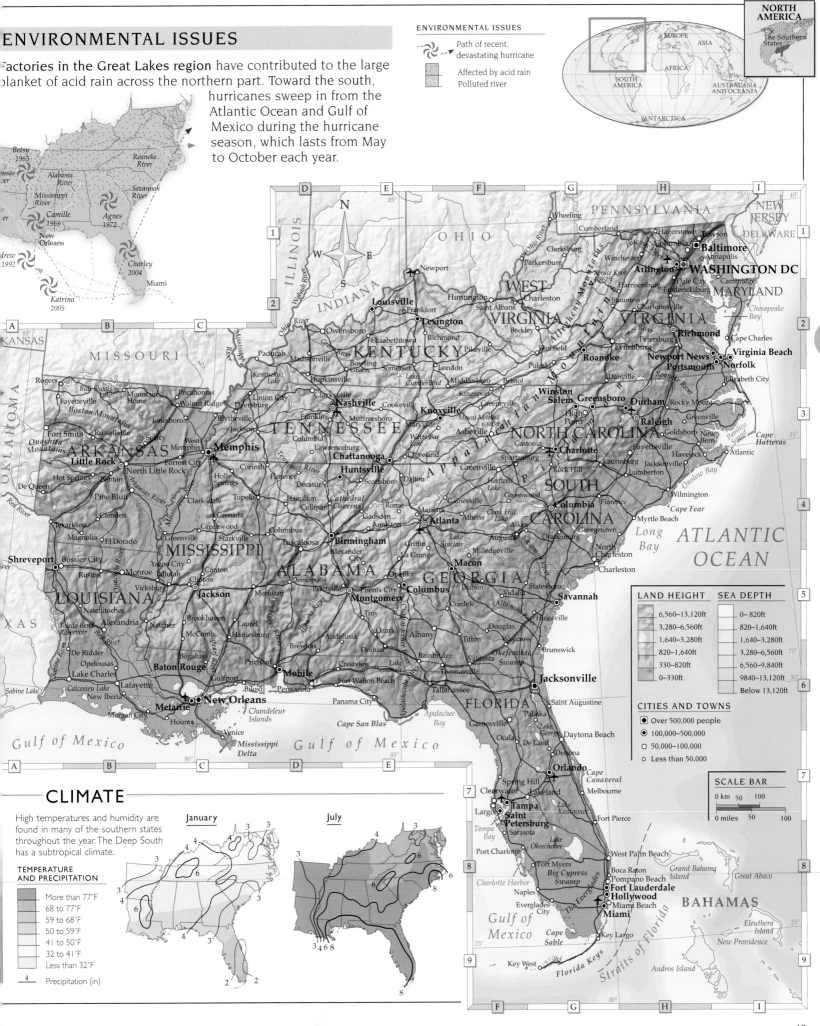

## CLIMATE

High temperatures and humidity are found in many of the southern states throughout the year. The Deep South has a subtropical climate.

**TEMPERATURE AND PRECIPITATION**

More than 77°F
68 to 77°F
59 to 68°F
50 to 59°F
41 to 50°F
32 to 41°F
Less than 32°F

4 — Precipitation (in)

January

July

**LAND HEIGHT**

6,560–13,120ft
3,280–6,560ft
1,640–3,280ft
820–1,640ft
330–820ft
0–330ft

**SEA DEPTH**

0–820ft
820–1,640ft
1,640–3,280ft
3,280–6,560ft
6,560–9,840ft
9840–13,120ft
Below 13,120ft

**CITIES AND TOWNS**

Over 500,000 people
100,000–500,000
50,000–100,000
Less than 50,000

**SCALE BAR**

0 km   50   100

0 miles   50   100

# US: THE GREAT LAKES STATES

ILLINOIS, INDIANA, MICHIGAN, OHIO, WISCONSIN

**Good transportation links**, excellent farmland, and a wealth of natural resources drew settlers from Europe and the south and east of the US to the Great Lakes states during the late 19th century. By the 1930s, they had become one of the world's most prosperous industrial and agricultural regions. In recent years, the decline in traditional heavy industries has hit some cities hard, leading to unemployment and a rising crime rate.

## POPULATION

The Great Lakes states are one of the most densely populated parts of the US. Many of the largest cities in this region – Chicago, Detroit, and Milwaukee – grew up on the banks of the lakes and are connected to each other and the rest of the US by an impressive road and rail network.

**INHABITANTS PER SQ MILE**

- More than 520
- 260–520
- 130–260
- 65–130
- Less than 65
- ● Major city

**URBAN/RURAL POPULATION DIVISION**

Detroit 2% | Chicago 6.3%
Indianapolis 1.7%
Other towns and cities 66%
Rural population 24%

## CLIMATE

Plentiful rainfall waters the agricultural lands. In winter, strong winds sweep across the lakes, and water close to the shore may freeze.

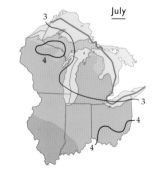

January

July

**TEMPERATURE AND PRECIPITATION**

| | |
|---|---|
| More than 77°F | 23 to 32°F |
| 68 to 77°F | 14 to 23°F |
| 59 to 68°F | Less than 14°F |
| 32 to 41°F | |

4 — Precipitation (in)

**SCALE BAR**

0 km 50 100

0 miles 50 100

**CITIES AND TOWNS**

- ● Over 500,000 people
- ◉ 100,000–500,000
- ○ 50,000–100,000
- ○ Less than 50,000

**LAND HEIGHT**

- 1,640–3,280ft
- 820–1,640ft
- 330–820ft
- 0–330ft

NORTH AMERICA

US: The Great Lake States

# FARMING AND LAND USE

**Michigan is renowned** for its cherries and apples. Corn and soybeans are the main crops produced in the region's southern states. Livestock-rearing includes pig and poultry farms – many very large – in Illinois, Indiana, and Ohio. Cattle rearing and dairy farming are common in Michigan and Wisconsin.

**LAND USE**

Pasture 8%
Other 16%
Cropland 47%
Forest 29%

Milwaukee
Chicago
Detroit
Cleveland
Indianapolis
Columbus

**FARMING AND LAND USE**

- 🐄 Cattle
- 🐖 Pigs
- 🦃 Poultry
- 🌽 Corn
- 🍎 Fruit
- 🌱 Soybeans
- 🌲 Timber
- 🍂 Tobacco
- 🍇 Vineyards
- 🌾 Wheat
- Cropland
- Forest
- Pasture
- ● Major conurbation

## THE LANDSCAPE

**Until about 10,000 years ago**, much of this region was covered by great ice sheets that extended south to Illinois and Ohio. When the ice melted the Great Lakes were left in large hollows that the ice had scoured. The ice sheets changed the course of many rivers, so today most rivers flow south into the Mississippi/Missouri River system.

**Lakes and marshes (B3)**
Wisconsin is scattered with thousands of smaller lakes and many marshy areas. Like the Great Lakes, they were formed by erosion by the retreating ice at the end of the last Ice Age.

**Underground water**
In northern Illinois much of the water is pumped from underground reservoirs. In some places, the water table has dropped by 700 ft over the last century, so many areas now face a water shortage.

**Moraines**
When the last ice age ended, the retreating ice sheets left long ridges and piles of rock to the south of Lake Michigan. Some of these ridges, known as moraines, can be up to 300 ft high.

**Limestone region**
Limestone in the hills of southern Indiana has been dissolved by acid rainwater. This has produced features such as sinkholes and underground caves.

**Lake Erie (F5)**
Lake Erie is the shallowest of the Great Lakes. Its average depth is about 62 ft. Storms that sweep across from Canada have eroded its shores and caused the silting of its harbors.

# INDUSTRY

**The US automobile industry** grew up on the banks of the Great Lakes, supported by the manufacture of iron and steel. Both industries have suffered in recent years from competition from cheap foreign imports. Meat packing has moved out from cities such as Chicago closer to the farms. New industries which have developed since the 1970s include electronics, service, and finance industries.

Milwaukee
Saginaw
Grand Rapids
Lansing
Rockford
Detroit
Chicago
Toledo
Cleveland
Gary
Fort Wayne
Youngstown
Peoria
Indianapolis
Dayton
Columbus
Cincinnati
Evansville

**STRUCTURE OF INDUSTRY**

Primary 1%
Services 73%
Manufacturing 26%

**INDUSTRY**

- 🍶 Brewing
- 🚗 Car manufacturing
- ⚗️ Chemicals
- ⚙️ Engineering
- 🗄️ Food processing
- 🚃 Iron and steel
- Ⓢ Finance
- 🖥️ High-tech
- ✪ Research and development
- ⱺ Tourism
- ▣ Major industrial center / area
- — Major road

# ENVIRONMENTAL ISSUES

**The heavy industries** on the banks of the Great Lakes have caused terrible pollution over the last century. Industrial effluent has polluted the lakes themselves, and factory emissions have led to severely acidic rain, which affects forests and lakes both here and farther away in Canada.

Milwaukee
Detroit
Chicago
Gary
Cleveland
Mississippi River
Ohio River

**ENVIRONMENTAL ISSUES**

- 😷 Urban air pollution
- Affected by acid rain
- Severely affected by acid rain
- Polluted rivers
- Lake pollution
- Severe lake pollution
- ● Major industrial center

# US: THE CENTRAL STATES

IOWA, KANSAS, MINNESOTA, MISSOURI, NEBRASKA,
NORTH DAKOTA, OKLAHOMA, SOUTH DAKOTA

**The prairie states** of the central US became one of America's richest agricultural regions in the mid-19th century. Despite the "Dustbowl" crisis of the 1930s, which led many farmers to leave their ruined lands, agriculture is still crucial to the economy, and one third of the people still live in rural areas rather than large cities.

## FARMING AND LAND USE

**Wheat and corn** grow on the fertile plains. Kansas is the leading grower of wheat in the entire US, while Iowa is one of the leaders in corn and livestock. Irrigation projects to combat drought are crucial in large areas. Livestock – including cattle in vast herds; pigs, particularly in Iowa, the Dakotas, and Nebraska; sheep; and turkeys – are raised throughout these states.

### LAND USE

Other 37%
Cropland 43%
Forest 11%
Pasture 9%

### FARMING AND LAND USE

- Cattle
- Pigs
- Poultry
- Sheep
- Corn
- Soybeans
- Wheat
- Cropland
- Forest
- Pasture
- Major conurbation

## INDUSTRY

**Industries related to agriculture**, such as food processing and the production of farm machinery, are traditional in these states but high-tech industries – such as aeronautical engineering – are increasing and large aerospace plants are found in Wichita and Saint Louis. Oil and gas are extracted in great quantities toward the south of the region, especially in Oklahoma and Kansas.

### STRUCTURE OF INDUSTRY

Primary 4%
Services 76%
Manufacturing 20%

### INDUSTRY

- ✈ Aerospace
- 🚗 Car manufacturing
- 🧪 Chemicals
- ⚙ Engineering
- Food processing
- Iron and steel
- 👕 Textiles
- Oil and gas
- S Finance

- ⊡ Major industrial center / area
- — Major road

## THE LANDSCAPE

**Most of the eastern edge** of this region is marked by the Mississippi River, while the Missouri bisects it, running from northwest to southeast. The Great Plains cover most of this area, gradually rising toward the Rocky Mountains at the far western edge of the Central States.

**The Badlands** (A 4)
The Badlands cover an area of about 2,000 sq miles in South Dakota. Heavily eroded by wind and water, almost nothing grows there.

**Minnesota**
Minnesota is filled with lakes, hills strewn with boulders, and mineral-rich deposits that have been left behind by the scouring movement of glaciers.

## ENVIRONMENTAL ISSUES

**Intensive agriculture** requires large quantities of water to grow crops. Overintensive use of the land has destroyed the balance of soil and water in the past, leading to fertile farmland being turned into useless areas of "Dustbowl." These states have a great underground store of water known as the Ogallala Aquifer, but overextraction for irrigation is reducing the amount of available water.

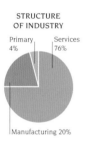

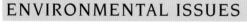

### ENVIRONMENTAL ISSUES

- 😷 Urban air pollution
- Affected by acid rain
- Aquifer
- Polluted river
- Risk of desertification
- • Major industrial center

**Chimney Rock** (A-5)
Chimney Rock stands 500-ft above the plains. It is a remnant of an ancient land surface that was eroded by the North Platte River.

**Great Plains** (D 7)
Little more than a century ago the great flat plains that cover most of these states were home to wild grasses and massive herds of buffalo. In areas where lack of water has made farming impossible, large tracts of land are being allowed to return to grassland.

**Great Salt Plains** (D 7)
These arid salt plains cover about 45-sq-miles of northern Oklahoma. An ancient salt lake once occupied the area. When the salt evaporated, only the salt flats were left.

# POPULATION

The inhabitants are largely the descendants of Europeans who came to the region in the late 1800s. The entire region is primarily rural, with enormous tracts of land devoted to growing crops. North Dakota has no city with a population greater than 100,000.

URBAN/RURAL POPULATION DIVISION

Kansas City 1.9%
Oklahoma City 2.3%
Omaha 1.8%
Other towns and cities 60%
Rural population 34%

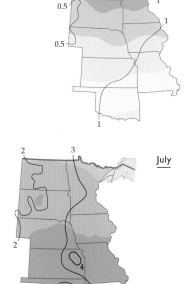

INHABITANTS PER SQ MILE

- More than 130
- 65–130
- Less than 65
- ● Major city

# CLIMATE

The Central States have a continental climate, with hot, dry summers and long, cold winters. Unreliable rainfall can be a problem for farmers on the Great Plains.

January

July

TEMPERATURE AND PRECIPITATION

- More than 77°F
- 68 to 77°F
- 59 to 68°F
- 50 to 59°F
- 41 to 50°F
- 32 to 41°F
- 23 to 32°F
- 14 to 23°F
- 5 to 14°F
- Less than 5°F
- 4 — Precipitation (in)

NORTH AMERICA

US: The Central States

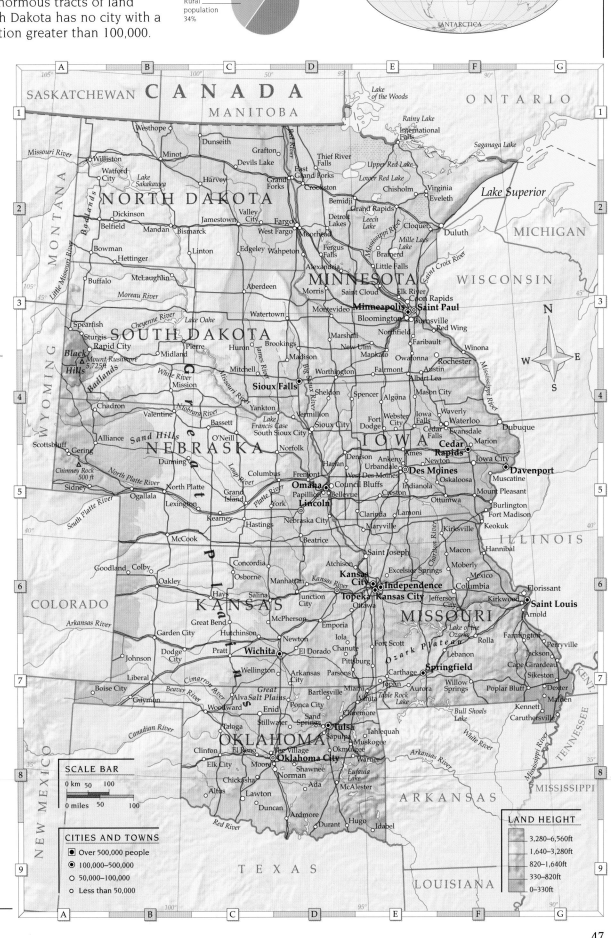

SCALE BAR

0 km 50 100
0 miles 50 100

CITIES AND TOWNS
- ■ Over 500,000 people
- ◉ 100,000–500,000
- ○ 50,000–100,000
- ○ Less than 50,000

LAND HEIGHT
- 3,280–6,560ft
- 1,640–3,280ft
- 820–1,640ft
- 330–820ft
- 0–330ft

# US: THE SOUTHWESTERN STATES

## ARIZONA, NEW MEXICO, TEXAS

**Large parts of the southwestern states** were purchased from Mexico in 1848. This land of expansive plateaus, spectacular canyons, prairies, and deserts is home to several distinct peoples, whose customs and traditions are still practiced. The Navaho and Hopi own one-third of the land in Arizona, and the ruins of thousand-year-old cliff dwellings built by the Anasazi people are still preserved there today.

## ENVIRONMENTAL ISSUES

**Desertification is a serious problem** in the southwestern states. Lack of water combined with intensive farming has allowed soils to erode. Drought is held at bay by irrigation, but falling water table levels are a cause for concern. New Mexico was the site for many of the earliest nuclear weapons tests, and some places remain contaminated.

### ENVIRONMENTAL ISSUES

- Urban air pollution
- Former nuclear test site
- Desert area
- Risk of desertification
- Polluted river
- Major industrial center

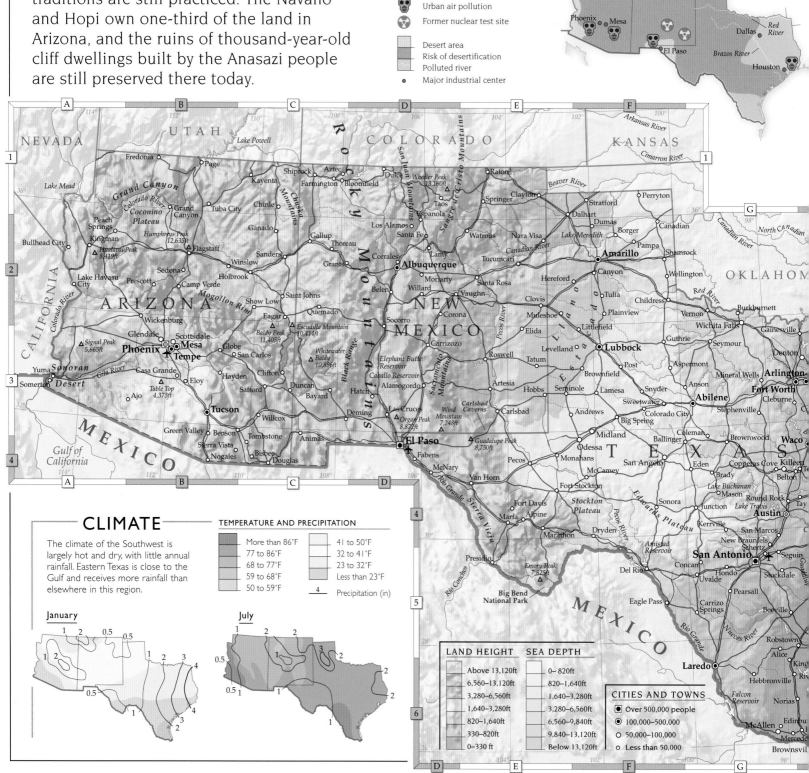

## CLIMATE

The climate of the Southwest is largely hot and dry, with little annual rainfall. Eastern Texas is close to the Gulf and receives more rainfall than elsewhere in this region.

### TEMPERATURE AND PRECIPITATION

- More than 86°F
- 77 to 86°F
- 68 to 77°F
- 59 to 68°F
- 50 to 59°F
- 41 to 50°F
- 32 to 41°F
- 23 to 32°F
- Less than 23°F
- 4 — Precipitation (in)

January

July

### LAND HEIGHT

- Above 13,120ft
- 6,560–13,120ft
- 3,280–6,560ft
- 1,640–3,280ft
- 820–1,640ft
- 330–820ft
- 0–330 ft

### SEA DEPTH

- 0–820ft
- 820–1,640ft
- 1,640–3,280ft
- 3,280–6,560ft
- 6,560–9,840ft
- 9,840–13,120ft
- Below 13,120ft

### CITIES AND TOWNS

- Over 500,000 people
- 100,000–500,000
- 50,000–100,000
- Less than 50,000

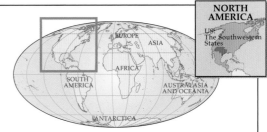

NORTH AMERICA

US: The Southwestern States

## THE LANDSCAPE

The arid, mountainous Colorado Plateau covers nearly half of Arizona, dipping toward the south to form desert basins. Parts of northern New Mexico are forested, but the south consists primarily of semiarid plains. Eastern Texas is bordered by the waters of the Gulf of Mexico, and the farmland of this area is well watered. Western Texas is covered by the Llano Estacado and, in the south, much of the land is arid.

**Big Bend** (E 5)
Big Bend National Park gets its name from the 90° bend that the Rio Grande makes there.

**Invading sea**
The crust of southeastern Texas is warping, causing the land to subside and allowing the sea to invade. Hurricanes make the situation worse.

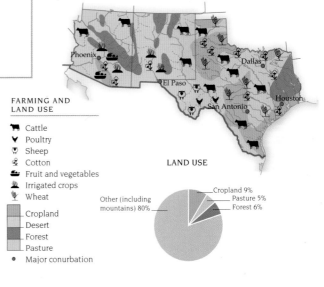

**Grand Canyon** (B 1)
The Grand Canyon is a dramatic gorge cut in the rock by the Colorado River. It is about 217 miles long, 418 miles wide, and up to one-mile deep.

**Carlsbad Caverns** (B 3)
Carlsbad Caverns are a series of underground caves, consisting of a three-level chain of limestone chambers studded with towering stalactites and stalagmites. They are millions of years old.

**Rio Grande** (G 5)
The Rio Grande, or "Great River" forms all of the border between Texas and Mexico. It flows from its source high up in the Rocky Mountains, to the Gulf of Mexico.

## FARMING AND LAND USE

**Many cattle and sheep ranches** have been set up on the open plateaus. Fruit and vegetables, grown in hothouses and cotton, hay, and wheat are among the major crops. Beef cattle and broiler chickens are raised on huge farms while sheep graze the drier parts of Texas. Extensive irrigation has made farming possible in even the most arid areas.

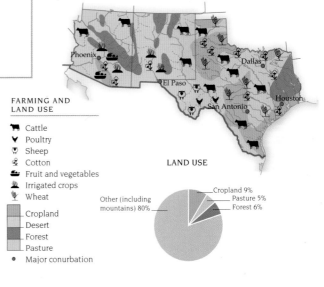

### FARMING AND LAND USE

- 🐄 Cattle
- 🦃 Poultry
- 🐑 Sheep
- ❀ Cotton
- 🍓 Fruit and vegetables
- 🌾 Irrigated crops
- 🌿 Wheat

- Cropland
- Desert
- Forest
- Pasture
- • Major conurbation

**LAND USE**

Other (including mountains) 80%
Cropland 9%
Pasture 5%
Forest 6%

## INDUSTRY

**Mining and related industries** are one of the most important sources of income in the Southwest. Great deposits of oil lie under about 65% of Texas; copper and coal are mined in Arizona and New Mexico. Defense-related industries, including NASA have encouraged the development of many high-tech companies in Texas – and high-tech is also growing in larger cities such as Santa Fe and Phoenix.

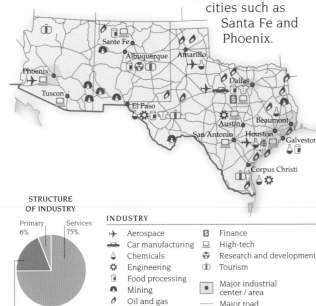

## POPULATION

**The descendants of Mexican** and Spanish settlers and numerous groups of Native Americans live in the southwestern states. The great cities of Texas grew up on income from cattle-ranching and the oil industry. Much of Arizona and New Mexico is sparsely populated, but today people are moving to these states to escape the cold winters elsewhere.

**STRUCTURE OF INDUSTRY**

Primary 6%
Services 75%
Manufacturing 19%

### INDUSTRY

- ✈ Aerospace
- 🚗 Car manufacturing
- ⚗ Chemicals
- ⚙ Engineering
- 🥫 Food processing
- ⛏ Mining
- 🛢 Oil and gas
- ⚙ Defense

- 💲 Finance
- 🖥 High-tech
- ◉ Research and development
- 🏛 Tourism

- ⊡ Major industrial center / area
- — Major road

**URBAN/RURAL POPULATION DIVISION**

Pheonix 4.7%
Houston 6.8%
San Antonio 4.1%
Other towns and cities 62.4%
Rural population 22%

**INHABITANTS PER SQ MILE**

- More than 130
- 65–130
- Less than 65
- • Major city

ARKANSAS

LOUISIANA

Arkansas River

Red River

Toledo Bend Reservoir

Sam Rayburn Reservoir

Sabine River

Lake Livingston

Texarkana
Atlanta
Marshall
Carthage
Henderson
Nacogdoches
Pineland
Livingston
The Woodlands
**Beaumont**
**Houston**
Port Arthur
Baytown
**Pasadena**
Texas City
Galveston
Lake Jackson
Freeport

*Gulf of Mexico*

N
W E
S

SCALE BAR

# US: THE MOUNTAIN STATES

COLORADO, IDAHO, MONTANA, NEVADA, UTAH, WYOMING

**These states are home** to some of the nation's most fantastic landscapes: endless treeless plains, craggy peaks, incredible desert landforms, and the salt flats of Utah. Although this was one of the last regions of the US to be settled, great mineral reserves have been exploited here in recent years, and new industries have grown up in some of the larger cities. Utah is the headquarters of the Mormon religion.

## INDUSTRY

Rich mineral reserves, including coal, oil, and gas, are mined throughout the region and forests are a source of good-quality timber. In the larger cities of Colorado and Utah, growing industries include high-tech computer firms. Many tourists are drawn to this region to ski in the resorts of Colorado and to explore the wilderness.

### INDUSTRY

- ♨ Chemicals
- 🍴 Food processing
- ⛀ Textiles
- ⚒ Coal
- ⛏ Mining
- ⬦ Oil and gas
- ♣ Timber processing
- ⛃ Gambling
- ⬜ High-tech
- ⊗ Research and development
- ⬤ Tourism

**STRUCTURE OF INDUSTRY**

Manufacturing 16%  Primary 4%

Services 80%

- ⊙ Major industrial center / area
- — Major road

## FARMING AND LAND USE

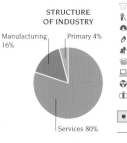

**In the southern** mountain states, cattle ranching is the main form of farming. Wheat and corn are grown in the eastern states, and the fertile soils of the Snake River valley in Idaho produce large crops of potatoes and many other vegetables. The northern states have many large commercial forests.

### FARMING AND LAND USE

- 🐄 Cattle
- 🌽 Corn
- 🌾 Irrigated crops
- ♣ Potatoes
- 🌿 Timber
- 🌾 Wheat

- ▫ Cropland
- ▫ Desert
- ▪ Forest
- ▫ Pasture
- • Major conurbation

**LAND USE**

Other (including mountains) 85%

Cropland 9%
Pasture 2%
Forest 4%

**Colorado, with the growing city** of Denver, is the most populous of the mountain states. In other states, people have settled close to sources of water such as Great Salt Lake in Utah. Many towns have less than 10,000 people and are far apart.

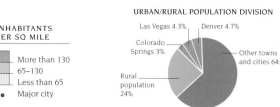

**INHABITANTS PER SQ MILE**

- ▪ More than 130
- ▪ 65–130
- ▫ Less than 65
- • Major city

**URBAN/RURAL POPULATION DIVISION**

Las Vegas 4.3%  Denver 4.7%
Colorado Springs 3%
Other towns and cities 64%
Rural population 24%

## THE LANDSCAPE

The great Rocky Mountains and many smaller mountain ranges cover almost all of this region.
Only eastern Montana is not mountainous. Here western parts of the Great Plains rise to meet the mountains. Parts of the southern mountain states are very arid with spectacular scenery, including blocklike *mesas*, formed by erosion.

### Continental Divide
From this watershed, crossing the Lewis Range, rivers flow in different directions across North America. Some flow east to Hudson Bay, some south to the Gulf of Mexico and others west to the Pacific Ocean.

### Yellowstone National Park (D 3)
Yellowstone was set up in 1872 as the first national park in the US. Water from hot springs has deposited minerals as it cools, forming white rock terraces close to the springs.

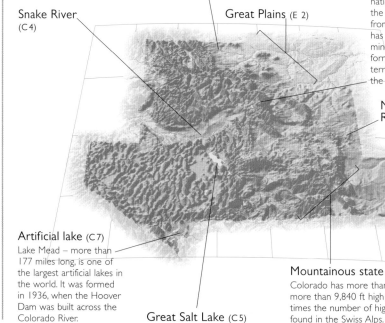

Snake River (C 4)

Great Plains (E 2)

North Platte River (F 4)

### Artificial lake (C 7)
Lake Mead – more than 177 miles long, is one of the largest artificial lakes in the world. It was formed in 1936, when the Hoover Dam was built across the Colorado River.

Great Salt Lake (C 5)

### Mountainous state
Colorado has more than 1,500 peaks more than 9,840 ft high – this is six times the number of high mountains found in the Swiss Alps.

NORTH
AMERICA

USA:
The Mountain
States

## ENVIRONMENTAL ISSUES

Parts of the Rocky Mountains, including the National Parks, have become major centers for outdoor pursuits. The sheer number of people puts pressure on the land leading to soil erosion, and increasing the possibility of landslides. Nevada remains the main testing ground for the US nuclear arsenal, and there are many older, disused sites here.

Glacier

Yellowstone
Grand Teton

Salt Lake
City
Rocky
Mountains
Denver

Capitol Reef
Canyonlands
Zion Bryce
Canyon
Mesa Verde

### ENVIRONMENTAL ISSUES

⊗ Former nuclear test site
⊗ Nuclear test site
☠ Urban air pollution
⚑ National Park
● Major industrial center

## CLIMATE

In the lowland areas, particularly in the south, summers are often very hot and dry. Parts of the Rocky Mountains are permanently covered by snow, and some of the high passes are cut off by snow in the winter.

January

July

### TEMPERATURE AND PRECIPITATION

| | | |
|---|---|---|
| More than 86°F | | 32 to 41°F |
| 77 to 86°F | | 23 to 32°F |
| 68 to 77°F | | 14 to 23°F |
| 59 to 68°F | | Less than 14°F |
| 50 to 59°F | | 4 — Precipitation (in) |
| 41 to 50°F | | |

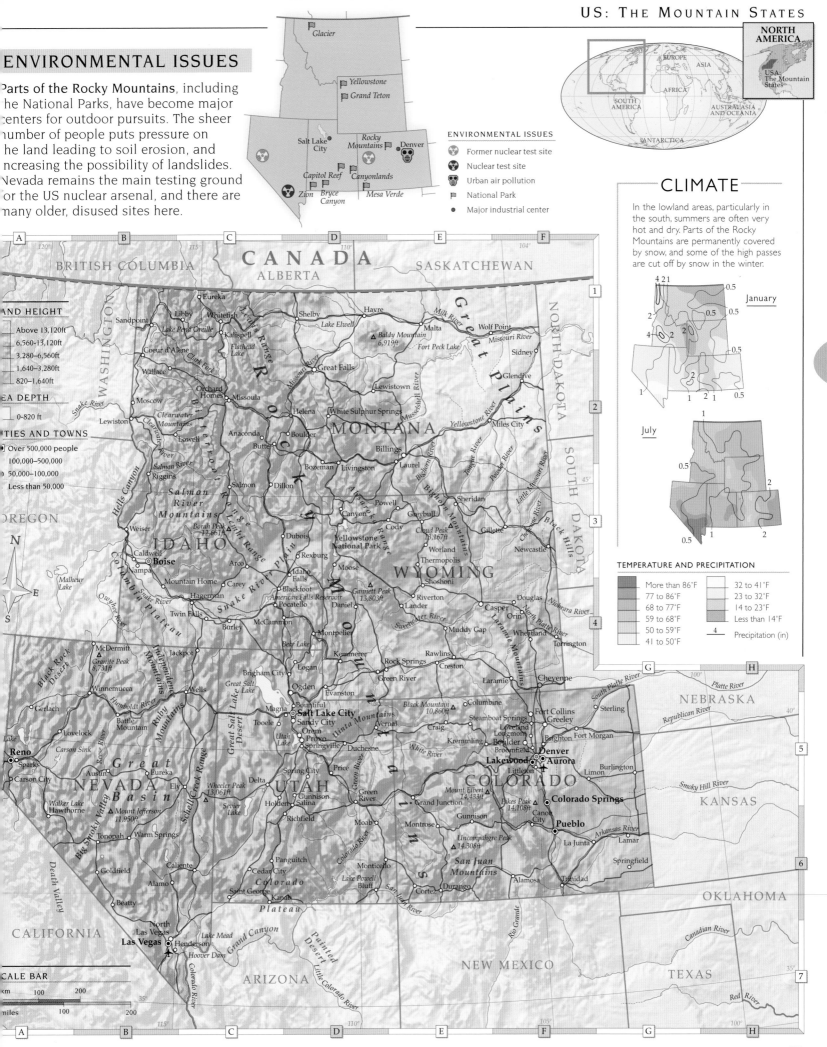

LAND HEIGHT
Above 13,120ft
6,560–13,120ft
3,280–6,560ft
1,640–3,280ft
820–1,640ft

SEA DEPTH
0–820 ft

CITIES AND TOWNS
● Over 500,000 people
● 100,000–500,000
● 50,000–100,000
● Less than 50,000

SCALE BAR

# US: THE PACIFIC STATES

## CALIFORNIA, OREGON, WASHINGTON

**The earliest European visitors** to the West Coast were fur-trappers and miners, but the Gold Rush of 1849 brought in the first major wave of settlers. Drawn by tales of the beautiful scenery, pleasant climate, and fertile valleys, more people arrived on the newly built railroads. People from all over the world are still moving into this region, seeking jobs in the dynamic economy and the famous laid-back lifestyle.

## INDUSTRY

**The Pacific States** are the center of the high-tech computer industry with Silicon Valley between San Francisco and San Jose, and electronics industries growing in Portland and Seattle. Other major industries include research and development for the defense industry, filmmaking in Los Angeles, food processing and lumbering. Tourism is well developed throughout the Pacific States.

### STRUCTURE OF INDUSTRY

Primary 2%
Services 81%
Manufacturing 17%

### INDUSTRY

- ✈ Aerospace
- ⚗ Chemicals
- ⚙ Engineering
- 🗎 Food processing
- ⛴ Iron and steel
- ⚓ Shipbuilding
- 👕 Textiles
- 🌲 Timber processing
- 🎬 Film industry
- 💻 High-tech
- ☢ Research and development
- 🎡 Tourism
- ⊡ Major industrial center / area
- — Major road

## FARMING AND LAND USE

**California's Central Valley** and the river valleys of Washington and Oregon provide ideal conditions for a wide range of fruit and vegetables, including citrus fruit and grapes. Poultry farming is widespread in the northwest and there are many large cattle ranches. Millions of acres of commercial forest are located in this region.

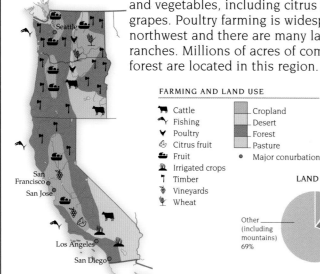

### FARMING AND LAND USE

- 🐄 Cattle
- 🐟 Fishing
- 🦃 Poultry
- 🍊 Citrus fruit
- 🍇 Fruit
- 🌾 Irrigated crops
- 🌲 Timber
- 🍇 Vineyards
- 🌾 Wheat
- Cropland
- Desert
- Forest
- Pasture
- Major conurbation

### LAND USE

Cropland 10%
Pasture 2%
Forest 19%
Other (including mountains) 69%

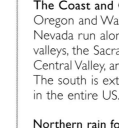

## ENVIRONMENTAL ISSUES

**Some of the** great national parks of the US, including Yosemite and Sequoia, are found here. The immense numbers of visitors put great pressure on the landscape. Water is in short supply in large parts of California, and desertification, caused by overintense farming methods, is a problem. Wind farms have been set up on the hills above the San Joaquin valley to provide alternative energy.

### ENVIRONMENTAL ISSUES

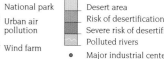

- ⚑ National park
- ☠ Urban air pollution
- 🌀 Wind farm
- Desert area
- Risk of desertification
- Severe risk of desertification
- Polluted rivers
- ● Major industrial center

## THE LANDSCAPE

**The Coast and Cascade ranges** run north–south through Oregon and Washington while further south, the high Sierra Nevada run along California's eastern fringes. Two broad valleys, the Sacramento and San Joaquin, are known as the Central Valley, and form a trough beneath the Sierra Nevada. The south is extremely dry – Death Valley is the hottest place in the entire US.

**Northern rain forest** (B 2)
The ocean-facing side of the Olympic Mountains receives 142 in of rain every year, supporting the only true temperate rain forest in the Northern Hemisphere.

**Hells Canyon** (D 3)
Hells Canyon is North America's deepest gorge. Running through part of Oregon, it was created as the Snake River cut down through the land.

**Volcanic eruption** (B 2)
Mount St. Helens erupted in 1980, killing 57 people and destroying a vast area.

**San Andreas Fault**
The San Andreas Fault runs for 650 miles underneath California. When both sides of the fault move at different rates, tremors and earthquakes result.

**Hottest place** (D 7)
In 1913, Death Valley set the record for the highest temperature ever recorded in the US, at 134° F.

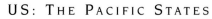

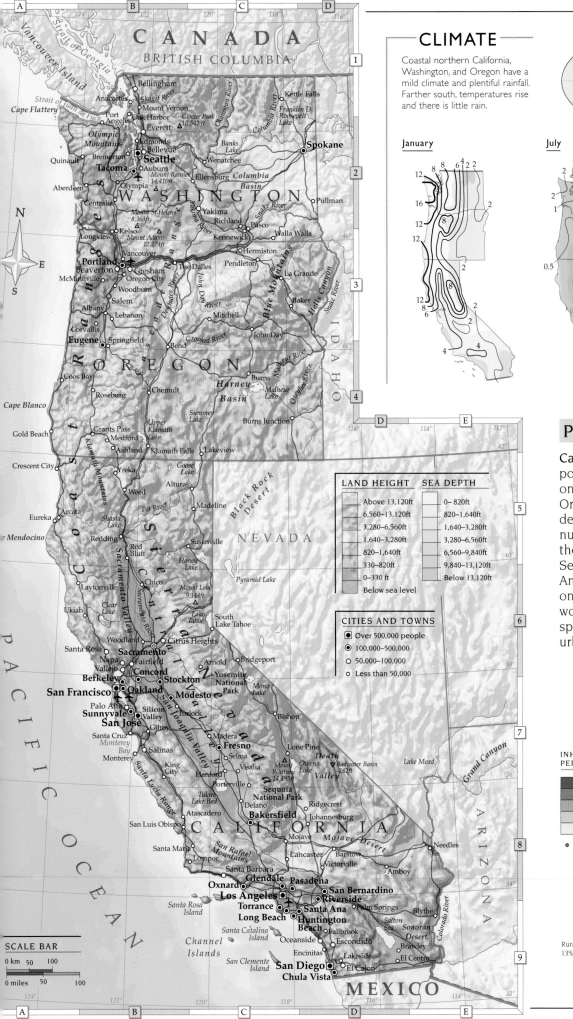

## Map labels

CANADA
BRITISH COLUMBIA
Vancouver Island
Strait of Georgia
Strait of Juan de Fuca
Cape Flattery
Bellingham
Anacortes
Skagit River
Mount Vernon
Oak Harbor
Port Angeles
Edmonds
Bellevue
Bremerton
Seattle
Tacoma
Auburn
Quinault
Aberdeen
Olympic Mountains
Olympia
Mount Rainier 14,410ft
Centralia
Ellensburg
Banks Lake
Wenatchee
Spokane
Kettle Falls
Franklin D. Roosevelt Lake
Columbia River
Okanogan River
Glacier Peak 10,542 ft
WASHINGTON
Columbia Basin
Yakima
Richland
Pasco
Kennewick
Walla Walla
Pullman
Snake River
Yakima River
Mount St.Helens 8,363ft
Longview
Kelso
Mount Adams 12,274ft
Vancouver
Portland
Beaverton
Gresham
Oregon City
The Dalles
Pendleton
Hermiston
La Grande
McMinnville
Woodburn
Salem
Albany
Lebanon
Corvallis
Eugene
Springfield
OREGON
John Day River
Deschutes River
Crooked River
Mitchell
John Day
Bend
Blue Mountains
Baker
Hells Canyon
Snake River
Malheur River
Burns
Chemult
Harney Basin
Malheur Lake
Coos Bay
Roseburg
Summer Lake
Burns Junction
Owyhee River
Cape Blanco
Gold Beach
Grants Pass
Medford
Ashland
Upper Klamath Lake
Klamath Falls
Lakeview
Goose Lake
Crescent City
Yreka
Weed
Alturas
Madeline
Black Rock Desert
Eureka
Arcata
Cape Mendocino
Redding
Shasta Lake
Pit River
Susanville
Honey Lake
Pyramid Lake
NEVADA
Klamath Mountains
Coast Ranges
Sierra Nevada
Laytonville
Ukiah
Clear Lake
Red Bluff
Chico
Mount Lola 9,144ft
Santa Rosa
Napa
Vallejo
Fairfield
Sacramento
Woodland
Citrus Heights
Sacramento River
South Lake Tahoe
Lake Tahoe
Berkeley
Concord
Oakland
San Francisco
Stockton
Arnold
Bridgeport
Palo Alto
Silicon Valley
Sunnyvale
San Jose
Modesto
Yosemite National Park
Mono Lake
Santa Cruz
Monterey
Monterey Bay
Salinas
King City
Turlock
Gilroy
Madera
Fresno
Selma
Bishop
Central Valley
San Joaquin Valley
Santa Lucia Range
Hanford
Visalia
Lone Pine
Owens Lake
Death Valley
Mount Whitney 14,495ft
Badwater Basin -282ft
Lake Mead
Grand Canyon
Porterville
Delano
Sequoia National Park
Tulare Lake Bed
Ridgecrest
Johannesburg
Atascadero
Bakersfield
San Luis Obispo
CALIFORNIA
Santa Maria
Mojave
Mojave Desert
Lancaster
Barstow
Victorville
Amboy
Needles
ARIZONA
San Rafael Mountains
Lompoc
Santa Barbara
Glendale
Oxnard
Pasadena
Los Angeles
Torrance
Santa Ana
Long Beach
Huntington Beach
San Bernardino
Riverside
Palm Springs
Blythe
Colorado River
Salton Sea
Sonoran Desert
Santa Rosa Island
Santa Catalina Island
Channel Islands
Fallbrook
Oceanside
Escondido
Encinitas
Lakeside
El Centro
Brawley
San Clemente Island
San Diego
Chula Vista
El Cajon
MEXICO
IDAHO
PACIFIC OCEAN

### Scale Bar
SCALE BAR
0 km 50 100
0 miles 50 100

## CLIMATE

Coastal northern California, Washington, and Oregon have a mild climate and plentiful rainfall. Farther south, temperatures rise and there is little rain.

January

July

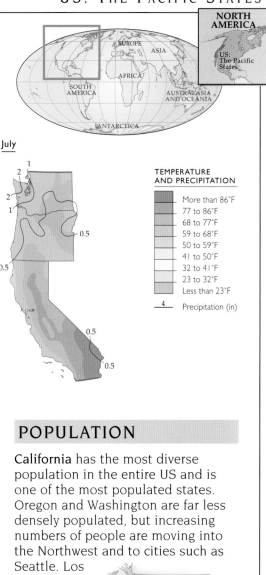

### TEMPERATURE AND PRECIPITATION
More than 86°F
77 to 86°F
68 to 77°F
59 to 68°F
50 to 59°F
41 to 50°F
32 to 41°F
23 to 32°F
Less than 23°F
—4— Precipitation (in)

### LAND HEIGHT
Above 13,120ft
6,560–13,120ft
3,280–6,560ft
1,640–3,280ft
820–1,640ft
330–820ft
0–330 ft
Below sea level

### SEA DEPTH
0– 820ft
820–1,640ft
1,640–3,280ft
3,280–6,560ft
6,560–9,840ft
9,840–13,120ft
Below 13,120ft

### CITIES AND TOWNS
■ Over 500,000 people
◉ 100,000–500,000
◎ 50,000–100,000
○ Less than 50,000

## POPULATION

**California** has the most diverse population in the entire US and is one of the most populated states. Oregon and Washington are far less densely populated, but increasing numbers of people are moving into the Northwest and to cities such as Seattle. Los Angeles is one of the world's most sprawling urban centers.

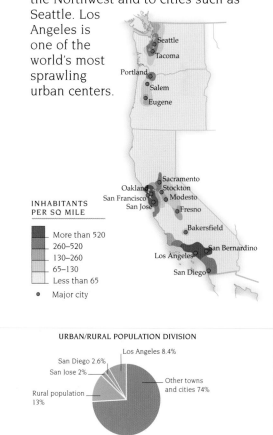

### INHABITANTS PER SQ MILE
More than 520
260–520
130–260
65–130
Less than 65
• Major city

### URBAN/RURAL POPULATION DIVISION
Los Angeles 8.4%
San Diego 2.6%
San Jose 2%
Rural population 13%
Other towns and cities 74%

NORTH AMERICA
US: The Pacific States

# ALASKA

A **magnificent land** of mountains, forests, and snowfields, with rich oil and mineral reserves, Alaska was purchased from Russia for $1 million in 1867. Almost 650,000 people live here, many drawn by the oil industry. Some of Alaska's native peoples like the Aleuts and Inupiaq still live by hunting and fishing.

## ENVIRONMENTAL ISSUES

**Much of northern Alaska** is covered by permafrost (permanently frozen ground). The Trans-Alaska Pipeline, which brings oil from Prudhoe Bay to Valdez, was built above ground to stop the permafrost melting. A number of major oil spills have threatened Alaska's unique envrionment.

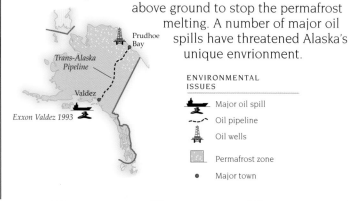

Prudhoe Bay

Trans-Alaska Pipeline

Valdez

*Exxon Valdez 1993*

**ENVIRONMENTAL ISSUES**

- 🛢 Major oil spill
- ---- Oil pipeline
- ⛽ Oil wells
- ▦ Permafrost zone
- • Major town

## INDUSTRY

Prudhoe Bay

Anchorage

Valdez

Juneau

**The Alaskan economy** is dominated by the oil business. The oilfields of Alaska are of a similar size to those in the Persian Gulf. Minerals including gold are mined in the mountains and paper products are exported to countries on the Pacific Rim.

**INDUSTRY**

- 🛢 Chemicals
- 🗻 Mining
- 🛢 Oil and gas
- 🌲 Timber processing
- ▣ Major industrial center
- — Major road

## FARMING AND LAND USE

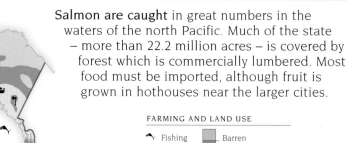

Anchorage

**Salmon are caught** in great numbers in the waters of the north Pacific. Much of the state – more than 22.2 million acres – is covered by forest which is commercially lumbered. Most food must be imported, although fruit is grown in hothouses near the larger cities.

**FARMING AND LAND USE**

- 🐟 Fishing
- 🚢 Fruit
- 🌾 Timber
- ▦ Barren
- ▦ Forest
- ▦ Mountains
- ▦ Tundra
- • Major conurbation

## CLIMATE

Parts of northern Alaska are frozen year-round and can be cut off entirely in the winter. Summers are milder – especially in the Aleutians.

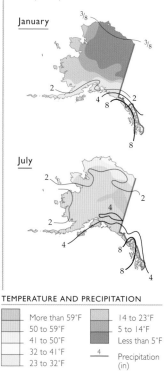

January

July

**TEMPERATURE AND PRECIPITATION**

- More than 59°F
- 50 to 59°F
- 41 to 50°F
- 32 to 41°F
- 23 to 32°F
- 14 to 23°F
- 5 to 14°F
- Less than 5°F
- 4 — Precipitation (in)

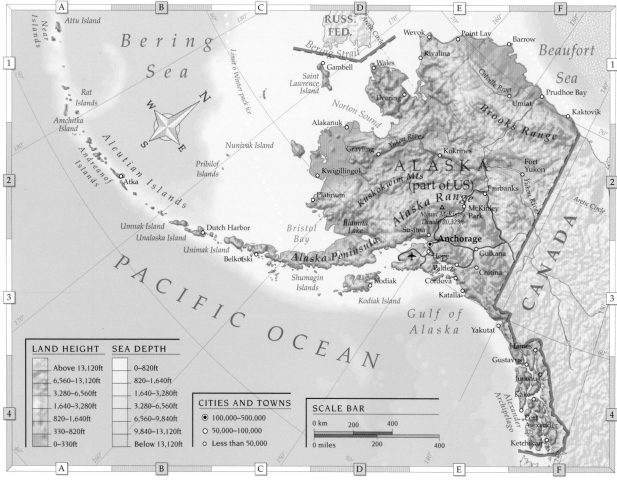

Attu Island
Near Islands
*Bering Sea*
Rat Islands
Amchitka Island
Andreanof Islands
*Aleutian Islands*
Atka
Umnak Island
Unalaska Island
Unimak Island
Dutch Harbor
Belkofski
*Bristol Bay*
*Shumagin Islands*
Pribilof Islands
Nunivak Island
Kwigillingok
Platinum
Iliamna Lake
Kodiak
Kodiak Island
*PACIFIC OCEAN*
RUSS. FED.
Arctic Creek
Bering Strait
Wales
Gambell
Saint Lawrence Island
Deering
*Norton Sound*
Alakanuk
Grayling
Yukon River
Kokrines
Wevok
Kivalina
Point Lay
Barrow
*Beaufort Sea*
Colville River
Umiat
Prudhoe Bay
Kaktovik
*Brooks Range*
Fort Yukon
Fairbanks
Yukon River
ALASKA (part of US)
*Kuskokwim Mts*
*Alaska Range*
Mount McKinley (Denali) 20,320ft
McKinley Park
Susitna
**Anchorage**
Hope
Valdez
Gulkana
Chitina
Cordova
Katalla
*Gulf of Alaska*
Yakutat
CANADA
Arctic Circle
Haines
Gustavus
Juneau
Kake
*Alexander Archipelago*
Port Alexander
Ketchikan

**LAND HEIGHT**
- Above 13,120ft
- 6,560–13,120ft
- 3,280–6,560ft
- 1,640–3,280ft
- 820–1,640ft
- 330–820ft
- 0–330ft

**SEA DEPTH**
- 0–820ft
- 820–1,640ft
- 1,640–3,280ft
- 3,280–6,560ft
- 6,560–9,840ft
- 9,840–13,120ft
- Below 13,120ft

**CITIES AND TOWNS**
- ◉ 100,000–500,000
- ○ 50,000–100,000
- ○ Less than 50,000

**SCALE BAR**
0 km    200    400
0 miles    200    400

# HAWAI'I

Hawai'i is the 50th US state. It lies far from the mainland in the middle of the Pacific Ocean. The island chain was formed by volcanoes, only one of which, Mauna Loa, remains active today. The islands' indigenous peoples are Polynesians, but continued immigration means that they now make up only 9% of the population.

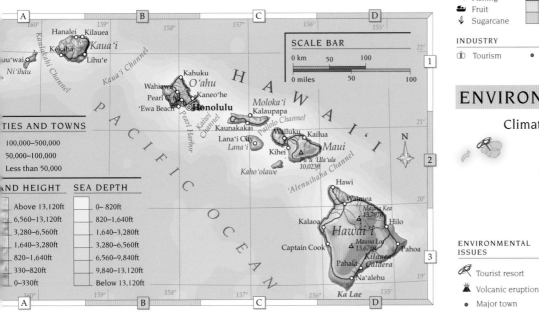

SCALE BAR
| 0 km | 50 | 100 |
| 0 miles | 50 | 100 |

CITIES AND TOWNS
- ● 100,000–500,000
- ● 50,000–100,000
- ○ Less than 50,000

LAND HEIGHT
- Above 13,120ft
- 6,560–13,120ft
- 3,280–6,560ft
- 1,640–3,280ft
- 820–1,640ft
- 330–820ft
- 0–330ft

SEA DEPTH
- 0–820ft
- 820–1,640ft
- 1,640–3,280ft
- 3,280–6,560ft
- 6,560–9,840ft
- 9,840–13,120ft
- Below 13,120ft

## INDUSTRY AND LAND USE

**Tourism is the most important** industry in Hawai'i, accounting for one in every three jobs. The naval base at Pearl Harbor also provides jobs for numerous people. The many large plantations grow sugarcane, bananas, and tropical fruit for export.

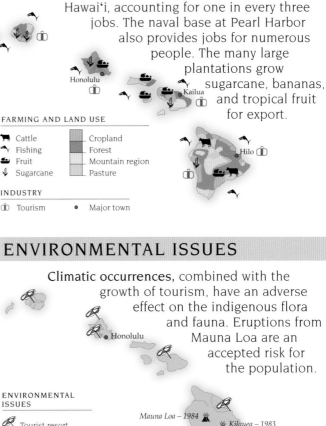

FARMING AND LAND USE
- Cattle
- Fishing
- Fruit
- Sugarcane
- Cropland
- Forest
- Mountain region
- Pasture

INDUSTRY
- Tourism
- ● Major town

## ENVIRONMENTAL ISSUES

**Climatic occurrences,** combined with the growth of tourism, have an adverse effect on the indigenous flora and fauna. Eruptions from Mauna Loa are an accepted risk for the population.

ENVIRONMENTAL ISSUES
- Tourist resort
- Volcanic eruption
- ● Major town

Mauna Loa – 1984
Kilauea – 1983

# US OVERSEAS TERRITORIES

America's overseas territories have traditionally been seen as strategically or economically important. In most cases, the local population has been given a say in deciding whether it wants to govern itself. A US commonwealth territory has a greater level of independence than a US unincorporated or external territory. The US has 13 overseas territories: the four largest are shown here.

AMERICAN SAMOA

American Samoa consists of five volcanic islands and two coral atolls in the south Pacific. The people are among the last true Polynesians.

GUAM

The US military base that covers one-third of the island makes Guam strategically important to the US. The Chamorro, the indigenous people, are in charge of political and social life.

US VIRGIN ISLANDS

There are 53 volcanic islands in the US Virgin Islands. Most people live on the main islands of St.-John, St.-Thomas, and St.-Croix, which has a vast oil refinery.

PUERTO RICO

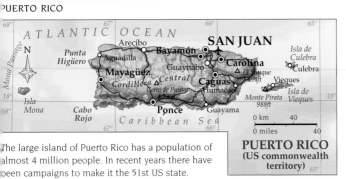

The large island of Puerto Rico has a population of almost 4 million people. In recent years there have been campaigns to make it the 51st US state.

# MEXICO

Mexico is a large country with a rich mixture of traditions and cultures. The ancient civilization of the Aztecs that flourished here was crushed by Spanish invaders in the 16th century. Spain ruled Mexico until its independence in 1836, and today the country has the world's largest Spanish-speaking population. Mexico is mostly dry and mountainous, and farmland is limited, so the country has to import most of the basic foods it needs to feed its people.

## FARMING AND LAND USE

Most of the land suitable for farming is planted with corn – a big part of the Mexican diet. Along the Gulf coast coffee, sugarcane, and cotton are grown on plantations for export. Parts of the dry north are irrigated to grow cotton, but most of the land is taken up by large cattle ranches. Fishing, especially for shellfish such as lobster and shrimp is important in coastal areas.

**FARMING AND LAND USE**

- Cattle
- Fishing
- Sheep
- Bananas
- Coffee
- Corn
- Cotton
- Fruit
- Grapes
- Shellfish
- Sugarcane
- Timber

- Cropland
- Desert
- Forest
- Pasture
- Wetland
- Major conurbation

*Cities on farming map:* Ciudad Juárez, Chihuahua, Monterrey, San Luis Potosí, Guadalajara, Mexico City, Puebla, Mérida, Acapulco

**LAND USE**

- Cropland 14%
- Pasture 42%
- Forest 29%
- Other 15%

## THE LANDSCAPE

Much of Mexico is made up of a high plateau. The climate there is very dry and varies between true desert in the north, and semidesert farther south. The plateau is separated from the coastal plains by two long, rugged mountain chains: the Eastern Sierra Madre and the Western Sierra Madre. Toward the south, the mountain ranges join, meeting in the region of high volcanic peaks that surround Mexico City.

**Baja (Lower) California** (B 3)
This long and very dry peninsula separates the Gulf of California from the Pacific Ocean. The Gulf was formed after the last Ice Age, when the sea rose to flood a major rift valley.

**The Rio Grande** (D 2)
This river flows from Colorado in the US and forms much of Mexico's northern border. It crosses a vast arid area on its way to the Gulf of Mexico.

**Earthquakes and volcanoes**
Volcanic activity is common in Mexico. Popocatépetl (F 5) and Volcán El Chichónal (G 5) have erupted recently, and Mexico City was hit by a devastating earthquake in 1985.

**Eastern Sierra Madre** (D 5).

**Western Sierra Madre** (C 3).

**Yucatan Peninsula (H 4)**
The Yucatan Peninsula is a low, wide tableland, formed by layers of limestone. Limestone absorbs water, so there are few rivers on the peninsula, and the tropical rainforests found there are fed mainly by streams and underground water.

## POPULATION

Most of the north is sparsely populated due to the hot, dry climate and lack of cultivable farmland. As people have migrated from the countryside in search of work, the cities have grown dramatically; almost 75% of Mexicans now live in urban areas. Mexico City is home to almost a fifth of the population and is one of the world's largest cities.

*Cities on population map:* Chihuahua, Monterrey, Guadalajara, Mérida, Puebla, MEXICO CITY, Acapulco

**INHABITANTS PER SQ MILE**
- More than 520
- 260–520
- 130–260
- Less than 130
- Capital city
- Major city

**URBAN/RURAL POPULATION DIVISION**
- Mexico City 17.1%
- Guadalajara 3.5%
- Monterrey 3.1%
- Other towns and cities 50.3%
- Rural population 26%

## ENVIRONMENTAL ISSUES

Fast, unplanned growth has led to poor sanitation and water supplies in Mexico City, while the wall of mountains that surrounds the city traps pollution from cars and factories, giving it some of the world's worst air pollution. Much of Mexico's tropical rainforest has been felled, leading to increased soil erosion. Land clearance farther north is also causing desertification.

**ENVIRONMENTAL ISSUES**
- Risk of desertification
- Deforested areas
- Remaining tropical forests
- Path of recent, devastating hurricane
- Major industrial city
- Volcanic eruption
- Urban air pollution

*Labels on environmental map:* Guadalajara, Mexico City, Nevado de Colima 1994, Popocatépetl 1994, Volcán El Chichónal 1994, Mitch 1998

*Map inset (right margin):* A, CALIFORNIA, 115°, 1, Tijuana, Mexicali, Rosarito, Ensenada, Sierra San Pedro Mártir, 2, 30°, Isla Cedros, Guerrero, 3, 25°, Tropic of Cancer, 4, 20°, 5, Isla Clari, 6, A

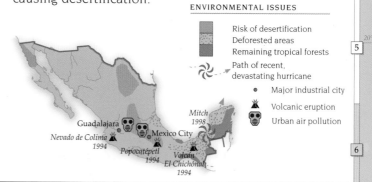

# INDUSTRY

**Oil and gas** on the Gulf coast are the biggest source of income. Mexico is also rich in other minerals; it is the world's top silver producer. Manufacturing is centered around Mexico City and along the US border, where mainly foreign-owned factories assemble products for export. Tourism is also very important to Mexico.

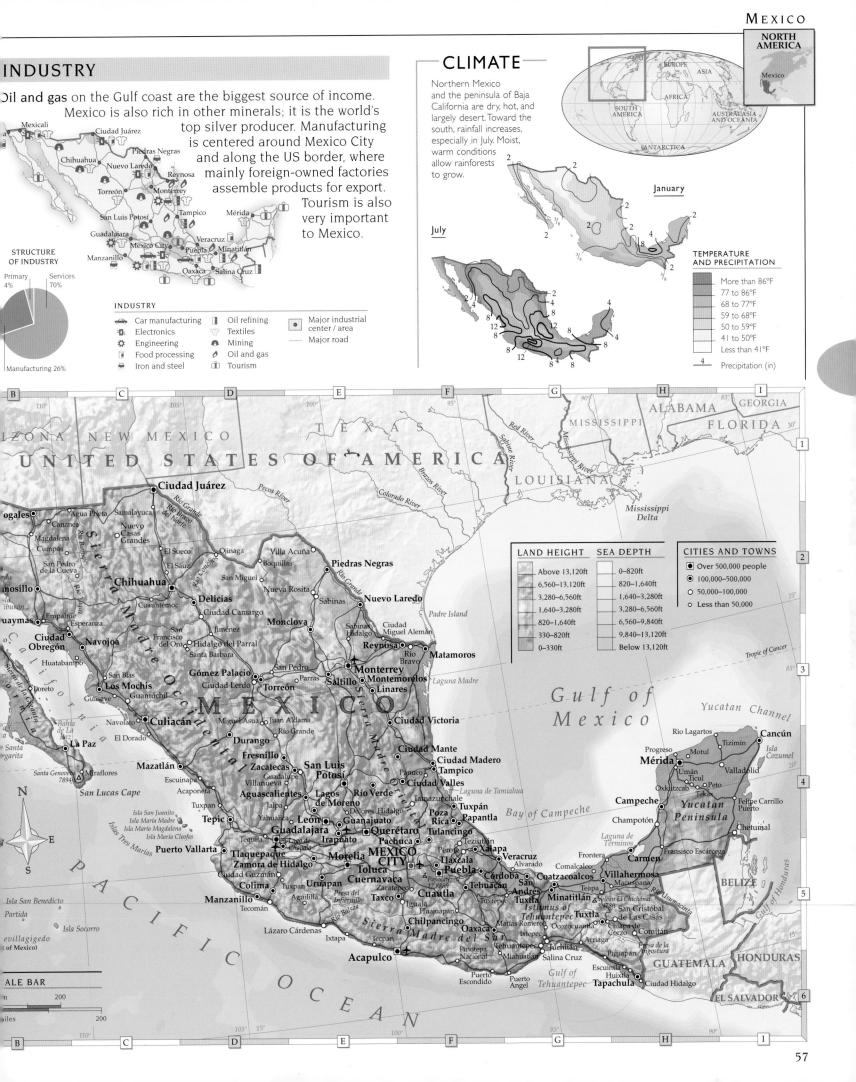

Mexicali
Ciudad Juárez
Chihuahua
Piedras Negras
Nuevo Laredo
Reynosa
Torreón
Monterrey
Tampico
Mérida
San Luis Potosí
Guadalajara
Veracruz
Mexico City
Puebla
Minatitlán
Manzanillo
Oaxaca
Salina Cruz

## STRUCTURE OF INDUSTRY

Primary 4%
Services 70%
Manufacturing 26%

### INDUSTRY

- 🚗 Car manufacturing
- ⚡ Electronics
- ⚙ Engineering
- 🏭 Food processing
- Iron and steel
- 🛢 Oil refining
- 👕 Textiles
- ⛏ Mining
- Oil and gas
- 🧳 Tourism
- ⊙ Major industrial center / area
- — Major road

# CLIMATE

Northern Mexico and the peninsula of Baja California are dry, hot, and largely desert. Toward the south, rainfall increases, especially in July. Moist, warm conditions allow rainforests to grow.

January

July

## TEMPERATURE AND PRECIPITATION

- More than 86°F
- 77 to 86°F
- 68 to 77°F
- 59 to 68°F
- 50 to 59°F
- 41 to 50°F
- Less than 41°F

—4— Precipitation (in)

EUROPE
ASIA
AFRICA
NORTH AMERICA
SOUTH AMERICA
AUSTRALASIA AND OCEANIA
ANTARCTICA

---

ALABAMA   GEORGIA
MISSISSIPPI   FLORIDA
30°

ARIZONA   NEW MEXICO
TEXAS
Red River
UNITED STATES OF AMERICA
LOUISIANA
Sabine River
Mississippi River
1

Ciudad Juárez
Pecos River
Brazos River
Colorado River
Mississippi Delta
25°
2

Nogales
Agua Prieta
Samalayuca
Río Grande del Norte
Ojinaga
Villa Acuña
Boquillas
Piedras Negras
Río Grande
Padre Island

Cananea
Magdalena
Cumpas
Nuevo Casas Grandes
El Sueco
El Sáuz
San Miguel
Nueva Rosita
Sabinas
Nuevo Laredo

San Pedro de la Cueva
Chihuahua
Cuauhtémoc
Delicias
Ciudad Camargo
Jiménez
Monclova
Sabinas Hidalgo
Ciudad Miguel Alemán
somosillo

## LAND HEIGHT
- Above 13,120ft
- 6,560–13,120ft
- 3,280–6,560ft
- 1,640–3,280ft
- 820–1,640ft
- 330–820ft
- 0–330ft

## SEA DEPTH
- 0–820ft
- 820–1,640ft
- 1,640–3,280ft
- 3,280–6,560ft
- 6,560–9,840ft
- 9,840–13,120ft
- Below 13,120ft

## CITIES AND TOWNS
- Over 500,000 people
- 100,000–500,000
- 50,000–100,000
- Less than 50,000

Tropic of Cancer
85°
3

Isla Tiburón
Empalme
uaymas
Ciudad Obregón
Navojoa
San Francisco del Oro
Hidalgo del Parral
Santa Barbara
Gómez Palacio
Ciudad Lerdo
San Pedro
Parras
Torreón
Saltillo
Monterrey
Montemorelos
Reynosa
Río Bravo
Matamoros

Huatabampo
Loreto
San Blas
Los Mochis
Guamúchil
Linares
Laguna Madre

Bahía de La Paz
Guasave
Navolato
Culiacán
Miguel Asua
Juan Aldama
Ciudad Victoria

Gulf of Mexico

La Paz
El Dorado
Durango
Río Grande
Ciudad Mante
Yucatan Channel

Santa Margarita
Santa Genoveva 7894ft
Miraflores
Mazatlán
Fresnillo
Zacatecas
San Luis Potosí
Ciudad Madero
Tampico
Pánuco
Río Lagartos
Tizimín
Cancún
Isla Cozumel
20°
4

San Lucas Cape
Escuinapa
Guadalupe
Villanueva
Ciudad Valles
Progreso
Motul
Mérida
Umán
Valladolid

Acaponeta
Aguascalientes
Lagos de Moreno
Río Verde
Tamazunchale
Laguna de Tamiahua
Ticul
Peto
Oxkutzcab
Tekax

Isla San Juanito
Isla María Madre
Isla María Magdalena
Isla María Cleofas
Islas Tres Marías
Tuxpan
Jalpa
Yahualica
Dolores Hidalgo
Tuxpán
Papantla
Bay of Campeche
Campeche
Yucatan Peninsula
Felipe Carrillo Puerto

Tepic
León
Guanajuato
Poza Rica
Champotón
Chetumal

Puerto Vallarta
Guadalajara
Tequila
Lago de Chapala
Irapuato
Querétaro
Pachuca
Tulancingo
Teziutlán
Laguna de Términos
Frontera
Francisco Escárcega

Tlaquepaque
Zamora de Hidalgo
Morelia
Ciudad Guzmán
MEXICO CITY
Toluca
Perote
Xalapa
Veracruz
Alvarado
Comalcalco
Carmen
BELIZE
15°
5

PACIFIC OCEAN
Colima
Tuxpan
Zacatepec
Uruapan
Cuernavaca
Taxco
Iguala
Tlaxcala
Puebla
Córdoba
Coatzacoalcos
Villahermosa
Macuspana

Isla San Benedicto
Partida
Manzanillo
Tecomán
Aguililla
Presa del Infiernillo
Cuautla
Popocatépetl 17,888ft
San Andrés Tuxtla
Minatitlán
Volcán El Chichónal
San Cristóbal de Las Casas
Chiapa de Corzo
Comitán

Isla Socorro
Lázaro Cárdenas
Ixtapa
Chilpancingo
Oaxaca
Matías Romero
Ixtepec
Ozocoautla
Tuxtla
Río Usumacinta
Presa de la Angostura

evillagigedo
of Mexico)
Tecpan
Sierra Madre del Sur
Huajuapan
Tehuantepec
Isthmus of Tehuantepec
Juchitán
Pijijiapán

Acapulco
Pinotepa Nacional
Miahuatlán
Salina Cruz
Gulf of Tehuantepec
Escuintla
Huixtla
GUATEMALA
HONDURAS

Puerto Escondido
Puerto Angel
Tapachula
Ciudad Hidalgo
EL SALVADOR
6

SIERRA MADRE OCCIDENTAL
SIERRA MADRE ORIENTAL
Gulf of California
MEXICO

N W E S

SCALE BAR
200
200 miles

110°   105°   15°   100°   95°   90°

# CENTRAL AMERICA

BELIZE, COSTA RICA, EL SALVADOR, GUATEMALA,
HONDURAS, NICARAGUA, PANAMA

**Central America lies** on a narrow bridge of land which links North and South America. All the countries here, except Belize, were once governed by Spain. Today, most of their people are *mestizos* – a mix of the original Maya Indian inhabitants and Spanish settlers. The hot, steamy climate is ideal for growing tropical crops, such as coffee and bananas, which are exported worldwide.

## FARMING AND LAND USE

**About half of all** the agricultural products grown here are exported. The Pacific coast has fertile, well-watered land suitable for growing cotton and sugarcane. In the central highlands are big coffee plantations and ranches where beef cattle are raised. Bananas grow well along the humid Caribbean coastal plain, and shrimp and lobster are caught offshore.

### FARMING AND LAND USE

- 🐂 Cattle
- 🦐 Shellfish
- 🍌 Bananas
- ☕ Coffee
- 🌽 Corn
- Cotton
- 🌾 Sugarcane
- ⌃ Timber

- Cropland
- Forest
- Pasture
- • Major conurbation

#### LAND USE

Pasture 27%
Forest 35%
Cropland 15%
Other 23%

## ENVIRONMENTAL ISSUES

**Central America's rain forests** are rapidly being cut down for timber and to make way for farmland and land for building. Over half of Guatemala's forests have been felled, mostly in the last 30 years. The situation is also bleak in Honduras, Costa Rica, and Nicaragua. Central America has a line of volcanoes running through the region which, are still active.

*Mitch 1998*

*Volcán Tacaná 1986*
*Volcán de Fuego 1974*
*Volcán de Izalco 1958*
*Volcán San Cristobal 2000*
*Volcán Masaya 2001*
*Volcán Cerro Negro 1995*
*Volcán Concepcion 1986*
*Volcán Arenal 1998, 2000*
*Volcán Rincon de la Vieja 1998*

### ENVIRONMENTAL ISSUES

- 🌋 Volcanic eruption
- Deforested areas
- Remaining forests
- Path of recent, devastating hurricane

## POPULATION

**Central America's people** live mainly in the valleys of the central highlands or along the Pacific coastal plains. Despite the threat of volcanic eruptions and earthquakes, towns and cities were developed in these areas because of the fertile volcanic soils found there. Around half the population still lives in rural areas, mostly in small villages or remote settlements, but the cities have expanded rapidly and overcrowding has become a serious problem.

BELMOPAN
GUATEMALA CITY
TEGUCIGALPA
SAN SALVADOR
MANAGUA
SAN JOSÉ
PANAMA CITY

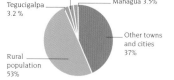

### INHABITANTS PER SQ MILE

- More than 130
- 52–130
- Less than 52
- ■ Capital city

### URBAN/RURAL POPULATION DIVISION

San Salvador 3.3%
Tegucigalpa 3.2%
Managua 3.5%
Other towns and cities 37%
Rural population 53%

## THE LANDSCAPE

**The Sierra Madre** in the north and the Cordillera Central to the south form a mountainous ridge that stretches down most of Central America. Along the Pacific coast north of Panama is a belt of more than 40 active volcanoes. The mountains are broken by valleys and basins with large, fertile areas of rich, volcanic soil.

Barillas
Jacaltenango
Huehuetenango
Volcán Tacaná 13,429ft
Santa Cruz del Quiché
San Marcos
Quezalter
Champerico
GUATEMALA C
Chajul
Neb
MEXICO
Yu
Río Usumacinta
GUA

### Coral reef (C 2)

Off the coast of Belize is a 180 mile-long coral reef – the second longest in the world. Its waters contain spectacular marine life. In places, the reef has become built up into dozens of small sandy islands called cayes.

**Sierra Madre (A 3)**

### The Mosquito Coast (E 4)

The Mosquito Coast is a remote area of tropical rain forests, lagoons, and rivers lined with mangroves. Most of it is uninhabited by humans, but there is a huge variety of animal species, including monkeys and alligators.

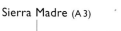

### Lake Nicaragua (E 5)

This large freshwater lake contains about 400 islands, some of which are active volances like Volcán Concepcion. The lake is also home to the world's only freshwater sharks.

**Cordillera Central (G 6)**

### Panama Canal (H 6)

The Panama Canal links the Atlantic and Pacific oceans along a distance of 51 miles. Half of its route passes through Lake Gatún, a freshwater lake that acts as a reservoir for the canal, providing water to operate the locks.

# CLIMATE

Temperatures are high all year round, although in January the Caribbean side of Central America is cooler and wetter than the Pacific side. Summers are generally much wetter, especially in the Sierra Madre in Guatemala and on the Pacific coasts of Costa Rica and Panama.

**TEMPERATURE AND PRECIPITATION**

More than 77°F
68 to 77°F
Less than 68°F
4 — Precipitation (in)

January

July

# INDUSTRY

Coffee, fish, and timber processing, fruit exporting, and textile-weaving are typical of the small-scale industries found in Central America. Most industries are based in the capital cities and larger towns. In Panama, many people work at the Panama Canal, which is one of the world's busiest shipping routes. The country is also a major financial center, with many banking and insurance companies.

**INDUSTRY**

- Chemicals
- Coffee processing
- Fish processing
- Food processing
- Textiles
- Banana exporting
- Timber processing
- Finance
- Major industrial center / area
- Major road

**STRUCTURE OF INDUSTRY**

Primary 18%
Services 60%
Manufacturing 22%

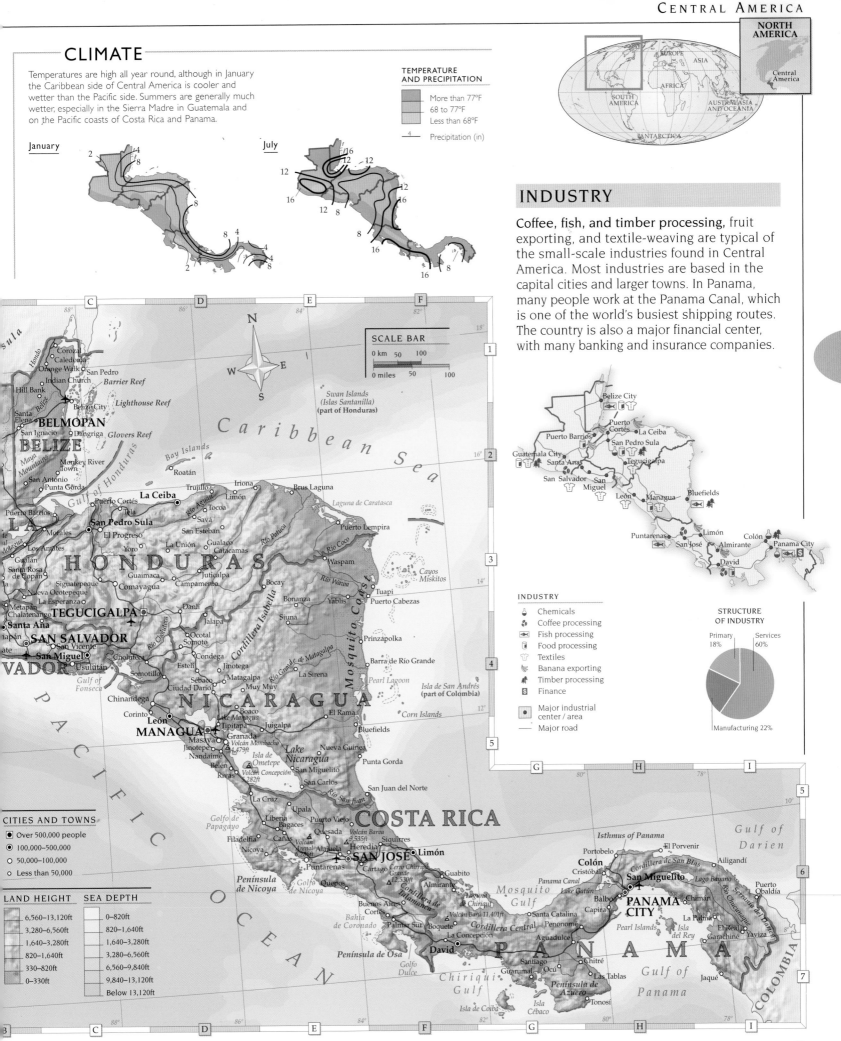

**CITIES AND TOWNS**
- Over 500,000 people
- 100,000–500,000
- 50,000–100,000
- Less than 50,000

**LAND HEIGHT**
6,560–13,120ft
3,280–6,560ft
1,640–3,280ft
820–1,640ft
330–820ft
0–330ft

**SEA DEPTH**
0–820ft
820–1,640ft
1,640–3,280ft
3,280–6,560ft
6,560–9,840ft
9,840–13,120ft
Below 13,120ft

# THE CARIBBEAN

**The Caribbean Sea** is enclosed by an arc of many hundreds of islands, islets, and offshore reefs that reach from Florida in the US, round to Venezuela in South America. From 1492, Spain, France, Britain, and the Netherlands claimed the islands as colonies. Most of the islands' original inhabitants were wiped out by disease and a wide mixture of peoples – of African, Asian, and European descent – now make up the population. The islands are prone to earthquakes, hurricanes, and volcanic eruptions.

## THE LANDSCAPE

### The Bahamas
The Bahamas are low-lying islands formed from limestone rock. Their coastlines are fringed by coral reefs, lagoons, and mangrove swamps. Some of the bigger islands are covered by forests.

**The islands are formed** from two main mountain chains: the Greater Antilles, which are part of a chain running from west to east, and the Lesser Antilles, which run from north to south. The mountains are now almost submerged under the Atlantic Ocean and Caribbean Sea. Only the higher peaks reach above sea level to form islands.

### Hispaniola (F4)
Two countries, Haiti and the Dominican Republic, occupy the island of Hispaniola. The land is mostly mountainous, broken by fertile valleys.

### Cuba (C3)
Cuba is the largest island in the Antilles. Its landscape is made up of wide, fertile plains with rugged hills and mountains in the southeast.

### The Lesser Antilles
Most of these small volcanic islands have mountainous interiors. Barbados and Antigua and Barbuda are flatter, with some higher volcanic areas. Monserrat was evacuated in 1997, following volcanic eruptions on the island.

## FARMING AND LAND USE

**Agriculture is an important source of income**, with over half of all produce exported. Many islands have fertile, well-watered land and large areas are set aside for commercial crops such as sugarcane, tobacco, and coffee. Some islands rely heavily on a single crop; in Dominica, bananas provide over half the country's income. Cuba is one of the world's biggest sugar producers.

Havana
Kingston
Port-au-Prince
San Juan

**FARMING AND LAND USE**

- 🐄 Cattle
- 🎣 Fishing
- 🐖 Pigs
- 🦃 Poultry
- 🦐 Shellfish
- 🍌 Bananas
- ☕ Coffee
- Sugarcane
- Tobacco

- Cropland
- Forest
- Pasture
- Major conurbation

## ENVIRONMENTAL ISSUES

**The islands of the Caribbean** are often under threat from hurricane storm systems which sweep in from the Atlantic Ocean between May and October. The winds can reach speeds of up to 156 miles per hour, devastating everything that lies in their path and causing severe flooding. The storms themselves are enormous; a hurricane can extend outward for 406 miles from its calm center, which is known as the "eye."

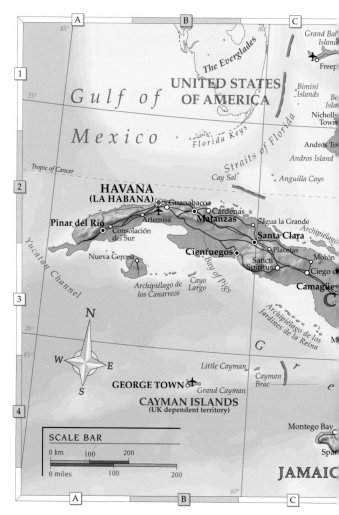

## TOURISM

**Tourism is thriving** in the Caribbean, often bringing more income to the region than other, traditional industries. Long sandy beaches, clear, warm waters, and the climate are the main attractions. In Cuba and the Dominican Republic, tourism is expanding at some of the fastest rates in North America. As hotel complexes and new roads and airports are developed, the environment is often damaged. Local people who work in the industry often receive little of the extra cash brought in by the tourists.

**TOURISM**

🦋 Major tourist destinations

Bahamas
Cuba
Jamaica
Puerto Rico
Virgin Islands
Antigua & Barbuda
Dominican Republic
Guadeloupe
St Lucia
Barbados
Aruba
Grenada
Trinidad & Tobago

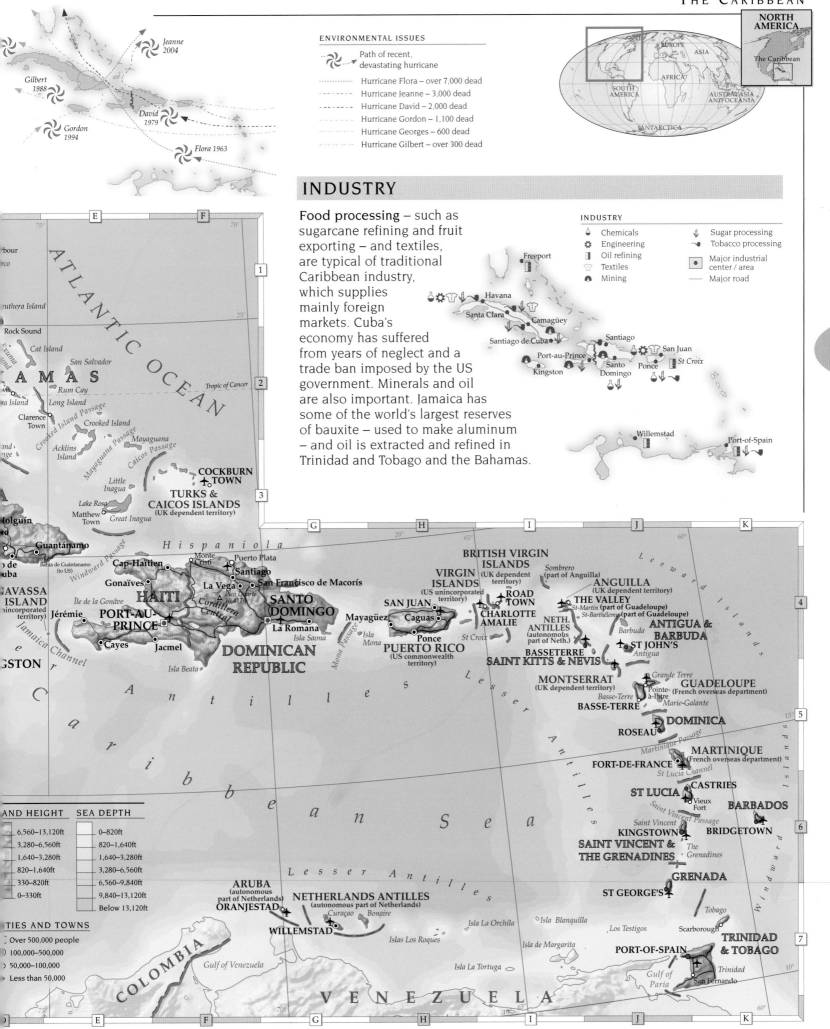

NORTH AMERICA

The Caribbean

## ENVIRONMENTAL ISSUES

- Path of recent, devastating hurricane
- Hurricane Flora – over 7,000 dead
- Hurricane Jeanne – 3,000 dead
- Hurricane David – 2,000 dead
- Hurricane Gordon – 1,100 dead
- Hurricane Georges – 600 dead
- Hurricane Gilbert – over 300 dead

Jeanne 2004
Gilbert 1988
Gordon 1994
David 1979
Flora 1963

## INDUSTRY

**Food processing** – such as sugarcane refining and fruit exporting – and textiles, are typical of traditional Caribbean industry, which supplies mainly foreign markets. Cuba's economy has suffered from years of neglect and a trade ban imposed by the US government. Minerals and oil are also important. Jamaica has some of the world's largest reserves of bauxite – used to make aluminum – and oil is extracted and refined in Trinidad and Tobago and the Bahamas.

### INDUSTRY

- Chemicals
- Engineering
- Oil refining
- Textiles
- Mining
- Sugar processing
- Tobacco processing
- Major industrial center / area
- Major road

Freeport · Havana · Santa Clara · Camagüey · Santiago de Cuba · Santiago · San Juan · Port-au-Prince · Santo Domingo · Ponce · St Croix · Kingston · Willemstad · Port-of-Spain

### LAND HEIGHT
- 6,560–13,120ft
- 3,280–6,560ft
- 1,640–3,280ft
- 820–1,640ft
- 330–820ft
- 0–330ft

### SEA DEPTH
- 0–820ft
- 820–1,640ft
- 1,640–3,280ft
- 3,280–6,560ft
- 6,560–9,840ft
- 9,840–13,120ft
- Below 13,120ft

### CITIES AND TOWNS
- Over 500,000 people
- 100,000–500,000
- 50,000–100,000
- Less than 50,000

ATLANTIC OCEAN

Eleuthera Island · Rock Sound · Cat Island · San Salvador · BAHAMAS · Long Island · Rum Cay · Clarence Town · Crooked Island · Acklins Island · Mayaguana · Little Inagua · Lake Rosa · Great Inagua · Matthew Town

Tropic of Cancer

COCKBURN TOWN · TURKS & CAICOS ISLANDS (UK dependent territory)

Crooked Island Passage · Mayaguana Passage · Caicos Passage

Holguín · Guantánamo · Santiago de Cuba · Bahía de Guantánamo (to US) · Windward Passage · Hispaniola · Monte Cristi · Cap-Haïtien · Puerto Plata · Santiago · San Francisco de Macorís · Gonaïves · La Vega · Pico Duarte 10,417ft · HAITI · Cordillera Central · NAVASSA ISLAND (US unincorporated territory) · Île de la Gonâve · Jérémie · PORT-AU-PRINCE · SANTO DOMINGO · La Romana · DOMINICAN REPUBLIC · Cayes · Jacmel · Isla Saona · Isla Beata · Kingston · Jamaica Channel

VIRGIN ISLANDS (US unincorporated territory) · BRITISH VIRGIN ISLANDS (UK dependent territory) · Sombrero (part of Anguilla) · ANGUILLA (UK dependent territory) · THE VALLEY · ROAD TOWN · St-Martin (part of Guadeloupe) · St-Barthélemy (part of Guadeloupe) · SAN JUAN · Caguas · CHARLOTTE AMALIE · St Croix · NETH. ANTILLES (autonomous part of Neth.) · ANTIGUA & BARBUDA · Barbuda · Mayagüez · Isla Mona · Ponce · St Croix · BASSETERRE · SAINT KITTS & NEVIS · ST JOHN'S · Antigua · PUERTO RICO (US commonwealth territory) · Mona Passage · MONTSERRAT (UK dependent territory) · Grande Terre · GUADELOUPE (French overseas department) · BASSE-TERRE · Basse-Terre · Pointe-à-Pitre · Marie-Galante · DOMINICA · ROSEAU · Martinique Passage · MARTINIQUE (French overseas department) · FORT-DE-FRANCE · St Lucia Channel · ST LUCIA · CASTRIES · Vieux Fort · Saint Vincent Passage · BARBADOS · KINGSTOWN · BRIDGETOWN · SAINT VINCENT & THE GRENADINES · Saint Vincent · The Grenadines · GRENADA · ST GEORGE'S · Leeward Islands · Windward Islands

Antilles · Caribbean Sea · Lesser Antilles

ARUBA (autonomous part of Netherlands) · NETHERLANDS ANTILLES (autonomous part of Netherlands) · ORANJESTAD · Curaçao · Bonaire · Isla La Orchila · WILLEMSTAD · Islas Los Roques · Isla Blanquilla · Isla La Tortuga · Los Testigos · Isla de Margarita · Tobago · Scarborough · TRINIDAD & TOBAGO · PORT-OF-SPAIN · Trinidad · Gulf of Paria · San Fernando

COLOMBIA · Gulf of Venezuela · VENEZUELA

# CONTINENTAL EUROPE

**Europe is the world's** second smallest continent, occupying the western tip of the vast Eurasian landmass. To the north and west are old highlands, with the high peaks of the Alps in the south. Most people live on the densely populated North European Plain, which extends from southern England, through northern France, across Germany into Russia.

**3,360 miles**
**3,140 miles**

## CROSS-SECTION THROUGH EUROPE

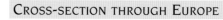
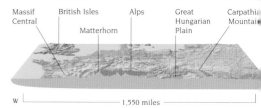

Massif Central | British Isles | Alps | Great Hungarian Plain | Carpathia Mountain

Matterhorn

W ├──────── 1,550 miles ────────┤

In the west, the land rises up from the Atlantic coast toward the Massif Central in France, and the high peaks of the Alps. Between the Alps and the Carpathian Mountains is the Great Hungarian Plain, where the Danube River flows on its way to the Black Sea.

## PHYSICAL EUROPE

**The ancient mountains** of northwest Europe were scoured and smoothed by glaciers in the last Ice Age. The Alps are newer and more jagged – pushed up when Africa collided with Europe. In between is the North European Plain, where thick layers of fertile soils allow many different crops to be grown.

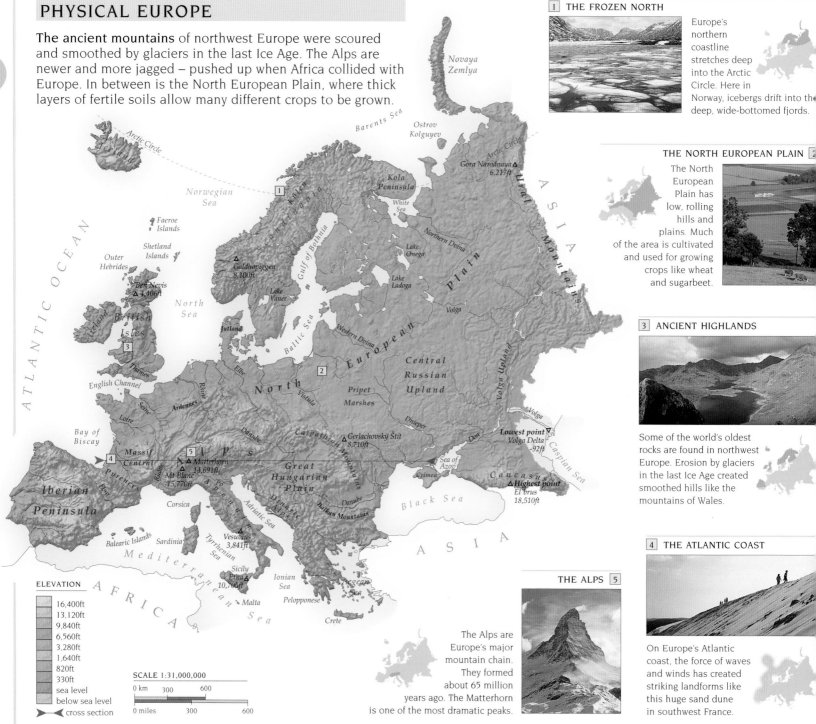

**1 THE FROZEN NORTH**

Europe's northern coastline stretches deep into the Arctic Circle. Here in Norway, icebergs drift into the deep, wide-bottomed fjords.

**THE NORTH EUROPEAN PLAIN 2**

The North European Plain has low, rolling hills and plains. Much of the area is cultivated and used for growing crops like wheat and sugarbeet.

**3 ANCIENT HIGHLANDS**

Some of the world's oldest rocks are found in northwest Europe. Erosion by glaciers in the last Ice Age created smoothed hills like the mountains of Wales.

**4 THE ATLANTIC COAST**

On Europe's Atlantic coast, the force of waves and winds has created striking landforms like this huge sand dune in southwest France.

**THE ALPS 5**

The Alps are Europe's major mountain chain. They formed about 65 million years ago. The Matterhorn is one of the most dramatic peaks.

### Map labels

Novaya Zemlya
Barents Sea
Ostrov Kolguyev
Arctic Circle
Iceland
Norwegian Sea
Kölen
Scandinavia
Kola Peninsula
White Sea
Gora Narodnaya △ 6,217ft
Arctic Circle
ASIA
Faeroe Islands
Shetland Islands
Outer Hebrides
Galdhøpiggen 8,100ft
Gulf of Bothnia
Northern Dvina
Lake Onega
Lake Ladoga
Ural Mountains
Ben Nevis △ 4,406ft
North Sea
Lake Vänern
Volga
Ireland
British Isles
Jutland
Baltic Sea
European Plain
Central Russian Upland
Volga Upland
ATLANTIC OCEAN
English Channel
Thames
Elbe
North European Plain
Vistula
Pripet Marshes
Dnieper
Volga
Seine
Rhine
Ardennes
Danube
Carpathian Mountains
Gerlachovský Štít 8,710ft
Don
Lowest point Volga Delta -92ft
Caspian Sea
Loire
Bay of Biscay
Massif Central
Rhine
Matterhorn 14,691ft
Alps
Mt Blanc 15,770ft
Po
Apennines
Great Hungarian Plain
Sea of Azov
Crimea
Caucasus
△ Highest point El'brus 18,510ft
Pyrenees
Ebro
Dinaric Alps
Adriatic Sea
Danube
Balkan Mountains
Black Sea
ASIA
Iberian Peninsula
Corsica
Balearic Islands
Sardinia
Tyrrhenian Sea
Vesuvius 3,841ft
Sicily
Etna △ 10,705ft
Ionian Sea
Aegean Sea
Peloponnese
Mediterranean Sea
Malta
Crete
AFRICA

### ELEVATION

- 16,400ft
- 13,120ft
- 9,840ft
- 6,560ft
- 3,280ft
- 1,640ft
- 820ft
- 330ft
- sea level
- below sea level
- ✕ cross section

SCALE 1:31,000,000

0 km   300   600

0 miles   300   600

# POLITICAL EUROPE

Europe's population increased rapidly during the 18th and 19th centuries, following the Industrial Revolution. In the 20th century, Europe suffered a series of wars which redrew the political map. From 1989–1991, communist governments in eastern Europe and the former Soviet Union collapsed, as political reform swept through the countries behind the 'Iron Curtain'. In 2004 the European Union admitted 10 more states in a further expansion.

## EUROPEAN UNION

- six original members, 1957
- nine further members, 1973 – 1995
- ten new members, 2004

### REGIONAL IDENTITY

Throughout Europe, there is a growing call to recognize regional cultural identity. The Basque region, straddling southwest France and Spain, is one example.

### RURAL LIFE

Away from Europe's bustling cities, traditional rural lifestyles survive. Here in the Ireland, a winter shelter is being made for cattle.

## STANDARDS OF LIVING

Living standards are generally much lower in eastern Europe than in the wealthier west. Homelessness and unemployment are still common, even in the most prosperous countries.

## POPULATION

Capital cities
- ◉ Above 500,000
- ◉ 100,000 to 500,000
- ● 50,000 to 100,000

SCALE 1:27,500,000

0 km   300   600

0 miles   300   600

## POPULATION

More than 725 million people live in Europe, and its population is highly urbanized. In Belgium and the Netherlands, almost 90% of people live in cities. In the south and east, more people still live in rural areas. The northern countries have the smallest populations because much of the land is too cold to be habitable.

POPULATION DENSITY
(People per sq mile)
- Below 127
- 127–257
- 258–386
- 387–515
- 516–774
- Above 774

### SPREADING CITIES

Largest city
MOSCOW
10.1 million people

Amsterdam, in the Netherlands, is part of a conurbation, a large built-up area where several towns or cities have merged together to form a single urban area.

STANDARD OF LIVING
(UN Human Development Index)
low          high

# EUROPEAN GEOGRAPHY

Europe is blessed with a temperate climate, ample mineral reserves, and good transportation links. During the 18th and 19th centuries the continent was transformed, as new methods of production made industry and farming more efficient and productive. Today, in many countries, heavy industries have been replaced by high-tech and service industries. Agriculture is still important, and many crops thrive on Europe's fertile plains.

## INDUSTRY

Western Europe has some of the world's wealthiest countries. In countries such as France, Germany, and the UK, traditional industries like iron and steel-making are now being replaced by light industries, such as electronics, and services like finance and insurance. In Eastern Europe, industry was subsidized by the communist governments for years. Many factories are old-fashioned and need investment to improve their equipment and production methods.

## MINERAL RESOURCES

Europe has few sizable reserves of metallic minerals; most were used up by industry during the 19th century. Oil, gas, and coal are found in large quantities – gas in the North Sea and oil in the Volga basin. Coal, although abundant, is being steadily depleted.

**MINERAL RESOURCES**

- Bauxite
- Chromium
- Copper
- Iron
- Manganese
- Nickel
- Uranium
- Oil/gas field
- Coal field

**OIL AND GAS**

Oil and gas reserves are plentiful in the Russian Federation. South of Rostov-on-Don, oil is pumped from the ground and piped to nearby refineries.

**CAR MANUFACTURING**

Germany is one of the world's largest manufacturers of cars. Companies like BMW, Mercedes-Benz, and Volkswagen export cars across the world.

**FINANCE**

London, Frankfurt and Paris are among the most important financial centers in the world. Many banks and financial institutions have their headquarters here. At the London Stock Exchange, people buy and sell stocks and shares.

**ECONOMIC ACTIVITY**

- Aerospace
- Vehicle manufacturing
- Chemicals
- Coal
- Defense
- Electronics
- Engineering
- Finance
- Food processing
- High-tech industry
- Iron and steel
- Oil and gas
- Printing and publishing
- Textiles
- Timber processing

**GNI per capita (US$)**

- Below 1,999
- 2,000–4,999
- 5,000–9,999
- 10,000–19,999
- 20,000–24,999
- Above 25,000
- Industrial center

## CLIMATE

Europe's climate is temperate with few climatic extremes. In the far north, Europe extends into the Arctic Circle and the climate is so cold that the Baltic Sea freezes over in the winter. Toward the Atlantic coast in the west, the climate becomes wetter and warmer because of a warm ocean current, known as the Gulf Stream. Countries such as Italy and Spain that border the Mediterranean Sea have long, hot summers and low rainfall, which can sometimes lead to such problems as drought.

### EXTREME WEATHER EVENTS

Symbols indicate climatic extremes

### CLIMATE

- Tundra
- Subarctic
- Cool continental
- Temperate/humid
- Mediterranean
- Semiarid

Coldest place
UST' SHCHUGOR (Russ. Fed.)
Temperature -67F

Driest place
ASTRAKHAN (Russ. Fed.)
Annual rainfall 6 in

Hottest place
SEVILLE (Spain)
Temperature 122F

Wettest place
CRKVICE (Serbia & Montenegro)
Annual rainfall 183 in

### THE MEDITERRANEAN CLIMATE

The mild, warm climate around the Mediterranean Sea allows olives, citrus fruits, and grapes to thrive. Long, sunny days also help the fruits ripen. Grapes are harvested and crushed to make many different wines.

## LAND USE AND AGRICULTURE

Europe's agricultural heart is the North European Plain, where fertile soils and ample rainfall allow a variety of crops to be grown. Wheat is the main grain crop, and a wide range of fruit and vegetables are also grown. Dairy and beef cattle are raised for their milk and meat throughout Europe. In the south, the Mediterranean climate is ideal for citrus fruits and olives. Forests cover much of northern Scandinavia, while sheep farming is common in the hills of the British Isles.

### FISHING

The north Atlantic Ocean provides a rich marine harvest for fishermen. Today the cod, haddock and mackerel stocks have to be protected from over-fishing.

### LAND USE AND AGRICULTURE

- Cattle
- Goats
- Pigs
- Reindeer
- Sheep
- Cereals
- Citrus fruits
- Fishing
- Fruit
- Olive oil
- Potatoes
- Root crops
- Shellfish
- Sunflowers
- Timber
- Vineyards

- Cropland
- Forest
- Ice cap
- Mountain region
- Pasture
- Tundra
- Wetland
- Major conurbation

### CROPLANDS

Many different crops are grown on the North European Plain. Sunflowers, wheat, and sugar beets – used to make sugar – are among the main crops grown there.

### DAIRY FARMING

Dairy farming is very common across northern Europe. Cows grazed on rich pastures produce milk used for making butter and cheese.

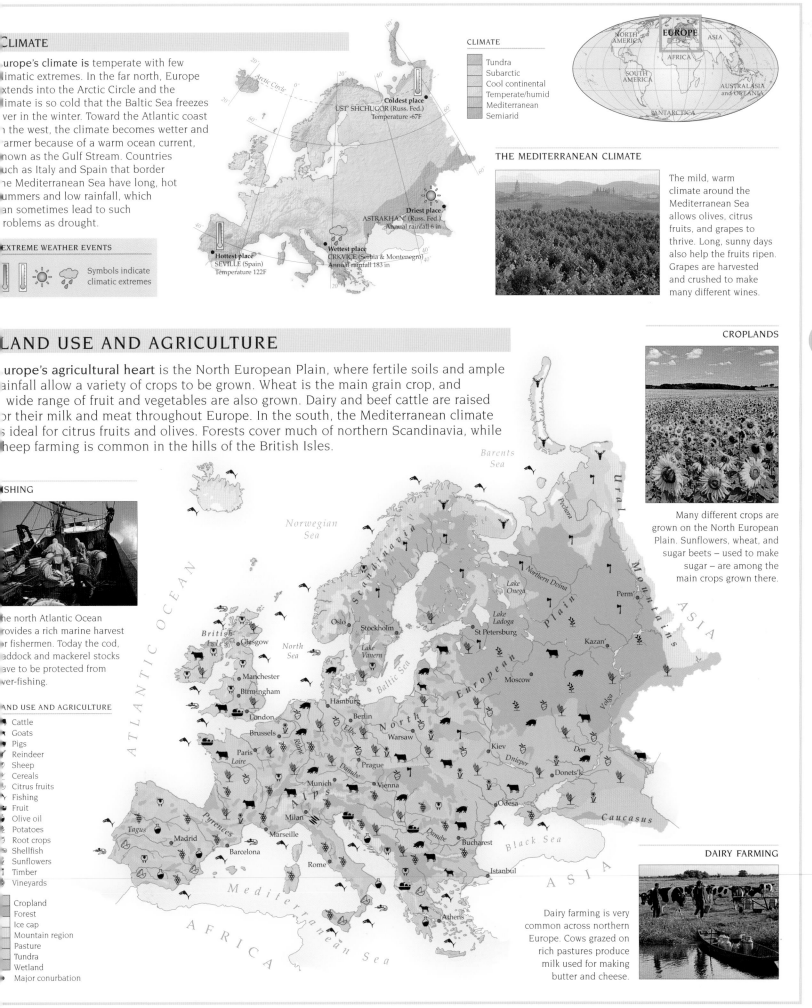

# NORTHERN EUROPE

DENMARK, ESTONIA, FINLAND, ICELAND, LATVIA, LITHUANIA, NORWAY, SWEDEN

**Denmark, Sweden, and Norway** are together known as Scandinavia. These countries, along with the North Atlantic island of Iceland, have similar languages and cultures. Finland has a very different language and a separate identity from its Scandinavian neighbors. Estonia, Latvia, and Lithuania, known as the Baltic states, were part of the Soviet Union until 1989, when each became an independent country.

## INDUSTRY

**In Scandinavia,** many natural resources are used in industry: timber for paper and furniture; iron ore for steel and cars; and fish and natural gas from the seas. Hydroelectric power is generated by water flowing down steep mountain slopes. The Baltic states still rely on Russia to supply their raw materials and energy.

### INDUSTRY

- 🚗 Car manufacturing
- 🚙 Chemicals
- ⚙ Engineering
- 🐟 Fish processing
- ⊞ Hydroelectric power
- ⚓ Shipbuilding
- ⚒ Timber processing
- 🏛 Tourism
- ▣ Major industrial center / area
- — Major road

### STRUCTURE OF INDUSTRY

Primary 4%
Services 65%
Manufacturing 31%

## POPULATION

**The population is distributed** mainly along the warmer and flatter southern and coastal areas. Population totals and densities are low for all of the countries, and Iceland has the lowest population density in Europe, with just seven people per sq mile. Many Scandinavians have holiday homes on the islands, along the lake shores, or in coastal areas.

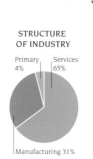

### INHABITANTS PER SQ MILE

- More than 520
- 260–520
- 130–260
- Less than 130
- ■ Capital city
- • Major city

### URBAN/RURAL POPULATION DIVISION

Copenhagen 3.4%   Stockholm 3.8%
Helsinki 3.3%
Other towns and cities 66.5%
Rural population 23%

## FARMING AND LAND USE

**Southern Denmark and Sweden** are the most productive areas, with pig farming, dairy farming, and crops such as wheat, barley, and potatoes. Sheep farming is important in southern Norway and Iceland. In the Baltic states, cereals, potatoes, and sugar beets are the main crops, and cattle graze on damp pasture.

### FARMING AND LAND USE

- 🐄 Cattle
- 🐟 Fishing
- 🐖 Pigs
- 🐑 Sheep
- 🌾 Cereals
- 🌱 Root crops
- 🌲 Timber

- Pasture
- Cropland
- Forest
- Ice cap
- Mountain region
- Tundra
- • Major conurbation

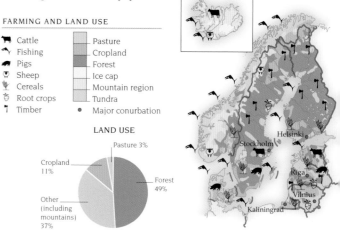

### LAND USE

Pasture 3%
Cropland 11%
Forest 49%
Other (including mountains) 37%

## THE LANDSCAPE

**The north and west** of Scandinavia is extremely rugged and mountainous, with landscapes eroded by ice. In the south of Scandinavia the land is flatter, with fertile soils deposited by glaciers. Much of Finland, Norway, and Sweden is covered by dense forests. The Baltic states are much lower, with rounded hills and many lakes and marshes.

**The land of ice and fire.** Iceland is one of the world's most active volcanic areas. There are about 200 volcanoes on the island, along with bubbling hot springs, mud-holes, and geysers that spurt boiling water and steam high into the air.

**Fjords**
Norway has many fjords: deep, wide valleys, drowned by seawater when the ice melted at the end of the last Ice Age.

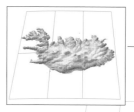

**Baltic Sea (D7)**
Ships from Finland, Sweden, and the Baltic states use the Baltic Sea as their route to the north Atlantic Ocean. In winter, much of the sea is frozen.

**Glacial lakes**
Finland and Sweden have many thousands of lakes. During the last Ice Age, glaciers scoured hollows that filled with water when the ice melted.

**Courland Spit (D7**
This wide sandspit run 62-miles along the Balt coast of Lithuania and Russian enclave of Kalin It encloses a huge lago

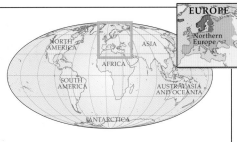

# ENVIRONMENTAL ISSUES

Northern Europe has been badly affected by industrial pollution from other parts of Europe. Polluted air moves north and mixes with the rain to create acid rain. This poisons forests and lakes, destroying the plants and animals living in them. In Norway and Sweden, electricity is produced by dams that obtain power from plentiful water. Hydro-electric power is a clean, alternative energy source.

## ENVIRONMENTAL ISSUES

- Major dams
- Urban air pollution
- Volcanic eruption
- Affected by acid rain
- Sea pollution
- Major industrial center

# CLIMATE

Warm ocean currents flowing north along the coasts of Norway and Iceland make the climate mild and wet. Away from the sea, the climate is generally colder and drier.

January

July

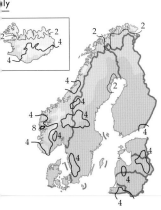

## TEMPERATURE AND PRECIPITATION

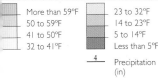

| | |
|---|---|
| More than 59°F | 23 to 32°F |
| 50 to 59°F | 14 to 23°F |
| 41 to 50°F | 5 to 14°F |
| 32 to 41°F | Less than 5°F |

4 — Precipitation (in)

### ICELAND

### SCALE BAR

0 km   100   200
0 miles   100   200

### LAND HEIGHT

| | |
|---|---|
| | 6,560–13,120ft |
| | 3,280–6,560ft |
| | 1,640–3,280ft |
| | 820–1,640ft |
| | 330–820ft |
| | 0–330ft |

### SEA DEPTH

| | |
|---|---|
| | 0–160ft |
| | 160–330ft |
| | 330–820ft |
| | 820–1,640ft |
| | 1,640–3,280ft |
| | 3,280–6,560ft |
| | Below 6,560ft |

### CITIES AND TOWNS

- Over 500,000 people
- 100,000–500,000
- 50,000–100,000
- Less than 50,000

# THE LOW COUNTRIES

BELGIUM, LUXEMBOURG, NETHERLANDS

**Belgium, Luxembourg, and the Netherlands** are called the Low Countries because most of their land is flat and low-lying. Much of the Netherlands lies below sea level, and over hundreds of years the Dutch have built dikes and dams to prevent flooding, and have pumped water off large areas of land to reclaim them from the sea. The Low Countries are Europe's most densely populated countries, but most of their people have a high living standard.

## ENVIRONMENTAL ISSUES

**Huge land reclamation** projects in the Netherlands, such as the IJsselmeer project, have created some new land for agricultural use, and also for houses, roads, and open spaces. Heavy industry has caused serious air pollution in cities such as Amsterdam and Rotterdam, and added to Europe's acid rain problem.

ENVIRONMENTAL
ISSUES

- 🙂 Urban air pollution
- Built-up areas
- Reclaimed land
- Polluted river
- • Major industrial center

## CLIMATE

The Low Countries share a similar climate, with mild winters and warm summers. Only in the upland Ardennes region does rainfall increase and temperatures decrease.

January

July

Less than 2

Less than 2

4

4

TEMPERATURE
AND PRECIPITATION

- More than 59°F
- 50 to 59°F
- 41 to 50°F
- 32 to 41°F
- Less than 32°F

4 — Precipitation (in)

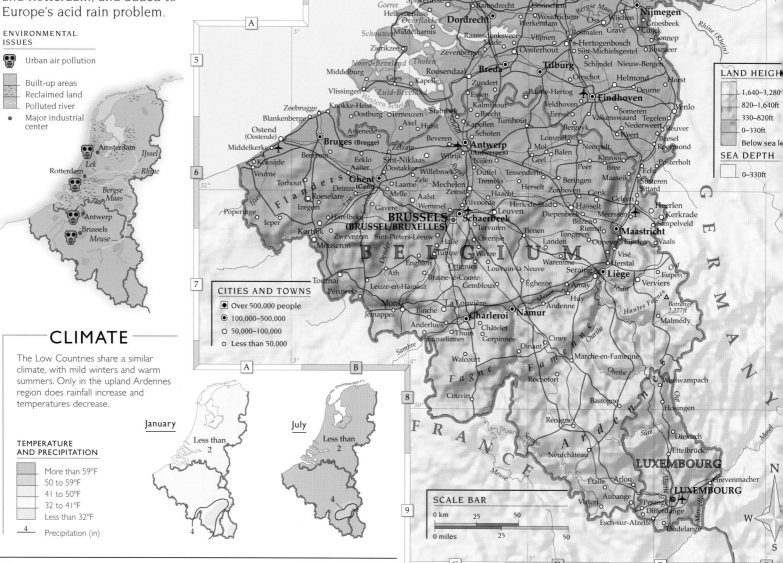

NETHERLANDS'
TWO CAPITALS
AMSTERDAM - capital
THE HAGUE - seat of govern

CITIES AND TOWNS
- ■ Over 500,000 people
- ◉ 100,000–500,000
- ◉ 50,000–100,000
- ○ Less than 50,000

LAND HEIGH
- 1,640–3,280
- 820–1,640ft
- 330–820ft
- 0–330ft
- Below sea le

SEA DEPTH
- 0–330ft

SCALE BAR

0 km   25   50

0 miles   25   50

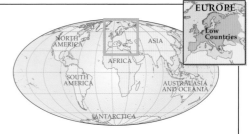

## POPULATION

More than 27 million people live in the
Low Countries, and nine out of every
ten people live in a town or city. The
largest urban area – known as the
Randstad Holland – is in the Netherlands.
It runs in an unbroken line from
Rotterdam in the south, to
Amsterdam in the west.
Even most rural areas
in the Low Countries
are densely
populated.

INHABITANTS
PER SQ MILE

- More than 520
- 260–520
- 130–260
- 0–130

■ Capital city
● Major city

THE HAGUE
AMSTERDAM
Groningen
Randstad Holland
Utrecht
Arnhem
Rotterdam
Ghent
Antwerp
BRUSSELS
Liège
Charleroi
LUXEMBOURG

Amsterdam 2.8%  Brussels 3.9%
Rotterdam 2.3%
Rural
population
8%

Other towns
and cities 83%

## FARMING AND LAND USE

The Low Countries' fertile soils and flat
plains provide excellent conditions for
farming. The main crops grown are barley,
potatoes, and flax for making linen.
In the Netherlands, much
farmland is used for dairy
farming. The country is
also famous for growing
flowers, which are
exported around the
world. Flowers and
vegetables are
grown either in
open fields or
in enormous
greenhouses,
which allow
production
year-round.

Amsterdam
The Hague
Rotterdam
Brussels

LAND USE

Forest
16%

Other
(including
urban)
29%

Pasture
26%

Cropland
29%

FARMING AND LAND USE

🐄 Cattle
🐖 Pigs
🌾 Cereals
❋ Flax
🌷 Flowers
🐏 Market gardening
🥬 Sugar beet

 Pasture
Cropland
Forest
Wetland
● Major
conurbation

## THE LANDSCAPE

The Low Countries are largely flat
and low-lying. The ancient hills of
the Ardennes, in the far southeast,
are the only higher region. They
rise to heights of more than 1,640 ft.
Two major rivers – the Meuse and
the Rhine – flow across the Low
Countries to their mouths in the
North Sea. At the coast, the Rhine
deposits large quantities of sediment
to form a delta.

### Polders

In the Netherlands, land has been
reclaimed from the sea since the
Middle Ages by building dikes
and drainage ditches. These
areas of land are called polders.
They are very fertile.

### Rhine River (E4)

The River Rhine erodes
and carries large amounts
of sediment along its
course. When it reaches
the Netherlands it divides
into three rivers. As they
approach the North Sea,
the rivers slow down,
depositing the sediment
to form a delta.

### Low-lying
Netherlands

Over two-
thirds of the
Netherlands
lies at or below
sea level. This
makes flooding a
constant threat
in coastal areas.

## INDUSTRY

The Low Countries are an important center for the high-tech
and electronics industries. Good transportation links to the
rest of Europe allow them to sell their products
in other countries. The built-up
area stretching from Amsterdam in the
Netherlands to Antwerp in Belgium
has the greatest number of factories.
Luxembourg is also an important
banking center; many international
banks have their headquarters in
its capital city.

STRUCTURE
OF INDUSTRY

Primary 2%
Services
73%

Manufacturing 25%

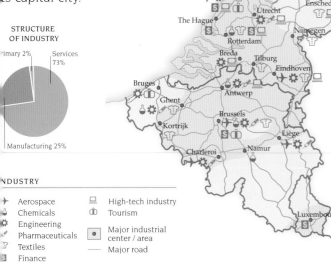

Groningen
Amsterdam
Enschede
The Hague
Utrecht
Nijmegen
Rotterdam
Breda
Tilburg
Eindhoven
Bruges
Antwerp
Ghent
Brussels
Kortrijk
Liège
Charleroi
Namur
Luxembourg

INDUSTRY

✈ Aerospace
⚗ Chemicals
⚙ Engineering
Pharmaceuticals
👕 Textiles
Finance
💻 High-tech industry
🏛 Tourism

🔲 Major industrial
center / area
— Major road

### Flanders (B6)

The plains of Flanders
in western Belgium
have fertile soils which
were deposited by
glaciers during the last
Ice Age. They provide
excellent land for
growing crops.

### Heathlands

The heathlands on
the Dutch-Belgian
border have thin,
sandy soils. The only
plants that grow
well here are
heathers and gorse.

### Ardennes (D8)

The hills of the Ardennes
were formed over 300
million years ago. They
have many deep valleys,
which have been eroded
by rivers like the Meuse.

69

# THE BRITISH ISLES

IRELAND, UNITED KINGDOM

**The British Isles** lie off the northwest coast of mainland Europe. They are made up of two large islands and more than 5,000 smaller ones. Politically, the region is divided into two countries: the United Kingdom – England, Wales, Scotland, and Northern Ireland – and the Republic of Ireland. Geographically, the British Isles are divided between highlands to the north and west, and lowlands to the south and east.

## THE LANDSCAPE

**Low rolling hills**, high moorlands, and small fields with high hedges are all typical of the British Isles. Ireland is known as the Emerald Isle because heavy rainfall gives it a lush, green appearance. Scotland and Wales are mountainous; the rocks forming the mountains there are some of the oldest in the world.

### Indented coastlines

The west coast of the British Isles faces the Atlantic Ocean, and more than 1,860 miles of open sea to the North American continent. Storms and high waves constantly batter the hard, rocky coastline, giving it a jagged outline.

### Ben Nevis (C 4)

This mountain is the highest point in the British Isles. It is 4,406 ft above sea level.

### The Lake District (D 5)

The Lake District National Park has England's highest peak, Scafell Pike, at 3,209 ft, its deepest lake, Wast Water (260 ft), and its largest lake, Windermere (10 miles long).

### The Pennines (D 6)

The Pennines are a chain of high hills, topped by moorland. They run for more than 250 miles, and are known as the "backbone of England."

### The Burren (A 6)

The Burren is a large area of limestone in the west of Ireland. Its flat surfaces are known as limestone "pavements." There are also many caves and sinkholes in the area.

### Rias

Rias are river valleys that have been drowned by rising sea levels. The southern coast of southwest England has many good examples.

### The Fens (E 6)

This is the flattest area in England. Much of the land here has been reclaimed from the sea.

## FARMING AND LAND USE

**The English lowlands** and the wide, flat stretches of land in East Anglia are the agricultural heartland of the United Kingdom. The country is no longer self-sufficient in food, but wheat, potatoes and other vegetables, and fruits, are widely grown. In Ireland, and in central and southern England, dairy and beef cattle feed off grassy pastures. In the hilly and mountainous areas, sheep farming is more usual.

FARMING AND LAND USE

- 🐂 Cattle
- 🐟 Fishing
- 🐑 Sheep
- 🌾 Cereals
- 🐄 Market gardening
- 🌱 Root crops

- ☐ Pasture
- ☐ Cropland
- ☐ Forest
- ☐ Mountain region
- ● Major conurbation

LAND USE

Cropland 24%
Pasture 50%
Other (including urban) 17%
Forest 9%

## INDUSTRY

**The United Kingdom's** traditional industries, such as coal mining, iron- and steel-making, and textiles, have declined in recent years. Today, newer industries make cars, chemicals, and electronic and high-tech goods. Service industries, especially banking and insurance, have grown in importance. The country's most valuable natural resource is its large North Sea oil and gas fields.

INDUSTRY

- ✈ Aerospace
- 🚗 Car manufacturing
- 🜀 Chemicals
- ⚙ Engineering
- Textiles
- 🅂 Finance
- 🖥 High-tech industry
- ⚓ Tourism

☐ Major industrial center / area
— Major road

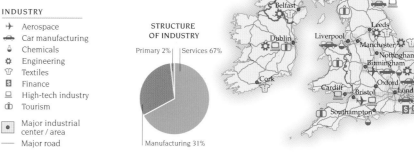

STRUCTURE OF INDUSTRY

Primary 2% | Services 67%
Manufacturing 31%

## POPULATION

**The United Kingdom** is densely populated, with most of the people living in urban areas. The southeast is the most crowded part of the country. The Scottish Highlands are less populated today than they were 200 years ago. Ireland is still mainly rural, with many Irish people making their living from farming.

URBAN/RURAL POPULATION DIVISION

Birmingham 1.6%
London 11.4%
Glasgow 1%
Rural population 12%
Other towns and cities 74%

INHABITANTS PER SQ MILE

- ☐ More than 520
- ☐ 260–520
- ☐ 130–260
- ☐ Less than 130
- ■ Capital city
- ● Major city

EUROPE

British Isles

## LAND HEIGHT

- 3,280–6,560ft
- 1,640–3,280ft
- 820–1,640ft
- 330–820ft
- 0–330ft

## SEA DEPTH

- 0–160ft
- 160–330ft
- 330–820ft
- 820–1,640ft
- 1,640–3,280ft
- 3,280–6,560ft
- Below 6,560ft

## CITIES AND TOWNS

- ■ Over 500,000 people
- ● 100,000–500,000
- ◎ 50,000–100,000
- ○ Less than 50,000

## ENVIRONMENTAL ISSUES

Air pollution is becoming a serious problem in many British cities, as the number of vehicles using the roads increases. The seas around the British Isles have been polluted by sewage and industrial waste. In recent years, several major oil spills have occurred off the coast of the United Kingdom.

Shetland Islands 1993

Milford Haven 1996

Glasgow

Newcastle upon Tyne

Dublin

Tyne

Manchester

Mersey

Birmingham

London

Thames

## ENVIRONMENTAL ISSUES

- Major oil spill
- Urban air pollution
- Sea pollution
- Polluted rivers
- ● Major industrial center

## CLIMATE

The British Isles' climate is moderated by the warm Atlantic ocean current called the Gulf Stream. The west is generally wetter than the east, and the south is warmer than the north.

January

July

## TEMPERATURE AND PRECIPITATION

- More than 59°F
- 50 to 59°F
- 41 to 50°F
- 37 to 41°F
- Less than 37°F
- —4— Precipitation (in)

### Map labels

Shetland Islands
Yell
Unst
Fetlar
Mainland
Lerwick

Fair Isle

Orkney Islands
Sanday
Kirkwall
Hoy
Mainland
Thurso
John o'Groats

Isle of Lewis
Stornoway
The Minch

St Kilda
North Uist
Outer Hebrides
South Uist

Ben Hope 3,042ft
Ullapool
Moray Firth
Elgin
Fraserburgh
Peterhead
Inverness
Loch Ness
Stronferry
Aviemore
Spey
Dee
Aberdeen

The Little Minch
Isle of Skye
Rhum
Eigg
Coll
Mallaig
Fort William
Ben Nevis 4,406ft
SCOTLAND
Forfar
Montrose
Arbroath
Dundee
St Andrews

Tiree
Isle of Mull
Oban
Firth of Lorn
Perth
Dunfermline
Firth of Forth

Jura
Loch Lomond
Stirling
Forth
Inner Hebrides
Islay
Greenock
Glasgow
Edinburgh
Berwick-upon-Tweed
Paisley
Hamilton
East Kilbride
Galashiels
Kilmarnock
Prestwick
Hawick
Isle of Arran
Ayr
Kintyre
Dumfries

ATLANTIC OCEAN

North Sea

Newcastle upon Tyne
South Shields
Sunderland
Hartlepool
Middlesbrough
Whitby

Coleraine
Londonderry
Strabane
NORTHERN IRELAND
Newtownabbey
Bangor
Carlisle
Penrith
Tees
Darlington
Durham
Stranraer
Workington
Whitehaven
Northallerton
Scarborough
Donegal
Omagh
Lough Neagh
Belfast
Newtownards
Lower Lough Erne
Enniskillen
Portadown
Armagh
Downpatrick
Newry
Barrow-in-Furness
Lancaster
Ribble
Harrogate
York
Castleford
Bridlington
Beverley

Donegal Bay
Sligo
Upper Lough Erne
Dundalk
DOUGLAS
ISLE OF MAN (UK crown dependency)
Blackpool
Preston
Bolton
Bradford
Leeds
Huddersfield
Kingston upon Hull
Grimsby

Castlebar
Connaught
Longford
Drogheda
Irish Sea
Manchester
Doncaster
Sheffield
Lincoln
Louth
Skegness

Lough Corrib
Galway
Athlone
Newbridge
Lucan
IRELAND
Liverpool
Anglesey
Holyhead
Birkenhead
Mersey
The Wash
Boston
Galway Bay
Lough Derg
Leinster
Chester
Crewe
ENGLAND
Nottingham
Stoke-on-Trent
Shrewsbury
Derby
Ennis
Port Laoise
Bangor
Snowdon 3,560ft
Stafford
Leicester
Norwich
Great Yarmouth
King's Lynn
Tralee
Clonmel
Kilkenny
Carlow
Wexford
Barmouth
Wolverhampton
Nuneaton
Peterborough
East Anglia
Lowestoft
Munster
Blackwater
Waterford
Tywyn
Cardigan Bay
Birmingham
Coventry
Kettering
Newmarket
Carrantuohill 3,406ft
Aberystwyth
WALES
Kidderminster
Northampton
Bedford
Cambridge
Ipswich
Killarney
St George's Channel
Worcester
Milton Keynes
Stevenage
Harlow
Felixstowe
Harwich
Cork
Fishguard
Carmarthen
Gloucester
Cheltenham
Luton
Colchester
Haverfordwest
Llanelli
Cotswold Hills
Oxford
St Albans
Watford
Southend-on-Sea
Milford Haven
Swansea
Port Talbot
Newport
Swindon
Thames
LONDON
Margate
Cardiff
Bristol
Reading
Windsor
Croydon
Canterbury
Bristol Channel
Bath
Basingstoke
Woking
Maidstone
Folkestone
Dover
Ilfracombe
Weston-super-Mare
Andover
Guildford
Crawley
Celtic Sea
Barnstaple
Taunton
Salisbury
Winchester
Brighton
Channel Tunnel
Bideford
Yeovil
Eastleigh
Havant
Hastings
Tiverton
Bridport
Southampton
Hove
Eastbourne
Bodmin
Exmouth
Portsmouth
Newport
Newquay
Exeter
Bournemouth
Poole
Weymouth
Isle of Wight
Saltash
Torquay
St Austell
Plymouth
Lyme Bay
Truro
Penzance
Falmouth
Land's End
Isles of Scilly

English Channel

GUERNSEY (UK crown dependency)
ST PETER PORT
Sark
Channel Islands
Alderney
Seine
ST HELIER
JERSEY (UK crown dependency)

FRANCE

## SCALE BAR

0 km   50   100

0 miles   50   100

N
W   E
S

# FRANCE

ANDORRA, FRANCE, MONACO

**France has helped shape** the history and culture of Europe for centuries. Today, as a founder-member of the European Union, France is an avid supporter of the eventual political and economic integration of Europe's different countries. France is Western Europe's leading farming nation and one of the world's top industrial powers. Its cultural attractions and scenery draw tourists from around the world.

## FARMING AND LAND USE

**France is able** to produce a variety of crops because of its rich soils and mild climate. Wheat is grown in many parts of the north, along with potatoes and other vegetables. Fields of corn and sunflowers and fruit orchards are found in the south, while grapes for the famous wine industry are grown across the country. Beef and dairy cattle are grazed on low-lying pasture.

### FARMING AND LAND USE

- Cattle
- Fishing
- Cereals
- Market gardening
- Root crops
- Tobacco
- Vineyards

- Pasture
- Cropland
- Forest
- Mountain region
- Wetland
- Major conurbation

### LAND USE

- Other (including urban) 18%
- Cropland 35%
- Forest 27%
- Pasture 20%

## THE LANDSCAPE

**The north and west** of France is made up of mainly flat, grassy plains or low hills. Wooded mountains line the country's borders in the south and east, and much of central France is taken up by the Massif Central, an enormous plateau cut by deep river valleys and scattered with extinct volcanoes. Three major rivers, the Loire, Seine, and Garonne, drain the lowland basins.

### Paris Basin

The Paris Basin is a saucer-shaped hollow made up of layers of hard and soft rock, covered with very fertile soils. It runs across about 38,600 sq miles of northern France.

### Alps (E 5)

The western end of the European Alpine mountain chain stretches into southeast France. The French Alps can be crossed by several passes, which give access to Italy and Switzerland.

### Normandy

The coast of Normandy is lined with high chalk cliffs.

### Pyrenees (C 7)

These mountains form a natural barrier between France and Spain. Several peaks reach heights of over 9,480 ft. The Pyrenees are difficult to cross, due to their height, and because they have few low passes.

### Massif Central (D 5)

This vast granite plateau was formed over 200 million years ago. Volcanic activity here stopped only within the last 10,000 years, and the region's rounded hills are the worn-down remains of volcanic mountains.

### Camargue (D 7)

The Camargue is an area of marshes, pastures, sand dunes, and salt flats at the mouth of the Rhône River. Rare animal and plant species are found there.

### Mont Blanc (E 5)

This mountain in the French Alps is the tallest in Western Europe. It is 15,771 ft high.

## INDUSTRY

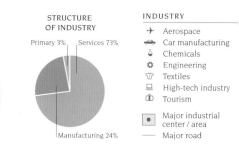

**France is one of the world's** top manufacturing nations, with a variety of both traditional and high-tech industries. Cars, machinery, and electronic products are exported worldwide, along with luxury goods such as perfumes, fashions, and wines. Fossil fuels provide some energy, but France is currently the world's second-biggest producer of nuclear power.

### STRUCTURE OF INDUSTRY

- Primary 3%
- Services 73%
- Manufacturing 24%

### INDUSTRY

- Aerospace
- Car manufacturing
- Chemicals
- Engineering
- Textiles
- High-tech industry
- Tourism
- Major industrial center / area
- Major road

## POPULATION

**In the past 50 years,** most people have moved from the countryside into urban areas. Paris and its suburbs, the industrial cities, and the Côte d'Azur in the southeast are the most economically developed parts of France and now have the biggest populations.

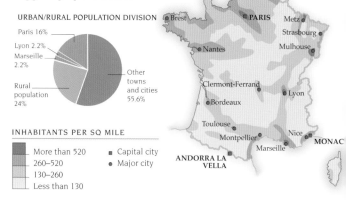

### URBAN/RURAL POPULATION DIVISION

- Paris 16%
- Lyon 2.2%
- Marseille 2.2%
- Rural population 24%
- Other towns and cities 55.6%

### INHABITANTS PER SQ MILE

- More than 520
- 260–520
- 130–260
- Less than 130
- Capital city
- Major city

EUROPE
France

# ENVIRONMENTAL ISSUES

Many of France's coastal areas have been polluted by industry and tourism. The French government has recently introduced policies that aim to protect the country's environment. France's reliance on nuclear energy – 75% of its electricity is generated by nuclear power – causes it to suffer less from the pollution caused by burning fossil fuels than many other countries in Europe.

NORTH AMERICA • ASIA • AFRICA • SOUTH AMERICA • AUSTRALASIA AND OCEANIA • ANTARCTICA

## CLIMATE

In winter, the coldest areas of France are the mountains of the Massif Central and the Alps. Summers are hottest on the Mediterranean coast.

**TEMPERATURE AND PRECIPITATION**

- More than 68°F
- 59 to 68°F
- 50 to 59°F
- 41 to 50°F
- 32 to 41°F
- 23 to 32°F
- Less than 23°F

— 4 — Precipitation (in)

January

July

### ENVIRONMENTAL ISSUES

- ⌐ Nuclear power station
- Sea pollution
- Polluted rivers
- • Major industrial center

**SCALE BAR**
0 km 50 100
0 miles 50 100

**LAND HEIGHT**
- Above 13,120ft
- 6,560–13,120ft
- 3,280–6,560ft
- 1,640–3,280ft
- 820–1,640ft
- 330–820ft
- 0–330ft

**SEA DEPTH**
- 0–160ft
- 160–330ft
- 330–820ft
- 820–1,640ft
- 1,640–3,280ft
- 3,280–6,560ft
- Below 6,560ft

**CITIES AND TOWNS**
- ● Over 500,000 people
- ● 100,000–500,000
- ○ 50,000–100,000
- ○ Less than 50,000

# SPAIN AND PORTUGAL

PORTUGAL, SPAIN

**Spain and Portugal** occupy the Iberian Peninsula, which is cut off from the rest of Europe by the Pyrenees. Over the centuries, Iberia has been invaded and settled by many different peoples. The Moors, who arrived from North Africa in the 8th century, ruled much of Spain for almost 800 years, and their influence can still be seen in Spanish culture. Portugal has modernized its economy since joining the European Union, and both countries have changed their currencies to the euro.

## FARMING AND LAND USE

Cereals, especially wheat and barley, are Iberia's chief crops. In the dry south of Spain, the land is irrigated to citrus fruits, particularly oranges, and a variety of vegetables. In both countries, olive trees and vineyards occupy large areas of land; olive oil and wine are important exports. Cork oak trees from Iberia's forests supply 80% of the world's cork.

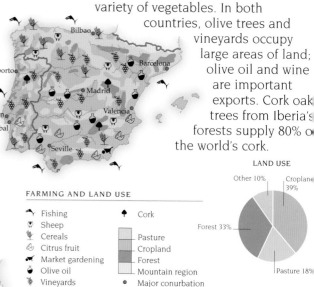

### FARMING AND LAND USE

- Fishing
- Sheep
- Cereals
- Citrus fruit
- Market gardening
- Olive oil
- Vineyards
- Cork
- Pasture
- Cropland
- Forest
- Mountain region
- Major conurbation

**LAND USE**

Other 10%
Cropland 39%
Forest 33%
Pasture 18%

## INDUSTRY

**Madrid, Barcelona,** and the northern ports are Spain's industrial centers. Here, iron ore from Spanish mines is used to make steel, and factories produce cars, machinery, and chemicals. Portugal exports textiles, clothing, and footwear, along with fish, such as sardines and tuna, caught off the Atlantic coast. In both countries, tourism is very important to the economy.

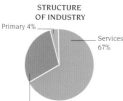

**STRUCTURE OF INDUSTRY**

Primary 4%
Services 67%
Manufacturing 29%

### INDUSTRY

- Car manufacture
- Chemicals
- Engineering
- Fish processing
- Shipbuilding
- Steel
- Textiles
- Mining
- Publishing
- Tourism
- Major industrial center / area
- Major road

## THE LANDSCAPE

**Most of inland Spain is taken up** by the Meseta, a dry, almost treeless plateau surrounded by steep mountain ranges. The only lowlands, apart from narrow strips along the Mediterranean coast, are the valleys of the Ebro, Tagus, Guadiana, and Guadalquivir Rivers. Portugal's coast is lined by wide plains. Inland, the Tagus River divides the country in two. To the north the land is hilly and wooded; to the south it is low-lying and drier.

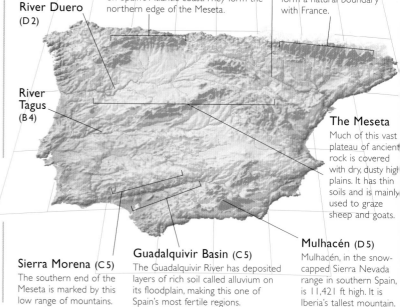

**Westward-flowing rivers**
The Duero, Tagus, and Guadalquivir Rivers flow across the Meseta on their courses to the Atlantic Ocean.

**Ebro River** (E 2)
The Ebro River carries vital irrigation water to Spain's northeastern plains before flowing into the Mediterranean Sea.

**Cordillera Cantábrica** (C 1)
These rugged, forested mountains rise on Spain's Atlantic coast. They form the northern edge of the Meseta.

**The Pyrenees** (F 2)
These high mountains form a natural boundary with France.

**River Duero** (D 2)

**River Tagus** (B 4)

**The Meseta**
Much of this vast plateau of ancient rock is covered with dry, dusty high plains. It has thin soils and is mainly used to graze sheep and goats.

**Sierra Morena** (C 5)
The southern end of the Meseta is marked by this low range of mountains.

**Guadalquivir Basin** (C 5)
The Guadalquivir River has deposited layers of rich soil called alluvium on its floodplain, making this one of Spain's most fertile regions.

**Mulhacén** (D 5)
Mulhacén, in the snow-capped Sierra Nevada range in southern Spain, is 11,421 ft high. It is Iberia's tallest mountain.

## POPULATION

**In the first half** of the 20th century, most Spaniards lived in villages or small towns scattered around the country. Today, tourism and industry have drawn most of the population to the cities and coastal areas. Most Portuguese live in cities, but one third still live in rural areas along the coast or in the river valleys.

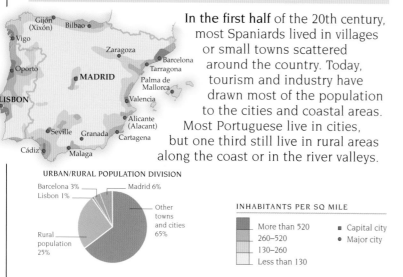

**URBAN/RURAL POPULATION DIVISION**

Barcelona 3%
Lisbon 1%
Madrid 6%
Other towns and cities 65%
Rural population 25%

**INHABITANTS PER SQ MILE**

- More than 520
- 260–520
- 130–260
- Less than 130
- Capital city
- Major city

## ENVIRONMENTAL ISSUES

Soil erosion – where the top layer of soil has been worn away by wind and rain – has affected much of the Iberian Peninsula. This is caused by farming, combined with drought and deforestation. In Spain, a national tree-planting program has been started to combat this problem. Industrial and tourist development along the Mediterranean coast of Spain and in the Balearic Islands has damaged natural habitats on both land and sea.

### ENVIRONMENTAL ISSUES

- Major oil spill
- Overbuilding
- Soil degradation
- Severe soil degradation
- Polluted rivers

## CLIMATE

Northern Spain is wetter and cooler than the south. On the central plateau, summers are very hot and dry, and winters often freezing. The north of Portugal is cooled by winds blowing off the Atlantic Ocean. The south is warmer, with dry, mild winters.

EUROPE

Spain and Portugal

January

July

### TEMPERATURE AND PRECIPITATION

- More than 77°F
- 68 to 77°F
- 59 to 68°F
- 50 to 59°F
- 41 to 50°F
- 32 to 41°F
- 23 to 32°F
- 14 to 23°F
- Less than 14°F

4 — Precipitation (in)

### LAND HEIGHT

- 6,560–13,120ft
- 3,280–6,560ft
- 1,640–3,280ft
- 820–1,640ft
- 330–820ft
- 0–330ft

### SEA DEPTH

- 0–820ft
- 820–1,640ft
- 1,640–3,280ft
- 3,280–6,560ft
- 6,560–9,840ft
- 9,840–13,120ft
- Below 13,120ft

### CITIES AND TOWNS

- Over 500,000 people
- 100,000–500,000
- 50,000–100,000
- Less than 50,000

### SCALE BAR

0 km 50 100

0 miles 50 100

# GERMANY AND THE ALPINE STATES

AUSTRIA, GERMANY, LIECHTENSTEIN, SLOVENIA, SWITZERLAND

**Germany lies at the heart** of Europe and is the biggest industrial power in the continent. In 1945, Germany was divided into two separate countries, East and West Germany, which were reunited in 1990. To the south, the snow-capped peaks of the Alps, Europe's highest mountains, tower over the Alpine states – Switzerland, Austria, Liechtenstein, and the former Yugoslavian state of Slovenia.

## INDUSTRY

**Germany is a leading** manufacturer of cars, chemicals, machinery, and transportation equipment. Switzerland and Liechtenstein make high-value products such as watches and pharmaceuticals and provide services such as banking. The Alpine states are a popular tourist location year-round.

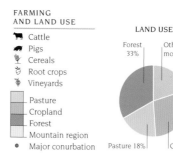

### INDUSTRY

🚗 Car manufacture
🍾 Chemicals
⚙ Engineering
🏭 Iron & steel
⚓ Shipbuilding
💊 Pharmaceuticals
$ Finance
🖥 Hi-tech industry
⛵ Tourism

■ Major industrial center / area

— Major road

#### STRUCTURE OF INDUSTRY

Primary 1%  Services 68%

Manufacturing 31%

## POPULATION

**Western and central Germany** are the most densely populated areas in this region – particularly in and around the Rhine and Ruhr valleys, where there are many industries. In the south, the steep slopes of the Alps and permanent snow cover on the higher peaks means that most large towns and cities are in scattered lowland areas.

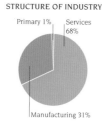

### INHABITANTS PER SQ MILE

More than 520
260–520
130–260
Less than 130

■ Capital city
● Major city

#### URBAN/RURAL POPULATION DIVISION

Hamburg 1.8%   Berlin 3.5%
Vienna 1.7%
Rural population 16%
Other towns and cities 77%

## FARMING AND LAND USE

**Germany produces** three-quarters of its own food. Crop farming is widespread, with cereals and root crops grown in flat, fertile areas. Cattle and pig farming supplies meat and dairy products. Across the Alps, the mountains limit farming, although grapes are grown on the warmer, south-facing slopes. The rich pastures of the lower slopes are used to graze beef and dairy cattle.

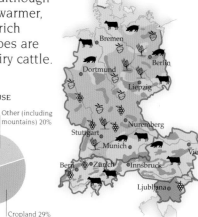

### FARMING AND LAND USE

🐄 Cattle
🐖 Pigs
🌾 Cereals
🌱 Root crops
🍇 Vineyards

Pasture
Cropland
Forest
Mountain region
● Major conurbation

#### LAND USE

Forest 33%
Other (including mountains) 20%
Cropland 29%
Pasture 18%

## THE LANDSCAPE

**To the north, flat plains** and heathlands surround the North Sea coast. Farther south are Germany's central uplands, which are lower and older than the jagged peaks of the Alps, which began to form about 65 million years ago. From its source in the Black Forest, the Danube River flows eastward across Germany and Austria on its course to the Black Sea. The other major river, the Rhine, flows northward.

**Harz mountains** (C 4)
These rugged, wooded mountains are much older than the Alps. They were formed over 300 million years ago.

**Rhine River** (B 5)
The Rhine is Germany's main waterway. It is an important transportation route to and from northern ports. It twists and turns across 820 miles of Europe, from its source in southeast Switzerland, to the North Sea.

**Karst region** (E 8)
Most of the water in this limestone region of Slovenia flows underground, through huge caves and caverns.

**Danube River** (B 7)
The Danube is Europe's second-longest river, flowing 1,765 miles.

**Lake Constance** (B 7)
Lake Constance covers 210 sq miles and is Germany's largest lake, although its waters are shared by Austria and Switzerland.

**Alps** (C 8)
The Alps were formed when the African Plate collided with the Eurasian Plate, pushing up and crushing huge amounts of rock, to form mountains.

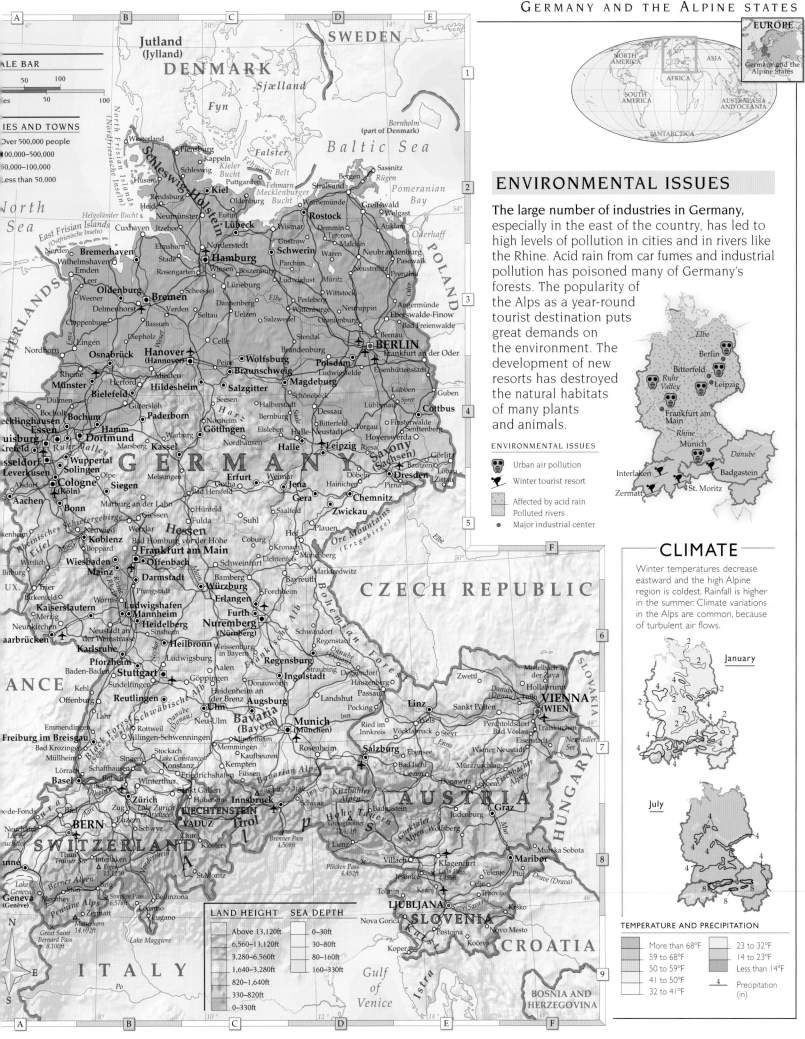

EUROPE

Germany and the Alpine States

## ENVIRONMENTAL ISSUES

The large number of industries in Germany, especially in the east of the country, has led to high levels of pollution in cities and in rivers like the Rhine. Acid rain from car fumes and industrial pollution has poisoned many of Germany's forests. The popularity of the Alps as a year-round tourist destination puts great demands on the environment. The development of new resorts has destroyed the natural habitats of many plants and animals.

### ENVIRONMENTAL ISSUES

- 😷 Urban air pollution
- 🎿 Winter tourist resort
- Affected by acid rain
- Polluted rivers
- • Major industrial center

## CLIMATE

Winter temperatures decrease eastward and the high Alpine region is coldest. Rainfall is higher in the summer. Climate variations in the Alps are common, because of turbulent air flows.

January

July

### TEMPERATURE AND PRECIPITATION

| | |
|---|---|
| More than 68°F | 23 to 32°F |
| 59 to 68°F | 14 to 23°F |
| 50 to 59°F | Less than 14°F |
| 41 to 50°F | —4— Precipitation (in) |
| 32 to 41°F | |

### LAND HEIGHT
- Above 13,120ft
- 6,560–13,120ft
- 3,280–6,560ft
- 1,640–3,280ft
- 820–1,640ft
- 330–820ft
- 0–330ft

### SEA DEPTH
- 0–30ft
- 30–80ft
- 80–160ft
- 160–330ft

### CITIES AND TOWNS
- ◼ Over 500,000 people
- ◼ 100,000–500,000
- ◼ 50,000–100,000
- ◻ Less than 50,000

SCALE BAR

# ITALY

ITALY, SAN MARINO, VATICAN CITY

**Italy has played** an important role in Europe since the Romans based their mighty empire here over 2,000 years ago. The famous boot shape divides into two very different halves. Northern Italy has a varied range of industries and agriculture. Beautiful cities like Venice, Florence, and Rome draw tourists from all over the world. Southern Italy is poorer and less developed than the north, with a hotter, drier climate and less productive land.

## THE LANDSCAPE

**Italy is a peninsula** jutting south from mainland Europe into the Mediterranean Sea. In northern and central Italy the land is mainly mountainous. Most of the flat land is in the Po Valley and along the eastern coast. Italy lies within an earthquake zone, which makes the land unstable, and there are also a number of active volcanoes.

### Italian lakes
Great lakes like Garda (B3) and Como (B2) fill several south-facing valleys once occupied by glaciers.

### The Dolomites (D 2)
These high mountains are part of the same range as the Alps. They were formed 65 million years ago.

### Po Valley (C 2)
The basin of the Po River has the best soils in Italy. Rich alluvium is washed from the mountains by the river to form a wide plain.

### The Apennines (C 4)
This mountain range forms the "backbone" of Italy, dividing the rocky west coast from the flatter, sandy east coast.

### Tyrrhenian Sea (C 6)
This sea, which divides the Italian mainland from Sardinia, is gradually filling with sediment from the rivers which flow into it.

### Earthquakes
The southern Apennines, as well as coastal areas of southwestern Italy, often experience earthquakes and mudslides.

### Sardinia
The island of Sardinia is made from very old rocks that were thrust up to form mountains.

### Sicily
Sicily is the largest island in the Mediterranean. It has a famous active volcano called Mount Etna and often experiences earthquakes.

### Gulf of Taranto (F 7)
During earthquakes, great blocks of land have broken away and sunk into the sea, forming the Gulf's square shape.

## FARMING AND LAND USE

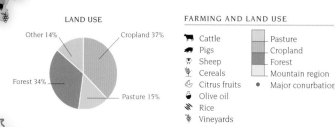

**The Po Valley is a** broad, flat plain in the north of Italy. It contains the most fertile land in the country, and wheat and rice are the main cereal crops grown here. Grapes for wine are grown everywhere in Italy. In much of the south, the land must be irrigated to support crops. Where there is enough water, citrus fruits, olives, and many kinds of tomatoes are grown.

### LAND USE
- Other 14%
- Cropland 37%
- Forest 34%
- Pasture 15%

### FARMING AND LAND USE
- Cattle
- Pigs
- Sheep
- Cereals
- Citrus fruits
- Olive oil
- Rice
- Vineyards
- Pasture
- Cropland
- Forest
- Mountain region
- Major conurbation

## INDUSTRY

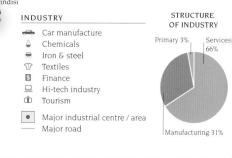

**Italian industry is located** mainly in the north. Design is extremely important to Italians, and they are proud of the elegant designs of their furniture, clothes, and shoes. Although many firms are small, they are very efficient. Italy has few mineral resources, so it needs to import raw materials to make cars, engines, and other high-tech products.

### INDUSTRY
- Car manufacture
- Chemicals
- Iron & steel
- Textiles
- Finance
- Hi-tech industry
- Tourism
- Major industrial centre / area
- Major road

### STRUCTURE OF INDUSTRY
- Primary 3%
- Services 66%
- Manufacturing 31%

## POPULATION

**Most of Italy's population** lives in the north, mainly in and around the Po Valley, which is home to over 25 million people. Most people here have a high standard of living. Southern Italy is much more rural: towns are smaller and life is often much harder.

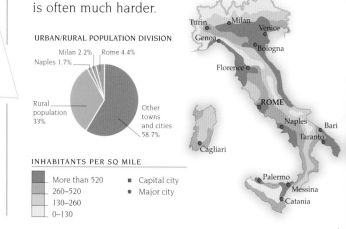

### URBAN/RURAL POPULATION DIVISION
- Milan 2.2%
- Rome 4.4%
- Naples 1.7%
- Rural population 33%
- Other towns and cities 58.7%

### INHABITANTS PER SQ MILE
- More than 520
- 260–520
- 130–260
- 0–130
- Capital city
- Major city

EUROPE
Italy

## ENVIRONMENTAL ISSUES

Sewage and chemical by-products from industry have polluted the Mediterranean and Adriatic Seas. In many northern cities, severe air pollution is a health hazard. Southern Italy is subject to natural dangers like earthquakes and mudslides.

ENVIRONMENTAL ISSUES
- Catastrophic earthquakes
- Urban air pollution
- Acid rain
- Sea pollution
- Major industrial center

## CLIMATE

The Alpine north has cold winters, often with snow. Farther south, temperatures are higher. Sicily has Italy's highest temperatures, because of the warm African winds.

January

July

TEMPERATURE AND PRECIPITATION
- More than 77°F
- 68 to 77°F
- 59 to 68°F
- 50 to 59°F
- 41 to 50°F
- 32 to 41°F
- 23 to 32°F
- 14 to 23°F
- Less than 14°F
- 4 — Precipitation (in)

LAND HEIGHT
- Above 13,120ft
- 6,560–13,120ft
- 3,280–6,560ft
- 1,640–3,280ft
- 820–1,640ft
- 330–820ft
- 0–330ft

SEA DEPTH
- 0–160ft
- 160–330ft
- 330–820ft
- 820–1,640ft
- 1,640–3,280ft
- 3,280–6,560ft
- Below 6,560ft

SCALE BAR
0 km   40   80
0 miles   40   80

CITIES AND TOWNS
- Over 500,000 people
- 100,000–500,000
- 50,000–100,000
- Less than 50,000

# CENTRAL EUROPE

CZECH REPUBLIC, HUNGARY, POLAND, SLOVAKIA

**Central Europe** has been invaded many times throughout history. The countries have changed shape frequently as their borders have shifted back and forth. From the end of World War Two until 1989, they were ruled by communist governments, which were supported by the Soviet Union. In 1993, the state of Czechoslovakia voted to split into two separate nations, called the Czech Republic and Slovakia.

## INDUSTRY

**Brown coal, or lignite,** is central Europe's main fuel, and one of Poland's major exports. A variety of minerals are mined in the mountains of the Czech Republic and Slovakia. Hungary has a wide range of industries producing vehicles, metals, and chemicals, as well as textiles and electrical goods. The Czech Republic is famous for its breweries and glass-making.

STRUCTURE
OF INDUSTRY

Primary 3%
Services 65%
Manufacturing 32%

INDUSTRY

- 🛢 Brewing
- 🚗 Car manufacturing
- ⚗ Chemicals
- ⚙ Engineering
- 🥫 Food processing
- 🏭 Iron and steel
- ⛏ Coal mining
- ⊙ Major industrial center / area
- — Major road

## ENVIRONMENTAL ISSUES

**The growth of heavy industries** that took place under communist rule has caused terrible environmental pollution in some places. Hungary's oil and Poland's brown coal have a high sulfur content. Burning these fuels to produce electricity causes air pollution, and the sulfur dioxide produced combines with moisture in the air, leading to acid rain.

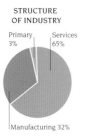

ENVIRONMENTAL ISSUES

- ☁ Severe industrial pollution
- 👹 Urban air pollution
- Affected by acid rain
- Polluted rivers
- ● Major industrial center

## FARMING AND LAND USE

**Central Europe's** main crops are cereals such as corn, wheat and rye, along with sugar beets and potatoes. Sweet peppers grow in Hungary, helped by the warm summers and mild winters. They are used to make paprika. Grapes are also grown, to make wine. Large areas of the plains of Hungary and Poland are used for rearing pigs and cattle. Trees for timber grow in the mountains of Slovakia and the Czech Republic.

FARMING AND LAND USE

- 🐄 Cattle
- 🐖 Pigs
- 🌾 Cereals
- 🌰 Root crops
- 🥔 Potatoes
- 🌲 Timber
- 🍇 Vineyards
- Pasture
- Cropland
- Forest
- ● Major conurbation

LAND USE

Other 11%
Cropla 47%
Forest 29%
Pasture 13%

## THE LANDSCAPE

**The high Carpathian Mountains** sweep across northern Slovakia. The lower Sudeten Mountains lie on the border of the Czech Republic and Poland. Together, these mountains form a barrier that divides the Great Hungarian Plain and the Danube River basin in the south from Poland and the vast rolling lowlands of the North European Plain.

### Pomerania (C 2)
This is a sandy coastal area with lakes formed by glaciers. It stretches west from the River Vistula to just beyond the German border.

### Vistula River (F 4)
Poland's largest river is the Vistula. It flows northward, passing through the capital, Warsaw, on its way to the Baltic Sea.

North European Plai

### Hot springs
The Sudeten mountains (C5) are famous for their hot mineral springs. These occur where water heated deep within the Earth's crust finds its way to the surface along fractures in the rock.

### Danube River (D 7)
The Danube River forms the border between Slovakia and Hungary for over 100 miles. It then turns south to flow across the Great Hungarian Plain.

### Great Hungarian Plain (E 8)
This huge plain covers almost half of Hungary's land area. It is a mixture of farmland and steppe.

### Tatra Mountains (E 6)
The Tatra Mountains are a sma range at the northern end of the Carpathian Mountains. They include Gerlachovsky Stit, which is Central Europe's highest point at 8,711 ft.

# POPULATION

Most people in central Europe live in low-lying areas – for example, along the Vistula River in Poland, and in the lowlands of the Czech Republic. In mountainous Slovakia, many people still live in rural towns and villages. The industrial areas and capital cities have the highest population densities.

**URBAN/RURAL POPULATION DIVISION**

Warsaw 2.6%
Budapest 2.7%
Prague 1.7%
Other towns and cities 59%
Rural population 34%

EUROPE
Central Europe

NORTH AMERICA
ASIA
AFRICA
SOUTH AMERICA
AUSTRALASIA AND OCEANIA
ANTARCTICA

**INHABITANTS PER SQ MILE**

More than 520
260–520
130–260
Less than 130

■ Capital city
● Major city

Gdynia
Łódź
WARSAW
Rybnik  Chorzów
PRAGUE  Hradec Králové  Kraków
Brno
BRATISLAVA
BUDAPEST

## CLIMATE

The Carpathian Mountains are both the coldest and the wettest part of central Europe. Temperatures plunge below freezing across the whole region during winter. In summer, eastern Hungary is the hottest place.

January

July

**TEMPERATURE AND PRECIPITATION**

More than 68°F
59 to 68°F
50 to 59°F
41 to 50°F
32 to 41°F
23 to 32°F
Less than 23°F

—4— Precipitation (in)

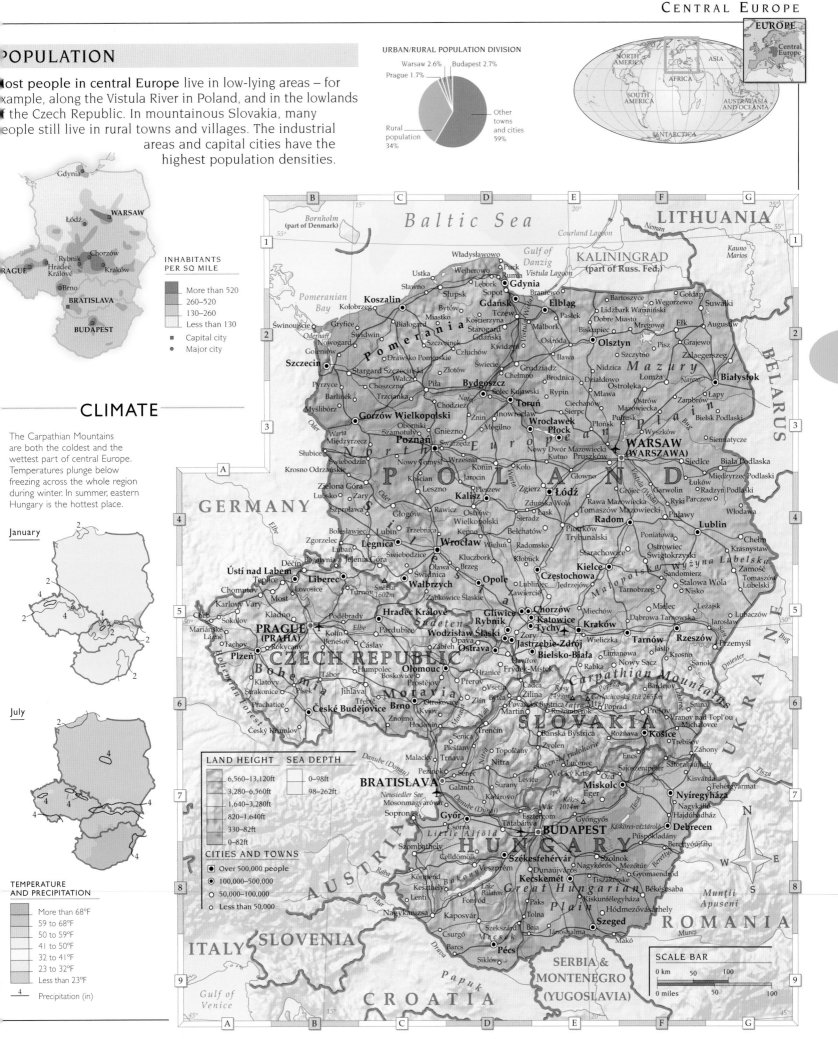

**LAND HEIGHT**
6,560–13,120ft
3,280–6,560ft
1,640–3,280ft
820–1,640ft
330–82ft
0–82ft

**SEA DEPTH**
0–98ft
98–262ft

**CITIES AND TOWNS**
● Over 500,000 people
◉ 100,000–500,000
○ 50,000–100,000
○ Less than 50,000

**SCALE BAR**
0 km    50    100
0 miles    50    100

# SOUTHEAST EUROPE

ALBANIA, BOSNIA AND HERZEGOVINA, BULGARIA, CROATIA, GREECE, MACEDONIA, YUGOSLAVIA (SERBIA & MONTENEGRO)

**Southeast Europe extends inland** from the coasts of the Aegean, Adriatic, and Black Seas. Ancient Greece was the birthplace of European civilization. Albania and Bulgaria were ruled by communists for over 50 years, until the early 1990s. The rest of the region was part of a communist union of states called Yugoslavia. The collapse of this union in 1991 led to a civil war, after which five separate countries emerged.

## THE LANDSCAPE

**Southeast Europe** is largely mountainous, with ranges running from northwest to southeast. The Dinaric Alps run parallel to the Dalmatian coast, and the Pindus Mountains continue this line into Greece. In the Aegean Sea, the drowned peaks of an old mountain chain form thousands of islands.

### Earthquakes
Bulgaria, Greece, and Macedonia lie in earthquake zones. Major earthquakes have hit the Ionian Islands in 1953 and Macedonia in 1963.

### Great Hungarian Plain (D 1)
The Vojvodina region of Yugoslavia is the southern part of the Great Hungarian Plain. The plain is flat, and fertile soil enables crops like corn and wheat to be grown.

### Dinaric Alps (C 2)

**STRUCTURE OF INDUSTRY**

Primary 10%
Services 64%
Manufacturing 26%

### Balkan Mountains (F 3)
The mountains form a spur running east to west through Bulgaria and separate the two main rivers, the Danube and the Maritsa.

### Dalmatian coast (B 2)
The Dalmatian coast has many long, narrow islands near the shore. These were formed as the Adriatic Sea flooded the river valleys that ran parallel to the coast.

### Greek Islands

### The Peloponnese (E 6)
The Peloponnese is a mountainous peninsula linked to the Greek mainland only by a narrow strip of land, only 6 km wide, called the Isthmus of Corinth.

### Greek Islands
There are two groups of Greek Islands, the Ionian Islands to the west of mainland Greece, and the more numerous islands to the east in the Aegean Sea.

## FARMING AND LAND USE

Cereals like wheat, and fruits, vegetables, and grapes are grown in the fertile north of the region. The band of mountains across southeast Europe is used mainly for grazing sheep and goats. Farther south, and in coastal areas, the warm Mediterranean climate is ideal for growing grapes, olives, and tobacco.

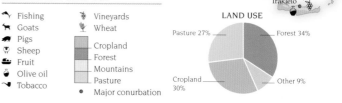

**FARMING AND LAND USE**

- 🐟 Fishing
- 🐐 Goats
- 🐖 Pigs
- 🐑 Sheep
- 🦀 Fruit
- 🫒 Olive oil
- 🌿 Tobacco
- 🍇 Vineyards
- 🌾 Wheat
- ▨ Cropland
- ▨ Forest
- ▨ Mountains
- ▨ Pasture
- ● Major conurbation

**LAND USE**

Pasture 27%
Forest 34%
Cropland 30%
Other 9%

## INDUSTRY

**Mainland Greece and the many islands** in the Aegean Sea are centers of a thriving tourist trade, while tourism on the Black Sea coast continues to grow. The Dalmatian coast's growing tourist industry is recovering, after the civil war in former Yugoslavia disrupted it, and other industries. Heavy industries like chemicals, engineering, and shipbuilding remain an important source of income in Bulgaria.

**INDUSTRY**

- 🧪 Chemicals
- ⚙ Engineering
- ▤ Food processing
- △ Metal refining
- ⚓ Shipbuilding
- 👕 Textiles
- ⛏ Mining
- 🛍 Tourism
- ▣ Major industrial center / area
- — Major road

## POPULATION

**Greece's population** is two thirds urban; over 35% live in the capital, Athens, and in Salonica. In Bulgaria, most people live in cities. About half of Albania's and Macedonia's people are still rural. Since the civil war, the different ethnic groups in Bosnia and Herzegovina, Yugoslavia, and Croatia have lived apart from one another.

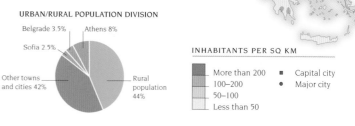

**URBAN/RURAL POPULATION DIVISION**

Belgrade 3.5%
Athens 8%
Sofia 2.5%
Other towns and cities 42%
Rural population 44%

**INHABITANTS PER SQ KM**

- ▨ More than 200
- ▨ 100–200
- ▨ 50–100
- ▨ Less than 50
- ■ Capital city
- ● Major city

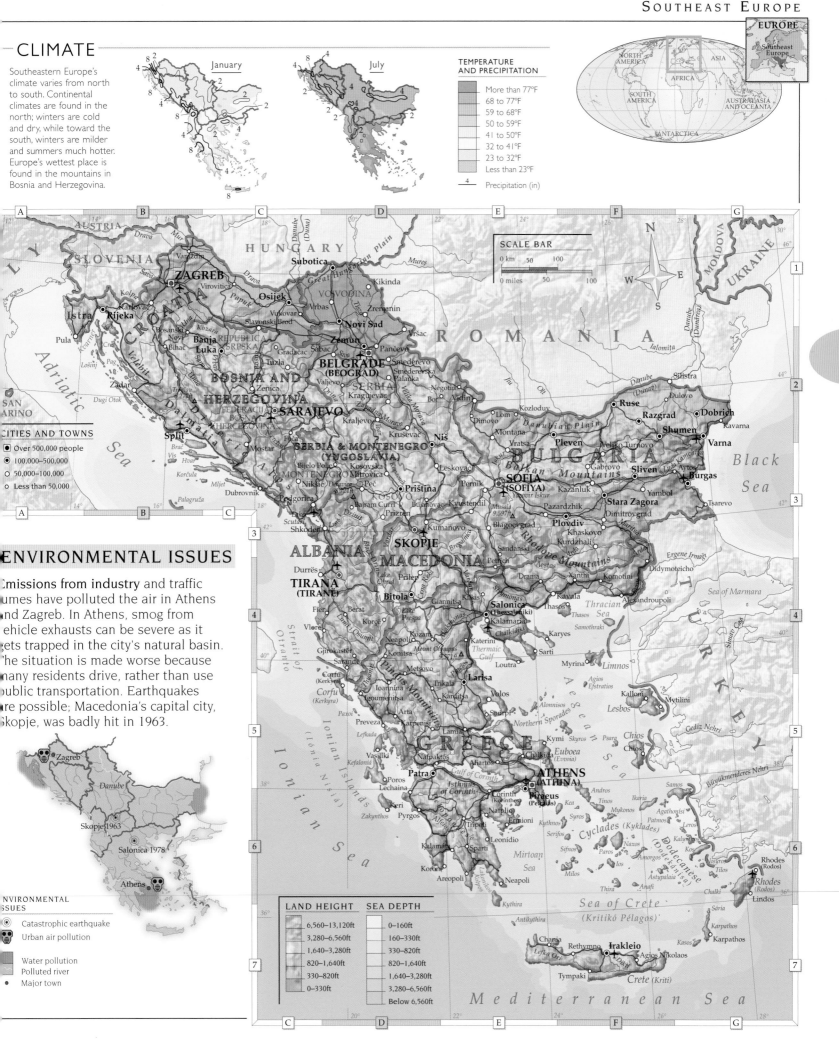

## CLIMATE

Southeastern Europe's climate varies from north to south. Continental climates are found in the north; winters are cold and dry, while toward the south, winters are milder and summers much hotter. Europe's wettest place is found in the mountains in Bosnia and Herzegovina.

January

July

**TEMPERATURE AND PRECIPITATION**

More than 77°F
68 to 77°F
59 to 68°F
50 to 59°F
41 to 50°F
32 to 41°F
23 to 32°F
Less than 23°F

4 —— Precipitation (in)

**CITIES AND TOWNS**
- Over 500,000 people
- 100,000–500,000
- 50,000–100,000
- Less than 50,000

## ENVIRONMENTAL ISSUES

Emissions from industry and traffic fumes have polluted the air in Athens and Zagreb. In Athens, smog from vehicle exhausts can be severe as it gets trapped in the city's natural basin. The situation is made worse because many residents drive, rather than use public transportation. Earthquakes are possible; Macedonia's capital city, Skopje, was badly hit in 1963.

**ENVIRONMENTAL ISSUES**
- Catastrophic earthquake
- Urban air pollution
- Water pollution
- Polluted river
- Major town

Zagreb
Danube
Skopje 1963
Salonica 1978
Athens

**SCALE BAR**
0 km  50  100
0 miles  50  100

**LAND HEIGHT**
- 6,560–13,120ft
- 3,280–6,560ft
- 1,640–3,280ft
- 820–1,640ft
- 330–820ft
- 0–330ft

**SEA DEPTH**
- 0–160ft
- 160–330ft
- 330–820ft
- 820–1,640ft
- 1,640–3,280ft
- 3,280–6,560ft
- Below 6,560ft

# EASTERN EUROPE

BELARUS, MOLDOVA, ROMANIA, UKRAINE

**Much of Eastern Europe,** which extends north from the Danube River and the Black Sea, is covered by open grasslands called steppe. Ukraine's excellent farmland and large mineral reserves make it one of the strongest new countries to emerge from the former Soviet Union. Moldova and Belarus were also part of the USSR until they became independent in 1991. Romania was a strict communist regime from 1945 until 1989.

## INDUSTRY

**In Ukraine,** most industry is based around the country's mineral reserves. The Donbass region has Europe's largest coalfield and is an important center for iron and steel production. The main industries of Belarus are chemicals, machine building, and food-processing. Romania's manufacturing industries are growing, with the help of foreign investment.

**STRUCTURE OF INDUSTRY**

Primary 15%
Manufacturing 42%
Services 43%

### INDUSTRY

- 🚗 Car manufacturing
- ⚗ Chemicals
- ⚙ Engineering
- Food processing
- Iron and steel
- 👕 Textiles
- Coal
- ⚒ Mining
- Oil and gas
- Tourism
- Major industrial center / area
- — Major road

## FARMING AND LAND USE

**The black soils** found across much of Ukraine are very fertile and the country is a big producer of cereals, sugar beets, and sunflowers, which are grown for their oil. In Moldova and southern Romania, the warm summers are ideal for growing grapes for wine, along with sunflowers and a variety of vegetables. Cattle and pigs are farmed throughout Eastern Europe.

**LAND USE**

Other 11%
Forest 24%
Pasture 15%
Cropland 50%

### FARMING AND LAND USE

- 🐄 Cattle
- 🐖 Pigs
- 🐑 Sheep
- Root crops
- Sunflowers
- Vineyards
- Wheat
- Cropland
- Forest
- Pasture
- Wetland
- • Major conurbation

## POPULATION

**Many Romanians** still live in rural areas, although Bucharest, the capital, is home to six times as many people as the next largest city. In Ukraine, two-thirds of the population live in cities such as those in the Donbass industrial area. Most of Belarus's people are city dwellers. Moldova is the most rural country in Eastern Europe; over half live in the countryside.

**URBAN/RURAL POPULATION DIVISION**

Bucharest 2.3%   Kiev 3.1%
Minsk 2.1%
Rural population 36%
Other towns and cities 56.5%

**INHABITANTS PER SQ MILE**

- More than 520
- 260–520
- 130–260
- Less than 130
- ■ Capital city
- ● Major city

## THE LANDSCAPE

**Flat or rolling grasslands,** marshes, and river flood plains cover almost all of Ukraine and Belarus. The Carpathian Mountains cross the southwestern corner of Ukraine and continue in a large arc-shaped chain of high peaks at the heart of Romania. Along the southern part of this chain, the Carpathians are called the Transylvanian Alps.

### Pripet Marshes (C 3)

The Pripet Marshes in Belarus and Ukraine form the largest area of marshland in Europe.

### The steppes

The steppes are great, wide grasslands that are found across eastern Europe and central Asia. Over 70% of the Ukrainian landscape is steppe. Little rain falls throughout the steppes.

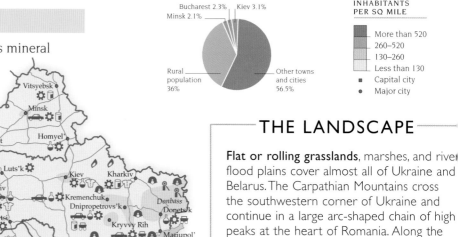

### Carpathian Mountains (C 5)

The Carpathians are the largest mountain range in Eastern Europe. They are a rich source of timber and minerals.

### Dnieper (E 5) and Dniester (D 5) Rivers

The Dnieper and Dniester run south and east toward the Black Sea. They flow slowly across huge areas of low-lying land.

### The Crimea (F 6)

This peninsula divides the Sea of Azov from the Black Sea. The steep mountains of Kryms'ki Hory run along the southeastern coast of the Crimea.

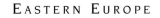

EUROPE

Eastern
Europe

## CLIMATE

January

July

The climate is continental, with warm, dry summers and very cold, dry winters. Temperatures are higher along the fringes of the Black Sea, while the Carpathian Mountains are colder and wetter all year round.

Less than 2

2
2

Less than 2

2
2
2

2

4
4

2

2
2

4

TEMPERATURE
AND PRECIPITATION

More than 68°F
59 to 68°F
50 to 59°F
41 to 50°F
32 to 41°F
23 to 32°F
Less than 23°F

4 — Precipitation (in)

## ENVIRONMENTAL ISSUES

**The worst nuclear accident** in history happened at Chernobyl nuclear power plant in northern Ukraine in 1986. Around 70% of the nuclear fallout was received by Belarus, contaminating its farmland, forests, and water supplies. Four million Ukrainians still live in dangerously radioactive areas.

ENVIRONMENTAL
ISSUES

Destroyed nuclear reactor
Urban air pollution

Levels of nuclear fallout
Very high
High
Moderate
Polluted river
Major industrial center

Minsk

Chornobyl
Kiev
Kharkiv
Dnipropetrovs'k
Donets'k
Târgu
Mures
Arad
Dnieper
Bucharest

LAND HEIGHT

6,560–13,120ft
3,280–6,560ft
1,640–3,280ft
820–1,640ft
330–820ft
0–330ft

SEA DEPTH

0–160ft
160–330ft
330–820ft
820–1,640ft
1,640–3,280ft
3,280–6,560ft
Below 6,560ft

CITIES AND TOWNS

Over 500,000 people
100,000–500,000
50,000–100,000
Less than 50,000

LATVIA

LITHUANIA

RUSSIAN FEDERATION

Western Dvina

Bihosava
Drysa
Haradok
Navapolatsk
Polatsk
Vitsyebsk
Hlybokaye
Lyepyel'
Bacheykava
Bahushewsk
Myadzyel
Chashniki
Orsha
Dnieper
Neris
Maladzyechna
Barysaw
Horki
Zhodzina
Byerazino
Viliya
Lida
Minskaya
Wzvyshsha
MINSK
Mahilyow
Hrodna
Shchuchyn
BELARUS
Neman
Vawkavysk
Asipovichy
Babruysk
Kastsyukovichy
Baranavichy
Slutsk
Byelaruskaya Hrada
Salihorsk
Svyetlahorsk
Zhlobin
Yasyel'da
Luninyets
Mazyr
Homyel'
Brest
Drahichyn
Pinsk
Pripet
Bug
Kobryn
Marshes
Narowlya
Shchors
Shostka
Makrany
Pripet
Chornobyl'
Chernihiv
Hlukhiv
POLAND
Kovel'
Horyn
Sarny
Olevs'k
Korosten'
Kiev Reservoir
Nizhyn
Konotop
Romny
Sumy
Vistula (Wisła)
Styr
Sluch
Volodymyr-Volyns'kyy
Kiev Lowland
Pryluky
Okhtyrka
Wyżyna Lubelska
Luts'k
Rivne
KIEV (KYYIV)
Lubny
Kharkiv
Dubno
Fastiv
Psel
Starobil's'k
Zhovkva
Zhytomyr
Bila Tserkva
Kup"yans'k
L'viv
UKRAINE
Poltava
Donets
Kreminna
Rubizhne
Sambir
Khmel'nyts'kyy
Kaniv's'ke Vodoskhovyshche
Slov"yans'k
Syeverodonets'k
Lysychans'k
Ternopil'
Vinnytsya
Cherkasy
Kremenchuk
Kramators'k
Stakhanov
Luhans'k
Stryy
Zvenyhorodka
Dniprodzerzhyns'ke Vodoskhovyshche
Kostyantynivka
Horlivka
Ivano-Frankivs'k
Podil's'ka Vysochyna
Uman'
Oleksandriya
Novomoskovs'k
Pavlohrad
Yenakiyeve
Krasnyy Luch
Uzhhorod
Haysyn
Dnipropetrovs'k
Makiyivka
Mukacheve
Kamyanets'-Podil's'kyy
Dniprodzerzhyns'k
Donets'k
Khust
Chernivtsi
Dnister
Pervomays'k
Kirovohrad
Zhovti Vody
Volnovakha
Piatra Mountains
Hora Hoverla 6,762ft
Kotovs'k
Kryvyy Rih
Zaporizhzhya
Orikhiv
Novoazovs'k
SLOVAKIA
Carpathian Mountains
Botoşani
Bălţi
Novyy Buh
Kakhovs'ke Vodoskhovyshche
Nikopol'
Don
HUNGARY
Satu Mare
Suceava
MOLDOVA
Kotovs'k
Dniprorudne
Mariupol'
Gulf of Taganrog
Yeya
Baia Mare
Bistriţa
Siret
Prodovchyy Buh
Berdyans'k
Oradea
Transylvania
Iaşi
CHIŞINĂU
Mykolayiv
Black Sea Lowland
RUSSIAN FEDERATION
Zalău
Piatra-Neamţ
Roman
Dniester
Melitopol'
Cluj-Napoca
Muntii Apuseni
Turda
Târgu Mureş
Bacău
Vaslui
Tighina (Bendery)
Tiraspol
Odesa
Kherson
Heniches'k
Arad
Alba Iulia
Mediaş
Bârlad
Basarabeasca
Illichivs'k
Armyans'k
Sea of Azov
Great Hungarian Plain
ROMANIA
Bârlad
Cahul
Artsyz
Dzhankoy
Zatoka Syvash
Mureş
Humedoara
Sighişoara
Miercurea-Ciuc
Ozero Shahany
Kerch
Timişoara
Deva
Sibiu
Vârful Moldoveanu 8,347ft
Sfântu Gheorghe
Focşani
Karkinits'ka Zatoka
Kerch Strait
Reşiţa
Lugoj
Braşov
Galaţi
Izmayil
Tulcea
Crimea
Feodosiya
Kuban'
Târgu Jiu
Transylvanian Alps
Râmnicu Vâlcea
Brăila
Buzău
Lacul Razim
Yevpatoriya
Caucasus
SERB. & MON. (YUGO.)
Drobeta-Turnu Severin
Pitești
Ploieşti
Târgovişte
Simferopol'
Kryms'ki Hory
Wallachia
Strehaia
Slatina
Sevastopol'
Yalta
GEORGIA
Craiova
BUCHAREST (BUCUREȘTI)
Călăraşi
Constanţa
Caracal
Danube (Dunărea)
Giurgiu
Lacul Sinoie
Black Sea
Velika Morava
BULGARIA

N
W E S

SCALE BAR

0 km 50 100

0 miles 50 100

# EUROPEAN RUSSIA

## RUSSIAN FEDERATION

European Russia is separated from the Asiatic part of the Russian Federation by the Ural Mountains. It is home to two-thirds of the country's population. Russia was the largest and most powerful republic of the communist Soviet Union, which collapsed in 1991. New businesses were set up when communism ended, but many old state industries closed down, causing unemployment and further hardship for many people.

## INDUSTRY

European Russia is rich in natural resources. Minerals are mined on the Kola Peninsula and in the Urals, while dense forests are felled and processed in many of the larger northern cities. The Volga basin is one of Europe's largest sources of oil and gas. Moscow and the cities near the Volga are centers of skilled labor for a wide range of manufacturing industries like cars, chemicals, and heavy engineering and steel production.

### INDUSTRY

| | |
|---|---|
| Car manufacturing | Oil and gas |
| Chemicals | Timber processing |
| Engineering | |
| Iron and steel | Major industrial center/area |
| Textiles | Major road |
| Mining | |

## FARMING AND LAND USE

Russia's best farmland lies within this region. Big crops of wheat, barley and oats, potatoes and sunflowers are produced in the fertile black soil that forms a thick band across the country to the south of Moscow. The far north is cold and frozen, with bare mountains and tundra making cultivation impossible. Farther south there are extensive forests, and rough pastures that are used for herding and hunting.

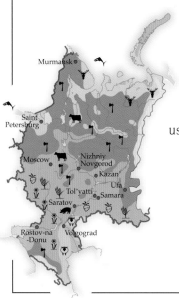

### FARMING AND LAND USE

| | | |
|---|---|---|
| Cattle | | Barren land |
| Fishing | | Cropland |
| Pigs | | Forest |
| Reindeer | | Mountain region |
| Sheep | | Pasture |
| Cereals | | Tundra |
| Root crops | | Wetland |
| Sunflowers | • | Major conurbation |
| Timber | | |

## POPULATION

Three-quarters of European Russia's people live in towns and cities, most in a broad band stretching south from St. Petersburg to Moscow, and eastward to the Urals. The capital, Moscow, and St. Petersburg are very crowded cities. Living conditions there are cramped, with two families often sharing one apartment. The southeast is also heavily populated. Over 12 million people live in the cities and towns that line the banks of the Volga River.

### INHABITANTS PER SQ MILE

| | |
|---|---|
| | More than 260 |
| | 130–260 |
| | 30–130 |
| | Less than 30 |
| ▪ | Capital city |
| ● | Major city |

## THE LANDSCAPE

European Russia lies on the North European Plain, a huge, rolling lowland with wide river basins. The northern half of the plain, which was once covered by glaciers, has many lakes and swamps. The Volga River drains much of the plain as it flows south to the Caspian Sea. The Caucasus and Ural Mountains form natural boundaries in the south and east.

### Northern European Russia (C 3)

Northern European Russia reaches into the Arctic Circle. It is a region of pine and birch forests, marshes, and tundra. There are also tens of thousands of lakes, including the biggest in Europe, Ladoga, which covers about 6,830 sq miles.

### Ural Mountains (E 5)

The Ural Mountains run from north to south, stretching almost 2,500 mil

**Lake Ladoga (B 4)**

### Valdai Hills (A 5)

The Valdai Hills are a high, swampy region of the North European Plain. Two of Europe's biggest rivers, the Volga and the Western Dvina, have their sources here.

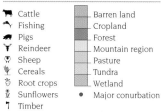

### Caucasus (A 9)

This massive barrier of mountains stretches from the Black Sea to the Caspian Sea. It includes El'brus, the highest peak in Europe, at 18,511 feet.

### Caspian Sea (C 9)

### Volga River (C 7)

The Volga River flows for 2,292 miles, making it Europe's longest river and Russia's most important inland waterway. It is used for transportation and to generate hydro-electric power.

### North European Plain (C 4)

The North European Plain sweeps west from the Ural Mountain all the way to the Rhine River in Germany. In European Russia it includes a number of hill ranges, such as the Volga Uplands and the Central Russian Upland.

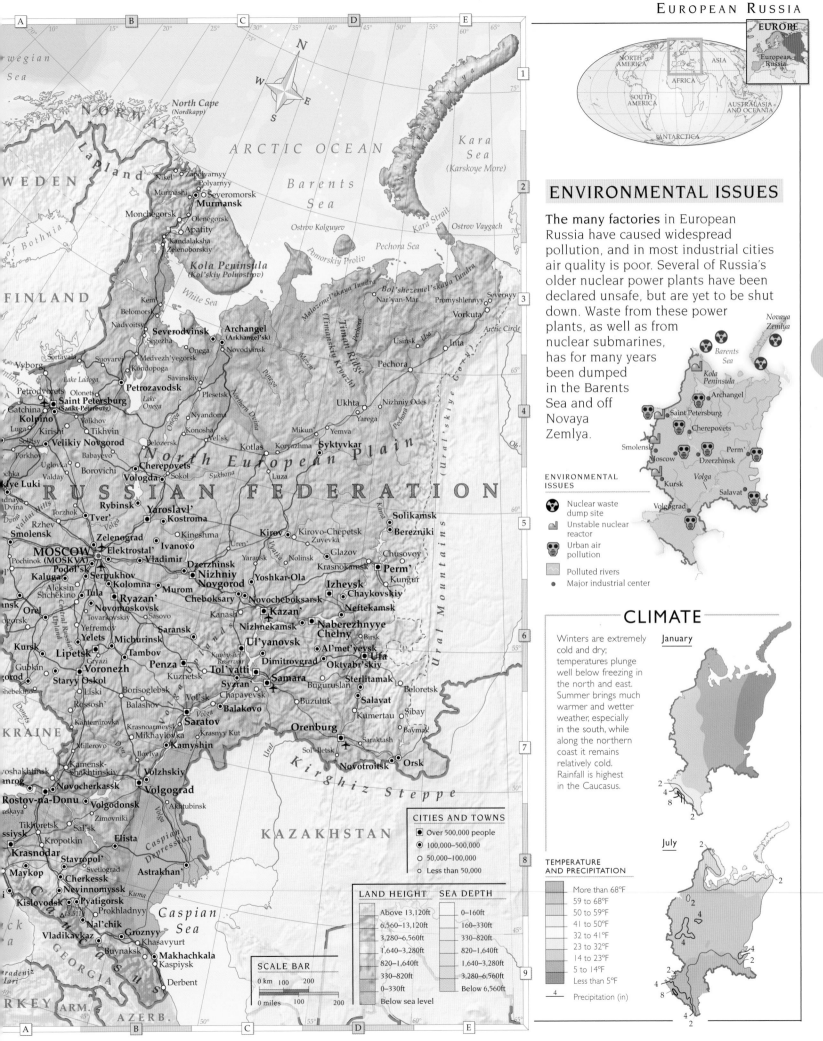

## ENVIRONMENTAL ISSUES

**The many factories** in European Russia have caused widespread pollution, and in most industrial cities air quality is poor. Several of Russia's older nuclear power plants have been declared unsafe, but are yet to be shut down. Waste from these power plants, as well as from nuclear submarines, has for many years been dumped in the Barents Sea and off Novaya Zemlya.

**ENVIRONMENTAL ISSUES**

- ☢ Nuclear waste dump site
- ⚒ Unstable nuclear reactor
- ☻ Urban air pollution
- Polluted rivers
- • Major industrial center

## CLIMATE

Winters are extremely cold and dry; temperatures plunge well below freezing in the north and east. Summer brings much warmer and wetter weather, especially in the south, while along the northern coast it remains relatively cold. Rainfall is highest in the Caucasus.

January

July

**TEMPERATURE AND PRECIPITATION**

- More than 68°F
- 59 to 68°F
- 50 to 59°F
- 41 to 50°F
- 32 to 41°F
- 23 to 32°F
- 14 to 23°F
- 5 to 14°F
- Less than 5°F

— 4 — Precipitation (in)

**CITIES AND TOWNS**
- ■ Over 500,000 people
- ⊙ 100,000–500,000
- ○ 50,000–100,000
- ○ Less than 50,000

| LAND HEIGHT | SEA DEPTH |
|---|---|
| Above 13,120ft | 0–160ft |
| 6,560–13,120ft | 160–330ft |
| 3,280–6,560ft | 330–820ft |
| 1,640–3,280ft | 820–1,640ft |
| 820–1,640ft | 1,640–3,280ft |
| 330–820ft | 3,280–6,560ft |
| 0–330ft | Below 6,560ft |
| Below sea level | |

**SCALE BAR**

0 km 100 200

0 miles 100 200

# THE MEDITERRANEAN

**The Mediterranean Sea** separates Europe from Africa. It stretches more than 2,500 miles from east to west and is almost completely enclosed by land. Many great civilizations, including the Greek and Roman empires, grew up around the Mediterranean. It has been a crossroads of international trade routes for many centuries. More than 100 million people live in the 28 countries that border the sea, and their numbers are increased by the large crowds of tourists who regularly visit the area.

## ENVIRONMENTAL ISSUES

**Water pollution is widespread** in the Mediterranean, especially near the large coastal resorts where raw sewage and industrial effluent is pumped out to sea, and often ends up on the beaches. Oil refining and oil spills have also increased pollution.

**ENVIRONMENTAL ISSUES**

- 🐚 Oil spill
- ▨ Mild water pollution
- ▨ Severe water pollutio

**SCALE BAR**

0 km 100 200

0 miles 100 200

**MALTA**

Victoria · Nadur

Gozo · Mgarr · Comino

Mellieha

Mosta · St Julian's

Sliema

Naxxar · Paola · VALLETTA

Malta · Rabat

Birżebbuġa

0 km 10

0 miles 10

**CYPRUS**

*Mediterranean Sea*

Agialousa (Yenierenköy)

Lápithos (Lapta) · Kyrenia (Girne)

Mórfou (Güzelyurt) · Kythrea (Değirmenlik)

Pólis · NICOSIA · Famagusta (Ammochostos)

Larnaca (Lárnaka) · Famagusta Bay

Páfos · Dhekelia Sovereign Base Area (to UK)

**TURKISH REPUBLIC OF NORTHERN CYPRUS** (recognized only by Turkey)

Akrotiri Sovereign Base Area (to UK)

Troodos · Limassol (Lemesós)

0 km 25

0 miles 25

| LAND HEIGHT | SEA DEPTH |
| --- | --- |
| Above 13,120ft | 0–820ft |
| 6,560–13,120ft | 820–1,640ft |
| 3,280–6,560ft | 1,640–3,280ft |
| 1,640–3,280ft | 3,280–6,560ft |
| 820–1,640ft | 6,560–9,840ft |
| 330–820ft | 9,840–13,120ft |
| 0–330ft | Below 13,120ft |
| Below sea level | |

**CITIES AND TOWNS**

- ■ Over 500,000 people
- ⬤ 100,000–500,000
- ◯ 50,000–100,000
- ○ Less than 50,000

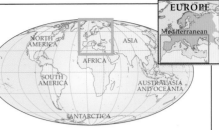

# THE LANDSCAPE

**The Mediterranean Sea** would be an enormous lake if it were not for the Strait of Gibraltar, a narrow opening only 8 miles wide, which joins it to the Atlantic Ocean. The Mediterranean lies over the boundary of two continental plates. Where they meet, earthquakes and volcanoes are common.

**Strait of Gibraltar**

**Sandy beaches**
The Mediterranean coasts are bordered by several thousand miles of sandy beaches.

**Shallow shelves**
The area of water off the coast of Tunisia, and also the Adriatic Sea, are shallower than the rest of the Mediterranean.

**Greek islands**
Greece has thousands of islands that lie both in the Mediterranean and in the smaller Aegean Sea. Some of them are the remains of old volcanoes which have left black sand on the beaches.

**Suez Canal**
The Suez Canal links the Mediterranean to the Gulf of Suez and the Red Sea. Before it was built, ships had to sail around all of Africa to reach Asia.

**Atlas Mountains**
The rugged Atlas Mountains run through most of Morocco and Algeria. They form a barrier between the Mediterranean coast and the Sahara, which lies to the south.

# TOURISM

**The tourist industry in and around the Mediterranean** is one of the most highly developed in the world. More than half the world's income from tourism is generated here. Resorts have grown up along the northwest coast of Africa, and in Egypt, southern Spain, France, Italy, Greece, and Turkey. Tourism brings huge economic benefits, but the ever-increasing number of visitors has also damaged the environment.

TOURISM
- Major tourist destinations/resorts
- Tourist center

# INDUSTRY

**The Mediterranean has a large fishing industry,** although most of the fishing is small-scale. Tuna and sardines are caught throughout the region, and mussels are farmed off the coast of Italy. Fish canning and packing take place at most of the larger ports. Small oil and gas reserves are extracted off the coast of North Africa and near Greece, Spain, and Italy.

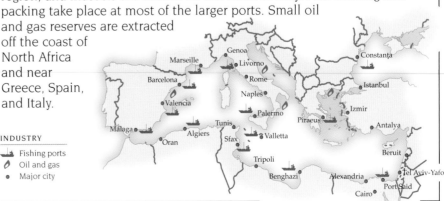

INDUSTRY
- Fishing ports
- Oil and gas
- Major city

# CONTINENTAL ASIA

**Asia is the world's largest continent**, and has the greatest range of physical extremes. Some of the highest, lowest, and coldest places on Earth are found in Asia: Mount Everest in the Himalayas is the highest, the Dead Sea in the west is the lowest, and the frozen wastes of northern Siberia are among the coldest. More people live in Asia than on any other continent – 1.3 billion of them in China, and 1.07 billion in India.

4,040 miles

6,030 miles

## CROSS-SECTION THROUGH ASIA

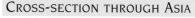

The Gulf | Iranian Plateau | Plateau of Tibet | Yellow River
Arabian Peninsula | Himalayas | Mouth of the Ganges | Taiwan

W ——— 4,800 miles ———

The Arabian Peninsula and the mountainous Iranian Plateau are divided by the Persian Gulf, fed by the Tigris and Euphrates Rivers. Farther east, the land begins to rise, the mountains spreading north to the Plateau of Tibet, and south to the Himalayas. The plains to the south of the Himalayas are drained by the Indus and Ganges, and to the east of the Plateau of Tibet by the Yellow River.

## PHYSICAL ASIA

**Northern Asia** is made up of old mountains and ancient, stable plateaus. The jagged Himalayan mountains dominate the central part of the continent, along with the Plateau of Tibet, which stretches north into China. In Southeast Asia, there are many islands. Volcanoes and earthquakes are common, and some of the islands are volcanically formed.

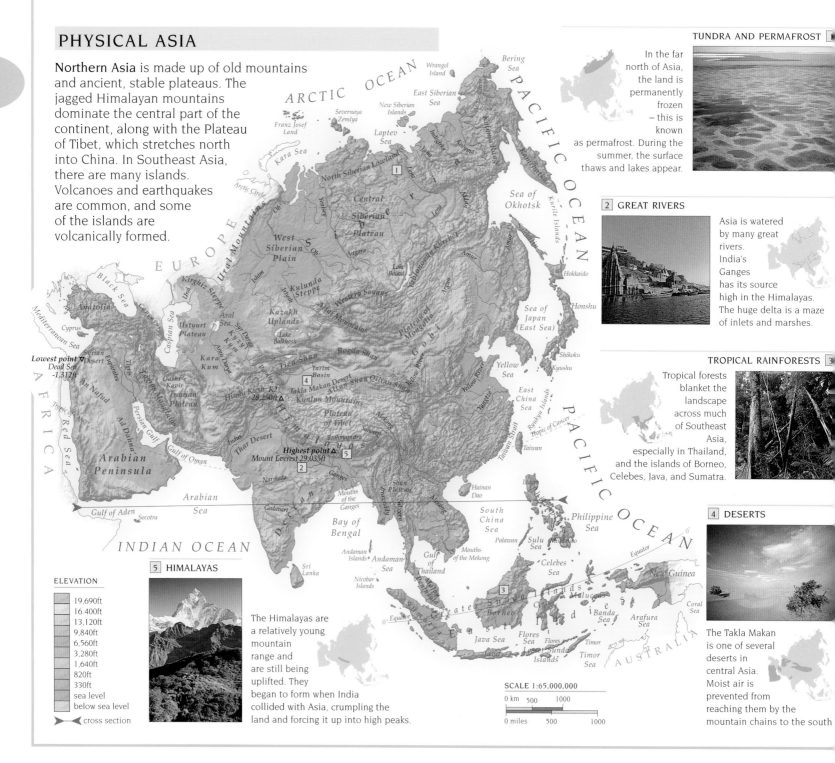

### TUNDRA AND PERMAFROST 1

In the far north of Asia, the land is permanently frozen – this is known as permafrost. During the summer, the surface thaws and lakes appear.

### 2 GREAT RIVERS

Asia is watered by many great rivers. India's Ganges has its source high in the Himalayas. The huge delta is a maze of inlets and marshes.

### TROPICAL RAINFORESTS 3

Tropical forests blanket the landscape across much of Southeast Asia, especially in Thailand, and the islands of Borneo, Celebes, Java, and Sumatra.

### 4 DESERTS

The Takla Makan is one of several deserts in central Asia. Moist air is prevented from reaching them by the mountain chains to the south.

**ELEVATION**

19,690ft
16,400ft
13,120ft
9,840ft
6,560ft
3,280ft
1,640ft
820ft
330ft
sea level
below sea level

✕ cross section

### 5 HIMALAYAS

The Himalayas are a relatively young mountain range and are still being uplifted. They began to form when India collided with Asia, crumpling the land and forcing it up into high peaks.

**SCALE 1:65,000,000**

0 km   500   1000

0 miles   500   1000

# POLITICAL ASIA

Asia is a continent of many contrasts: in its lands, its peoples, and its traditions. The break-up of the Soviet Union, which once stretched south from Russia to Iran, produced the new central Asian republics of Kazakhstan, Kyrgyzstan, Tajikistan, Turkmenistan, and Uzbekistan. The countries in southwest Asia are mainly Muslim, and include monarchies, republics and theocracies. India is the world's largest democracy, while China is a communist power regaining its economic influence in the world.

## POPULATION

Capital cities
● 50,000 to 100,000
▣ Above 500,000 ● Below 50,000
◉ 100,000 to 500,000

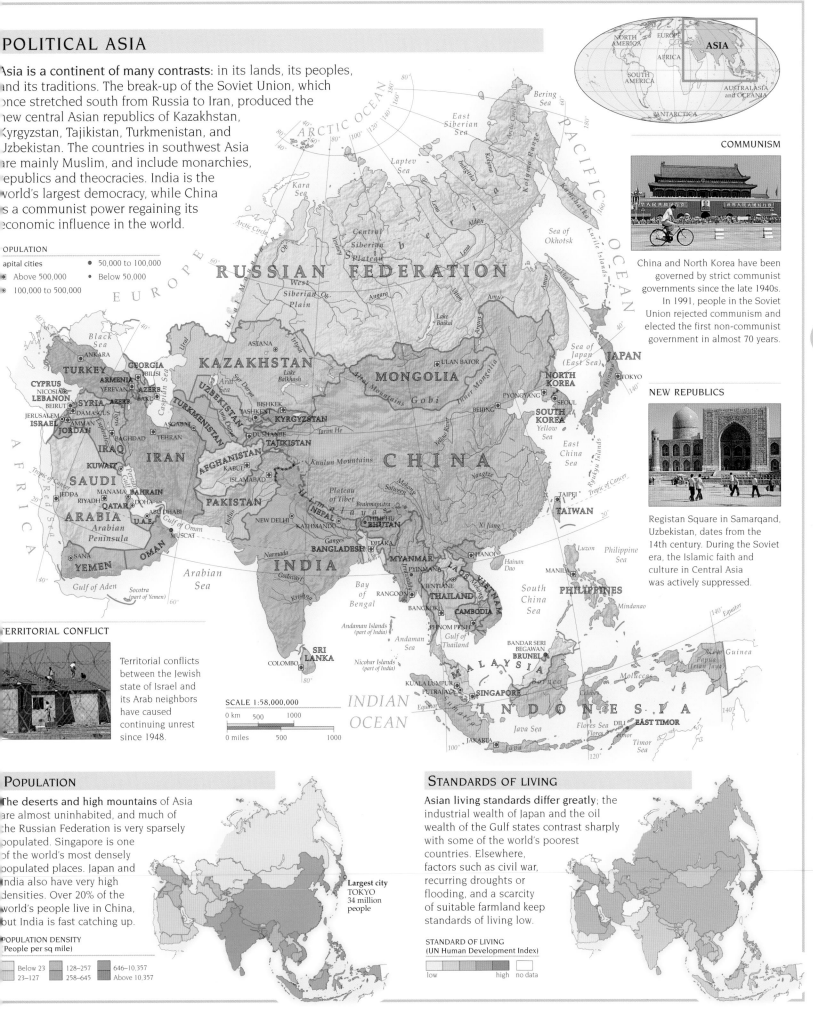

## COMMUNISM

China and North Korea have been governed by strict communist governments since the late 1940s. In 1991, people in the Soviet Union rejected communism and elected the first non-communist government in almost 70 years.

## NEW REPUBLICS

Registan Square in Samarqand, Uzbekistan, dates from the 14th century. During the Soviet era, the Islamic faith and culture in Central Asia was actively suppressed.

## TERRITORIAL CONFLICT

Territorial conflicts between the Jewish state of Israel and its Arab neighbors have caused continuing unrest since 1948.

SCALE 1:58,000,000

0 km    500    1000

0 miles    500    1000

## POPULATION

The deserts and high mountains of Asia are almost uninhabited, and much of the Russian Federation is very sparsely populated. Singapore is one of the world's most densely populated places. Japan and India also have very high densities. Over 20% of the world's people live in China, but India is fast catching up.

Largest city
TOKYO
34 million
people

POPULATION DENSITY
(People per sq mile)

Below 23
23–127
128–257
258–645
646–10,357
Above 10,357

## STANDARDS OF LIVING

Asian living standards differ greatly; the industrial wealth of Japan and the oil wealth of the Gulf states contrast sharply with some of the world's poorest countries. Elsewhere, factors such as civil war, recurring droughts or flooding, and a scarcity of suitable farmland keep standards of living low.

STANDARD OF LIVING
(UN Human Development Index)

low    high    no data

# ASIAN GEOGRAPHY

Asia's forbidding mountain ranges, barren deserts and fertile plains have affected the way in which people settled the continent. Intensive agriculture is found in the more fertile areas, and the largest concentrations of people grew up near fertile land, and close to great rivers. Asia's mineral wealth has brought people to the more inhospitable parts of the continent; the deserts of southwest Asia for oil, and frozen Siberia for oil, gas, and minerals.

## MINERAL RESOURCES

Over half of the world's oil and gas reserves are in Asia, most importantly around The Gulf, and in western Siberia. Coal in Siberia and China has provided power for steel industries. Metallic minerals are also abundant; tin in Southeast Asia, and platinum and nickel in Siberia.

**MINERAL RESOURCES**

- Chromium
- Tin
- Nickel
- Iron
- Platinum
- Gold
- Lead
- Oil/gas field
- Coal field

## INDUSTRY

Many people in Asia still rely on agriculture as a source of income, and some countries have very few industries. Heavy industry dominates eastern China and Russia, but Japan is the most industrially productive country. In recent years, booming 'tiger' economies have developed in countries such as Taiwan, which border the Pacific Ocean.

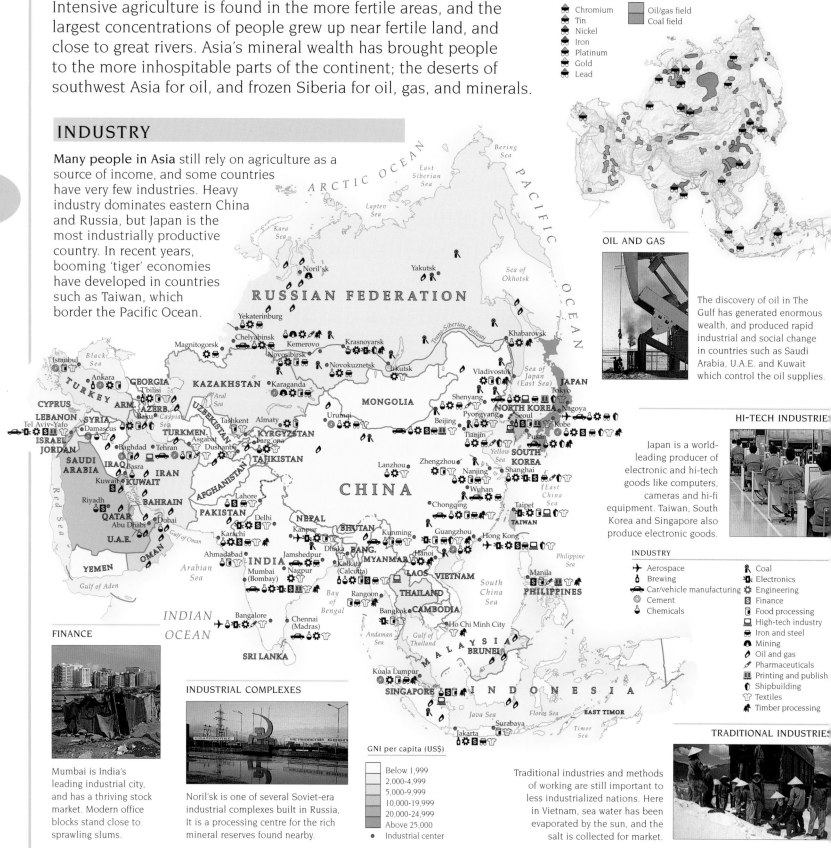

### OIL AND GAS

The discovery of oil in The Gulf has generated enormous wealth, and produced rapid industrial and social change in countries such as Saudi Arabia, U.A.E. and Kuwait which control the oil supplies.

### HI-TECH INDUSTRIES

Japan is a world-leading producer of electronic and hi-tech goods like computers, cameras and hi-fi equipment. Taiwan, South Korea and Singapore also produce electronic goods.

**INDUSTRY**

- ✈ Aerospace
- ♨ Brewing
- 🚗 Car/vehicle manufacturing
- ♻ Cement
- ⚗ Chemicals
- ⛏ Coal
- 🔌 Electronics
- ⚙ Engineering
- $ Finance
- 🍴 Food processing
- 💻 High-tech industry
- 🚂 Iron and steel
- ⚓ Mining
- ◊ Oil and gas
- ✐ Pharmaceuticals
- 🖥 Printing and publish
- ⚓ Shipbuilding
- 👕 Textiles
- 🌲 Timber processing

**GNI per capita (US$)**

- Below 1,999
- 2,000-4,999
- 5,000-9,999
- 10,000-19,999
- 20,000-24,999
- Above 25,000
- • Industrial center

### FINANCE

Mumbai is India's leading industrial city, and has a thriving stock market. Modern office blocks stand close to sprawling slums.

### INDUSTRIAL COMPLEXES

Noril'sk is one of several Soviet-era industrial complexes built in Russia, It is a processing centre for the rich mineral reserves found nearby.

### TRADITIONAL INDUSTRIES

Traditional industries and methods of working are still important to less industrialized nations. Here in Vietnam, sea water has been evaporated by the sun, and the salt is collected for market.

## CLIMATE

Most of Asia has a continental climate, apart from coastal areas. Without the moderating effects of the ocean, temperatures can soar during the day, and plummet at night; while rainfall is generally low – producing several large deserts. Temperatures as low as −90°F have been recorded in the frozen wastes of Siberia, while the islands in Southeast Asia have tropical climates. Southern and eastern Asia are also affected by a seasonal wind called the monsoon. This originates in the Indian Ocean and brings heavy rainfall and high winds, often devastating small coastal and low-lying villages and towns.

### EXTREME WEATHER EVENTS

Symbols indicate climatic extremes

**CLIMATE**
- Tundra
- Subarctic
- Cool continental
- Warm temperate
- Mediterranean
- Semiarid
- Arid
- Humid equatorial
- Tropical
- Hot humid

Coldest place
VERKHOYANSK (Russ. Fed.)
Temp −90°F

Hottest place
TIRAT TSVI (Israel)
Temp 129°F

Wettest place
CHERRAPUNJI (India)
Annual rainfall 45in

Driest place
ADEN (Yemen)
Annual rainfall 3/16in

### RAINFORESTS

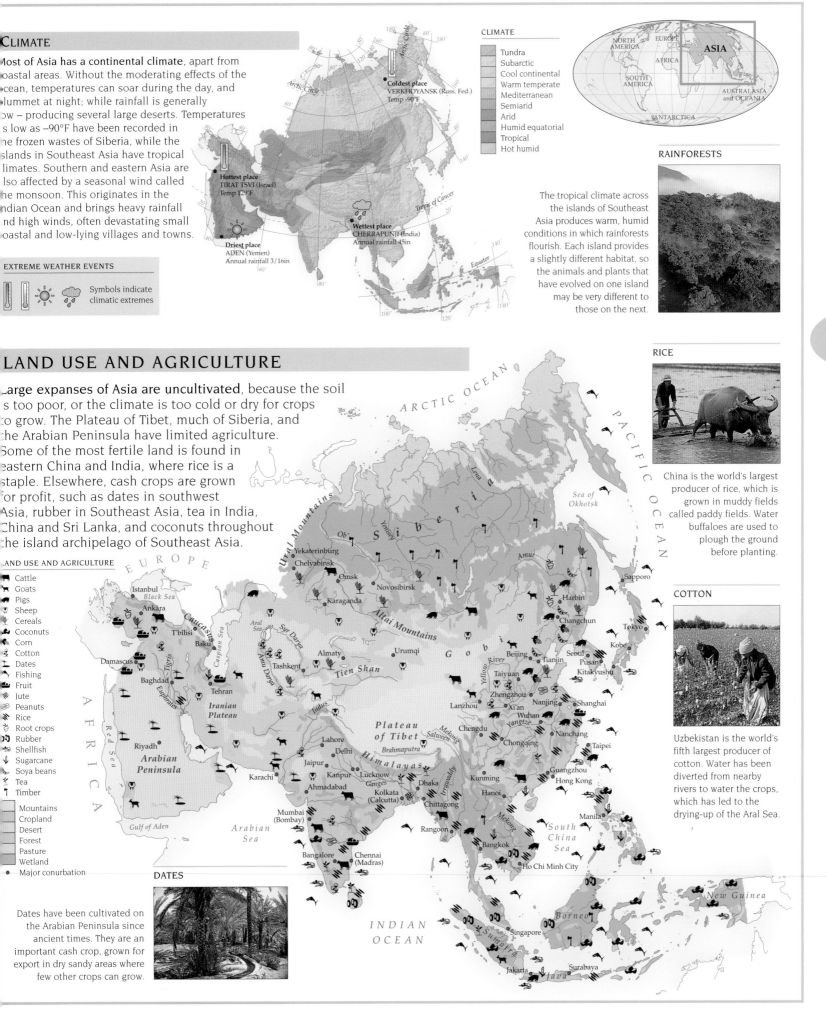

The tropical climate across the islands of Southeast Asia produces warm, humid conditions in which rainforests flourish. Each island provides a slightly different habitat, so the animals and plants that have evolved on one island may be very different to those on the next.

### RICE

China is the world's largest producer of rice, which is grown in muddy fields called paddy fields. Water buffaloes are used to plough the ground before planting.

## LAND USE AND AGRICULTURE

Large expanses of Asia are uncultivated, because the soil is too poor, or the climate is too cold or dry for crops to grow. The Plateau of Tibet, much of Siberia, and the Arabian Peninsula have limited agriculture. Some of the most fertile land is found in eastern China and India, where rice is a staple. Elsewhere, cash crops are grown for profit, such as dates in southwest Asia, rubber in Southeast Asia, tea in India, China and Sri Lanka, and coconuts throughout the island archipelago of Southeast Asia.

### LAND USE AND AGRICULTURE
- Cattle
- Goats
- Pigs
- Sheep
- Cereals
- Coconuts
- Corn
- Cotton
- Dates
- Fishing
- Fruit
- Jute
- Peanuts
- Rice
- Root crops
- Rubber
- Shellfish
- Sugarcane
- Soya beans
- Tea
- Timber

- Mountains
- Cropland
- Desert
- Forest
- Pasture
- Wetland
- Major conurbation

### COTTON

Uzbekistan is the world's fifth largest producer of cotton. Water has been diverted from nearby rivers to water the crops, which has led to the drying-up of the Aral Sea.

### DATES

Dates have been cultivated on the Arabian Peninsula since ancient times. They are an important cash crop, grown for export in dry sandy areas where few other crops can grow.

# RUSSIA AND KAZAKHSTAN

**Russia lies partly in Europe** but mostly in Asia. The land to the east of the Ural Mountains is called Siberia. This immense stretch of grasslands, thick, evergreen forest, and tundra is crossed by giant rivers. Vast areas of Siberia are almost untouched by human activity, yet in the industrial regions set up under communism (1922–1991), air, water, and soil are heavily polluted with harmful substances. Along with the former Soviet state of Kazakhstan, Siberia is rich in a huge variety of minerals.

## INDUSTRY

**The discovery of gold** in the 19th century opened Siberia up to economic and industrial development. Later, vast reserves of oil, coal, and gas were found, especially in the west, which is now the main center for oil extraction. Gold and diamonds are mined in the east. In Kazakhstan, mining and other industries are growing with the help of foreign investors.

STRUCTURE OF INDUSTRY

Primary 5%
Services 60%
Manufacturing 35%

INDUSTRY

- 🚗 Car manufacture
- ⚗ Chemicals
- ⚙ Engineering
- Iron & steel
- 👕 Textiles
- ◈ Diamonds
- ◊ Mining
- ♨ Oil and gas
- 🌲 Timber manufacturing
- ⊙ Major industrial center / area
- Major road

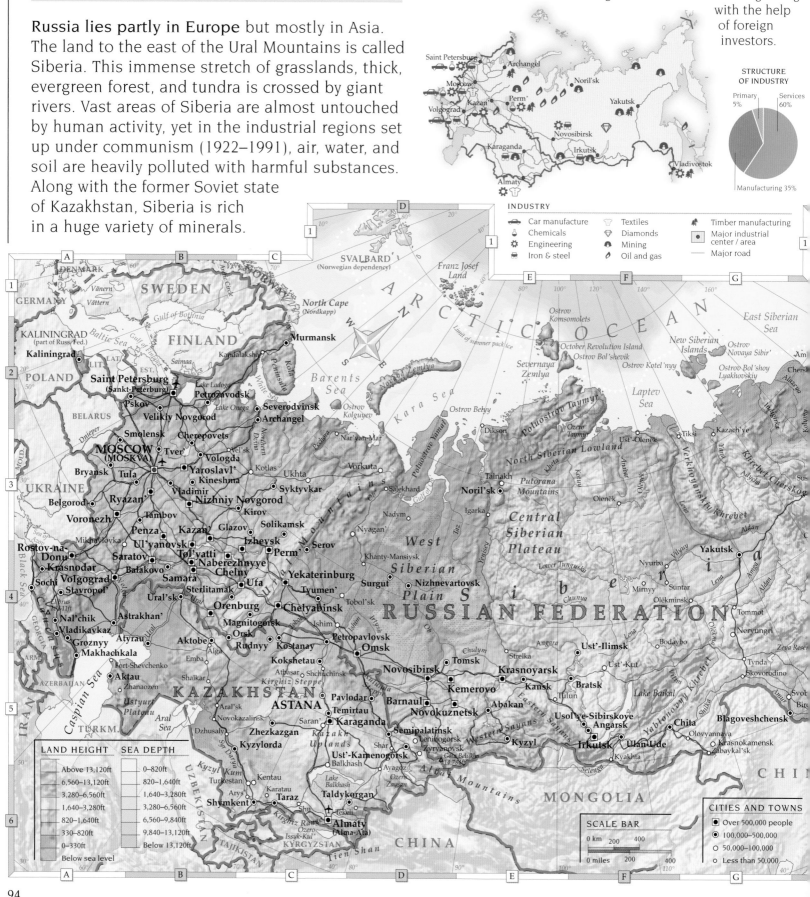

LAND HEIGHT

- Above 13,120ft
- 6,560–13,120ft
- 3,280–6,560ft
- 1,640–3,280ft
- 820–1,640ft
- 330–820ft
- 0–330ft
- Below sea level

SEA DEPTH

- 0–820ft
- 820–1,640ft
- 1,640–3,280ft
- 3,280–6,560ft
- 6,560–9,840ft
- 9,840–13,120ft
- Below 13,120ft

SCALE BAR

0 km  200  400
0 miles  200  400

CITIES AND TOWNS

- Over 500,000 people
- 100,000–500,000
- 50,000–100,000
- Less than 50,000

## THE LANDSCAPE

[E]ast of the Ural Mountains lies the West Siberian Plain – the [w]orld's largest area of flat ground. The plain gradually rises to [t]he Central Siberian Plateau and then again to highlands in [t]he southeast. Great coniferous forests called *taiga* stretch [a]cross most of this land. The far north of Siberia extends into [t]he Arctic Circle. [H]ere the landscape [is] made up of frozen [p]lains called tundra. [M]uch of Kazakhstan [is] covered by huge [r]olling grasslands, [o]r steppe. In the [s]outh are arid [s]andy deserts.

### Tundra and *taiga*
Stubby birch trees, dwarf bushes, moss and lichen huddle close to the ground in the frozen tundra wastes of northern Russia. They lie between the permanent ice and snow of the Arctic, and the thick *taiga* forests which cover an area greater than the Amazon rain forest.

### The Caspian Sea (A 5)
The Caspian Sea covers 143,243 sq miles and is the world's largest expanse of inland water. It is fed by the Volga and Ural Rivers, which flow in from the plains of the north.

### West Siberian Plain (D 4)
This vast, flat expanse is covered with a network of marshes and streams. The Ob' River, which winds its way north across the plains, is frozen for up to half the year.

### Lake Baikal (F 5)
Lake Baikal is the deepest lake in the world, and the largest freshwater one – it is more than 1 mile deep and covers 12,500 sq miles. It is fed by 336 rivers and contains around 20% of all the fresh water in the world.

## CLIMATE

Russia and Kazakhstan have continental climates, and their distance from seas and oceans means that temperatures fluctuate wildly, both daily and seasonally. Temperatures in eastern Siberia have been known to reach -90°F.

**January**

**July**

**TEMPERATURE AND PRECIPITATION**

- More than 86°F
- 77 to 86°F
- 68 to 77°F
- 59 to 68°F
- 50 to 59°F
- 41 to 50°F
- 32 to 41°F
- 23 to 32°F
- 14 to 23°F
- 5 to 14°F
- Less than 5°F
— 4 Precipitation (in)

## FARMING AND LAND USE

Siberia's harsh climate has restricted farming to the south, where there are a few areas warm enough to grow cereal crops such as wheat and oats and to raise cattle on the small pockets of pasture. The rest of the region is used for hunting, herding reindeer, and forestry – the *taiga* forests contain the world's largest timber reserves. In Kazakhstan, big herds of cattle, goats, and sheep are raised for wool and meat, and wheat is cultivated in the fertile north.

**FARMING AND LAND USE**

- Cattle
- Fishing
- Pigs
- Reindeer
- Sheep
- Root crops
- Timber
- Tobacco
- Wheat
- Barren land
- Cropland
- Desert
- Forest
- Mountains
- Pasture
- Tundra
- Wetland
- ● Major conurbation

**LAND USE**
- Cropland 9%
- Pasture 14%
- Forest 41%
- Other (including mountains) 36%

## POPULATION

Siberia has some of the world's largest areas of uninhabited land – the bitingly cold climate and harsh living conditions have kept the population small. The industrial cities in the west have the most people. Despite its huge size, Kazakhstan has only 16 million people, just over half live in urban areas.

**INHABITANTS PER SQ MILE**
- More than 260
- 13–260
- 30–130
- Less than 30
- ■ Capital city
- ● Major city

**URBAN/RURAL POPULATION DIVISION**
- Saint Petersburg 2.6%
- Moscow 6.4%
- Novosibirsk 1%
- Rural population 24%
- Other towns and cities 66%

## ENVIRONMENTAL ISSUES

Decades of industrial development during the communist regime brought new industries to undeveloped parts of the region, such as Siberia. This industrial development has now led to environmental degradation on a massive scale: river, air, and land pollution in Russia is among the worst in the world.

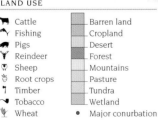

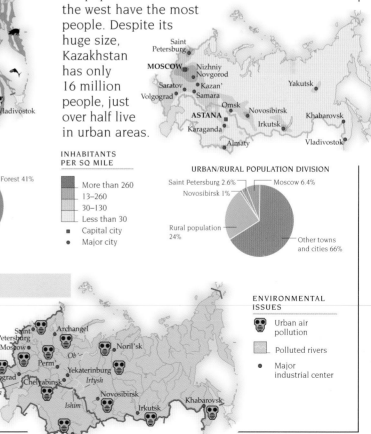

**ENVIRONMENTAL ISSUES**
- Urban air pollution
- Polluted rivers
- ● Major industrial center

# TURKEY AND THE CAUCASUS

ARMENIA, AZERBAIJAN, GEORGIA, TURKEY

**Turkey and the Caucasus** lie partly in Europe, and partly in Asia. Turkey has a long Islamic tradition, and although the country is now a secular (nonreligious) one, most. Turks are Muslims. Turkey is becoming more industrialized, although one third of its workforce is still employed in agriculture. The countries of the Caucasus were under Russian rule for 70 years, until 1991. They are home to more than 50 different ethnic groups.

## INDUSTRY

**Turkey has a wide range** of industries, including tourism and growing trade links with Europe. Azerbaijan has large oil reserves and is able to export oil. The other states use imported fuel and hydro-electric power generated by their rushing rivers. Georgia produces industrial machinery and chemicals. Armenia's economy is recovering from the conflict with Azerbaijan.

## FARMING AND LAND USE

**With its warm climate** and good soils, Turkey is able to produce all of its own food. Cattle and goats are kept on the central plateau. Along the Mediterranean coast, farmers grow olives, figs, grapes, and peaches. Hazelnuts are cultivated along the shores of the Black Sea. Across the Caucasus, the limited fertile land is used to grow wine grapes, tobacco, and cotton.

**FARMING AND LAND USE**

- 🐂 Livestock
- 🐟 Fishing
- ⚘ Cotton
- 🍎 Fruit
- 🌰 Hazelnuts
- 🥔 Root crops
- 🌿 Tobacco
- 🍇 Vineyards

- Pasture
- Cropland
- Forest
- • Major conurbation

**LAND USE**

Other 31%
Cropland 34%
Forest 15%
Pasture 20%

**INDUSTRY**

- ⚙ Cement manufacturing
- 🧪 Chemicals
- ⚙ Engineering
- 📷 Food processing
- 🎪 Textiles
- ⚓ Oil field
- 🏛 Tourism
- ▣ Major industrial center / area
- — Major road

**STRUCTURE OF INDUSTRY**

Primary 12%
Service 57%
Manufacturing 31%

## THE LANDSCAPE

**A huge semiarid plateau** called Anatolia runs across the center of Turkey. It is rimmed by several mountain ranges along the Black Sea coast and the steep Taurus Mountains in the south. A narrow strip of lowland separates the Caucasus and the Lesser Caucasus mountains in the northeast.

### Anatolia

Anatolia has large areas of soft limestone rock. Over a long period of time, layers of rock have been worn away by water to produce strange landscapes with caves and tall, isolated rock pinnacles.

**Caucasus Mountains** (H 1)

**Lesser Caucasus** (H 2)

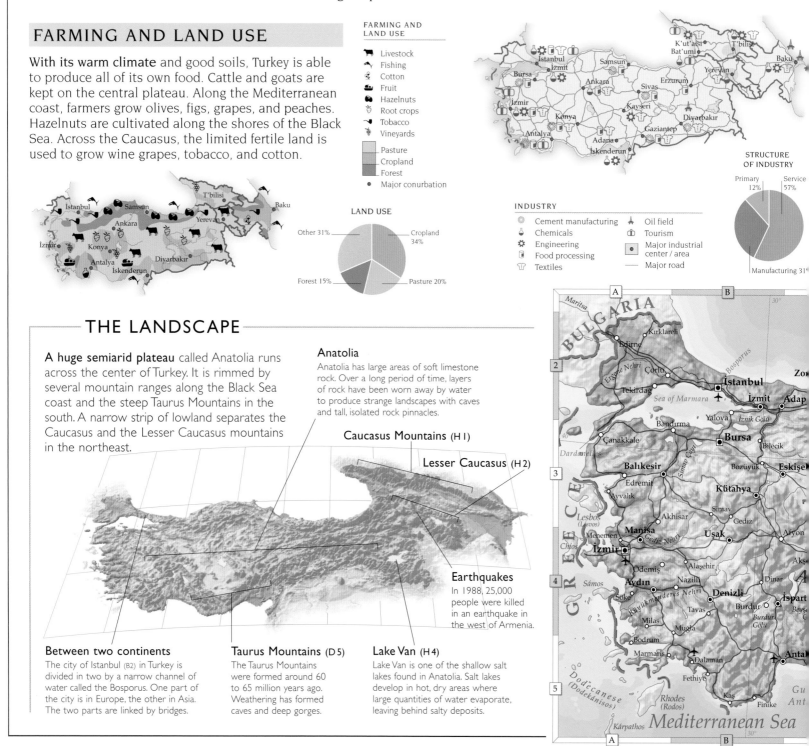

**Earthquakes**
In 1988, 25,000 people were killed in an earthquake in the west of Armenia.

### Between two continents

The city of Istanbul (B2) in Turkey is divided in two by a narrow channel of water called the Bosporus. One part of the city is in Europe, the other in Asia. The two parts are linked by bridges.

### Taurus Mountains (D 5)

The Taurus Mountains were formed around 60 to 65 million years ago. Weathering has formed caves and deep gorges.

### Lake Van (H 4)

Lake Van is one of the shallow salt lakes found in Anatolia. Salt lakes develop in hot, dry areas where large quantities of water evaporate, leaving behind salty deposits.

# POPULATION

Over 75% of Turks live in large towns or cities, mostly in the western half of the country. The eastern and southeastern parts of Anatolia are home to the Kurdish people. The Caucasian republics became more industrialized under Russian rule, and today, two thirds of their people live in urban places.

URBAN/RURAL
POPULATION DIVISION

Istanbul 10%
Ankara 3.7%
İzmir 2.5%
Other towns and cities 55.8%
Rural population 28%

INHABITANTS
PER SQ MILE

More than 520
260–520
130–260
Less than 130
Capital city
Major city

# ENVIRONMENTAL ISSUES

Turkey has built many large dams to use water from rivers – especially the Euphrates – to irrigate its farmland. Syria and Iraq, which lie downstream, have opposed the dams, because they will have less water flowing into their countries. The safety of old-style nuclear plants such as Metsamor in Armenia has caused concern.

İstanbul
1999
T'bilisi 1998
Metsamor
Yerevan
Atatürk Dam
Euphrates

ENVIRONMENTAL ISSUES

Earthquake zone
Major dam
Unstable nuclear power station
Urban air pollution
Major industrial center

ASIA
Turkey & the Caucasus

NORTH AMERICA
EUROPE
AFRICA
SOUTH AMERICA
AUSTRALASIA AND OCEANIA
ANTARCTICA

# CLIMATE

Winters are coldest in the Caucasus Mountains and in Anatolia, while the shores of the Mediterranean and Black Seas remain mild. Summers are hottest around the edge of the Mediterranean and near Turkey's border with Syria and Iraq.

January

July

TEMPERATURE AND PRECIPITATION

More than 86°F
77 to 86°F
68 to 77°F
59 to 68°F
50 to 59°F
41 to 50°F
32 to 41°F
23 to 32°F
14 to 23°F
Less than 14°F

4 Precipitation (in)

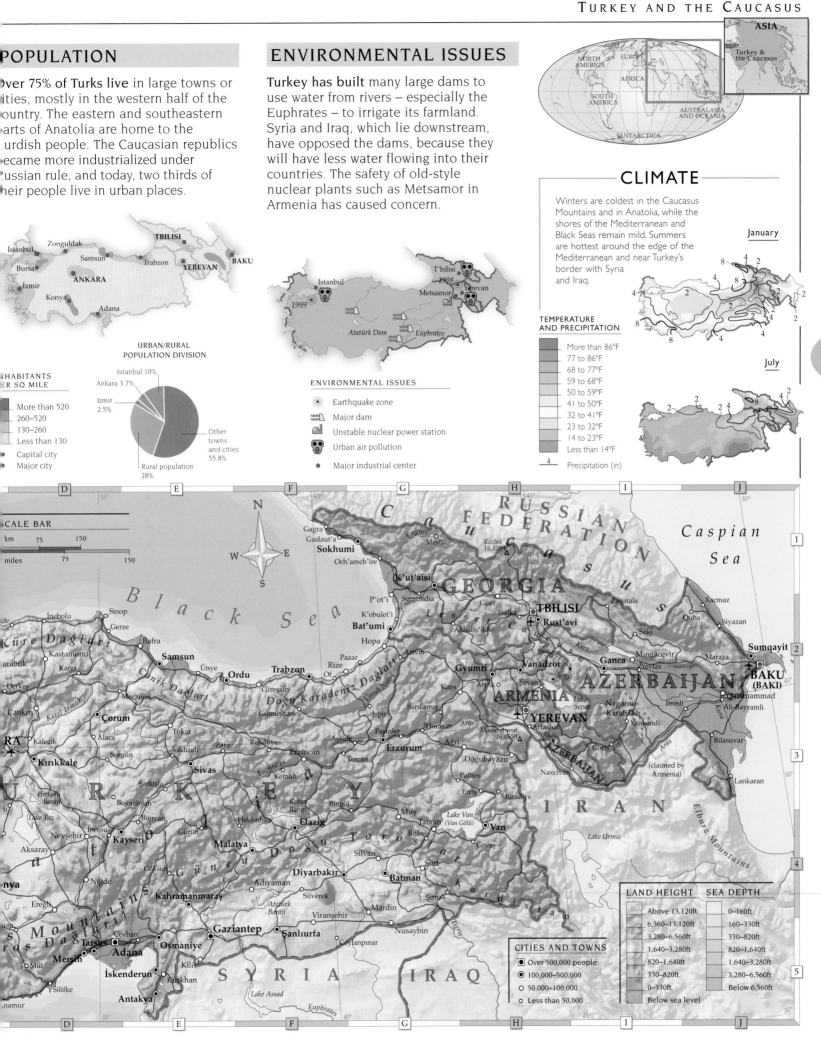

SCALE BAR

km  75  150
miles  75  150

N W E S

CITIES AND TOWNS

Over 500,000 people
100,000–500,000
50,000–100,000
Less than 50,000

| LAND HEIGHT | SEA DEPTH |
|---|---|
| Above 13,120ft | 0–160ft |
| 6,560–13,120ft | 160–330ft |
| 3,280–6,560ft | 330–820ft |
| 1,640–3,280ft | 820–1,640ft |
| 820–1,640ft | 1,640–3,280ft |
| 330–820ft | 3,280–6,560ft |
| 0–330ft | Below 6,560ft |
| Below sea level | |

# SOUTHWEST ASIA

BAHRAIN, IRAN, IRAQ, ISRAEL, JORDAN, KUWAIT, LEBANON, OMAN, QATAR, SAUDI ARABIA, SYRIA, UNITED ARAB EMIRATES, YEMEN

**Most of southwest Asia** is barren desert, yet the world's first cities originated here over 5,000 years ago. It was the birthplace of three major religions: Islam, Judaism, and Christianity. In recent years, the discovery of oil has brought great wealth to much of the region, but it has also been torn by internal conflicts and wars between neighboring countries. Most people here are Muslims, although Israel is the world's only Jewish state.

## ENVIRONMENTAL ISSUES

**Water shortages** are common because of the hot, dry climate and the lack of rivers. Desalination plants convert seawater into freshwater, and are found along the Red Sea and Gulf coasts. Lack of water also makes the risk of desertification greater. Iran has had many catastrophic earthquakes; in 1978 an earthquake killed 25,000 people.

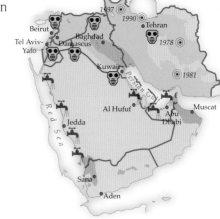

ENVIRONMENTAL ISSUES

💧 Area with many desalination plants

◉ Catastrophic earthquake

👥 Urban air pollution

▢ Existing desert
▩ Risk of desertification
• Major industrial center

## INDUSTRY

**Oil has made** the previously poor Arab states very wealthy. It and natural gas continue to be the main sources of income for many of the countries here. Other industries are being developed to support the region's economies when these resources run out. Iran is famous for its carpets, which are woven from wool or silk.

INDUSTRY

⚙ Cement manufacturing
🗋 Food processing
🚂 Iron and steel
🗋 Oil refining
👕 Textiles
🛢 Oil and gas
Ⓢ Finance

▣ Major industrial center / area
— Major road

STRUCTURE OF INDUSTRY

Primary 10%
Services 49%
Manufacturing 41%

## FARMING AND LAND USE

**The best farmland** is found along the Mediterranean coast and in the fertile valleys of the Tigris, Euphrates and Jordan Rivers. Wheat is the main cereal crop, and cotton, dates, and citrus and orchard fruits are grown for export. Elsewhere, modern irrigation techniques have created patches of fertile land in the desert. Dates, wheat, and coffee are cultivated in the oases and along the Persian Gulf coast.

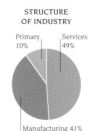

LAND USE

Forest 2%
Pasture 45%
Cropland 6%
Other (including desert) 47%

FARMING AND LAND USE

🐐 Goats
🐟 Fishing
🐑 Sheep
🍊 Citrus fruits
☕ Coffee
🌿 Cotton
🌱 Dates
🍎 Fruit
🍃 Tobacco
🌾 Wheat

▨ Cropland
▨ Desert
▨ Forest
▨ Pasture
▨ Wetland
• Major conurbation

## THE LANDSCAPE

**Great desert plateaus,** both sandy and rocky, cover much of southwest Asia. On the enormous Arabian Peninsula, which covers an area almost the size of India, narrow, sandy plains along the Red Sea and south coast rise to dry mountains. In the center a vast, high plateau that slopes gently down to the flat shores of the Persian Gulf. The mountainous areas of Iran experience frequent earthquakes.

### Wadis

Valleys or riverbeds, called *wadis*, are found in the Saudi Arabian desert. They are usually dry, but after heavy rains, they are briefly filled by fast flowing rivers.

### Syrian Desert (B2)

The Syrian Desert extends from the Jordan valley in the west to the fertile plains of the Tigris and Euphrates Rivers in the east. It is mainly a rocky desert, because the sand has been swept away by winds and occasional heavy rainstorms.

### Oases

Oases are areas within a desert where water is available for plants and human use. They are usually formed when a fault, or split, in the rock allows water to come to the surface. Oases can be no bigger than a few palm trees or cover several hundred sq miles.

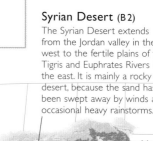

### Dead Sea (A2)

This large lake on the border between Israel and Jordan is the lowest point on the Earth's surface – its shores lie 1,286 ft below sea level. It is also the world's saltiest body of water, and cannot sustain any life.

### Ar Rub' al Khali (D5)

The Ar Rub' al Khali desert, also known as the "Empty Quarter," is the largest uninterrupted stretch of sand on Earth. It covers some 250,000 sq miles and is one of the world's driest and most hostile deserts.

### Iranian Plateau (E3)

Central Iran is taken up by a vast, semiarid plateau, that rises steeply from the coastal lowlands bordering the Persian Gulf. It is ringed by the high Zagros and Elburz mountains.

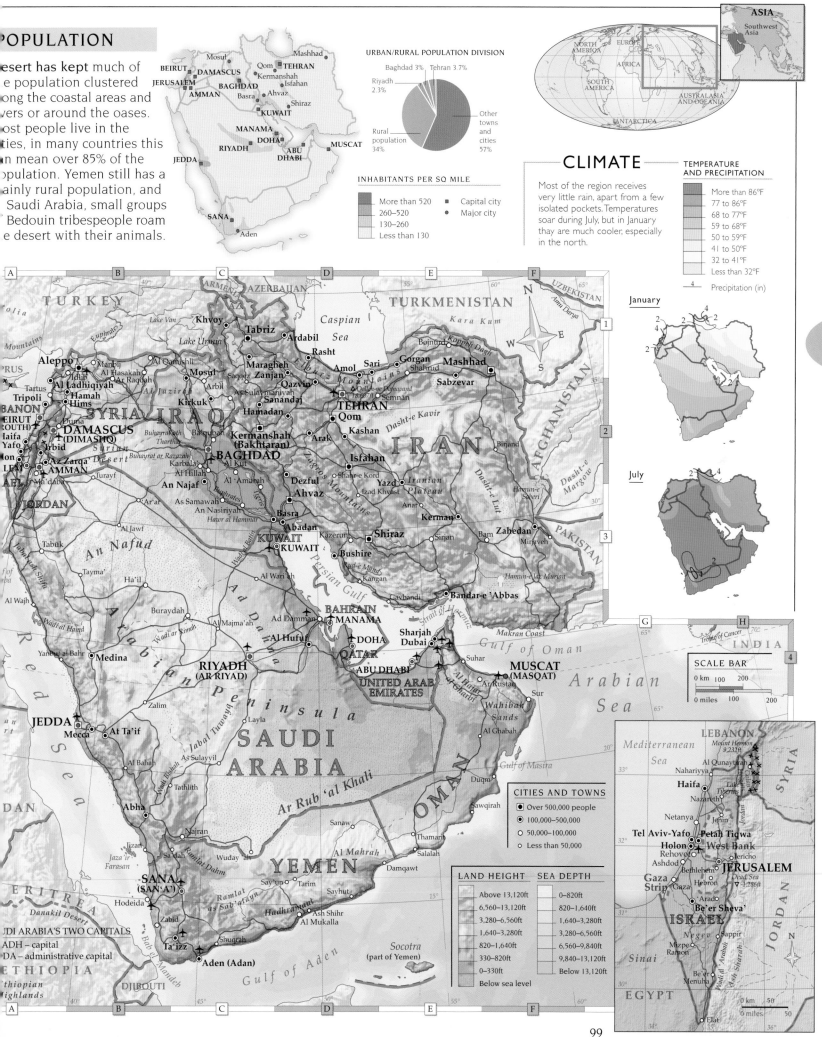

## POPULATION

esert has kept much of
e population clustered
ong the coastal areas and
vers or around the oases.
ost people live in the
ties, in many countries this
n mean over 85% of the
opulation. Yemen still has a
ainly rural population, and
Saudi Arabia, small groups
Bedouin tribespeople roam
e desert with their animals.

**URBAN/RURAL POPULATION DIVISION**

Baghdad 3%   Tehran 3.7%
Riyadh 2.3%
Rural population 34%
Other towns and cities 57%

**INHABITANTS PER SQ MILE**

- More than 520
- 260–520
- 130–260
- Less than 130
- Capital city
- Major city

## CLIMATE

Most of the region receives
very little rain, apart from a few
isolated pockets. Temperatures
soar during July, but in January
thay are much cooler, especially
in the north.

**TEMPERATURE AND PRECIPITATION**

- More than 86°F
- 77 to 86°F
- 68 to 77°F
- 59 to 68°F
- 50 to 59°F
- 41 to 50°F
- 32 to 41°F
- Less than 32°F
- 4 — Precipitation (in)

January

July

**CITIES AND TOWNS**

- Over 500,000 people
- 100,000–500,000
- 50,000–100,000
- Less than 50,000

**LAND HEIGHT**

- Above 13,120ft
- 6,560–13,120ft
- 3,280–6,560ft
- 1,640–3,280ft
- 820–1,640ft
- 330–820ft
- 0–330ft
- Below sea level

**SEA DEPTH**

- 0–820ft
- 820–1,640ft
- 1,640–3,280ft
- 3,280–6,560ft
- 6,560–9,840ft
- 9,840–13,120ft
- Below 13,120ft

UDI ARABIA'S TWO CAPITALS
ADH – capital
DA – administrative capital

**SCALE BAR**

0 km 100 200
0 miles 100 200

99

# CENTRAL ASIA

AFGHANISTAN, KYRGYZSTAN, TAJIKISTAN, TURKMENISTAN, UZBEKISTAN

**Central Asia** is a land of hot, dry deserts and high, rugged mountains. It lies on the ancient Silk Road, an important trade route between China and Europe for over 400 years, until the 15th century. All of the countries here, except for Afghanistan, were part of the Soviet Union from the 1920s until 1991, when they gained independence. Since then, their people have reestablished their local languages and Islamic faith, which were restricted under Russian rule.

## INDUSTRY

**Fossil fuels,** especially coal, natural gas, and oil, are extracted and processed throughout Central Asia. Agriculture supplies the raw materials for many industries, including food and textile processing, and the manufacture of leather goods and clothing. The region is famous for its colorful traditional carpets, hand-woven from the wool of the Karakul sheep. The Fergana Valley, southeast of Tashkent, is the main industrial area.

INDUSTRY

- ⚗ Chemicals
- ⚙ Engineering
- 🗋 Food processing
- ⚚ Textiles
- ⚒ Mining
- ⚘ Oil and gas
- ▣ Major industrial center / area
- — Major road

STRUCTURE OF INDUSTRY

Primary 39%
Manufacturing 29%
Services 32%

## POPULATION

**The peoples of Central Asia are mostly rural farmers,** living in the river valleys and in oases. There are few large cities. A few still lead a traditional nomadic lifestyle, moving from place to place with their animals in search of new pastures. Large areas of Afghanistan, the western deserts, and the mountain regions in the east, are virtually uninhabited.

INHABITANTS PER SQ MILE

- More than 260
- 130–260
- 30–130
- Less than 30
- ▪ Capital city
- ● Major city

URBAN/RURAL POPULATION DIVISION

Tashkent 3.2%
Kabul 4%
Bishkek 1.1%
Other towns and cities 22.7%
Rural population 69%

## FARMING AND LAND USE

**Farming is concentrated** around the fertile river valleys in the east, like the Fergana Valley. A variety of cereals and fruits – including peaches, melons, and apricots – are grown. In drier areas, animal breeding is important with goats, sheep, and cattle supplying wool, meat, and hides. Big crops of cotton, which is a major export, are produced on land irrigated by the Amu Darya River.

FARMING AND LAND USE

- 🐂 Cattle
- 🐐 Goats
- 🐑 Sheep
- 🐏 Cotton
- 🧺 Fruit
- 🌷 Opium poppies
- 🌿 Tobacco
- 🌾 Wheat

- Cropland
- Desert
- Mountains
- Pasture
- Wetland
- ● Major conurbation

LAND USE

Forest 5%
Cropland 9%
Pasture 51%
Other (including mountains and deserts) 35%

## THE LANDSCAPE

**Two of the world's great deserts,** the Kara Kum and the Kyzyl Kum, cover much of the western portion of Central Asia. In the east, a belt of high mountain ranges – the Hindu Kush, the Tien Shan, and the Pamirs – tower above the land. Few rivers cross the deserts, apart from the Amu Darya, which flows from the Pamirs to the shrinking Aral Sea.

### Aral Sea (D 1)
The Aral Sea was once the fourth largest lake in the world, but it has shrunk by 75% since 1960. Diversion of its water for irrigation has made the lake shallower, so its waters evaporate faster.

### Kara Kum (D 3)
The sandy desert of the Kara Kum occupies over 70% of Turkmenistan. Its surface consists of wind-shaped dunes and depressions. Human settlement is limited to the desert's fringes.

### Tien Shan (H 2)

### Fergana Valley (G 3)
Stresses and strain in the Earth create the Fergana Valley, a deep depression encircled by high mountains. The valley's fertile soils are irrigated by water from the Sy Darya River, and underground source

### Amu Darya river (E 3)

### Hindu Kush (G 4)

### Pamirs (G 4)
The Pamirs lie mainly in Tajikistan. Their highest point, at 24,590 ft, is Communism Peak, so named because it was the highest peak in the former Soviet Union.

# ENVIRONMENTAL ISSUES

he Aral Sea is rapidly drying up, because the rivers feeding it
re being diverted to irrigate cottonfields. Central Asia is a very
ry area, and desertification is a constant threat, especially
n Afghanistan. Severe urban and industrial air pollution
s a legacy from the
ommunist era, when
eavy industries
vere established in
he countries here.

ENVIRONMENTAL
ISSUES

Urban air pollution

Existing desert
Risk of desertification
Severe risk of desertification
Polluted river

Major industrial center

## CLIMATE

Central Asia's climate is
strongly inflenced by its
position deep within Asia,
far from the moderating
effects of the oceans.
Winters are cold, summers
are very hot everywhere.
Rainfall is virtually
nonexistent all
year round.

January

July

Less than
2in
precipitation

Less than
2in
precipitation

TEMPERATURE
AND PRECIPITATION

More than 86°F
77 to 86°F
41 to 50°F
32 to 41°F
Less than 32°F

ASIA

NORTH
AMERICA   EUROPE
AFRICA                    Central
                         Asia
SOUTH
AMERICA        AUSTRALASIA
               AND OCEANIA
      ANTARCTICA

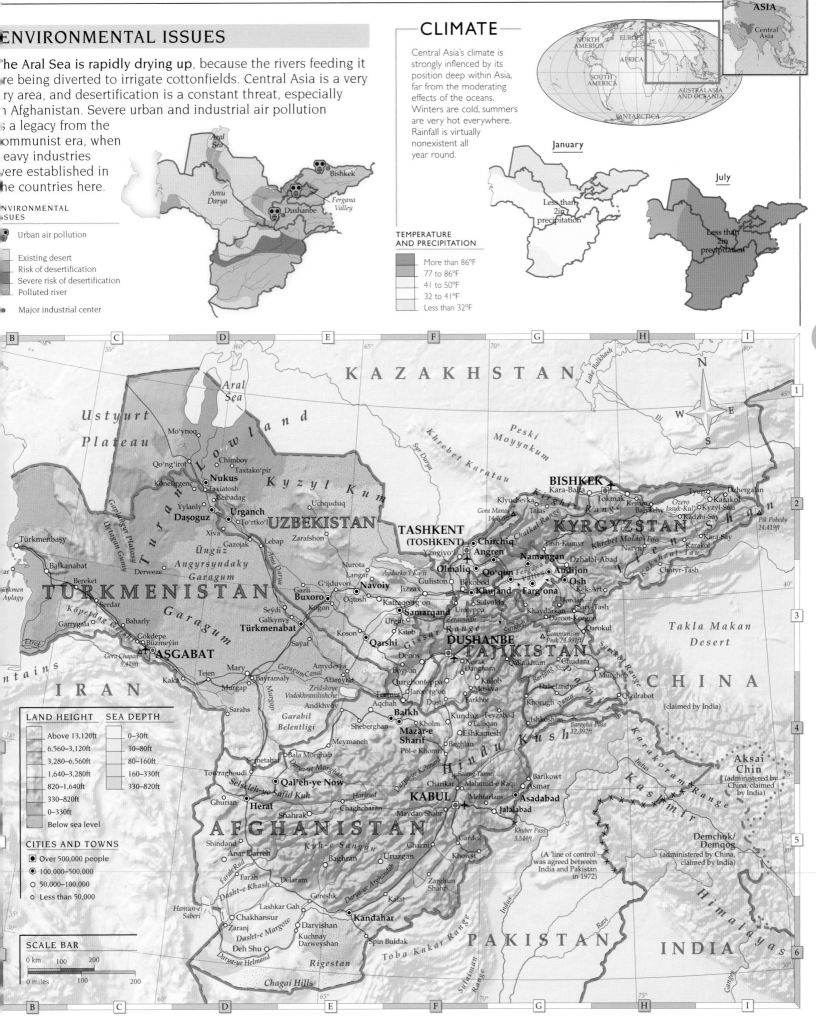

### LAND HEIGHT

Above 13,120ft
6,560–3,120ft
3,280–6,560ft
1,640–3,280ft
820–1,640ft
330–820ft
0–330ft
Below sea level

### SEA DEPTH

0–30ft
30–80ft
80–160ft
160–330ft
330–820ft

### CITIES AND TOWNS

Over 500,000 people
100,000–500,000
50,000–100,000
Less than 50,000

### SCALE BAR

0 km      100      200

0 miles    100     200

# JAPAN AND KOREA

JAPAN, NORTH KOREA, SOUTH KOREA

**Japan is a curved chain** of over 4,000 islands in the Pacific Ocean. To the west, Korea juts out from northern China. Japan has few natural resources, but it has become one of the world's most successful industrial nations, due to investment in new technology and a highly efficient workforce. North Korea is a communist state with limited contact with the outside world, while South Korea is a democracy with major international trade links.

## FARMING AND LAND USE

**Modern farming methods** allow Japan to grow much of its own food, despite a shortage of farmland. Rice is the main crop grown throughout the region. Japan has a large fishing fleet; the Japanese eat more fish than any other nation. In North Korea, farming is controlled by the government.

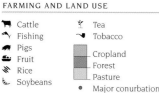

Sapporo
Sendai
Pyongyang
Seoul
Tokyo
Yokohama
Nagoya
Kobe
Pusan
Osaka
Kwangju
Hiroshima
Fukuoka

**FARMING AND LAND USE**

- 🐄 Cattle
- 🐟 Fishing
- 🐖 Pigs
- 🍓 Fruit
- 🌾 Rice
- 🫘 Soybeans
- 🍵 Tea
- 🚬 Tobacco
- Cropland
- Forest
- Pasture
- ● Major conurbation

**LAND USE**

- Pasture 1%
- Cropland 16%
- Other (including mountains) 18%
- Forest 65%

## POPULATION

**Most of Japan's** 128 million people live in crowded cities on the coasts of the four main islands. The Kanto Plain around Tokyo is Japan's biggest area of flat land, and the most populous part of the country. In South Korea, a quarter of the population lives in the capital, Seoul. Most North Koreans live on the coastal plains.

Sapporo
Hamhung
PYONGYANG
SEOUL
Taejŏn
Taegu
Kwangju
Pusan
Fukuoka
Kagoshima
Nagaoka
Sendai
TOKYO
Yokohama
Kobe
Nagoya
Osaka
Hiroshima

**URBAN/RURAL POPULATION DIVISION**

- Tokyo-Yokohama 5.9%
- Seoul 5.2%
- Kobe-Osaka 2.1%
- Rural population 22%
- Other towns and cities 64.8%

**INHABITANTS PER SQ MILE**

- More than 520
- 260–520
- 130–260
- Less than 130
- ■ Capital city
- ● Major city

## THE LANDSCAPE

**Most of Japan is covered** by forested mountains and hills, among which are many short, fast-flowing rivers and small lakes. Only about a quarter of the land is suitable for building and farming, and new land has been created by cutting back hillsides and reclaiming land from the sea. North and South Korea are mostly mountainous, with some coastal plains.

**Hokkaido, Honshu, Shikoku, and Kyushu**
Japan's four main islands were formed when two giant plates making up the Earth's crust collided, making their edges buckle upward.

**T'aebaek-sanmaek (C 5)**
This wooded mountain range forms the "backbone" of the Korean peninsula. It runs from north to south close to the east coast.

**Tsunamis**
Huge sea waves called tsunamis frequently threaten the east coast of Japan. They are set off by submarine earthquakes. The waves increase in size as they near the shore and can flood coastal areas and sink ships.

**Earthquakes**
In Japan, earthquakes are part of everyday life. The islands lie on a fault line, and earthquake tremors occur, on average, 5,000 times a year. Most of these are mild and may go unnoticed, but there is a constant threat of disaster.

**Volcanoes**
Japan's mountain ranges are studded with volcanoes, 60 of which are still active. Mount Fuji is a 12,389 ft snow-capped volcano and the highest mountain in Japan. It last erupted in 17██.

## INDUSTRY

**Japan is a world leader in** high-tech electronic goods like computers, televisions and cameras, as well as cars. South Korea also has a thriving economy. It produces ships, cars, high-tech goods, shoes, and clothes for worldwide export. Both countries have to import most of their raw materials and energy. North Korea has little trade with other countries, but it is rich in minerals such as coal and silver.

Kushiro
Sapporo
Hachinohe
Ch'ongjin
Sendai
Pyongyang
Nagaoka
Hitachi
Toyama
Tokyo
Seoul
Inch'on
Yokohama
Kyoto
Nagoya
Pusan
Kobe
Kwangju
Hiroshima
Osaka
Fukuoka
Kitakyushu

**STRUCTURE OF INDUSTRY**

- Primary 2%
- Services 70%
- Manufacturing 28%

**INDUSTRY**

- 🚗 Car manufacture
- 🧪 Chemicals
- ⚙️ Engineering
- 🍱 Food processing
- Iron & steel
- ⚓ Shipbuilding
- 👕 Textiles
- ⛏ Mining
- 💲 Finance
- 💻 Hi-tech
- 🔬 Research & Development
- ▪ Major industrial center / area
- — Major road

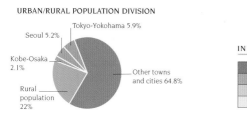

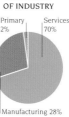

## ENVIRONMENTAL ISSUES

Industrial pollution from Korea and China has produced acid rain, and pollution in Japanese cities has led to people wearing masks to filter the air. Russia regularly dumps nuclear waste into the Sea of Japan. In 1995, an earthquake caused great destruction to the city of Kobe.

ENVIRONMENTAL ISSUES

- Catastrophic earthquake
- Nuclear waste dump site
- Urban air pollution
- Affected by acid rain
- Major industrial cent

## CLIMATE

Korea has hot summers and dry, very cold winters, especially in the north, where snow is common. In Japan, winters are less cold than on the Asian mainland; summers are hot, wet, and humid.

January

Less than 2

July

TEMPERATURE AND PRECIPITATION

| | |
|---|---|
| More than 68°F | 32 to 41°F |
| 59 to 68°F | 23 to 32°F |
| 50 to 59°F | Less than 23°F |
| 41 to 50°F | 4 Precipitation (in) |

ASIA
Japan and Korea

LAND HEIGHT
- 6,560–13,120ft
- 3,280–6,560ft
- 1,640–3,280ft
- 820–1,640ft
- 330–820ft
- 0–330ft

SEA DEPTH
- 0–820ft
- 820–1,640ft
- 1,640–3,280ft
- 3,280–6,560ft
- 6,560–9,840ft
- 9,840–13,120ft
- Below 13,120ft

CITIES AND TOWNS
- Over 500,000 people
- 100,000–500,000
- 50,000–100,000
- Less than 50,000

(North and South Korea have been divided by a ceasefire agreement since 1953)

# EAST ASIA

CHINA, MONGOLIA, TAIWAN

China is the world's fourth-largest country and its most populous – over one billion people live there. Under its communist government, which came to power in 1949, China has become a major industrial nation, but most of its people still live and work on the land as they have for thousands of years. Taiwan also has a booming economy and exports its products around the world. Mongolia is a vast, remote country with a small population, many of whom are nomads.

## INDUSTRY

Chemicals, iron and steel, engineering, and textiles are the main industries in China's east coast cities, and in industrial centers like Shenyang. Shanghai, Hong Kong, and Beijing are also important financial centers. In the interior, large deposits of coal support the heavy industries in major cities such as Chengdu and Wuhan. Taiwan specializes in textiles and shoe manufacture, along with electronic goods. Mongolia's economy is mainly agricultural.

STRUCTURE OF INDUSTRY

Services 37% | Manufacturing 50%
Primary 13%

### INDUSTRY

- 🚗 Car manufacture
- 🧪 Chemicals
- 🔌 Electronics
- 💻 Electronic goods
- ⚙️ Engineering
- 🍴 Food processing
- 🏭 Iron & steel
- ⚓ Shipbuilding
- 👕 Textiles
- ⛏️ Coal
- ⚒️ Mining
- Ⓢ Finance
- ⊡ Major industrial center / area
- — Major road

## POPULATION

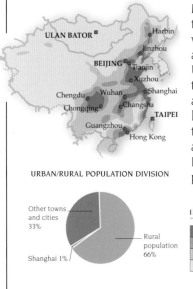

URBAN/RURAL POPULATION DIVISION

Other towns and cities 33%
Rural population 66%
Shanghai 1%

Most of China's people live in the eastern part of the country, where the climate, landscape and soils are most favorable. Urban areas there house more than 250 million people, but almost 70% of the population lives in villages and farms the land. Taiwan's lowlands are very densely populated. In Mongolia, one third of the people live in the countryside.

INHABITANTS PER SQ MILE
- More than 520
- 260–520
- 130–260
- Less than 130
- ■ Capital city
- ● Major city

## FARMING AND LAND USE

Despite its size, about 90% of China is unsuitable for farming. Either the soils and climate are poor, or the landscape is too mountainous. In the north and west, most farmers make their living by herding animals. On the fertile eastern plains, soybeans, wheat, corn, and cotton are grown. Farther south, rice becomes the main crop, and pigs are raised in large numbers.

### FARMING AND LAND USE

- 🐟 Fishing
- 🐖 Pigs
- 🐑 Sheep
- 🌽 Corn
- Cotton
- 🍒 Fruit
- 🌾 Rice
- Soybeans
- Sugarcane
- 🌿 Tea
- Tobacco
- 🌾 Wheat
- Cropland
- Desert
- Forest
- Mountain region
- Pasture
- ● Major conurbation

LAND USE

Cropland 14% | Pasture 49%
Other (including mountains) 21%
Forest 16%

## THE LANDSCAPE

China's landscape is divided into three areas. The vast Plateau of Tibet in the southwest is the highest and largest plateau on Earth. It contains both dry deserts and pockets of pasture surrounded by high mountains. Northwest China has dry highlands. The great plains of eastern China were formed from soils deposited by rivers like the Yellow River over thousands of years. Most of Mongolia is dry, grassland steppe and cold, arid desert.

### Tien Shan mountains (B 2)

The Tien Shan, or "Heavenly Mountains" reach heights of 24,419 ft. They surround fields of permanent ice and spectacular glaciers.

### Gobi (E2) and Takla Makan (B 3) deserts

The arid landscapes of the Gobi and Takla Makan deserts are made up of bare rock surfaces and huge areas of shifting sand dunes. They are hot in summer, but unlike most other deserts are extremely cold in winter.

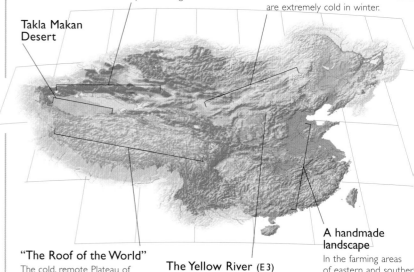

Takla Makan Desert

### "The Roof of the World"

The cold, remote Plateau of Tibet averages 13,000 ft in height. Many of China's great rivers have their sources here. The world's highest human settlement, a town called Wenquan, is found in the east of the plateau. It lies 16,729 ft above sea level.

### The Yellow River (E 3)

The Yellow River (Huang He) is the world's muddiest river, carrying hundreds of truckloads of sediment to the sea every minute. The river has burst its banks many times throughout history, causing enormous damage and claiming millions of human lives.

### A handmade landscape

In the farming areas of eastern and southern China, terraces have been carved into the hillsides to make them flat enough to grow rice and other crops. This method of farming has been used for over 7,000 years.

# ENVIRONMENTAL ISSUES

**The Three Gorges** hydroelectric program on the Yangtze River will be the world's largest. Nearly 350 miles of canyon will be flooded and 1.3 million people forced to move. Earthquakes are common in the area, and 100 million people downstream will be threatened if the dam breaks. In eastern China, many cities are affected by industrial pollution.

### ENVIRONMENTAL ISSUES

≋ Major dam

☠ Urban air pollution

● Industrial city

## CLIMATE

Two air masses control climate: one cold and dry from Siberia, and one moist and warm from the Pacific. Winters are long and cold away from the coast — especially on the Plateau of Tibet.

ASIA
East Asia

NORTH AMERICA  EUROPE  AFRICA  SOUTH AMERICA  ASIA  AUSTRALASIA AND OCEANIA  ANTARCTICA

**TEMPERATURE AND PRECIPITATION**

More than 86°F
68 to 86°F
50 to 68°F
32 to 50°F
14 to 32°F
-4 to 14°F
Less than -4°F

—4— Precipitation (in)

January

July

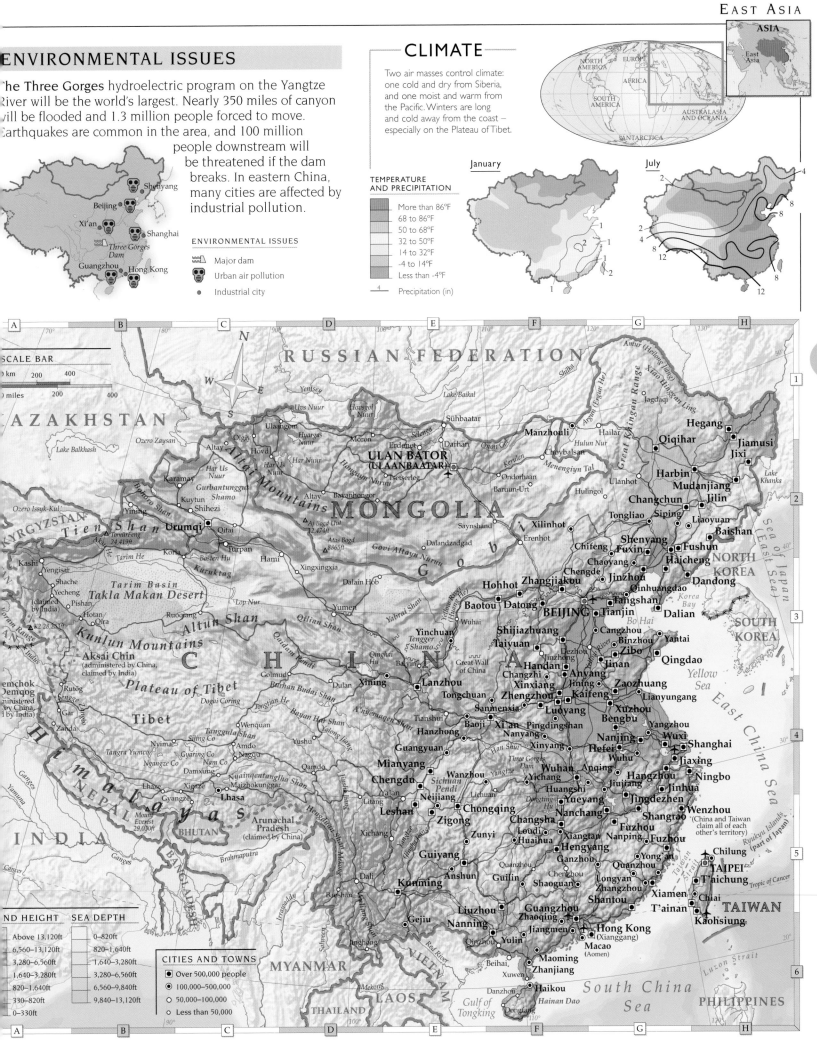

# SOUTH ASIA

BANGLADESH, BHUTAN, INDIA, NEPAL, PAKISTAN, SRI LANKA

**South Asia** is a land of many contrasts. Its landscape ranges from the mighty peaks of the Himalayas in the north through vast plains and arid deserts, to tropical forests and palm-fringed beaches in the south. More than one-fifth of the world's people live here, and a long history of foreign invasions has left a mosaic of vastly different cultures, religions, and traditions and thousands of languages and dialects.

## INDUSTRY

**Industry has expanded** in India in recent years. In the cities a variety of goods are produced and processed, including cars, airplanes, chemicals, food, and drink. Service industries such as tourism and banking are also growing. Elsewhere, small-scale cottage industries serve the needs of local people, but many products, mainly silk and cotton textiles, clothing, leather, and jewelry, are also exported.

STRUCTURE
OF INDUSTRY

Primary 23%
Services 49%
Manufacturing 28%

INDUSTRY

- ✈ Aerospace
- 🚗 Car manufacture
- ⚗ Chemicals
- ⚡ Electronics
- ⚙ Engineering
- 🍱 Food processing
- 🏭 Iron and steel
- 👕 Textiles
- ⛏ Mining
- Ⓢ Finance
- 🏛 Tourism
- ⦿ Major industrial center / area
- — Major road

## POPULATION

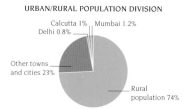

INHABITANTS
PER SQ MILE

- More than 520
- 260–520
- 130–260
- Less than 130
- ■ Capital city
- ● Major city

**Most of South Asia's people** live in villages scattered across the fertile river floodplains, in mountain valleys, or along the coasts, but increasing numbers are migrating to the cities in search of work. Overcrowding is a serious problem in both rural and urban areas; in many cities, thousands of people are forced to live in slums or on the streets.

URBAN/RURAL POPULATION DIVISION

Calcutta 1%   Mumbai 1.2%
Delhi 0.8%
Other towns and cities 23%
Rural population 74%

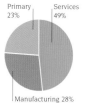

## FARMING AND LAND USE

**Over 60% of the population** is involved in agriculture, but most farms are small and produce only enough food to feed one family. Grains are the staple food crops – rice in the wetter part of the east and west, corn, and millet on the Deccan plateau, and wheat in the north. Peanuts are widely grown as a source of cooking oil. Cash crops include tea, which is grown on plantations, and jute.

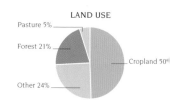

FARMING AND LAND USE

- 🐂 Cattle
- ⌐ Fishing
- 🐐 Goats
- 🌾 Cereals
- 🥜 Groundnuts
- ✽ Jute
- ⚘ Rice
- ⚜ Tea
- Cropland
- Desert
- Forest
- Pasture
- Wetland
- ● Major conurbation

LAND USE

Pasture 5%
Forest 21%
Other 24%
Cropland 50%

## THE LANDSCAPE

**A massive, towering wall** of snow-capped mountains stretches in an arc across the north, isolating South Asia from the rest of the continent. The huge floodplains and deltas of the Indus, Ganges, and Brahmaputra Rivers separate the mountains from the rest of the peninsula: a great rolling plateau, bordered on either side by coastal hills called the Eastern and Western Ghats.

### Himalayas (E 2)
The Himalayas are the highest mountain system in the world. They were formed about 40 million years ago when two of the Earth's plates collided, thrusting up huge masses of land.

### Mount Everest (F 3)
The northern ranges of the Himalayas average 23,000 ft in height. They include the highest point on Earth, Mount Everest on the Nepal–China border, which soars to 29,035 ft.

### Thar Desert (C 3)
The border between India and Pakistan runs through the arid, sandy Thar Desert.

### Western Ghats (C 5)
The Western Ghats run continuously along the Arabian Sea coast. The lower Eastern Ghats are interrupted by rivers that follow the gentle slope of the Deccan plateau and flow across broad lowlands into the Bay of Bengal. This is one of the wettest regions in the world.

### Eastern Ghats (E 5)

### Deccan plateau (D 5)
This giant plateau makes up most of central and southern India. Its volcanic rock has been deeply cut by rivers such as the Krishna, creating stepped valleys called *traps*.

### Bangladesh (G 3)
Much of Bangladesh lies in an enormous delta formed by the Brahmaputra and Ganges Rivers. During the summer monsoon, the rivers become swollen by the torrential rains – and meltwater from the Himalayas – and the delta floods. Over the years, millions of people have drowned or been made homeless by heavy flooding.

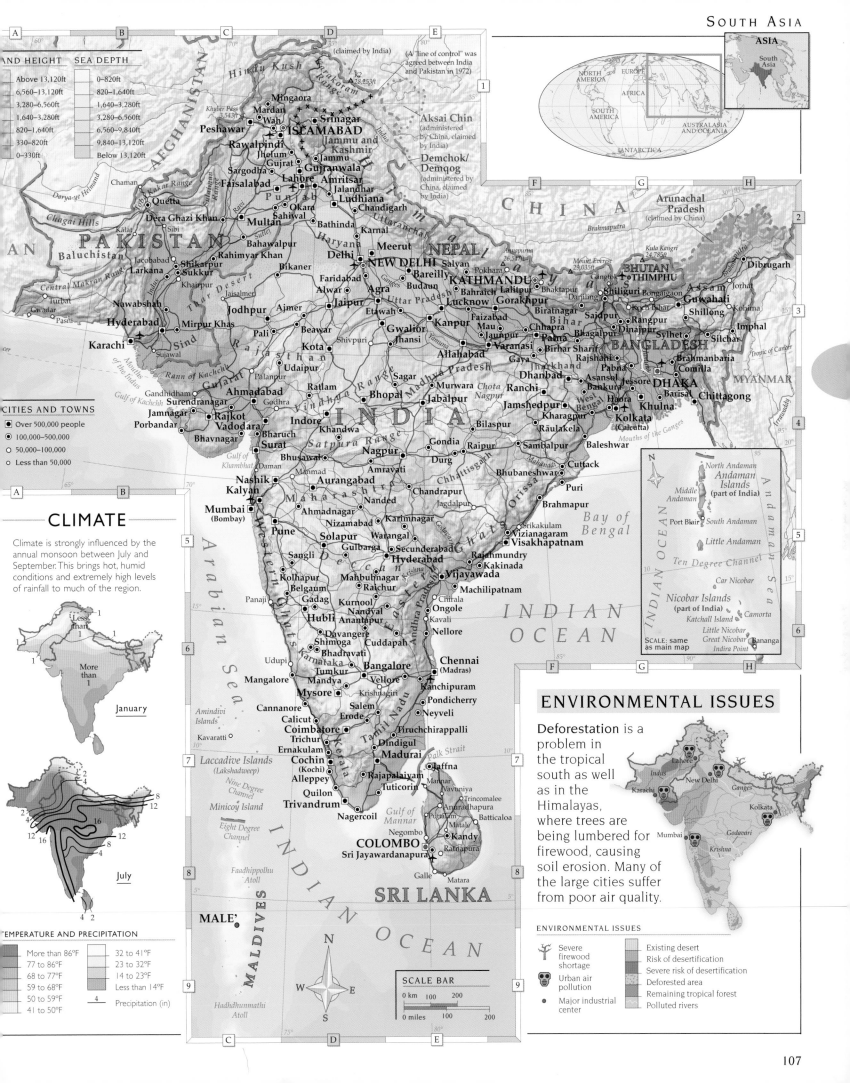

ASIA
South Asia

## LAND HEIGHT

Above 13,120ft
6,560–13,120ft
3,280–6,560ft
1,640–3,280ft
820–1,640ft
330–820ft
0–330ft

## SEA DEPTH

0–820ft
820–1,640ft
1,640–3,280ft
3,280–6,560ft
6,560–9,840ft
9,840–13,120ft
Below 13,120ft

## CITIES AND TOWNS

■ Over 500,000 people
● 100,000–500,000
◉ 50,000–100,000
○ Less than 50,000

## CLIMATE

Climate is strongly influenced by the annual monsoon between July and September. This brings hot, humid conditions and extremely high levels of rainfall to much of the region.

January

July

## TEMPERATURE AND PRECIPITATION

More than 86°F
77 to 86°F
68 to 77°F
59 to 68°F
50 to 59°F
41 to 50°F

32 to 41°F
23 to 32°F
14 to 23°F
Less than 14°F

4 — Precipitation (in)

## ENVIRONMENTAL ISSUES

Deforestation is a problem in the tropical south as well as in the Himalayas, where trees are being lumbered for firewood, causing soil erosion. Many of the large cities suffer from poor air quality.

## ENVIRONMENTAL ISSUES

⚘ Severe firewood shortage
☠ Urban air pollution
● Major industrial center

Existing desert
Risk of desertification
Severe risk of desertification
Deforested area
Remaining tropical forest
Polluted rivers

## SCALE BAR

0 km 100 200
0 miles 100 200

# SOUTHEAST ASIA

BRUNEI, CAMBODIA, EAST TIMOR, INDONESIA, LAOS, MALAYSIA, MYANMAR, PHILIPPINES, SINGAPORE, THAILAND, VIETNAM

**Southeast Asia** is made up of a mainland area and many thousands of tropical islands. The region has great natural wealth – from precious stones to oil – and has recently experienced fast industrial growth. Some countries here, especially Singapore and Malaysia, have become prosperous, but Laos and Cambodia remain poor and are still recovering from years of terrible warfare.

## ENVIRONMENTAL ISSUES

In Myanmar, Malaysia, and Indonesia, ancient rain forests are being cut down faster than they can grow back. The fantastic biodiversity of the forests, with their thousands of unique species of plants and animals, is severely threatened. Forest burning has recently caused terrible smog in Indonesia and Malaysia.

ENVIRONMENTAL ISSUES

- Urban air pollution
- Deforested area
  Remaining tropical forest
- Major industrial center

Rangoon
Bangkok
Manila
Kuala Lumpur
Singapore
Jakarta
Surabaya

## POPULATION

**On the mainland,** the population is concentrated in the river valleys, plateaus, or plains. Upland areas are inhabited by small groups of hill peoples. Most people still live in rural areas, but the cities are growing fast. In Indonesia and the Philippines, the population is unevenly distributed. Some islands, such as Java, are densely settled; others are barely occupied.

PYINMANA  HANOI
VIENTIANE
RANGOON  Da Nang  MANILA
BANGKOK  PHNOM PENH
Ho Chi Minh
Davao
KUALA  BANDAR
LUMPUR  SERI BEGAWAN
Medan
PUTRAJAYA  Manado
SINGAPORE
Palembang
JAKARTA  Surabaya  DILI

INHABITANTS PER SQ MILE

- More than 520
- 260–520
- 130–260
- Less than 130
- Capital city
- Major city

URBAN/RURAL POPULATION DIVISION

Bangkok 1.2%
Jakarta 1.5%
Manilla 1.8%
Rural population 37%
Other towns and cities 58.5%

## INDUSTRY

**Industries based** on the processing of raw materials, like metallic minerals, timber, oil and gas, and agricultural produce, are important here, but manufacturing has grown dramatically in recent years. Many foreign firms, attracted by low labor costs, have invested in the region. Malaysia and Singapore are major producers of electronic goods like disk drives for computers.

Mandalay
Hanoi
Rangoon
Da Nang
Bangkok
Manila
Phnom Penh
Ho Chi Minh
Davao
Medan
Kuala Lumpur
Singapore
Palembang
Jakarta
Bandung  Surabaya
Semarang

STRUCTURE OF INDUSTRY

Primary 19%
Services 45%
Manufacturing 36%

INDUSTRY

- Chemicals
- Engineering
- Food processing
- Textiles
- Mining
- Oil and gas
- Timber
- High-tech
- Tourism
- Major industrial center / area
- Major road

## THE LANDSCAPE

**On the mainland,** a belt of mountain ranges, cloaked in thick forest, runs north–south. The mountains are cut through by the wide valleys of five great rivers. On their way to the sea, these rivers have deposited sediment, forming immense, fertile flood plains and deltas. To the southeast of the mainland lies a huge arc of over 20,000 mountainous, volcanic islands.

### Borneo (D 7)
Borneo is the world's third-largest island, with a total area of 292,298 sq miles. Lying on the Equator and in the path of two monsoons, the island is hot and one of the wettest places on Earth. The landscape contains thickly forested central highlands and swampy lowlands.

### Mekong River (C 4)
The mighty Mekong River flows through southern China and Myanmar and forms much of the border between Laos and Thailand. It then travels through Cambodia before ending in a vast delta on the southern coast of Vietnam. This is one of the world's most productive rice-growing areas.

### Philippines (E 4)
The Philippines' 7,000 islands are mountainous and volcanic with narrow coastal plains.

### Irian Jaya (I 7)
Irian Jaya is a province of Indonesia. Its dense rain forests are some of the last unexplored areas on Earth and are inhabited by many rare plant and animal species.

### Volcanoes
Indonesia is the most active volcanic region in the world. Java alone has over 50 active volcanoes out of the country's total of more than 220.

### Indonesia (C 7)
Indonesia is an archipelago of 13,677 islands, scattered over almost 3,110 miles. The islands lie on the boundary between two of the Earth's tectonic plates and frequently experience earthquakes.

Hkakabo Razi 19,309ft
Brahmaputra
INDIA
Myitkyina
Banmauk
MYANM
Falam  Lashi
Monywa  Mand
Sagaing  Ma
Amara
Pakokku  Myingy
Taunggyi
Sittwe  Minbu
Ramree Island
Cheduba Island  PYINMAN
Sandoway  Prome
Henzada  Pegu
RANGOON
Bassein  Moulmein
Mouths of the Irrawaddy  Kyaik
Khao
Rese
Andaman Islands (part of India)  Ta
Mali
M
Letsok-aw I
Lanbi Ky
Zadetkyi I
Ko Phra T
Nicobar Islands (part of India)  Ko PI
Ph
Bandaaceh  Sigli
Meulaboh  Lang
Me
Pematang
Pulau Simeulue  Dar
Kepulauan Banyak  Pulau Nias
Equator
INDIA
Pulau

SCALE BAR
0 km  200  400
0 miles  200

# FARMING AND LAND USE

The staple crop here is rice, which grows in low-lying flooded fields called paddies, or on terraces cut into the hillsides. Sugarcane, coconuts, bananas, and pineapples are widely grown as cash crops, and Malaysia produces 25% of the world's rubber. Freshwater and marine fish are caught in large quantities; fish is one of the main foods in this region.

**FARMING AND LAND USE**

- Cattle
- Fishing
- Pigs
- Shellfish
- Coconuts
- Fruit
- Rice
- Rubber
- Sugarcane
- Timber

- Cropland
- Forest
- Pasture
- Wetland
- Major conurbation

**LAND USE**

Pasture 4%
Cropland 21%
Other 24%
Forest 51%

**ASIA**

Southeast Asia

NORTH AMERICA · EUROPE · ASIA · AFRICA · SOUTH AMERICA · AUSTRALASIA AND OCEANIA · ANTARCTICA

## CLIMATE

Southeast Asia's climate is strongly affected by the monsoon, which brings warm, humid air and high rainfall to mainland Southeast Asia during July and to maritime southeast Asia during January.

January

July

**TEMPERATURE AND PRECIPITATION**

- More than 86°F
- 68 to 86°F
- 50 to 68°F
- Less than 50°F
- Precipitation (in)

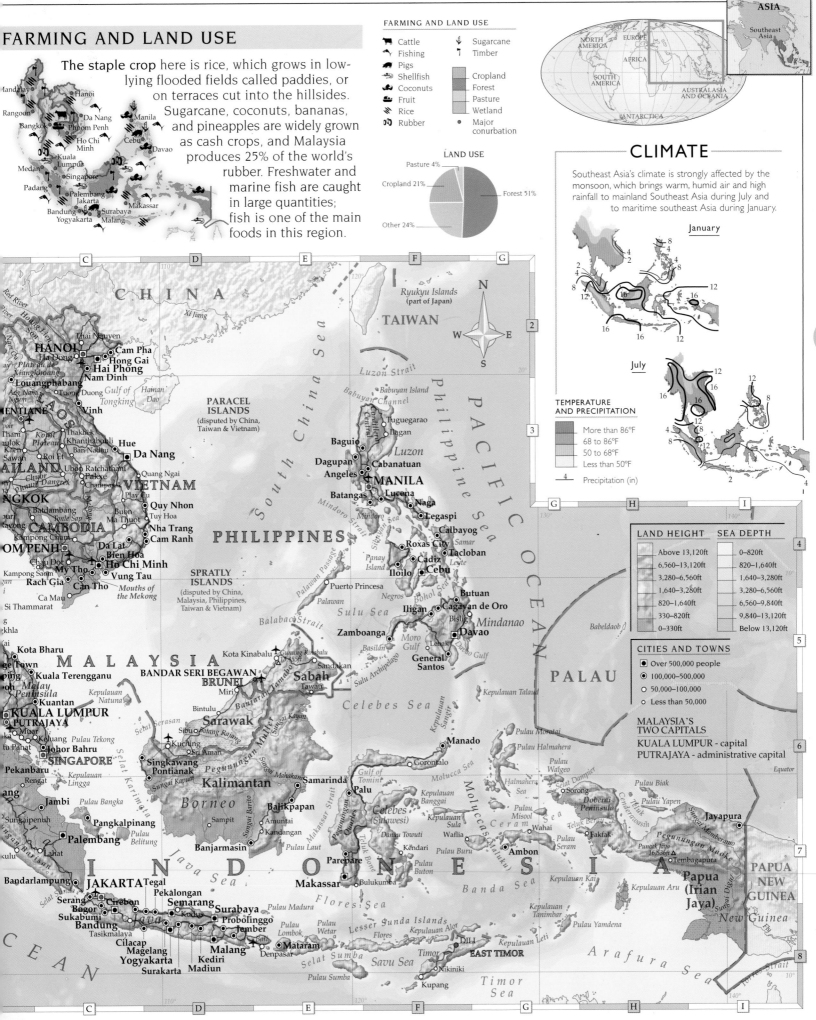

**LAND HEIGHT**

- Above 13,120ft
- 6,560–13,120ft
- 3,280–6,560ft
- 1,640–3,280ft
- 820–1,640ft
- 330–820ft
- 0–330ft

**SEA DEPTH**

- 0–820ft
- 820–1,640ft
- 1,640–3,280ft
- 3,280–6,560ft
- 6,560–9,840ft
- 9,840–13,120ft
- Below 13,120ft

**CITIES AND TOWNS**

- Over 500,000 people
- 100,000–500,000
- 50,000–100,000
- Less than 50,000

**MALAYSIA'S TWO CAPITALS**

KUALA LUMPUR - capital
PUTRAJAYA - administrative capital

109

# CONTINENTAL SOUTH AMERICA

**The towering peaks of the Andes** stand high above the western side of South America. They act as a barrier to the sparsely inhabited interior of the continent, which includes the dense rain forest of the Amazon Basin – one of the Earth's last great wildernesses. Most people live on South America's coastal fringes. Brazil is both the largest country and the most populous. Over half the continent's land area and half of its people are found there.

3,100 miles

4,750 miles

## CROSS-SECTION ACROSS SOUTH AMERICA

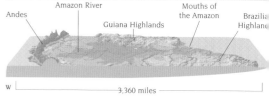

Andes · Amazon River · Guiana Highlands · Mouths of the Amazon · Brazilia Highland

W — 3,360 miles —

The high peaks of the Andes rise up from a narrow strip of land bordering the Pacific Ocean. East of the Andes, the land flattens into a broad, shallow basin into which the Amazon River flows. To the north are the older Guiana Highlands where rock has been eroded to form flat-topped "table" mountains.

## PHYSICAL SOUTH AMERICA

Ancient masses of rocks, like the Guiana and Brazilian highlands, which are known as shields, form the core of South America. The Andes are the solid backbone of the continent. They are relatively young, formed by collisions between different plates of the Earth's crust. The major rivers: the Paraná and the mighty Amazon, flow in deep depressions to the east of the mountains.

### ELEVATION

- 19,960ft
- 16,400ft
- 13,120ft
- 9,840ft
- 6,560ft
- 3,280ft
- 1,640ft
- 820ft
- 330ft
- sea level
- below sea level
- cross section

SCALE 1:40,000,000

0 km  400  800

0 miles  400  800

Caribbean Sea

Gulf of Darien · Lake Maracaibo · Central America · Gulf of Panama · Llanos · Orinoco · Cordillera Occidental · Cordillera Central · Cordillera Oriental · Guiana Highlands · **Highest waterfall Angel Falls** · Rio Negro · Branco · Japura · Equator · Cotopaxi 19,346ft · Chimborazo 20,701ft · Marañon · Putumayo · Amazon · Amazon Basin · Madeira · Represa Balbina · Amazon · Tapajós · Xingu · Tocantins · Mouths of the Amazon · Gulf of Guayaquil · Nevado Huascarán 22,204ft · Ucayali · Madre de Dios · Guaporé · Tocantins · Araguaia · São Francisco · Represa de Sobradinho · Lake Titicaca · Planalto de Mato Grosso · Brazilian Highlands · Andes · Lago Poopó · Pilcomayo · Paraná · Tropic of Capricorn · Atacama Desert · Gran Chaco · Pilcomayo · Paraguay · Parana · Mesopotamia · Uruguay · Lagoa dos Patos · Cerro Ojos del Salado 22,571ft · **Highest point Cerro Aconcagua 22,831ft** · Pampas · Salado · Mirim Lagoon · River Plate · **Lowest point Península Valdés -131ft** · Isla de Chiloé · Chico · Colorado · Río Negro · Patagonia · Gulf of San Jorge · Desaguadero · Bahía Grande · Falkland Islands · Strait of Magellan · Tierra del Fuego · Cape Horn · PACIFIC OCEAN · ATLANTIC OCEAN

### 5 VOLCANOES

The high Andes are lined with many volcanoes. Cotopaxi in Ecuador at 19,347 ft is one of South America's highest active volcanoes.

### 4 THE AMAZON BASIN

The Amazon River flows through a vast geological depression in the north of the continent, supporting thousands of square miles of tropical rainforest.

### 1 GUIANA HIGHLANDS

The Guiana Highlands are part of the ancient core of the continent. They are heavily eroded, with deep valleys and steep waterfalls.

### 2 MANGROVE SWAMPS

Dense mangrove swamps grow along the equatorial coast of Brazil, Colombia, and Ecuador. The delicate ecosystem of the mangrove swamp is easily destroyed by pollution.

### 3 THE ANDES

The Andes run the entire length of the continent – over 4,500 miles – from the storm-lashed island of Tierra del Fuego, to the tropical north. The mountains are on a volcanically active zone, and earthquakes are common.

# POLITICAL SOUTH AMERICA

In the 17th century, explorers from Spain and Portugal claimed most of South America for their rulers in Europe. Their influences are still strong today: Brazilians speak Portuguese, while much of the rest of the continent is Spanish-speaking. The small nations of the north, Suriname and Guyana, were Dutch and British colonies, and French Guiana is a French overseas department. The mix of peoples is mainly European, Native American, and African. Some native peoples still live in the dense Amazon rainforest.

SCALE 1:35,000,000

km  400        800

miles  400        800

## TRANSPORTATION LINKS

The Pan American Highway is a vital transportation link, running from the far south of the continent, northward along the Pacific coast. Its route takes it through sparsely populated areas like the Atacama Desert.

## POPULATION

Many South American countries have a similar pattern of population distribution. The largest concentrations of people are found near the coasts. Migration to the coastal cities has led to rocketing population figures and growing social problems. São Paulo is now one of the world's largest cities; its outskirts are fringed with sprawling, shanty town suburbs, known as *favelas*.

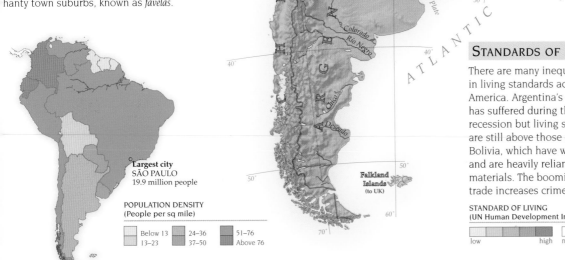

**Largest city**
SÃO PAULO
19.9 million people

POPULATION DENSITY
(People per sq mile)

Below 13      24–36      51–76
13–23         37–50      Above 76

## BORDER DISPUTES

Many of South America's borders have been, or remain, disputed. Bolivia is landlocked as a result of a dispute with Chile in 1883, when it lost its lands bordering the Pacific Ocean.

## URBAN GROWTH

Urban growth has transformed São Paulo into a major population and industrial center. Its rapid growth has created many problems, such as traffic congestion, overcrowding, and inadequate sewerage.

POPULATION

Capital cities
▣  Above 500,000
◉  100,000 to 500,000
●  50,000 to 100,000
•  Below 50,000

Other cities
▢  Above 500,000
○  50,000 to 100,000

## STANDARDS OF LIVING

There are many inequalities in living standards across South America. Argentina's economy has suffered during the regional recession but living standards are still above those of Guyana and Bolivia, which have weak economies and are heavily reliant upon trade in raw materials. The booming black-market drugs trade increases crime and corruption.

STANDARD OF LIVING
(UN Human Development Index)

low        high    no data

### Map labels

Caribbean Sea
Central America
CARACAS
Lake Maracaibo
VENEZUELA
(Venezuelan territorial claim)
GEORGETOWN
GUYANA
PARAMARIBO
SURINAME
French Guiana (to France)
CAYENNE
(Surinamese territorial claims)
BOGOTÁ
COLOMBIA
Orinoco
Rio Negro
Branco
Japurá
Represa Balbina
Amazon
Equator
QUITO
ECUADOR
Putumayo
Amazon
Marañón
Ucayali
Madeira
Tapajós
Xingu
Tocantins
Araguaia
Tocantins
São Francisco
Represa de Sobradinho
B R A Z I L
PERÚ
LIMA
Madre de Dios
BOLIVIA
LA PAZ
Lake Titicaca
Lago Poopó
SUCRE
Pilcomayo
Paraguay
PARAGUAY
São Paulo
BRASÍLIA
Tropic of Capricorn
ASUNCIÓN
Paraná
URUGUAY
Paraguay
Uruguay
SANTIAGO
BUENOS AIRES
MONTEVIDEO
River Plate
A R G E N T I N A
Salado
Colorado
Rio Negro
Chico
Desaguadero
Falkland Islands (to UK)

PACIFIC OCEAN
ATLANTIC OCEAN

# SOUTH AMERICAN GEOGRAPHY

**Agriculture is still the most** common form of employment in South America. Cattle and cash crops of coffee, cocoa, and, in some places, coca for cocaine, provide the main sources of income. Brazil has the greatest range of industries, followed by Argentina, Venezuela, and Chile. The large coastal cities such as Rio de Janeiro, Lima, and Buenos Aires are where most of the jobs are found. This encourages people to migrate from the country to the city, in search of employment.

## MINERAL RESOURCES

South America's mineral resources are highly localized. Few countries have both fossil fuels and metallic ores. The richest oilfields are in the north, especially in Venezuela. Coal, however, is scarce. When the Andes were formed, heat helped create the many metallic minerals that are mined today.

**MINERAL RESOURCES**

- Bauxite
- Copper
- Iron
- Lead
- Silver
- Tin
- Oil/Gas field
- Coal field

## INDUSTRY

**Brazil is the continent's** leading industrial producer, and São Paulo is the major industrial city. Manufactured products include iron and steel, automobiles, chemicals, textiles, and meat and leather products from the continent's vast cattle herds. In the mountains of Bolivia and Colombia, coca plants are grown to make cocaine, which has created a black market for this illegal drug.

### COPPER MINES

Metallic mineral reserves are abundant in the Andes. Chuquicamata, northern Chile, is one of the world's largest copper mines.

### OIL AND GAS

Under the waters of Lake Maracaibo, Venezuela, lie some of South America's biggest oil reserves. Oil exploitation has brought great wealth to Venezuela. The money has helped the country to build new roads and develop other industries.

### INDUSTRIAL CENTER

São Paulo, Brazil, is the largest city in South America and a leading industrial center. A wide range of goods is manufactured here, including automobiles, chemicals, textiles, and electronic products. São Paulo is also a leading financial center. Hundreds of people flock to the city daily in search of work.

### TRADE AND EXPORTS

The Chilean port of Valparaíso ships many different products out of South America. Trade is growing with Japan and other countries around the Pacific Ocean.

### Map labels

Caribbean Sea
Barranquilla
Maracaibo
Caracas
Cartagena
Barquisimeto
Valencia
Ciudad Guayana
Central America
Medellín
VENEZUELA
Georgetown
Paramaribo
Bogotá
GUYANA
SURINAME
French Guiana (to France)
Cali
COLOMBIA
ATLANTIC OCEAN
Quito
ECUADOR
Belém
Guayaquil
Amazon Basin
Manaus
Fortaleza
Chiclayo
Natal
Chimbote
Recife
BRAZIL
Lima
PERU
Cusco
Maceió
BOLIVIA
Salvador
Arequipa
La Paz
Santa Cruz
Brasília
Arica
Sucre
Iquique
Belo Horizonte
Chuquicamata
PARAGUAY
Antofagasta
São Paulo
Rio de Janeiro
Asunción
Curitiba
San Miguel de Tucumán
Córdoba
Corrientes
Porto Alegre
Valparaíso
Mendoza
Santa Fe
URUGUAY
Rio Grande
Santiago
Rosario
Montevideo
Buenos Aires
Talca
Concepción
ARGENTINA
Neuquén
Bahía Blanca
Valdivia
PACIFIC OCEAN
ATLANTIC OCEAN
Comodoro Rivadavia
Falkland Islands (to UK)
Punta Arenas
Cape Horn

**GNI per capita (US$)**

- Below 1,000
- 1,000–1,999
- 2,000–2,999
- 3,000–3,999
- 4,000–4,999
- Above 5,000
- Industrial center

**INDUSTRY**

- Aerospace
- Brewing
- Car/vehicle manufacture
- Chemicals
- Coal
- Electronics
- Engineering
- Finance
- Fish processing
- Food processing
- High-tech industry
- Iron and steel
- Metal refining
- Narcotics
- Oil and gas
- Pharmaceuticals
- Printing and publishing
- Shipbuilding
- Textiles
- Timber processing
- Tobacco processing

## CLIMATE

South America has four main climatic regions: tropical, arid, temperate, and the cold climate of the far south. The Amazon Basin, covered by massive rain forests, and the Guiana Highlands have a humid, tropical climate that allows vegetation to flourish. West of the Andes the climate tends to be very dry. Moist air flowing west from the Atlantic Ocean is prevented from reaching the shores of the Pacific Ocean by the Andes, and rain falls before it can pass over the mountains. This creates arid deserts like the Atacama.

### EXTREME WEATHER EVENTS

Symbols indicate climatic extremes

**Wettest place**
QUIBDO (Colombia)
Annual rainfall 354in

**Driest place**
ARICA (Chile)
Annual rainfall 1/4in

**Hottest place**
RIVADAVIA (Argentina)
Temp 120°F

**Coldest place**
SARMIENTO (Argentina)
Temp -27°F

### CLIMATE

- Subarctic
- Cool continental
- Warm temperate
- Semiarid
- Arid
- Temperate
- Tropical
- Humid equatorial

NORTH AMERICA | EUROPE | ASIA | AFRICA | SOUTH AMERICA | AUSTRALASIA and Oceania | ANTARCTICA

### PATAGONIAN ICEFIELDS

Toward the south of the continent, the climate becomes very cold. Large expanses of ice, forming glaciers, are found in southern Patagonia and on islands such as Tierra del Fuego at the tip of South America.

## LAND USE AND AGRICULTURE

Many plants now found throughout the world originated in South America, like the tomato, potato, and cassava. Today, coffee, cocoa, rubber, soybeans, corn, and sugarcane are widely cultivated, and grapes are grown in sheltered valleys in the Andes. Much of the Amazon Basin is covered by dense rain forest and is unsuitable for cultivation, although some farmers practice "slash and burn" techniques to make land for crops and cattle farming, which destroy ancient forest.

### LAND USE AND AGRICULTURE

- Cattle
- Pigs
- Sheep
- Bananas
- Corn
- Citrus fruits
- Coca
- Cocoa
- Cotton
- Coffee
- Fishing
- Oil palms
- Peanuts
- Rubber
- Shellfish
- Soybeans
- Sugarcane
- Vineyards
- Wheat

- Barren land
- Cropland
- Desert
- Forest
- Mountain region
- Pasture
- Wetland
- Major conurbation

### COFFEE

South America, and Brazil in particular, is a major producer of coffee. The plants thrive in the rich red soils of southern Brazil and are grown on huge plantations on the mountain slopes.

### LOCAL MARKETS

At traditional markets such as this one in Ecuador, high in the Andes, local people trade fruit, vegetables, and goods such as clothing, rugs, and blankets. Some goods produced by Ecuadorean Indians are now exported worldwide.

### CATTLE

The vast plains of the Pampas, to the west of Buenos Aires, support large herds of cattle. Meat processing and canning is a major industry in Argentina, Paraguay, and Uruguay.

### NARCOTICS

Coca, grown in forest clearings in remote mountain areas, is used to make the drug cocaine. Government troops burn any coca plants they discover to discourage production.

# NORTHERN SOUTH AMERICA

BRAZIL, COLOMBIA, ECUADOR, GUYANA, PERU, SURINAME, VENEZUELA

High mountains, rain forests, and hot, grassy plains cover much of northern South America. From the 16th century, after the conquest of the Incas, the western countries were ruled by Spain. Brazil was governed by Portugal, Guyana by Britain, and Suriname by the Dutch. The more recent history of some of these countries has included periods of civil war and military rule. Most are still troubled by widespread poverty.

## FARMING AND LAND USE

The variety of climates allows a wide range of crops, including sugarcane, cocoa, and bananas, to be grown for export. Coffee is the most important cash crop; Brazil is the world's leading coffee grower. Cattle are farmed on the plains of Colombia, Venezuela, and southern Brazil. Much of the good farmland is owned by a few rich landowners: many peasant farmers do not have enough land to make a living.

### FARMING AND LAND USE

- Cattle
- Fishing
- Goats
- Sheep
- Bananas
- Cocoa
- Cotton
- Coffee
- Rubber
- Sugarcane
- Timber

Cropland
Forest
Mountain region
Pasture
Wetland
• Major conurbation

LAND USE

Cropland 6%
Other (including mountains) 15%
Pasture 23%
Forest 56%

## INDUSTRY

Important oil reserves are found in Venezuela and parts of the Amazon Basin; Venezuela is one of the world's top oil producers. Brazil's cities have a wide range of industries including chemicals, clothes and shoes, and textiles. Metallic minerals, particularly iron ore, are mined throughout the area and specially built industrial centers like Ciudad Guayana have been developed to refine them.

### STRUCTURE OF INDUSTRY

Primary 11%
Services 50%
Manufacturing 39%

### INDUSTRY

- Chemicals
- Food processing
- Iron and steel
- Metal refining
- Textiles
- Mining
- Oil
- Timber processing
- Tourism
- Major industrial center / area
- Major road

## THE LANDSCAPE

The Andes run down the western side of South America. There are many volcanoes among their peaks and earthquakes are common. The tropical rain forests surrounding the Amazon River take up most of western Brazil. Huge, dry, flat grasslands called *llanos* cover central Venezuela and part of eastern Colombia.

### Angel Falls (D 2)
Venezuela's Angel Falls is the world's highest waterfall. Twenty times as high as Niagara Falls, it drops 3,212 ft from a spectacular plateau deep in the Guiana Highlands.

### Amazon River (D 4)
The Amazon is the longest river in South America, and the second longest in the world. It flows over 4,049 miles from the Peruvian Andes to the coast of Brazil. One-fifth of the world's freshwater is carried by the river.

## POPULATION

Most of the population lives in urban areas. Many cities are extremely overcrowded, with poor housing. São Paulo in Brazil is one of the world's fastest-growing cities. The rain forests of the interior and high Andes are sparsely populated. The few Native American peoples live in remote areas.

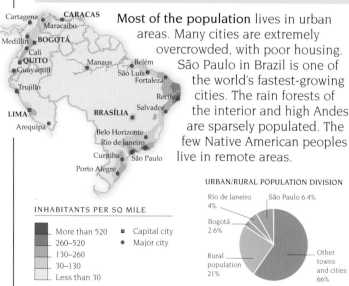

### INHABITANTS PER SQ MILE

- More than 520
- 260–520
- 130–260
- 30–130
- Less than 30
- ■ Capital city
- • Major city

### URBAN/RURAL POPULATION DIVISION

Rio de Janeiro 4%
São Paulo 6.4%
Bogotá 2.6%
Rural population 21%
Other towns and cities 66%

### Andes (B 5)
The snow-capped Andes are the longest mountain range on Earth. They stretch 4,500 miles down the whole length of South America.

### Lake Titicaca (C 6)
South America's largest lake is the highest navigable lake in the world at 12,500 ft above sea level. It lies across the border between Peru and Bolivia.

### Pantanal (E 6)
This is the largest area of wetlands in the world. It spreads across 50,000 sq miles of Brazil. Many hundreds of plant and animal species are found here.

### Amazon rain forest (D 4)
The enormous rain forest surrounding the Amazon River and its tributaries covers 2,510,000 sq miles, an area almost as big as Australia. It is estimated that at least half of all known living species are found in the forest.

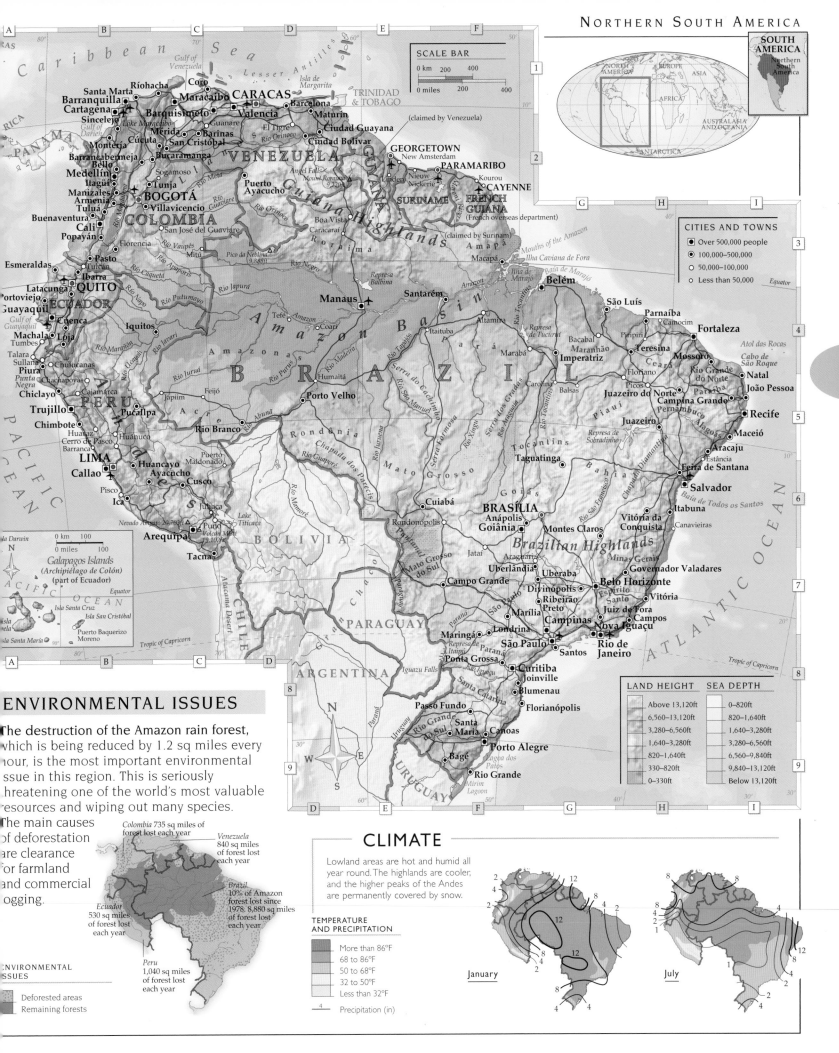

# SOUTHERN SOUTH AMERICA

ARGENTINA, BOLIVIA, CHILE, PARAGUAY, URUGUAY

**The southern half of South America** forms a long, narrow cone, with landscapes ranging from barren desert in the west to frozen glaciers in the far south. The whole area was governed by Spain until the early 19th century, and Spanish is still the main language spoken, although the few remaining Native American groups use their own languages. Most people now live in vast cities such as Buenos Aires and Santiago.

## POPULATION

Since the 1950s, there has been a tremendous move from the countryside to the cities. In Argentina, Chile, and Uruguay more than 85% of the people are now city dwellers. The capital cities of all these countries have grown enormously – Buenos Aires holds a third of Argentina's population, and two fifths of Uruguay's people live in the capital, Montevideo.

**INHABITANTS PER SQ MILE**
- More than 260
- 130–260
- 30–130
- Less than 30
- ■ Capital city
- • Major city

**URBAN/RURAL POPULATION DIVISION**
- Buenos Aires 16.8%
- Santiago 6.4%
- Montevideo 1.8%
- Rural population 17%
- Other towns and cities 58%

## INDUSTRY

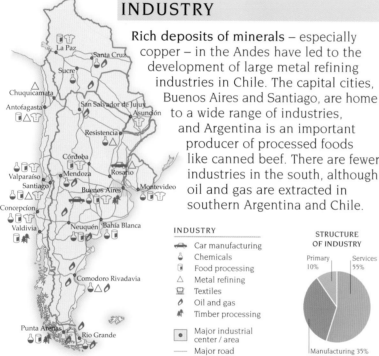

**Rich deposits of minerals** – especially copper – in the Andes have led to the development of large metal refining industries in Chile. The capital cities, Buenos Aires and Santiago, are home to a wide range of industries, and Argentina is an important producer of processed foods like canned beef. There are fewer industries in the south, although oil and gas are extracted in southern Argentina and Chile.

**INDUSTRY**
- 🚗 Car manufacturing
- ⚗ Chemicals
- 🥫 Food processing
- △ Metal refining
- 👕 Textiles
- ◊ Oil and gas
- 🌲 Timber processing
- ▣ Major industrial center / area
- — Major road

**STRUCTURE OF INDUSTRY**
- Primary 10%
- Services 55%
- Manufacturing 35%

## THE LANDSCAPE

**Southern South America's** landscape varies from tropical forest and dry desert in the north to subantarctic conditions in the south. The towering Andes divide Chile from Argentina. East of the Andes lie forests and rolling grasslands. To the west is a thin coastal strip. The wet, windswept, freezing southern tip of the continent has volcanoes alongside glaciers and fjords.

### Gran Chaco (C 3)
This huge stretch of forest and grassland runs from Bolivia, through Paraguay and into Argentina. The south and east provide grazing for cattle.

### Paraná River (C 4)
South America's second-longest river is the Paraná. It stretches 2,485 miles from the Brazilian Highlands, finally flowing into the Plate River near Buenos Aires in Argentina.

### Iguazu Falls (D 4)
The Iguazu River drops 860 ft over the Iguazu Falls. When the river is at its fullest, the water flowing over the falls could fill six Olympic swimming pools every second.

### Atacama Desert (A 3)
The Atacama Desert in northern Chile is the driest place on Earth. In some parts, rain has not fallen for hundreds of years.

### Pampas (B 5)
The grassy plains in central Argentina – known as the Pampas – cover 251,000 sq miles. The western part is semidesert, but the east gets plenty of rain.

### Chile
The far south of Chile has a dramatic landscape of fjords, lakes, jagged mountain peaks, and spectacular glaciers.

### Patagonia (B 8)
The high, windswept plateau of Patagonia covers 297,000 sq miles of southern Argentina. The south is dry and freezing cold, with very little vegetation.

## ENVIRONMENTAL ISSUES

**Many of** southern South America's rivers are polluted, particularly close to Buenos Aires. The Itaipú Dam on the Paraná River is the world's largest hydroelectric power plant. Deforestation is a persistent problem in Bolivia, Paraguay and northern Argentina with 2,320 sq miles cut down every year. Air quality in Buenos Aires and Santiago is poor, especially in Santiago, which is surrounded by mountains, making it difficult for pollution to escape.

**ENVIRONMENTAL ISSUES**
- Major dam
- Urban air pollution
- Deforested areas
- Polluted river
- • Major industrial center

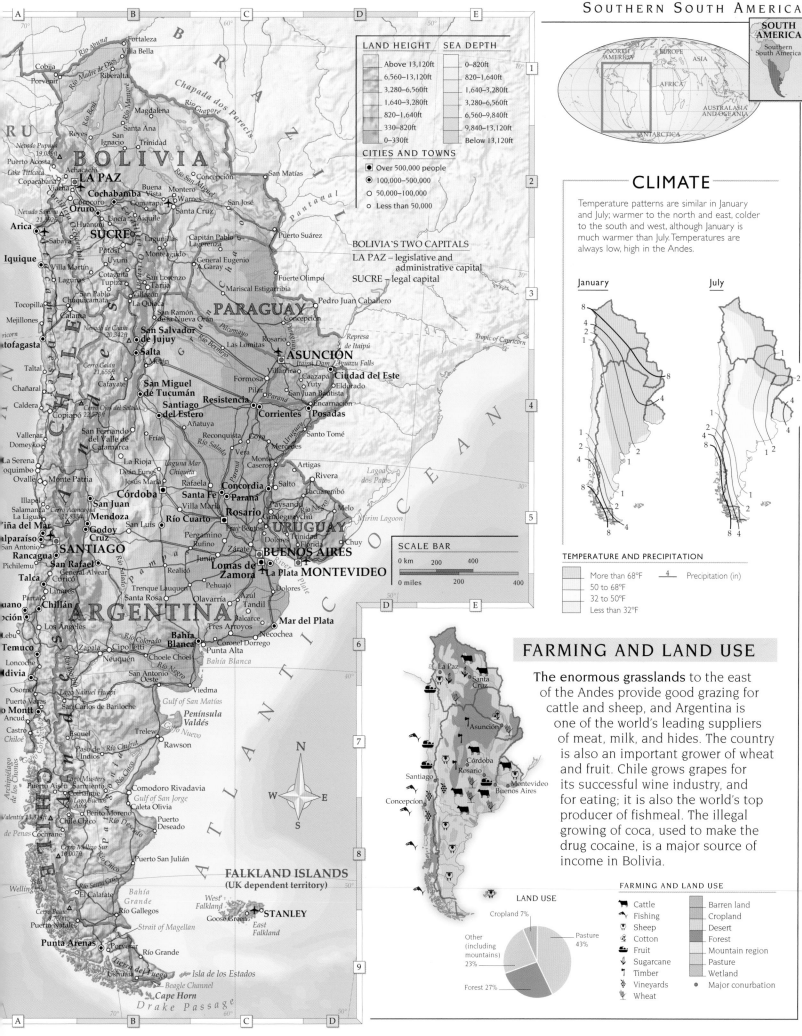

SOUTH
AMERICA
Southern
South America

**LAND HEIGHT**

- Above 13,120ft
- 6,560–13,120ft
- 3,280–6,560ft
- 1,640–3,280ft
- 820–1,640ft
- 330–820ft
- 0–330ft

**SEA DEPTH**

- 0–820ft
- 820–1,640ft
- 1,640–3,280ft
- 3,280–6,560ft
- 6,560–9,840ft
- 9,840–13,120ft
- Below 13,120ft

**CITIES AND TOWNS**

- Over 500,000 people
- 100,000–500,000
- 50,000–100,000
- Less than 50,000

**BOLIVIA'S TWO CAPITALS**

LA PAZ – legislative and
administrative capital

SUCRE – legal capital

## CLIMATE

Temperature patterns are similar in January and July; warmer to the north and east, colder to the south and west, although January is much warmer than July. Temperatures are always low, high in the Andes.

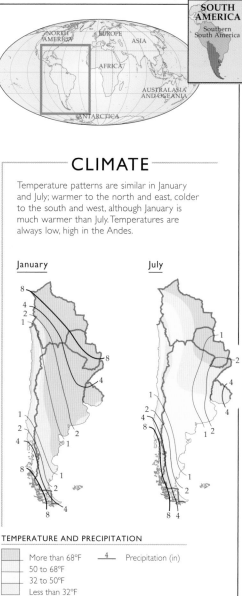

January

July

**TEMPERATURE AND PRECIPITATION**

- More than 68°F
- 50 to 68°F
- 32 to 50°F
- Less than 32°F

4 — Precipitation (in)

**SCALE BAR**

0 km    200    400

0 miles    200    400

## FARMING AND LAND USE

**The enormous grasslands** to the east of the Andes provide good grazing for cattle and sheep, and Argentina is one of the world's leading suppliers of meat, milk, and hides. The country is also an important grower of wheat and fruit. Chile grows grapes for its successful wine industry, and for eating; it is also the world's top producer of fishmeal. The illegal growing of coca, used to make the drug cocaine, is a major source of income in Bolivia.

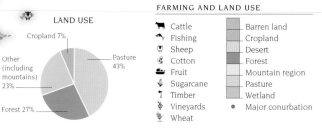

**LAND USE**

- Cropland 7%
- Pasture 43%
- Other (including mountains) 23%
- Forest 27%

**FARMING AND LAND USE**

- Cattle
- Fishing
- Sheep
- Cotton
- Fruit
- Sugarcane
- Timber
- Vineyards
- Wheat

- Barren land
- Cropland
- Desert
- Forest
- Mountain region
- Pasture
- Wetland
- Major conurbation

**FALKLAND ISLANDS**
(UK dependent territory)

# CONTINENTAL AFRICA

4,510 miles
4,737 miles

**Africa is the second-largest** continent in the world. Its dramatic landscapes include arid deserts, humid rain forests, and the valleys of the east African rift – where humans may have first evolved. Today, there are 53 separate countries in Africa, and its people speak a rich variety of languages. The world's highest temperatures have been recorded in Africa's deserts.

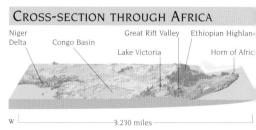

## CROSS-SECTION THROUGH AFRICA

Niger Delta · Congo Basin · Great Rift Valley · Ethiopian Highland · Lake Victoria · Horn of Afric

W — 3,230 miles —

In the west, the Niger River flows into the Atlantic Ocean through the swampy Niger Delta. Farther east is the immense Congo Basin, where the Congo River winds its way through thick rainforests. In the east is the Great Rift Valley and the Ethiopian Highlands. The Horn of Africa is Africa's most easterly point.

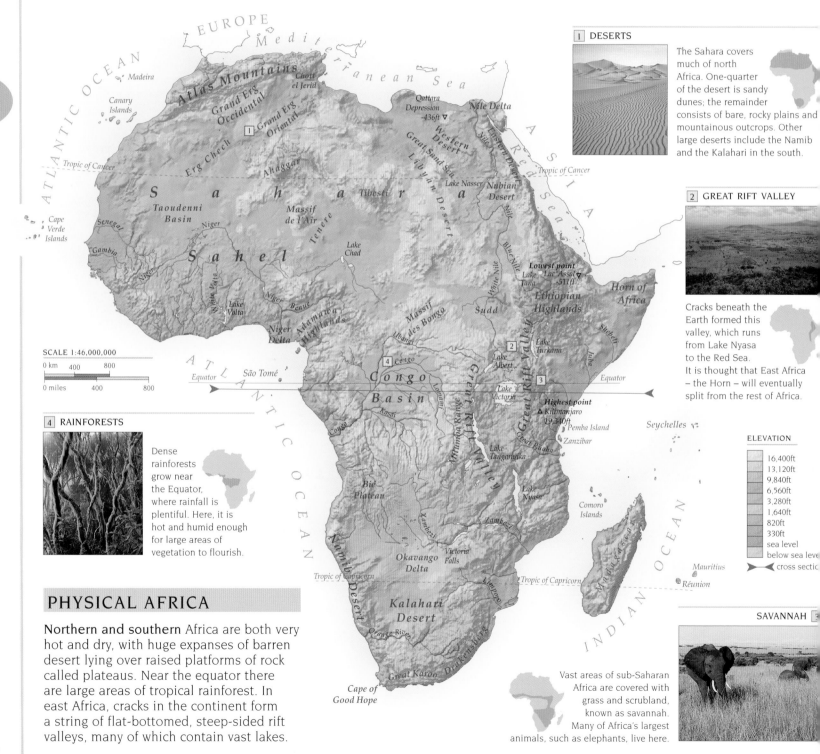

### 1 DESERTS

The Sahara covers much of north Africa. One-quarter of the desert is sandy dunes; the remainder consists of bare, rocky plains and mountainous outcrops. Other large deserts include the Namib and the Kalahari in the south.

### 2 GREAT RIFT VALLEY

Cracks beneath the Earth formed this valley, which runs from Lake Nyasa to the Red Sea. It is thought that East Africa – the Horn – will eventually split from the rest of Africa.

### 4 RAINFORESTS

Dense rainforests grow near the Equator, where rainfall is plentiful. Here, it is hot and humid enough for large areas of vegetation to flourish.

### SAVANNAH

Vast areas of sub-Saharan Africa are covered with grass and scrubland, known as savannah. Many of Africa's largest animals, such as elephants, live here.

SCALE 1:46,000,000

0 km  400  800
0 miles  400  800

**ELEVATION**

16,400ft
13,120ft
9,840ft
6,560ft
3,280ft
1,640ft
820ft
330ft
sea level
below sea leve

⊷ cross sectio

## PHYSICAL AFRICA

**Northern and southern** Africa are both very hot and dry, with huge expanses of barren desert lying over raised platforms of rock called plateaus. Near the equator there are large areas of tropical rainforest. In east Africa, cracks in the continent form a string of flat-bottomed, steep-sided rift valleys, many of which contain vast lakes.

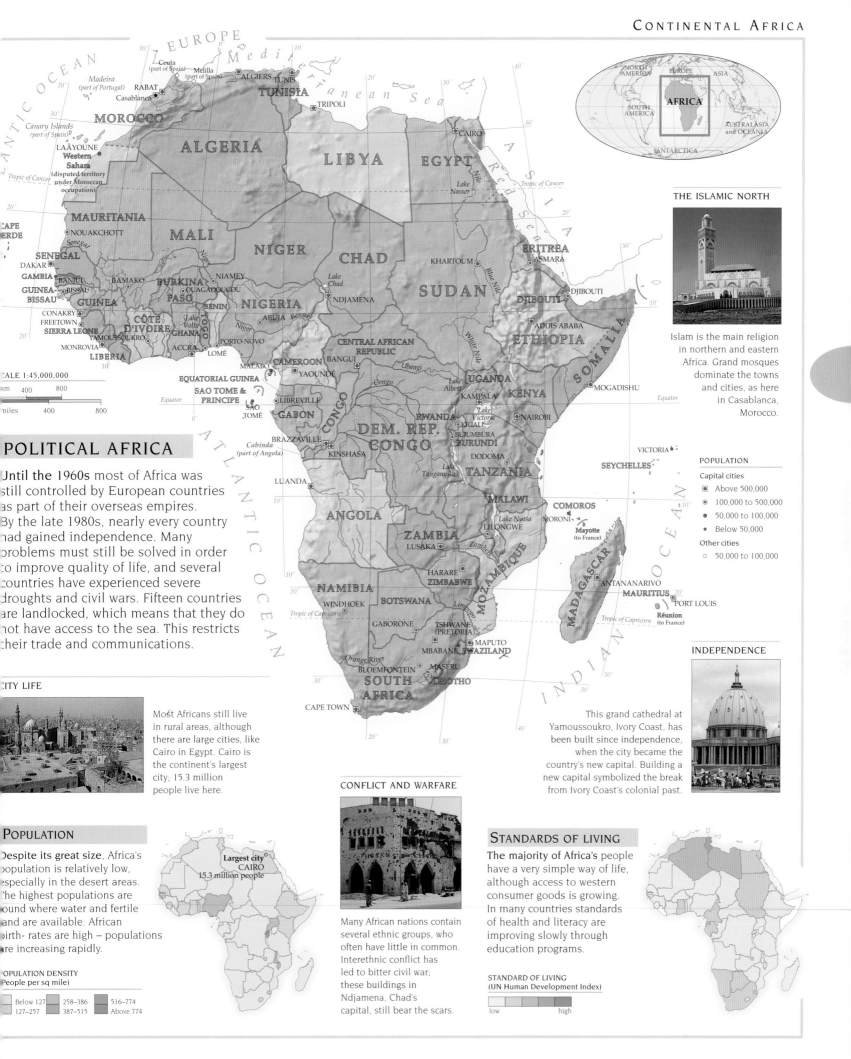

AFRICA

## THE ISLAMIC NORTH

Islam is the main religion in northern and eastern Africa. Grand mosques dominate the towns and cities, as here in Casablanca, Morocco.

# POLITICAL AFRICA

Until the 1960s most of Africa was still controlled by European countries as part of their overseas empires. By the late 1980s, nearly every country had gained independence. Many problems must still be solved in order to improve quality of life, and several countries have experienced severe droughts and civil wars. Fifteen countries are landlocked, which means that they do not have access to the sea. This restricts their trade and communications.

## POPULATION

### Capital cities
- ◉ Above 500,000
- ◉ 100,000 to 500,000
- ▪ 50,000 to 100,000
- ▪ Below 50,000

### Other cities
- ○ 50,000 to 100,000

## CITY LIFE

Most Africans still live in rural areas, although there are large cities, like Cairo in Egypt. Cairo is the continent's largest city; 15.3 million people live here.

## INDEPENDENCE

This grand cathedral at Yamoussoukro, Ivory Coast, has been built since independence, when the city became the country's new capital. Building a new capital symbolized the break from Ivory Coast's colonial past.

## POPULATION

Despite its great size, Africa's population is relatively low, especially in the desert areas. The highest populations are found where water and fertile land are available. African birth-rates are high – populations are increasing rapidly.

Largest city
CAIRO
15.3 million people

### POPULATION DENSITY
(People per sq mile)
- Below 127
- 127–257
- 258–386
- 387–515
- 516–774
- Above 774

## CONFLICT AND WARFARE

Many African nations contain several ethnic groups, who often have little in common. Interethnic conflict has led to bitter civil war; these buildings in Ndjamena, Chad's capital, still bear the scars.

## STANDARDS OF LIVING

The majority of Africa's people have a very simple way of life, although access to western consumer goods is growing. In many countries standards of health and literacy are improving slowly through education programs.

### STANDARD OF LIVING
(UN Human Development Index)
low —— high

# AFRICAN GEOGRAPHY

Africa's massive reserves of minerals, including oil, gold, copper, and diamonds, are among the largest in the world. Mining is a very important industry for many countries and has provided money for growth and development. Many different types of crops can be grown in Africa's wide range of environments. Rubber, bananas, and oil palms are grown for export in the Tropics, and east Africa is especially famous for its tea and coffee.

## INDUSTRY

Most African industries are based on processing raw materials such as food crops or mineral ores. Some African countries depend on one product or crop for most of their income, but in many larger cities different industries are developing. Northern Africa, Nigeria, and South Africa have the widest range of industries.

## MINERAL RESOURCES

The southern countries, in particular South Africa, have large reserves of diamonds, gold, uranium, and copper. The large copper deposits in Dem. Rep. Congo and Zambia are known as the "copper belt." Oil and gas are extracted in Algeria, Angola, Egypt, Libya, and Nigeria.

### MINING

One of the world's largest uranium mines is at Rossing, Namibia. Uranium is used to fuel nuclear power plants, and is also mined in Niger and South Africa.

### MINERAL RESOURCES

- Bauxite
- Copper
- Diamonds
- Iron
- Phosphates
- Gold
- Uranium
- Oil/gas field
- Coal field

### OIL AND GAS

In the desert wastes of Algeria, a drilling rig searches for new sources o oil in the rich north Africar oilfields. There are several large oil fields in the Niger delta and North Africa.

### INDUSTRY

- Brewing
- Car/vehicle manufacturing
- Cement
- Chemicals
- Coal
- Engineering
- Fish processing
- Finance
- Food processing
- Iron & steel
- Mining
- Oil & gas
- Pharmaceuticals
- Shipbuilding
- Textiles
- Timber processing

**GNI per capita (US$)**

- Below 500
- 500-999
- 1,000-1,999
- 2,000-2,999
- 3,000-3,999
- Above 4,000
- Industrial center

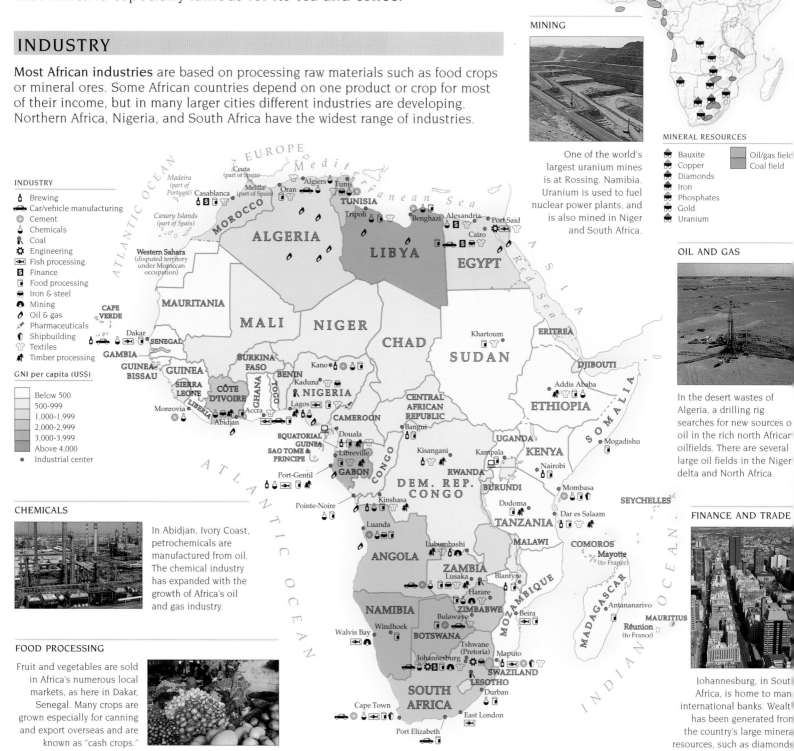

### CHEMICALS

In Abidjan, Ivory Coast, petrochemicals are manufactured from oil. The chemical industry has expanded with the growth of Africa's oil and gas industry.

### FOOD PROCESSING

Fruit and vegetables are sold in Africa's numerous local markets, as here in Dakar, Senegal. Many crops are grown especially for canning and export overseas and are known as "cash crops."

### FINANCE AND TRADE

Johannesburg, in Sout Africa, is home to man international banks. Wealt has been generated from the country's large minera resources, such as diamonds

# CLIMATE

Africa is the world's hottest continent: temperatures of more than 122°F have been recorded in the Sahara. The northern coast has a hot, dry climate with little rainfall. Farther inland, the Sahara is extremely arid, with strong, dry winds. South of the Sahara is the Sahel, where cutting down trees for fuel has turned farmland into desert. Close to the equator there is more rainfall, and huge rain forests can grow in western and central Africa. In the south, the climate is much drier, and drought is a problem.

**EXTREME WEATHER EVENTS**

Symbols indicate climatic extremes

**Coldest place**
IFRANE (Morocco)
Temp. -11°F

**Hottest place**
AL 'AZĪZĪYAH (Libya)
Temp. 136°F

**Driest place**
WADI HALFA (Sudan)
Annual rainfall 1/8in

**Wettest place**
CAPE DEBUNDSHA (Cameroon)
Annual rainfall 405in

Tropic of Cancer

Equator

Tropic of Capricorn

**CLIMATE**
- Warm temparate
- Mediterranean
- Semiarid
- Arid
- Humid equatorial
- Tropical

## THE ENCROACHING DESERT

Africa has three main desert areas: the Sahara in the north and the Namib and Kalahari deserts in the south. They are a mixture of sandy dunes and bare, rocky plateaus. At the desert's edges, low rainfall and land clearance is causing the deserts to expand into areas that were once grassland.

# LAND USE AND AGRICULTURE

The quality of land and the amount of rainfall has a great impact on the type of farming. In the mountain regions of countries such as Rwanda, Uganda, and Kenya, tea and coffee are grown. In the north, there is not enough water to produce staple crops such as wheat for all the population, but "cash crops" such as citrus fruits, dates, and olives are grown for export. Subtropical west Africa grows peanuts, cocoa, and coffee. In the southern part of the continent, South Africa grows many different crops: citrus fruits are grown for export, as well as grapes, which are used to make wine.

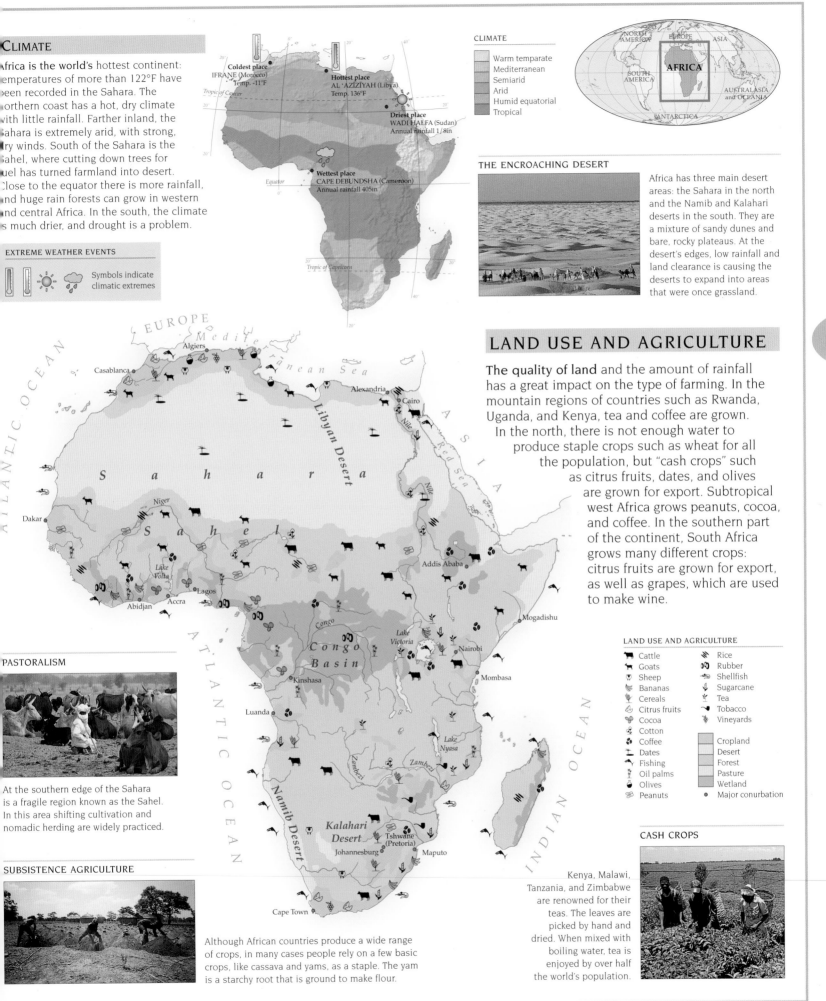

## PASTORALISM

At the southern edge of the Sahara is a fragile region known as the Sahel. In this area shifting cultivation and nomadic herding are widely practiced.

## SUBSISTENCE AGRICULTURE

Although African countries produce a wide range of crops, in many cases people rely on a few basic crops, like cassava and yams, as a staple. The yam is a starchy root that is ground to make flour.

**LAND USE AND AGRICULTURE**
- Cattle
- Goats
- Sheep
- Bananas
- Cereals
- Citrus fruits
- Cocoa
- Cotton
- Coffee
- Dates
- Fishing
- Oil palms
- Olives
- Peanuts
- Rice
- Rubber
- Shellfish
- Sugarcane
- Tea
- Tobacco
- Vineyards
- Cropland
- Desert
- Forest
- Pasture
- Wetland
- Major conurbation

## CASH CROPS

Kenya, Malawi, Tanzania, and Zimbabwe are renowned for their teas. The leaves are picked by hand and dried. When mixed with boiling water, tea is enjoyed by over half the world's population.

121

# NORTH AFRICA

ALGERIA, EGYPT, LIBYA, MOROCCO, TUNISIA.

**Sandwiched between** the Mediterranean and the Sahara, North Africa has a history dating back to the dawn of civilization. About 6,000 years ago, settlements were established along the banks of the Nile River. Since then, waves of settlers, including Romans, Arabs, and Turks, have brought a mix of different cultures to the area. In the 19th century, Spain, France, and Britain claimed colonies in the region, but today North Africa is independent, although Western Sahara is occupied by Morocco.

## FARMING AND LAND USE

Most farming in North Africa is restricted to the fertile Mediterranean coastal strip, and the banks of the Nile where it relies heavily on irrigation. In spite of these seemingly inhospitable conditions, the region is a major producer of dates, which grow in desert oases, and of cork, made from the bark of the cork oak tree. A wide variety of other crops is also grown, including grapes, olives, and cotton.

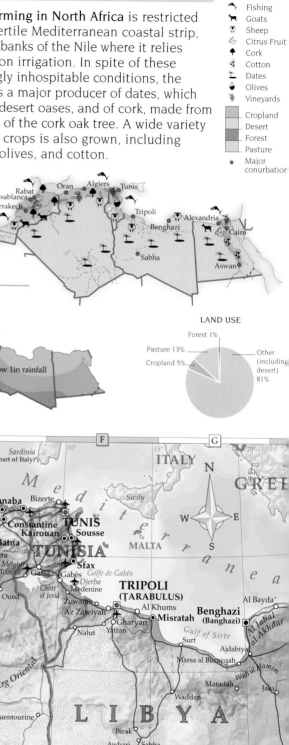

FARMING AND LAND USE

- Fishing
- Goats
- Sheep
- Citrus Fruit
- Cork
- Cotton
- Dates
- Olives
- Vineyards
- Cropland
- Desert
- Forest
- Pasture
- Major conurbation

## CLIMATE

Most of north Africa is desert, and the climate is harsh. Rainfall is scarce, and drought is common. Temperatures are freezing at night, scorching by day and have been known to climb to over 120°F.

January

July

whole area has below 1in rainfall

LAND USE

Forest 1%
Pasture 13%
Cropland 5%
Other (including desert) 81%

TEMPERATURE AND PRECIPITATION

- More than 95°F
- 86 to 95°F
- 77 to 86°F
- 68 to 77°F
- 59 to 68°F
- 50 to 59°F
- 41 to 50°F
- Less than 41°F
- 4 — Precipitation (in)

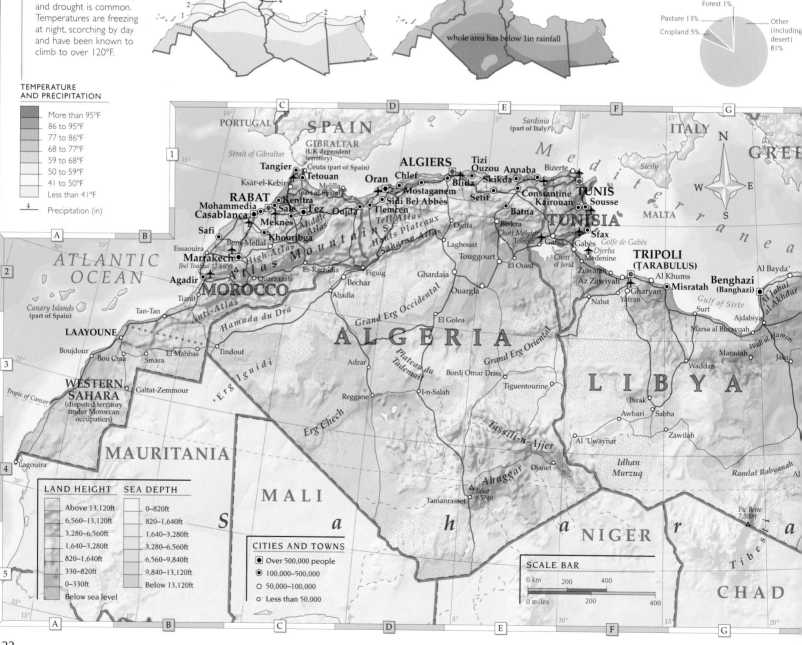

LAND HEIGHT
- Above 13,120ft
- 6,560–13,120ft
- 3,280–6,560ft
- 1,640–3,280ft
- 820–1,640ft
- 330–820ft
- 0–330ft
- Below sea level

SEA DEPTH
- 0–820ft
- 820–1,640ft
- 1,640–3,280ft
- 3,280–6,560ft
- 6,560–9,840ft
- 9,840–13,120ft
- Below 13,120ft

CITIES AND TOWNS
- Over 500,000 people
- 100,000–500,000
- 50,000–100,000
- Less than 50,000

SCALE BAR

0 km   200   400
0 miles   200   400

122

# POPULATION

The majority of the population, and all of the big towns and cities, are found on the coastal plains, or along the banks of the Nile – about 99% of Egyptians live along the river. Egypt's capital, Cairo, is Africa's largest city, with over 15 million people. Western Sahara and the southern portions of Egypt, Algeria, and Libya are sparsely populated by Tuareg nomads who roam the desert.

INHABITANTS PER SQ MILE

More than 520
260–520
130–260
30–130
Less than 30

- Capital city
- Major city

URBAN/RURAL POPULATION DIVISION

Alexandria 2.2%  Cairo 4.5%
Casablanca 2%
Rural population 46%
Other towns and cities 45.3%

# THE LANDSCAPE

The parched rocks and endless sandy expanses of the Sahara occupy much of North Africa. The only major river here is the Nile, with a delta that extends into the Mediterranean Sea. The old, eroded Atlas Mountains are the highest mountain range.

### Sand dunes
Winds blowing across the Sahara cause the sand to build up into dunes which can reach heights of up to 1,411 ft.

### Nile Delta (I 2)
As the Nile River nears the Mediterranean, it separates into many small streams, which flow over a fertile triangle of land. Mud and rock carried by the river and deposited in the delta have formed new land.

### Red Sea (J 3)
The Red Sea gets its name from red algae that live on the sea floor and make the water appear red.

### Atlas Mountains (C 2)
The Atlas Mountains are made up of a number of different ranges – the Anti-Atlas, High Atlas, Middle Atlas, Tell Atlas, and Saharan Atlas. They stretch some 1,400 miles from the north of Tunisia to the Atlantic coast of Morocco.

### Qattara Depression (I 3)
In the northwest of Egypt is a huge desert depression 200 miles long and 75 miles wide. Its floor, part of which is 440 ft below sea level, is covered with sand, brackish ponds and salt marshes.

### Nile River (I 3)
The world's longest river flows 4,160 miles to the Mediterranean Sea. The system of rivers and lakes that flow into the Nile drain some 1,100,000 sq miles – about 10% of the entire African continent.

# INDUSTRY

Oil and natural gas have brought wealth to the area, particularly to Libya, which has enough oil reserves to last into the middle of this century. Textile manufacture is widespread – North Africa is famous for its exotic cloths and rugs. Several large chemical refineries and steel plants have been established along the coast, especially in the major industrial cities like Alexandria and Cairo in Egypt.

STRUCTURE OF INDUSTRY

Primary 16%
Services 44%
Manufacturing 40%

INDUSTRY

- Chemicals
- Food processing
- Iron and steel
- Textiles
- Oil and gas
- Tourism
- Major industrial center / area
- Major road

# ENVIRONMENTAL ISSUES

Droughts, overgrazing, and the stripping of vegetation for firewood and animal food have caused the Sahara to expand northward. This has reduced the already limited amount of land available for farming. The risk of desertification is acute in many coastal areas. North Africa is very dry, and there are severe droughts periodically. Many of the larger cities like Alexandria and Cairo have very poor air quality.

ENVIRONMENTAL ISSUES

- Drought
- Urban air pollution
- Existing desert
- Risk of desertification
- Severe risk of desertification
- Unaffected area
- Major industrial center

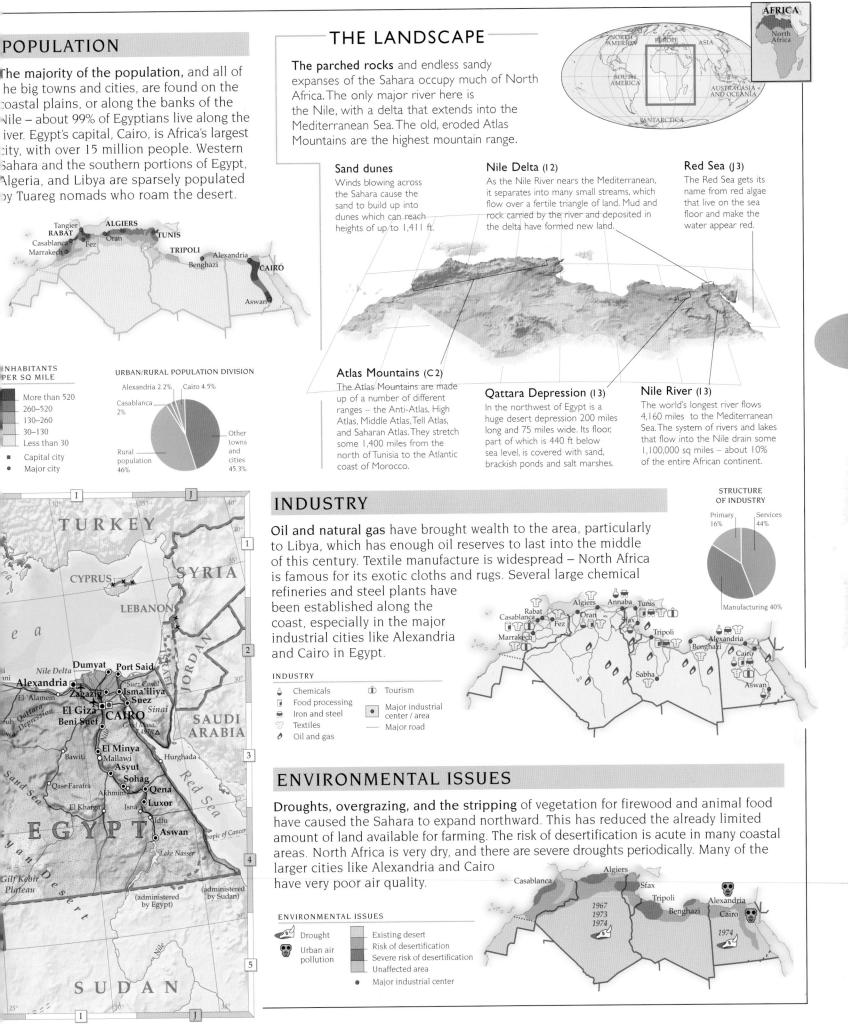

123

# WEST AFRICA

BENIN, BURKINA FASO, CAMEROON, CENTRAL AFRICAN REPUBLIC, CHAD, CÔTE D'IVOIRE, EQUATORIAL GUINEA, GAMBIA, GHANA, GUINEA, GUINEA-BISSAU, LIBERIA, MALI, MAURITANIA, NIGER, NIGERIA, SAO TOME & PRINCIPE, SENEGAL, SIERRA LEONE, TOGO

**West Africa's** varied climate and agricultural and mineral wealth have provided the foundation for some of Africa's greatest civilizations, like those of the Malinke and Asante people. The area remains ethnically and culturally diverse today as well as densely populated. Nigeria is the most populous country in Africa. Since independence from European colonial powers in the 1960s, political instability has been a reality for many countries here.

## INDUSTRY

**Agricultural products** still form the basis of most economies in West Africa. Food processing is widespread – oil palms and peanuts are processed for their valuable vegetable oils. Oil and gas are found off the coast of Côte D'Ivoire and around the Niger delta, where a large chemical industry has developed.

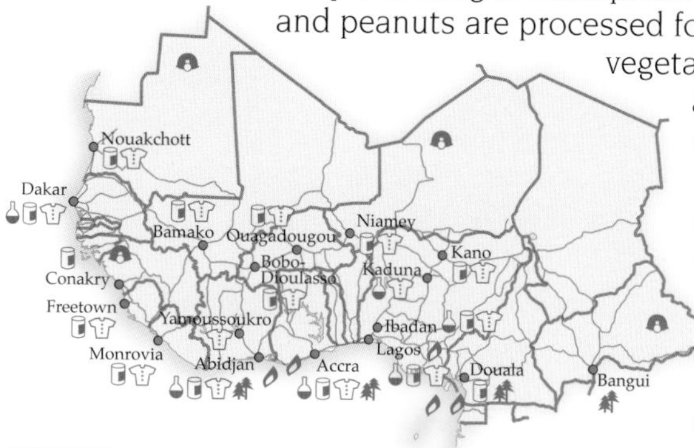

**INDUSTRY**
- Chemicals
- Food processing
- Textiles
- Timber
- Mining
- Oil and gas
- Major industrial center / area
- Major road

STRUCTURE OF INDUSTRY
- Primary 34%
- Manufacturing 30%
- Services 36%

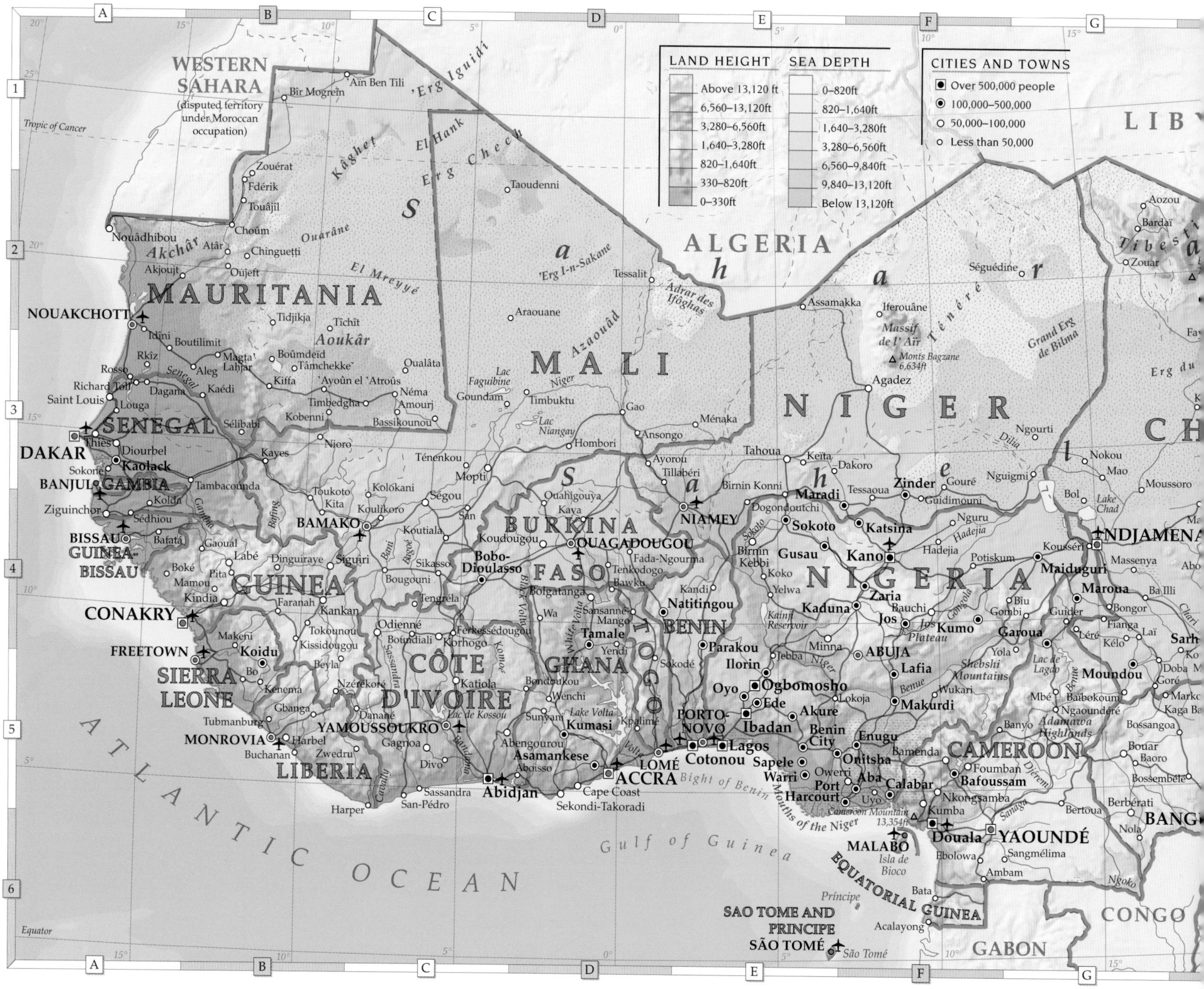

### Map

LAND HEIGHT
- Above 13,120 ft
- 6,560–13,120ft
- 3,280–6,560ft
- 1,640–3,280ft
- 820–1,640ft
- 330–820ft
- 0–330ft

SEA DEPTH
- 0–820ft
- 820–1,640ft
- 1,640–3,280ft
- 3,280–6,560ft
- 6,560–9,840ft
- 9,840–13,120ft
- Below 13,120ft

CITIES AND TOWNS
- Over 500,000 people
- 100,000–500,000
- 50,000–100,000
- Less than 50,000

WESTERN SAHARA (disputed territory under Moroccan occupation)

Tropic of Cancer

ALGERIA
LIBYA
MAURITANIA
MALI
NIGER
NOUAKCHOTT
DAKAR
SENEGAL
GAMBIA
BANJUL
GUINEA-BISSAU
BISSAU
GUINEA
CONAKRY
SIERRA LEONE
FREETOWN
LIBERIA
MONROVIA
CÔTE D'IVOIRE
YAMOUSSOUKRO
ABIDJAN
BURKINA FASO
OUAGADOUGOU
GHANA
ACCRA
TOGO
LOMÉ
BENIN
PORTO-NOVO
NIGERIA
ABUJA
LAGOS
CAMEROON
YAOUNDÉ
DOUALA
MALABO
EQUATORIAL GUINEA
SAO TOME AND PRINCIPE
SÃO TOMÉ
GABON
CONGO
NDJAMENA

ATLANTIC OCEAN

Gulf of Guinea

Equator

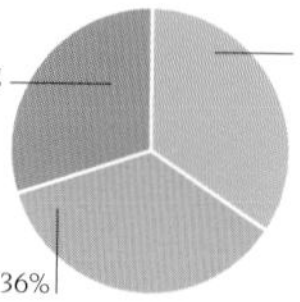

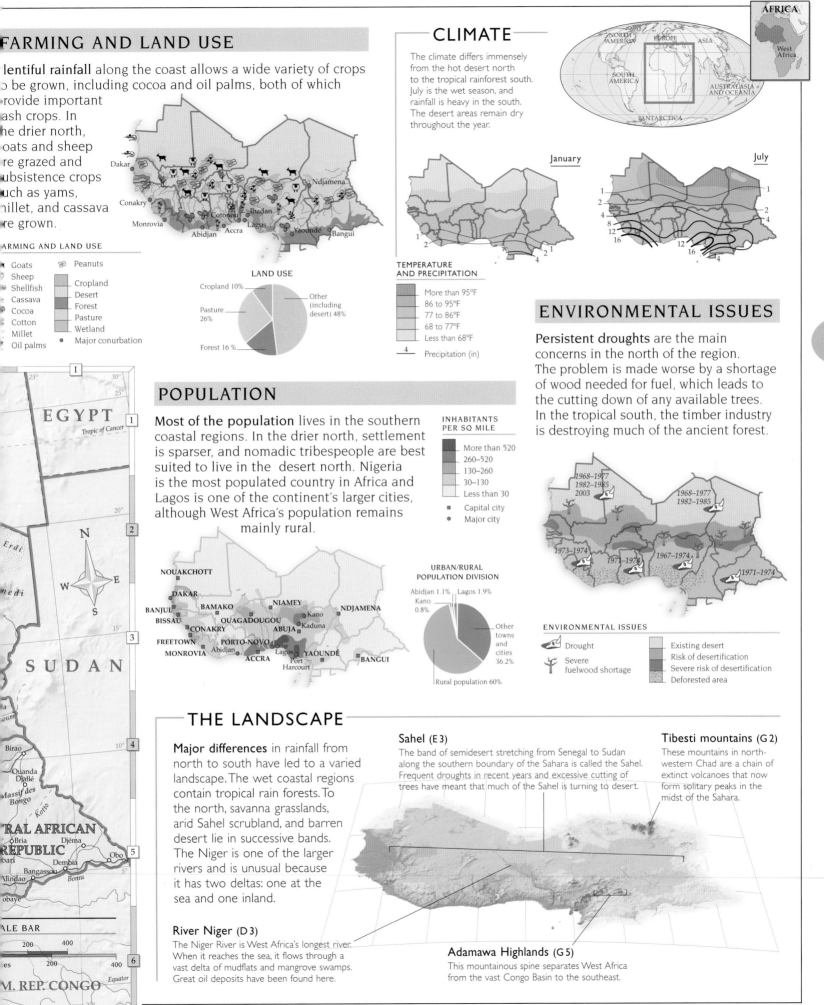

AFRICA
West Africa

# FARMING AND LAND USE

lentiful rainfall along the coast allows a wide variety of crops
o be grown, including cocoa and oil palms, both of which
rovide important
ash crops. In
he drier north,
oats and sheep
re grazed and
ubsistence crops
uch as yams,
illet, and cassava
re grown.

Dakar
Conakry
Monrovia
Abidjan
Cotonou
Accra
Ibadan
Lagos
Ndjamena
Yaoundé
Bangui

## ARMING AND LAND USE

- Goats
- Sheep
- Shellfish
- Cassava
- Cocoa
- Cotton
- Millet
- Oil palms

- Peanuts
- Cropland
- Desert
- Forest
- Pasture
- Wetland
- Major conurbation

### LAND USE

Cropland 10%
Pasture 26%
Forest 16 %
Other (including desert) 48%

# CLIMATE

The climate differs immensely
from the hot desert north
to the tropical rainforest south.
July is the wet season, and
rainfall is heavy in the south.
The desert areas remain dry
throughout the year.

NORTH AMERICA
EUROPE
ASIA
SOUTH AMERICA
AUSTRALASIA AND OCEANIA
ANTARCTICA

January

July

### TEMPERATURE AND PRECIPITATION

- More than 95°F
- 86 to 95°F
- 77 to 86°F
- 68 to 77°F
- Less than 68°F
- 4 — Precipitation (in)

# POPULATION

Most of the population lives in the southern
coastal regions. In the drier north, settlement
is sparser, and nomadic tribespeople are best
suited to live in the desert north. Nigeria
is the most populated country in Africa and
Lagos is one of the continent's larger cities,
although West Africa's population remains
mainly rural.

### INHABITANTS PER SQ MILE

- More than 520
- 260–520
- 130–260
- 30–130
- Less than 30
- Capital city
- Major city

NOUAKCHOTT
DAKAR
BANJUL
BISSAU
BAMAKO
CONAKRY
FREETOWN
MONROVIA
OUAGADOUGOU
NIAMEY
Kano
Kaduna
ABUJA
PORTO-NOVO
Abidjan
ACCRA
Lagos
Port Harcourt
YAOUNDÉ
NDJAMENA
BANGUI

### URBAN/RURAL POPULATION DIVISION

Abidjan 1.1%
Lagos 1.9%
Kano 0.8%
Other towns and cities 36.2%
Rural population 60%

# ENVIRONMENTAL ISSUES

Persistent droughts are the main
concerns in the north of the region.
The problem is made worse by a shortage
of wood needed for fuel, which leads to
the cutting down of any available trees.
In the tropical south, the timber industry
is destroying much of the ancient forest.

1968–1977
1982–1985
2003
1968–1977
1982–1985
1973–1974
1971–1974
1967–1974
1971–1974

### ENVIRONMENTAL ISSUES

- Drought
- Severe fuelwood shortage
- Existing desert
- Risk of desertification
- Severe risk of desertification
- Deforested area

EGYPT
Tropic of Cancer
SUDAN
RAL AFRICAN REPUBLIC
M. REP. CONGO
Equator

25°
30°
20°
15°
10°
5°

Erdi
nedi
Birao
Quanda Diallé
Massif des Bongo
Bria
Djéma
bari
Dembia
Obo
Bangassou
Bonnu
Alindao
obaye

ALE BAR
200    400
200    400
es

N    W    E    S

# THE LANDSCAPE

Major differences in rainfall from
north to south have led to a varied
landscape. The wet coastal regions
contain tropical rain forests. To
the north, savanna grasslands,
arid Sahel scrubland, and barren
desert lie in successive bands.
The Niger is one of the larger
rivers and is unusual because
it has two deltas: one at the
sea and one inland.

## Sahel (E 3)
The band of semidesert stretching from Senegal to Sudan
along the southern boundary of the Sahara is called the Sahel.
Frequent droughts in recent years and excessive cutting of
trees have meant that much of the Sahel is turning to desert.

## Tibesti mountains (G 2)
These mountains in north-
western Chad are a chain of
extinct volcanoes that now
form solitary peaks in the
midst of the Sahara.

## River Niger (D 3)
The Niger River is West Africa's longest river.
When it reaches the sea, it flows through a
vast delta of mudflats and mangrove swamps.
Great oil deposits have been found here.

## Adamawa Highlands (G 5)
This mountainous spine separates West Africa
from the vast Congo Basin to the southeast.

# EAST AFRICA

BURUNDI, DJIBOUTI, ERITREA, ETHIOPIA, KENYA, RWANDA, SOMALIA, SUDAN, TANZANIA, UGANDA

**Much of East Africa** is covered by long grass, scrub, and scattered trees, called savanna. This land is grazed by both domestic animals and a great variety of wild animals including lions, giraffes and elephants. The east of the region is known as the Horn of Africa, because it is shaped like an animal horn. Sudan, and the other countries there have recently been devastated by civil wars, and periods of drought and famine. In contrast, Kenya in the south is more stable but still has to battle with corruption.

## INDUSTRY

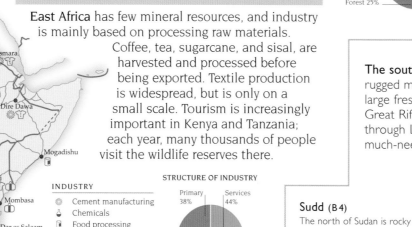

**East Africa** has few mineral resources, and industry is mainly based on processing raw materials. Coffee, tea, sugarcane, and sisal, are harvested and processed before being exported. Textile production is widespread, but is only on a small scale. Tourism is increasingly important in Kenya and Tanzania; each year, many thousands of people visit the wildlife reserves there.

### INDUSTRY

- ⚙ Cement manufacturing
- ⚗ Chemicals
- 🗄 Food processing
- 👕 Textiles
- 🎦 Tourism

- ▣ Major industrial center / area
- — Major road

### STRUCTURE OF INDUSTRY

Primary 38%
Services 44%
Manufacturing 18%

## ENVIRONMENTAL ISSUES

**Rapid population growth** has created a need for increasing amounts of land for farming. This, in addition to the need for firewood, has led to tree cover being stripped, allowing the soil to be washed or blown away. Over the past 30 years, East Africa has been stricken by many catastrophic droughts that have made desertification worse, and brought much human suffering.

### ENVIRONMENTAL ISSUES

- 🐟 Drought
- 🌳 Severe firewood shortage
- ▢ Existing desert
- ▢ Risk of desertification
- ▢ Severe risk of desertification

## FARMING AND LAND USE

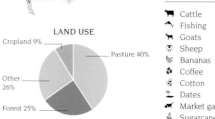

**Much of the north** and east is too dry for farming, but in Sudan, cotton is grown on land irrigated by the Nile River. The Lake Victoria basin and rich volcanic soils of the highlands in Kenya, Uganda, and Tanzania support staple food crops, and those grown for export, such as tea and coffee. Kenya also grows high-quality vegetables, like mangetout, and exports them by air to supermarkets abroad. Sheep, goats, and cattle are herded on the savanna.

### LAND USE

Cropland 9%
Pasture 40%
Other 26%
Forest 25%

### FARMING AND LAND USE

- 🐄 Cattle
- 🎣 Fishing
- 🐐 Goats
- 🐑 Sheep
- 🍌 Bananas
- ☕ Coffee
- 🌿 Cotton
- 🌴 Dates
- Market gardening
- Sugarcane
- Sisal
- Tea

- ▢ Cropland
- ▢ Desert
- ▢ Forest
- ▢ Pasture
- ▢ Wetland
- ● Major conurbation

## THE LANDSCAPE

**The south of East Africa** is savanna grassland, broken by the rugged mountains — some of them active volcanoes — and large fresh and saltwater lakes that make up part of the Great Rift Valley. The Nile River has its source here, flowing through Lakes Victoria, Kyoga, and Albert as it takes much-needed water to the arid desert areas in the north.

### Great Rift Valley (D 6) (D 4)
The Great Rift Valley is like a deep scar running 4,300 miles from north to south through East Africa. It has been formed by the movements of two of the Earth's plates over millions of years. If these movements continue East Africa may eventually become an island, separated by the ocean from the rest of the continent.

### Sudd (B 4)
The north of Sudan is rocky desert, but in the south, the waters of the White Nile run into a swampy area called the Sudd where much of its water disperses and evaporates.

### Juba River (E 5)
This river rises in the highlands of Ethiopia and flows some 750 miles southwards to the Indian Ocean. It, and the Shebeli River, which joins it about 19 miles from the coast, are the only permanent rivers in Somalia.

### Lake Victoria (C 5)
Lake Victoria is Africa's largest lake and the second largest freshwater lake in the world. It lies on the equator, between Kenya, Tanzania and Uganda, and covers 26,560 sq miles. Its only outlet is the Nile River in the north.

### Kilimanjaro (D 6)
This old volcano, made up of alternating layers of lava and ash, is Africa's highest mountain, rising to 19,341 ft. Although it lies only three degrees from the Equator, its peak is permanently covered with snow.

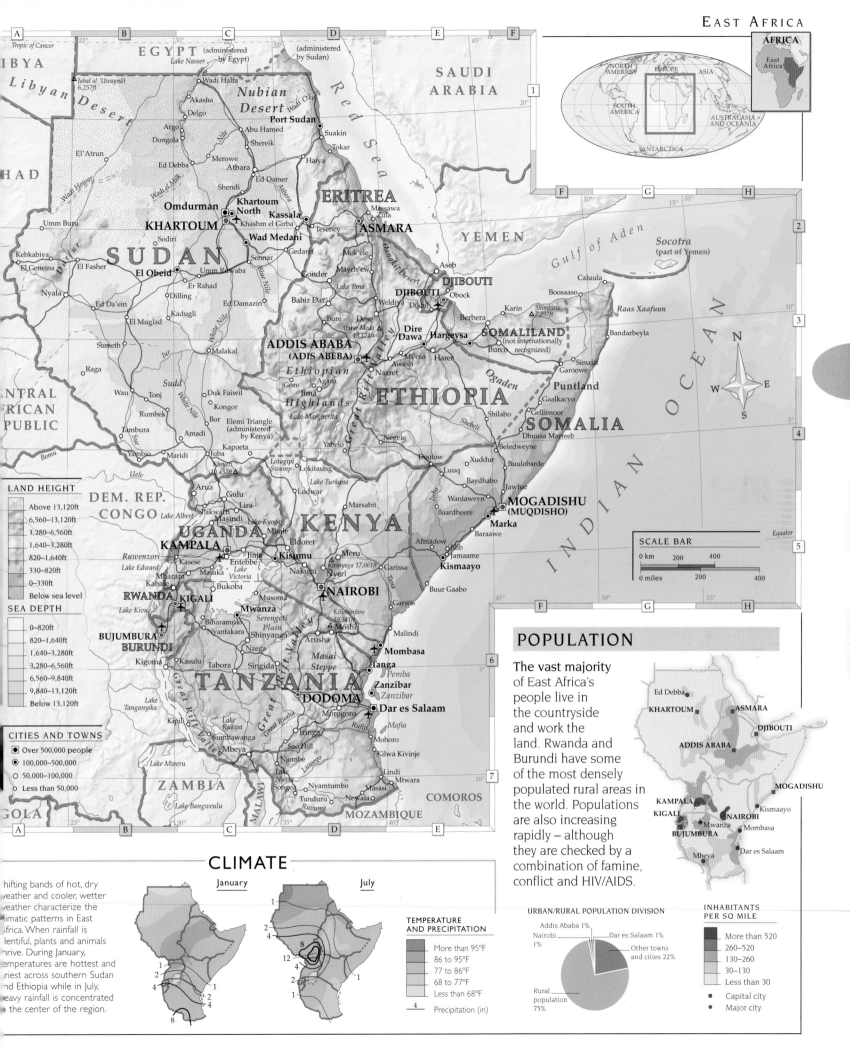

AFRICA
East Africa

# LAND HEIGHT
- Above 13,120ft
- 6,560–13,120ft
- 3,280–6,560ft
- 1,640–3,280ft
- 820–1,640ft
- 330–820ft
- 0–330ft
- Below sea level

## SEA DEPTH
- 0–820ft
- 820–1,640ft
- 1,640–3,280ft
- 3,280–6,560ft
- 6,560–9,840ft
- 9,840–13,120ft
- Below 13,120ft

## CITIES AND TOWNS
- Over 500,000 people
- 100,000–500,000
- 50,000–100,000
- Less than 50,000

## SCALE BAR
0 km   200   400
0 miles   200   400

# POPULATION

The vast majority of East Africa's people live in the countryside and work the land. Rwanda and Burundi have some of the most densely populated rural areas in the world. Populations are also increasing rapidly – although they are checked by a combination of famine, conflict and HIV/AIDS.

## INHABITANTS PER SQ MILE
- More than 520
- 260–520
- 130–260
- 30–130
- Less than 30
- ■ Capital city
- ● Major city

# CLIMATE

hifting bands of hot, dry weather and cooler, wetter weather characterize the limatic patterns in East frica. When rainfall is plentiful, plants and animals rive. During January, emperatures are hottest and riest across southern Sudan nd Ethiopia while in July, eavy rainfall is concentrated the center of the region.

January

July

## TEMPERATURE AND PRECIPITATION
- More than 95°F
- 86 to 95°F
- 77 to 86°F
- 68 to 77°F
- Less than 68°F
- —4— Precipitation (in)

## URBAN/RURAL POPULATION DIVISION
- Addis Ababa 1%
- Nairobi 1%
- Dar es Salaam 1%
- Other towns and cities 22%
- Rural population 75%

# SOUTHERN AFRICA

ANGOLA, BOTSWANA, COMOROS, CONGO, DEM. REP. CONGO (ZAIRE), GABON, LESOTHO, MADAGASCAR, MALAWI, MOZAMBIQUE, NAMIBIA, SOUTH AFRICA, SWAZILAND, ZAMBIA, ZIMBABWE

**Southern Africa** contains the richest deposits of valuable minerals on the continent. South Africa is the wealthiest and most industrialized country in the region. Most of the surrounding countries rely on it for trade and work. Racial segregation under apartheid operated from 1948 until 1994, when South Africa held its first multiracial elections.

## FARMING AND LAND USE

**Most of southern Africa's** farmers grow just enough food to feed their families, although much of the farmland is in the hands of a few wealthy landowners. In the tropical north, oil palms and rubber are grown on large commercial plantations. Fruits are cultivated in the south, and tea and coffee are important in the east. Cattle farming is widespread across the dry grasslands.

FARMING AND LAND USE

Cattle
Fishing
Cocoa
Coffee
Cotton
Fruit
Maize
Oil palms
Rubber
Tea
Timber
Vineyard

Cropland
Desert
Forest
Pasture
Wetland

Major conurbation

LAND USE

Cropland 5%
Other 17%
Pasture 38
Forest 40%

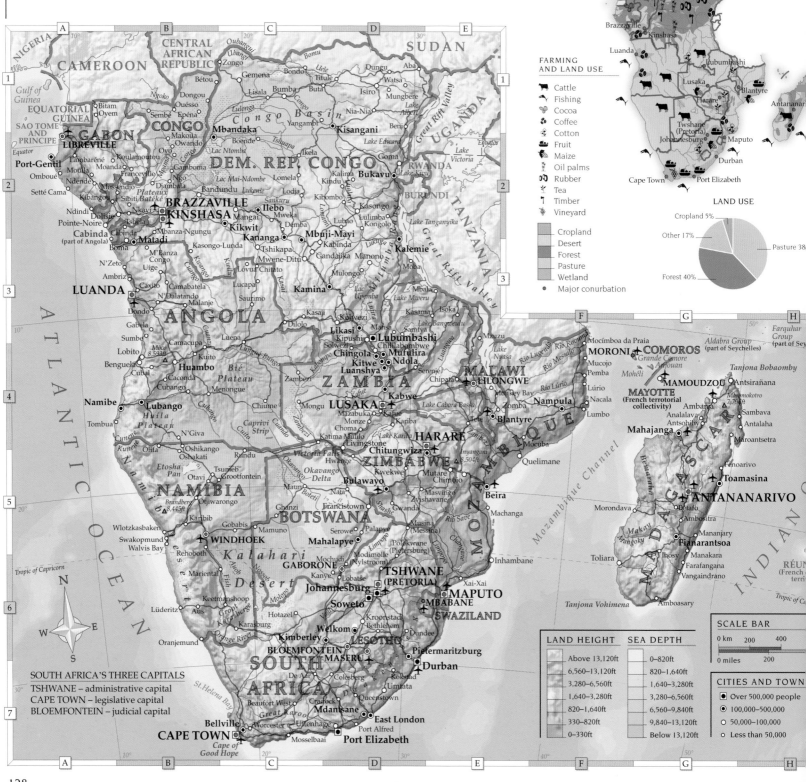

SOUTH AFRICA'S THREE CAPITALS
TSHWANE – administrative capital
CAPE TOWN – legislative capital
BLOEMFONTEIN – judicial capital

| LAND HEIGHT | SEA DEPTH |
|---|---|
| Above 13,120ft | 0–820ft |
| 6,560–13,120ft | 820–1,640ft |
| 3,280–6,560ft | 1,640–3,280ft |
| 1,640–3,280ft | 3,280–6,560ft |
| 820–1,640ft | 6,560–9,840ft |
| 330–820ft | 9,840–13,120ft |
| 0–330ft | Below 13,120ft |

SCALE BAR
0 km    200    400
0 miles    200

CITIES AND TOWN
Over 500,000 people
100,000–500,000
50,000–100,000
Less than 50,000

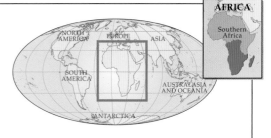

## CLIMATE

During January, temperatures are highest in the Kalahari Desert and rainfall is plentiful in the center of southern Africa. July is cooler and drier, with rainfall concentrated in the north of Dem. Rep. Congo (Zaire). The Atlantic coast of Namibia receives little rain all year round.

January / July

- More than 95°F
- 86 to 95°F
- 77 to 86°F
- 68 to 77°F
- 59 to 68°F
- Less than 59°F
- 4 — Precipitation (in)

## ENVIRONMENTAL ISSUES

he immense rainforests of the Congo Basin in the north emain relatively untouched, but deforestation is beginning to occur at its edges, with much more forest due to be cleared in the future. Large parts of Madagascar have also been deforested. Farther south, occasional drought and the clearing of bushlands for firewood can cause soil loss.

Congo Basin

1991–1992 2000–2002 2005
1971–1974 1979–1985 1991–1992 2002, 2005
1982–1984, 1992 1997–1998, 2001
1983–1985 1992–1993 2002–2003
1983 1985 2005

### ENVIRONMENTAL ISSUES

- Drought
- Severe firewood shortage
- Existing desert
- Risk of desertification
- Severe risk of desertification
- Deforested area
- Remaining tropical forest

## THE LANDSCAPE

outhern Africa stretches from just north of the quator down to the southern tip of the continent. It is n area with an extremely varied climate and geography. n the north are the tropical rainforests of the Congo asin, while arid desert covers much of the southwest. he eastern regions are mostly grasslands, with lush egetation found on the tropical coast of Mozambique.

### Congo Basin (C 1)
he Congo River s Africa's second ongest river, owing in an rc through the ense tropical orests of the Congo Basin before mptying into the tlantic Ocean.

### Namib Desert (B 5)
he Namib is one f the world's driest eserts. The only water receives is from mists hat roll in from the ea. Where the desert neets the coast is nown as the Skeleton Coast because of sailors vho were shipwrecked nd died there.

### Okavango Delta (C 5)
The Okavango River terminates in the Kalahari Desert, forming a vast, swampy inland delta.

### Victoria Falls (D 5)
On its way to the Indian Ocean, the Zambezi River plunges over a 420 ft cliff, into a narrow chasm. The resultant spray rises up to 1,600 ft, and the thunder of the water can be heard up to 25 miles away.

### Madagascar (G 5)
The world's fourth largest island lies in isolation 155 miles off the east coast of southern Africa. It became separated from the African continent 135 million years ago, and its plant and animal life are unique. The rich biodiversity of the rain forests is being threatened by uncontrolled lumbering.

### Drakensberg (D 4)
The Drakensberg are a chain of mountains that lie at the edge of a broad plateau that has tilted because of the movement of the Earth's plates. Rivers have carved through the high mountains, creating dramatic gorges and waterfalls.

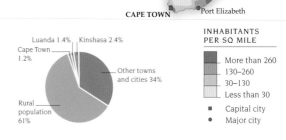

## INDUSTRY

Southern Africa has extraordinary mineral resources. Angola has large deposits of oil, and diamonds are found in Angola, Botswana, Namibia, and South Africa. Copper is mined in the region known as the "copper belt," that runs from Dem. Rep. Congo (Zaire) into Zambia. South Africa is the world's largest gold producer. Manufacturing, such as fruit canning and steel production, is most developed in South Africa.

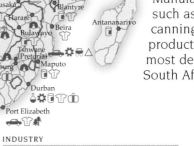 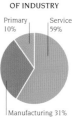

### INDUSTRY
- Car manufacturing
- Chemicals
- Engineering
- Food processing
- Iron and steel
- Metal refining
- Textiles
- Oil and gas
- Mining
- Timber processing
- Tourism
- Major industrial center / area
- Major road

### STRUCTURE OF INDUSTRY
Primary 10%
Services 59%
Manufacturing 31%

## POPULATION

The population is still mostly rural with two thirds of southern Africa's residents living in the countryside. Dense tropical rainforest in the north and arid desert in the southwest have kept habitation to a bare minimum. Malawi is the most densely populated country in the region.

### INHABITANTS PER SQ MILE
- More than 260
- 130–260
- 30–130
- Less than 30
- ■ Capital city
- ● Major city

Luanda 1.4%   Kinshasa 2.4%
Cape Town 1.2%
Other towns and cities 34%
Rural population 61%

# AUSTRALASIA & OCEANIA

Australasia and Oceania encompasses the ancient landmass of Australia, the islands of New Zealand, and the scattering of thousands of small islands that stretch out into the Pacific Ocean. Indigenous peoples of the South Pacific, such as the Aborigines, Maoris, Polynesians, Micronesians, and Melanesians, inhabit the region. In Australia and New Zealand, they live alongside people of European origin who settled in the 18th century, and more recent arrivals from East and Southeast Asia.

4,560 miles

6,125 miles

## PACIFIC ISLANDS

Micronesia is one of the Pacific's island nations, consisting of a group of volcanic islands, low-lying coral reefs, and lagoons. Many of the smaller Pacific islands are only a few feet above sea level.

## LAND USE AND AGRICULTURE

Much of the center of Australia is a dry, barren desert and unsuitable for agriculture. At its fringes, sheep farming is practiced, and both Australia and New Zealand are massive producers of wool and lamb. The Pacific islands export many exotic fruits and crops – especially oil palms and coconut palms. Oil from the palms is processed and sold as well as the fruits themselves. Small-scale fishing is common, but larger operations are run by foreign fishing fleets, especially the Japanese, who fish for tuna in the deeper waters of the Pacific.

### SHEEP FARMING

New Zealand and Australia are the world's biggest producers of wool. In New Zealand, sheep outnumber people by 12:1.

### POPULATION

**Capital cities**
- ◨ Above 500,000
- ◉ 100,000 to 500,000
- ● 50,000 to 100,000
- • Below 50,000

**State capitals**
- ◨ Above 500,000
- ◉ 100,000 to 500,000
- ○ 50,000 to 100,000

### BORDERS

| | |
|---|---|
| ⬛ | full international border |
| ⬛ | indication of maritime country extent |
| ⬛ | indication of maritime dependent territory extent |
| ⬛ | state border |

SCALE 1:37,250,000

0 km   300   600

0 miles   300   600

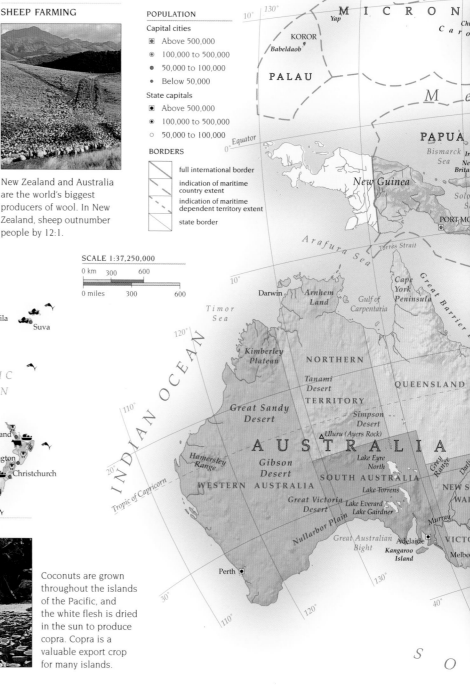

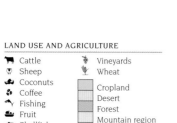

### COCONUTS

Coconuts are grown throughout the islands of the Pacific, and the white flesh is dried in the sun to produce copra. Copra is a valuable export crop for many islands.

### LAND USE AND AGRICULTURE

- 🐄 Cattle
- 🐑 Sheep
- 🥥 Coconuts
- ☕ Coffee
- 🎣 Fishing
- 🍓 Fruit
- 🦪 Shellfish
- 🌾 Sugarcane
- 🌲 Timber
- 🍇 Vineyards
- 🌾 Wheat

- Cropland
- Desert
- Forest
- Mountain region
- Pasture
- • Major conurbation

# MINERAL RESOURCES

**Mineral resources are not widespread**, but where they are found, they are in great abundance. Most of the small Pacific islands have no mineral resources, but Australia has enormous reserves of bauxite and iron ore, and also sizable reserves of gold and zinc. Copper is found in Papua New Guinea, and New Caledonia has large nickel reserves. There are ample supplies of fossil fuels, and although coal is plentiful in eastern Australia, oil and gas are found only in isolated pockets around Australia's coast.

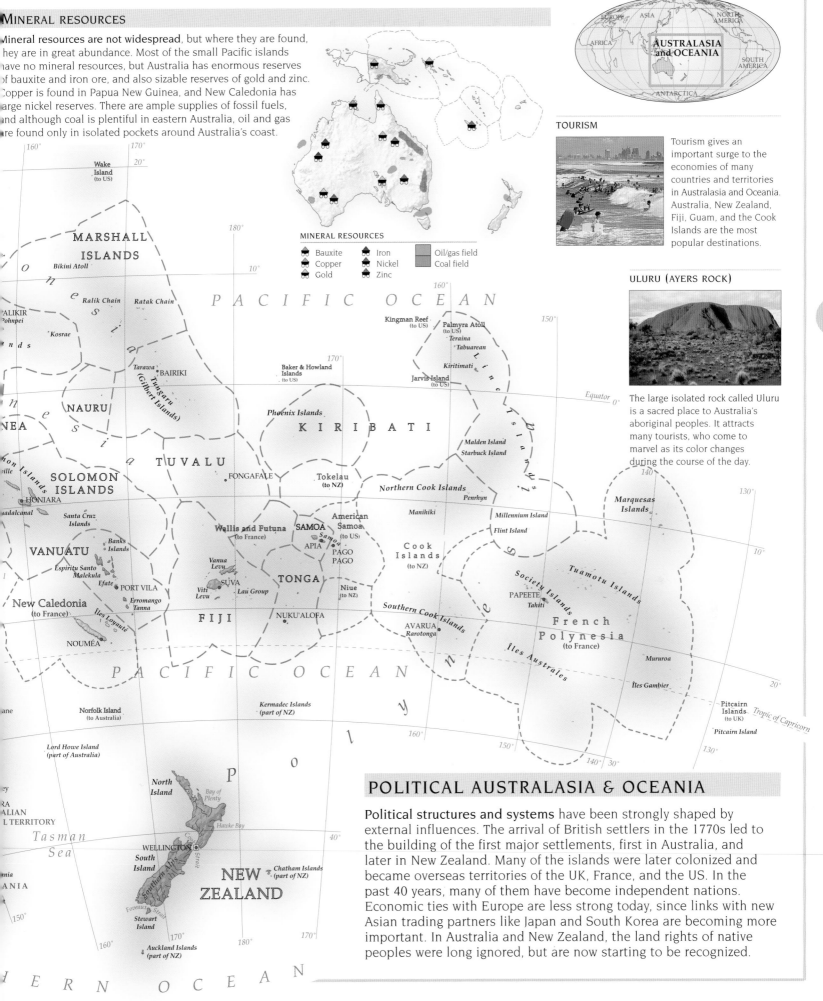

## MINERAL RESOURCES

- 🐚 Bauxite
- 🐚 Copper
- 🐚 Gold
- 🐚 Iron
- 🐚 Nickel
- 🐚 Zinc
- ▦ Oil/gas field
- ▦ Coal field

**AUSTRALASIA and OCEANIA**

## TOURISM

Tourism gives an important surge to the economies of many countries and territories in Australasia and Oceania. Australia, New Zealand, Fiji, Guam, and the Cook Islands are the most popular destinations.

## ULURU (AYERS ROCK)

The large isolated rock called Uluru is a sacred place to Australia's aboriginal peoples. It attracts many tourists, who come to marvel as its color changes during the course of the day.

# POLITICAL AUSTRALASIA & OCEANIA

**Political structures and systems** have been strongly shaped by external influences. The arrival of British settlers in the 1770s led to the building of the first major settlements, first in Australia, and later in New Zealand. Many of the islands were later colonized and became overseas territories of the UK, France, and the US. In the past 40 years, many of them have become independent nations. Economic ties with Europe are less strong today, since links with new Asian trading partners like Japan and South Korea are becoming more important. In Australia and New Zealand, the land rights of native peoples were long ignored, but are now starting to be recognized.

# AUSTRALIA

Australia is the world's sixth-largest country, and also the smallest, flattest continent, with the lowest rainfall. Most Australians are of European, mainly British, origin. However, since 1945 almost six million settlers from more than 170 countries have made Australia their home. The Aboriginal people, now only a tiny minority, were the first inhabitants. Recently, there have been several moves to restore their ancient lands.

## FARMING AND LAND USE

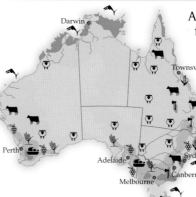

Away from the coasts, much of the land is too dry for agriculture. Fields of sugarcane grow close the east coast, and grapes for the thriving wine industry are cultivated in the south and west, along with wheat. Vast numbers of cattle and sheep are raised for their meat and wool – both of which are majo exports. They are grazed in the desert, on huge farms called "stations," and in more fertile area:

### FARMING AND LAND USE

- 🐂 Cattle
- 🐑 Sheep
- 🌾 Wheat
- Sugarcane
- Timber
- Vineyards

- Cropland
- Desert
- Forest
- Pasture
- • Major conurbation

**LAND USE**

Cropland 6%
Other (including desert) 21%
Forest 19%
Pasture 54%

## INDUSTRY

Australia has one of the world's biggest mining industries. Bauxite, coal, copper, gold, and iron ore are mined and exported, especially to Japan. In the cities, service industries, particularly tourism, are growing fast; Australia's sunshine and dramatic scenery are attracting an increasing number of overseas visitors.

### STRUCTURE OF INDUSTRY

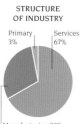

Primary 3%
Services 67%
Manufacturing 30%

### INDUSTRY

- 🍷 Brewing
- 🚗 Car manufacturing
- Chemicals
- Electronics
- ⚙ Engineering
- Food processing
- Coal

- Mining
- Oil and gas
- Tourism

- Major industrial center / area
- Major road

## POPULATION

Despite its vast size, Australia is sparsely populated. The desert outback, which covers most of the interior, is too dry and barren to support many people. About 85% of the population live in the cities and towns on the east and southeast coasts, and around Perth in the west.

### INHABITANTS PER SQ MILE

- More than 130
- 30–130
- 3–30
- Less than 3
- ▪ Capital city
- • Major city

### URBAN/RURAL POPULATION DIVISION

Sydney 17.8%
Melbourne 16%
Brisbane 7.7%
Other towns and cities 43.5%
Rural population 15%

## THE LANDSCAPE

Most of Australia is dry, flat, and barren; all of the wette fertile land is found along its coastline. Huge sun-baked deserts, fringed by semiarid plains of scrub and grassland cover most of the west and center of the country. In the east, the land rises to the highlands of the Great Dividing Range, which run the whole length of the east coast. Th tropical north coast has rainforests and mangrove swamps.

### Blue Mountains (G 6)

The Blue Mountains lie toward the southern end of the Great Dividing Range. They get their name from the blue haze of oil droplets given off by the eucalyptus trees covering their slopes.

### Great Barrier Reef (G 2)

This spectacular coral reef, which stretches for over 1,200 miles off the coast of Queensland, is the largest living structure on Earth. The reef has built up over millions of years and its waters are home to thousands of different species of coral and marine animals.

### Uluru (Ayers Rock) (D 4)

Uluru is an enormous block of red sandstone, standing almost in the middle of Australia. It is the world's biggest free-standing rock – 5.8 miles around the base, and 2,845 ft high. It is the summit of a sandstone hill that is buried beneath the sands of the desert.

### Simpson Desert (E 4)

The Simpson Desert covers around 50,000 sq miles. It contains long, parallel lines of sand dunes and is scattered with large salt pans and salt lakes, which were created when old rivers evaporated. They are now fed by the seasonal rains.

### Murray River (F 5)

Together with its tributaries, the Murray River is Australia's main river system. It winds slowly westward for more than 1,562 miles from the Great Dividing Range to the Indian Ocean. It is fed by snow from mountains in the far southeast.

### Great Dividing Range (H 5)

These highlands separate the desert regions from the fertile eastern plains. Rivers and streams have eroded them, creating deep valleys and gorges.

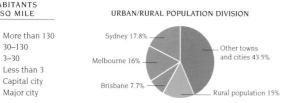

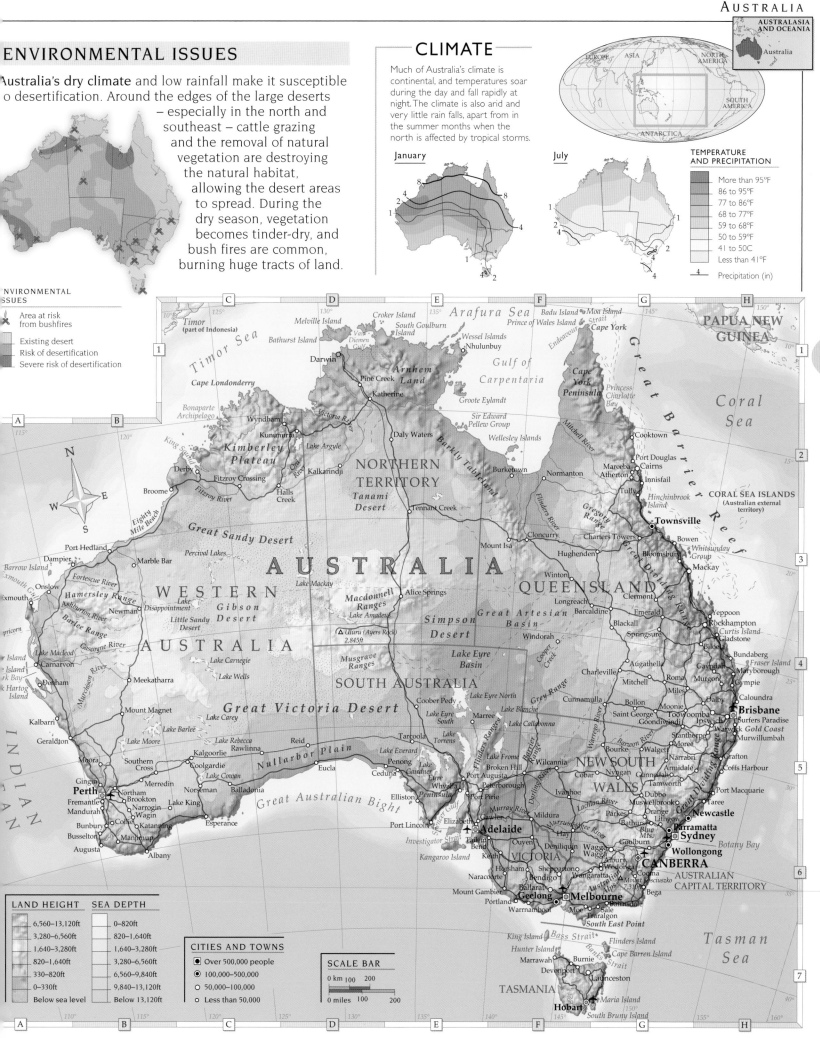

# ENVIRONMENTAL ISSUES

Australia's dry climate and low rainfall make it susceptible to desertification. Around the edges of the large deserts – especially in the north and southeast – cattle grazing and the removal of natural vegetation are destroying the natural habitat, allowing the desert areas to spread. During the dry season, vegetation becomes tinder-dry, and bush fires are common, burning huge tracts of land.

## CLIMATE

Much of Australia's climate is continental, and temperatures soar during the day and fall rapidly at night. The climate is also arid and very little rain falls, apart from in the summer months when the north is affected by tropical storms.

January

July

### AUSTRALASIA AND OCEANIA

Australia

### TEMPERATURE AND PRECIPITATION

- More than 95°F
- 86 to 95°F
- 77 to 86°F
- 68 to 77°F
- 59 to 68°F
- 50 to 59°F
- 41 to 50C
- Less than 41°F
- 4 — Precipitation (in)

### ENVIRONMENTAL ISSUES

- ✕ Area at risk from bushfires
- Existing desert
- Risk of desertification
- Severe risk of desertification

### LAND HEIGHT
- 6,560–13,120ft
- 3,280–6,560ft
- 1,640–3,280ft
- 820–1,640ft
- 330–820ft
- 0–330ft
- Below sea level

### SEA DEPTH
- 0–820ft
- 820–1,640ft
- 1,640–3,280ft
- 3,280–6,560ft
- 6,560–9,840ft
- 9,840–13,120ft
- Below 13,120ft

### CITIES AND TOWNS
- ■ Over 500,000 people
- ◉ 100,000–500,000
- ◎ 50,000–100,000
- ○ Less than 50,000

### SCALE BAR
0 km 100 200
0 miles 100 200

# NEW ZEALAND

New Zealand is one of the most remote populated places in the world, and was one of the last places on Earth to be inhabited by people. The first people to settle on the islands were the Maori, a Polynesian people. When European settlers arrived during the 19th century, the Maori became a minority and today make up only about 8% of the population. With few people and rich natural resources, New Zealand's inhabitants have high living standards.

## INDUSTRY

High-tech industries such as electronics and computing are growing in the major cities of Auckland and Wellington. Agricultural products such as meat, wool, and milk are still among New Zealand's major exports, and large pine forests supply wood for paper pulp and timber. The magnificent scenery and varied climate draw tourists from all over the world, especially for hiking and other special vacations.

**STRUCTURE OF INDUSTRY**

Primary 5%
Services 68%
Manufacturing 27%

**INDUSTRY**

- Chemicals
- Electronics
- Engineering
- Fish processing
- Food processing
- Iron and steel
- Textiles
- Timber
- Tourism
- Major industrial center / area
- — Major road

## POPULATION

Most of the population is descended from European settlers, although immigrants from Asia and the Pacific islands are increasing. About one-third of New Zealand's 4 million people live in Auckland on North Island, which also has the largest Polynesian population of any city in the Pacific. Elsewhere, the population is clustered along the coasts, where the land is lower.

**URBAN/RURAL POPULATION DIVISION**

Auckland 30.7%
Other towns and cities 36.8%
Wellington 9.3%
Christchurch 9.2%
Rural population 14%

**INHABITANTS PER SQ MILE**

- More than 130
- 30–130
- 3–30
- Less than 3
- ■ Capital city
- ● Major city

## ENVIRONMENTAL ISSUES

New Zealand is one of the world's least polluted countries, largely due to its small population and lack of heavy industries. Air quality is occasionally poor in Auckland and Christchurch. Environment-friendly geothermal energy is tapped to make electricity in the volcanic region of North Island. Recently, logging companies have begun to exploit the rich forest reserves, although this has been widely opposed.

**ENVIRONMENTAL ISSUES**

- Geothermal power generation
- Logging activity
- Urban air pollution
- ● Major industrial center

## THE LANDSCAPE

Two large, mountainous islands form New Zealand's main land areas. A large crack or fault – the Alpine Fault, in the west of South Island – is the boundary between two plates in the Earth's crust. Land on either side of the fault tends to move, causing earthquakes. Volcanoes, many of them still active, are also found on both islands. South Island has many high peaks, several more than 10,000 ft high.

### Geysers and boiling mud

Geysers occur when hot volcanic rocks come into contact with underground water. The water boils and turns to steam, forcing the water above it to burst through the Earth's surface into the air. There are many geysers and boiling mud pools in the areas around Rotorua and Taupo.

### Northland (C1)

This is a tropical region in the far northwest. Many of the inlets are fringed by mangrove swamps.

### Mount Taranaki (C4)

The dormant volcano of Mount Taranaki lies on New Zealand's North Island. It rises to a height of 8,262 ft.

### Probable location of Alpine Fault

### Lake Taupo (D3)

New Zealand's largest lake, Lake Taupo, covers 234 sq miles of North Island. It lies in the crater of an extinct volcano.

### Southern Alps

New Zealand's Southern Alps stretch more than 300 miles down the backbone of South Island. They were formed by the collision of the Indo-Australian and Pacific plates. Heavy snowfalls here, brought by westerly winds, feed the Fox Glacier, which moves at a speed of 1.5–15 ft a day.

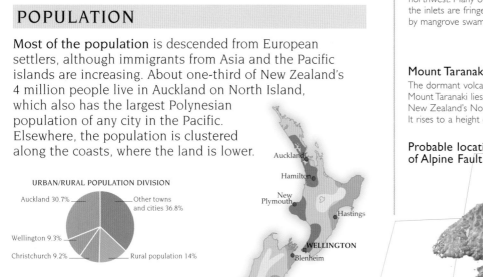

## FARMING AND LAND USE

**Large areas** of rich, sweet grasslands have made New Zealand one of the world's top regions for rearing sheep. There are around 12 sheep for every person, grazing alongside about ten million cattle. Fruits, including strawberries, apples, oranges, peaches, and the famous kiwi, are cultivated, particularly on South Island, and exported throughout the world. Fish caught off the Pacific coast are another important source of income.

### LAND USE

Other 8%
Cropland 14%
Forest 28%
Pasture 50%

### FARMING AND LAND USE

- Cattle
- Fishing
- Sheep
- Fruit
- Timber
- Wheat

- Cropland
- Forest
- Mountains
- Pasture
- ● Major conurbation

## CLIMATE

North Island has a generally warm climate that becomes tropical – hotter and more humid – toward the far north. South Island is cooler and wetter. There may be heavy snowfall in winter, particularly in the highlands, and many mountains are permanently snow-capped.

### TEMPERATURE AND PRECIPITATION

- More than 59°F
- 50 to 59°F
- 41 to 50°F
- 32 to 41°F
- 23 to 32°F
- Less than 23°F
- 4 — Precipitation (in)

January

July

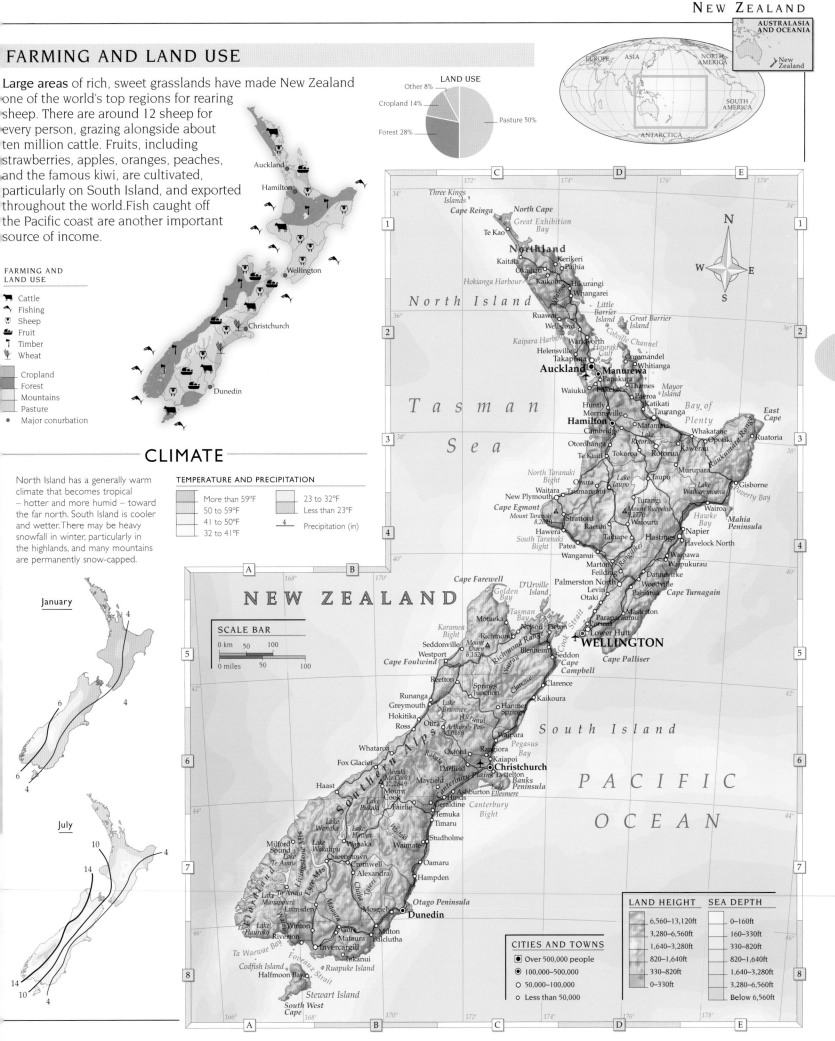

### AUSTRALASIA AND OCEANIA

### CITIES AND TOWNS
- ■ Over 500,000 people
- ◉ 100,000–500,000
- ○ 50,000–100,000
- ○ Less than 50,000

### LAND HEIGHT
- 6,560–13,120ft
- 3,280–6,560ft
- 1,640–3,280ft
- 820–1,640ft
- 330–820ft
- 0–330ft

### SEA DEPTH
- 0–160ft
- 160–330ft
- 330–820ft
- 820–1,640ft
- 1,640–3,280ft
- 3,280–6,560ft
- Below 6,560ft

# SOUTHWEST PACIFIC

**The many thousands** of islands in the Pacific Ocean are scattered across an enormous area. The original inhabitants, the Polynesians, Melanesians, and Micronesians, settled the islands following the last Ice Age. In the 1700s Europeans arrived. They colonized all of the Pacific islands, introducing their culture, languages, and religion. Today many, though not all, of the islands have become independent. Their economies are simple, based largely on fishing and agriculture. Many are increasingly relying on their beautiful scenery and tropical climates to attract tourists and give a valuable boost to their economies.

## LANDSCAPE

**Most of the Pacific islands** are extremely small, the largest landmass is the half of the island of New Guinea occupied by Papua New Guinea. The edges of the Indo-Australian and Pacific plates meet on the western edge of the area, leading to much volcanic and earthquake activity. Many of the islands are coral atolls, originally formed by volcanic activity, and some are no more than a few feet above sea level.

### New Guinea (A 2)
A mountainous spine runs through the center of the island, separating the northern coast from the dense forests and mangroves found in the south.

### Pacific Ocean
The Pacific Ocean is the Earth's oldest and deepest. Its name means peaceful, though it is far from being so; the highest wave ever recorded in open ocean – 112 ft – occurred during a hurricane in the Pacific.

### Kavachi
Kavachi is an underwater volcano lying off the coast of New Georgia, in the Solomon Islands. It still erupts every few years.

### Ring of Fire
The "Ring of Fire" is the term used to describe the string of volcanoes that surround the entire Pacific Ocean and erupt frequently because of intense stress and movement from within the Earth. The ring crosses the south Pacific, running between Vanuatu and New Caledonia, along the edge of the Solomon Islands, and between New Britain and New Guinea.

### Sea trenches
Deep trenches mark the seafloor boundary where the Indo-Australian plate "dives" under the Pacific plate.

### Coral atolls
Volcanic activity in the Pacific has led to the creation of many islands. These islands become fringed with a ring of coral. When the islands subside beneath the water once again, only the circle of coral is left, forming an atoll.

## INDUSTRY

**Today, the main industry** for many of the Pacific islands is tourism. Food processing and small-scale textile industries are also common on many islands.

INDUSTRY
- ⚗ Brewing
- ▣ Food processing
- ⌂ Textiles
- ♣ Timber processing
- ⬡ Mining
- ⬢ Tourism
- ▣ Major industrial center
- — Major road

# FARMING AND LAND USE

Most farming that takes place on the Pacific islands is at a subsistence level, and many people keep pigs and chickens. A few crops are grown for export, especially oil palms, and coconuts, which are dried in the sun to produce copra. Many islanders make their living from the rich fishing grounds of the Pacific. The thick forests of Papua New Guinea are increasingly cut down for timber.

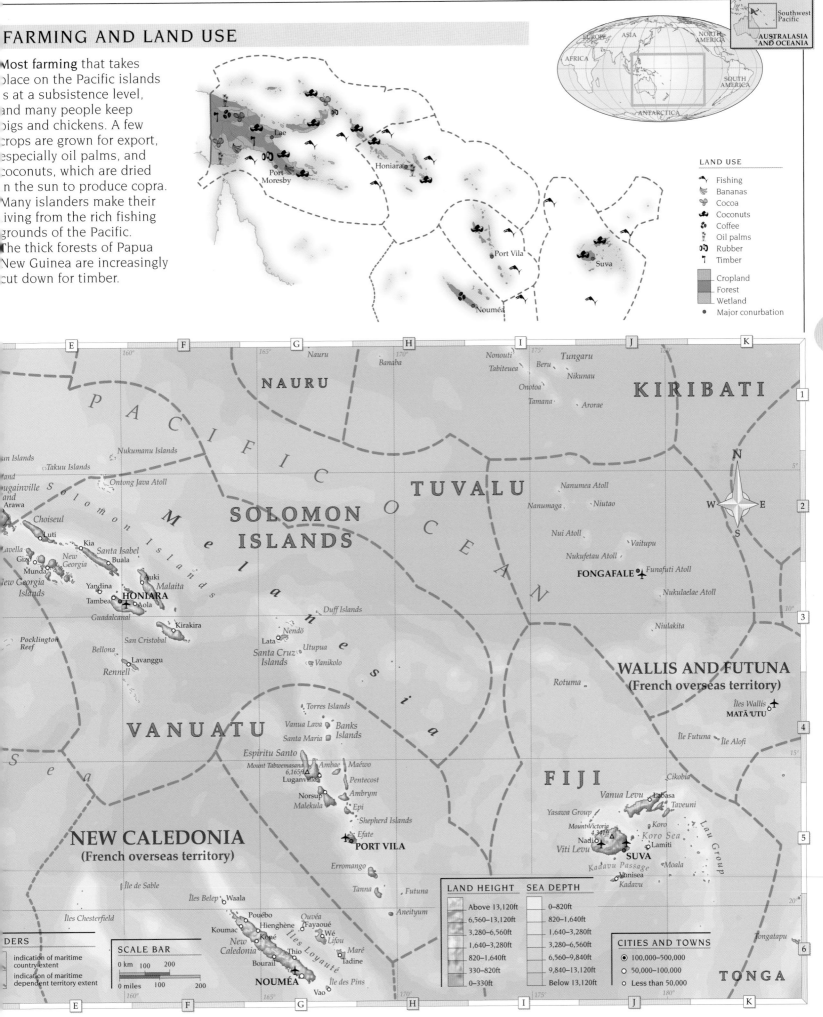

AUSTRALASIA AND OCEANIA

**LAND USE**

- Fishing
- Bananas
- Cocoa
- Coconuts
- Coffee
- Oil palms
- Rubber
- Timber

Cropland
Forest
Wetland
• Major conurbation

**LAND HEIGHT**

- Above 13,120ft
- 6,560–13,120ft
- 3,280–6,560ft
- 1,640–3,280ft
- 820–1,640ft
- 330–820ft
- 0–330ft

**SEA DEPTH**

- 0–820ft
- 820–1,640ft
- 1,640–3,280ft
- 3,280–6,560ft
- 6,560–9,840ft
- 9,840–13,120ft
- Below 13,120ft

**CITIES AND TOWNS**

- ◉ 100,000–500,000
- ◎ 50,000–100,000
- ○ Less than 50,000

**BORDERS**

- indication of maritime country extent
- indication of maritime dependent territory extent

**SCALE BAR**

0 km 100 200

0 miles 100 200

137

# ANTARCTICA

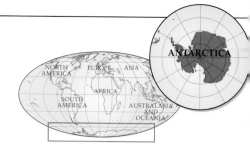

The continent of Antarctica has no permanent human population and very few animals can survive on the frozen land, although the surrounding waters teem with fish and mammals. Even in the summer, the temperature is rarely above freezing and the sea-ice only partly melts; in winter, temperatures plummet to –112°F. The only people who live in Antarctica are teams of scientists who study the wildlife and monitor the ice for changes in the Earth's atmosphere.

## THE LANDSCAPE

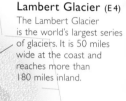

### Frozen seas
During the cold winter months, the water surrounding Antarctica freezes, almost doubling the size of the continent.

**Antarctica is the world's** most southerly continent. It is also the world's coldest continent and its highest, mainly due to the great ice sheet – up to 1.25 miles thick in parts – that lies over the mountains of the Antarctic Peninsula and the plateau of Greater Antarctica.

### Transantarctic Mountains (C 5)
The Transantarctic Mountains run across the continent, splitting it into Greater and Lesser Antarctica.

### Lambert Glacier (E 4)
The Lambert Glacier is the world's largest series of glaciers. It is 50 miles wide at the coast and reaches more than 180 miles inland.

### Ice sheet
A massive sheet of ice, about 15,700 ft thick at its deepest point, covers almost the entire area of Antarctica. It contains most of the freshwater on Earth. The weight of the ice pushes the land down below sea level.

### The Ross Ice Shelf (C 5)
The Ross Sea is part of the Pacific Ocean. This deep bay is covered with a thick sheet of ice that floats on the ocean.

## RESOURCES

**The mountains of Antarctica** have rich mineral reserves. Gold, iron, and coal are found, and there is natural gas in the surrounding water. The unique and abundant marine wildlife is Antarctica's greatest resource. Colonies of penguins breed on the ice sheet, and whales, seals, and many bird and fish species thrive in the icy waters.

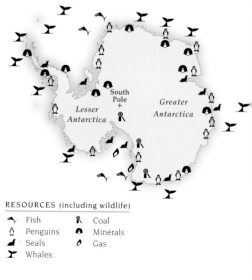

### RESOURCES (including wildlife)
- Fish
- Penguins
- Seals
- Whales
- Coal
- Minerals
- Gas

---

### Map

○ Research Station

| LAND HEIGHT | SEA DEPTH |
|---|---|
| Above 13,120ft | 0–820ft |
| 6,560–13,120ft | 820–1,640ft |
| 3,280ft–6,560ft | 1,640–3,280ft |
| 1,640–3,280ft | 3,280–6,560ft |
| 820–1,640ft | 6,560–9,840ft |
| 330–820ft | 9,840–13,120ft |
| 0–330ft | Below 13,120ft |

ATLANTIC OCEAN

SOUTH GEORGIA (to UK)
South Sandwich Trench
SOUTH SANDWICH ISLANDS (to UK)
America–Antarctica Ridge
Atlantic–Indian Basin
Scotia Sea
Antarctic Circle
Orcadas (to Argentina)
South Orkney Islands
Signy (to UK)
Lazarev Sea
Weddell Plain
Sanae (to South Africa)
Georg von Neumayer (to Germany)
Maitri (to India)
Novolazarevskaya (to Russian Federation)
Drake Passage
South Shetland Islands
Multinational Stations
Esperanza (to Argentina)
Capitan Arturo Prat (to Chile)
Weddell Sea
Halley (to UK)
Dronning Maud Land
Lutzow-Holm Bay
Molodezhnaya (to Russian Federation)
Syowa (to Japan)
Enderby Land
SOUTHERN OCEAN
Palmer (to US)
Antarctic Peninsula
Rothera (to UK)
San Martin (to Argentina)
Alexander Island
Palmer Land
Coats Land
Belgrano II (to Argentina)
Berkner Island
Ronne Ice Shelf
Kemp Land
Mawson (to Australia)
Cape Darnley
Lambert Glacier
Mackenzie Bay
Zhongshan (to China)
Prydz Bay
Bellingshausen Sea
Vinson Massif 16,067ft
ANTARCTICA
Princess Elizabeth Land
Davis (to Australia)
Davis Sea
PETER I ISLAND (to Norway)
Ellsworth Land
Amundsen-Scott (to US)
South Pole
Greater Antarctica
Mirny (to Russian Federation)
Limit of winter pack ice
Limit of summer pack ice
Lesser Antarctica
Transantarctic Mountains
South Geomagnetic Pole
Vostok (to Russian Federation)
Shackleton Ice Shelf
Marie Byrd Land
Mount Kirkpatrick 14,856ft
Mount Markham 14,276ft
Mount Sidley 13,718ft
Ross Ice Shelf
Victoria Land
Wilkes Land
Casey (to Australia)
Amundsen Sea
Mount Siple 10,171ft
Roosevelt Island
Scott Base (to NZ)
Cape Poinsett
SOUTHERN OCEAN
McMurdo Base (to US)
Mount Erebus 12,448ft
Terre Adélie
Ross Sea
George V Land
Cape Adare
Leningradskaya (to Russian Federation)
Dumont d'Urville (to France)
Amundsen Plain

SCALE BAR
0 km 500 1000
0 miles 500 1000

# THE ARCTIC

The ice-covered Arctic Ocean is encircled by the most northerly parts of Europe, North America, and Asia. Very few people live in the often-freezing conditions. Those who do, including the Sami of northern Scandinavia, the Siberian Yugyt and Nenet people, and the Canadian Inuit, were nomads who lived by hunting and herding. Some live like this today, but many have now settled in small towns.

## THE LANDSCAPE

**The Arctic Ocean** is the smallest ocean in the world, covering a total area of 5,440,000 sq miles. The ocean is divided into two large basins, divided by three great underwater mountain ranges including the Lomonosov Ridge which is more than 9,842 ft high on average.

### Lomonosov Ridge (C4)

### Arctic islands (A4)

In the far north of Canada, there are many thousands of islands including Baffin Island and Victoria Island. Many of them are almost entirely surrounded by pack ice.

### Pack ice

Much of the Arctic Ocean is permanently covered by pack ice. When the ice breaks up, it forms enormous floating ice masses called icebergs.

### Greenland (A3)

Greenland is the world's largest island. It is covered by a huge ice sheet, more than 649,960 sq miles across. The weight of the ice has pushed most of the land below sea level.

### Sastrugi

Snow, blown by strong winds, can scratch deep patterns in the snow. These patterns are known as sastrugi and line up with the direction of the wind.

## RESOURCES

**Coal, oil, and gas** are found beneath the Arctic Ocean and in Canada, Alaska, and Russia. Fears about damage to the environment and the cost of extracting these resources have restricted the quantities removed. Overfishing has reduced fish stocks to very low levels. Quotas have been put in place to allow them to revive.

SCALE BAR
0 km 250 500
0 miles 250 500

CITIES AND TOWNS
◉ 100,000–500,000
○ 50,000–100,000
○ Less than 50,000

SEA DEPTH
0–820ft
820–1,640ft
1,640–3,280ft
3,280–6,560ft
6,560–9,840ft
9,840–13,120ft
Below 13,120ft

RESOURCES
⌐ Fish
☂ Coal
♠ Minerals
◊ Oil and gas
● Major town/city

# GLOSSARY

This glossary defines certain geographical and technical terms used in this Atlas.

**Acid rain** Rain, sleet, snow or mist that has absorbed waste gases from fossil-fueled power stations and vehicle exhausts, becoming acidic and poisonous.

**Alluvium** Material deposited by a river, such as silt, sand, and mud

**Archipelago** A group, or chain, of islands.

**Atoll** A circular or horseshoe-shaped coral reef enclosing a shallow area of water (lagoon).

**Aquifer** A body of rock that can absorb water. It may be a source of water for wells or springs.

**Bar, coastal** An offshore strip of sand or shingle, either above or below the water.

**Biodiversity** The quantity of different animal or plant species in a given area.

**Birthrate** The number of live births per 1,000 individuals annually within a population.

**Cash crop** Agricultural produce grown for sale, often for foreign export, rather than to be consumed by the country or area where it was grown.

**Climate** The long term trends in weather conditions for an area.

**Coniferous forest** A type of forest containing trees or shrubs, like pines and firs, that have needles instead of leaves. They are found in temperate zones.

**Continental plates** The huge interlocking plates that make up the Earth's surface. A plate boundary is an area where two plates meet, and is the point at which earthquakes occur most frequently.

**Conurbation** A large urban area created by the merging of several towns.

**Coral reef** An underwater barrier created by colonies of coral polyps. The polyps secrete a protective skeleton of calcium carbonate, and reefs develop as live polyps build on the skeletons of dead generations.

**Core** The layers of liquid rock and solid iron at the center of the Earth.

**Crust** The hard, thin outer shell of the Earth. The crust floats on the mantle, which is softer, but more dense.

**Deciduous forest** A type of broadleaf forest found in temperate regions.

**Deforestation** Cutting down trees or forest for timber or farmland. It can lead to soil erosion, flooding, and landslides.

**Delta** A low-lying, fan-shaped area at a river mouth, formed by the deposition of successive layers of sediment. Slowing as it enters the sea, a river deposits sediment and may, as a result, split into many smaller channels called distributaries.

**Deposition** The laying down of material broken down by erosion or weathering and transported by the wind, water, or gravity.

**Desertification** The spread of desert conditions into a region that was not previously a desert.

**Drainage basin** The land drained by a river and its tributaries.

**Drought** A long period of continuously low rainfall.

**Earthquake** A trembling or shaking of the ground caused by the sudden movement of rocks in the Earth's crust – and sometimes deeper than the crust. Earthquakes occur most frequently along continental plate boundaries.

**Economy** The organization of a country's finances, exports, imports, industry, agriculture, and services.

**Ecosytem** A community of species dependent on each other and on the habitat in which they live.

**Equator** The 0° line of latitude. Equatorial climates are hot and there is plenty of rain.

**Erosion** The wearing down of the land surface by running water, waves, moving ice, wind, and weather.

**Estuary** The mouth of a river, where the saltwater from the sea meets the freshwater of the river.

**Fault** A crack or fracture in the Earth along which there has been movement of the rock masses relative to one another.

**Fjord** A coastal valley that was sculpted by glacial action.

**Flood plain** The broad, flat part of a river valley, next to the river itself, formed by sediment deposited during flooding.

**Geyser** A fountain of hot water or steam that erupts periodically as a result of underground streams coming into contact with hot rocks.

**GDP** Gross Domestic Product. The total value of goods and services produced by a country, excluding income from foreign countries.

**GIS** Geographic Information System. A computerized system for the collection, storage, and retrieval of geographic data.

**Glacier** A huge mass of ice made up of compacted and frozen snow, that moves slowly, eroding and depositing rock.

**Glaciation** The molding of the land by a glacier or ice sheet.

**GNI** Gross National Income. The total value of goods and services produced by a country.

**Groundwater** Water that has seeped into the pores, cavities, and cracks of rocks or into soil and water held in an aquifer or permeable rock.

**Gully** A deep, narrow chasm eroded in the landscape by a fast-flowing stream.

**Heavy industry** Industry that uses large amounts of energy and raw materials to produce heavy goods, such as machinery, ships, or locomotives.

**Humidity** The moisture content of the air.

**Hurricane** Violent tropical storms, also known as cyclones in the Indian Ocean and typhoons in the Pacific Ocean.

**Hydroelectric power** Energy produced by harnessing the rapid movement of water down steep mountain slopes to drive turbines to generate electricity.

**Ice Age** Periods of time in the past when much of the Earth's surface was covered by massive ice sheets. The most recent Ice Age began two million years ago and ended 10,000 years ago.

**Iceberg** A floating mass of ice that has broken off from a glacier or ice sheet.

**Ice sheet** A massive area of ice, thousands of feet thick.

**Irrigation** The artificial supply of water to dry areas – mainly for agricultural use. Water is carried or pumped to the area through pipes or ditches.

**Lagoon** A shallow stretch of coastal saltwater behind a partial barrier such as a sandbank or coral reef.

**Latitude** The distance north or south of the equator, measured in degrees, and shown on a globe as imaginary circles running around the Earth parallel to the equator.

**Lava** The molten rock, magma, that erupts onto the Earth's surface through a volcano, or through a fault or crack in the Earth's crust. Lava refers to the rock both in its liquid and its later, solidified form.

**Load** The material that is carried by a river or stream.

**Longitude** The distance, measured in degrees, east or west of the Prime Meridian.

**Limestone** A type of rock, formed by sediment, through which water can pass.

**Magma** Underground, molten rock, that is very hot and highly charged with gas. It originates in the Earth's lower crust or mantle.

**Mantle** The layer of the Earth's interior between the crust and the core. It is about 1,800 miles thick.

**Map projection** A mathematical formula that is used to show the curved surface of the Earth on a flat map.

**Market gardening** The intensive growing of fruit and vegetables close to large local markets.

**Meander** A looplike bend in a river. As a river nears the sea, it tends to wind more and more. The bigger the river and the shallower its slope, the more likely it is that meanders will form.

**Mediterranean climate** A temperate climate of hot, dry summers and warm, damp winters.

**Meltwater** Water that has melted from glaciers or ice sheets.

**Mestizo** A person of mixed native American and European origin.

**Mineral** A chemical compound that occurs naturally in the Earth.

**Monsoon** Winds that change direction according to the seasons. They are most common in South and East Asia, where they blow from the southwest in summer, bringing heavy rainfall, and the northeast in winter.

**Moraine** Sand and gravel that have been deposited by a glacier or ice sheet.

**Nomads (nomadic)** Wandering communities who move around in search of suitable pasture for their herds of animals.

**Oasis** A fertile area in a desert, usually watered by an underground aquifer.

**Pack ice** Ice masses more than 10 ft thick that form on the sea surface and are not attached to a landmass.

**Pacific Rim** The name given to the economically dynamic countries bordering the Pacific Ocean.

**Peat** Decomposed vegetation found in bogs. It can be dried and used as fuel.

**Per capita** A latin term meaning "for each person."

**Plantation** A large farm on which only one crop is usually grown, e.g. bananas or coffee.

**Plain** A flat, level region of land, often relatively low-lying.

**Plateau** A large area of high, flat land. When surrounded by steep slopes it is called a tableland.

**Peninsula** A thin strip of land surrounded on three of its sides by water. Large examples include Italy, Florida, and Korea.

**Permafrost** Permanently frozen ground, in which temperatures have remained below 32°F for more than two years.

**Precipitation** The fall of moisture from the atmosphere onto the surface of the Earth, as dew, hail, rain, sleet, or snow.

**Prairie** A Spanish-American term for grassy plains, with few or no trees.

**Prime Meridian** 0° longitude. Also known as the Greenwich Meridian because it runs through Greenwich in England.

**Rainforest** Dense forests in tropical zones with high rainfall, temperature and humidity.

**Rain shadow** An area downwind from high terrain that has little or no rainfall because it has fallen upon the high relief.

**Remote-sensing** A way of obtaining information about the environment by using unmanned equipment, such as a satellite, that relays the information to a point where it is collected.

**Ria** A flooded V-shaped river valley or estuary flooded by a rise in sea level or sinking land.

**Rift valley** A long, narrow depression in the Earth's crust, formed by the sinking of rocks between two faults.

**Savanna** Open grassland, where an annual dry season prevents the growth of most trees. They lie between the tropical rain-forest and hot desert regions.

**Scale** The relationship between distance on a map and on the Earth's surface

**Sediment** Grains of rock transported and deposited by rivers, sea, ice, or wind.

**Semiarid** Areas between deserts and better-watered areas, where there is sufficient moisture to support a little more vegetation than in a true desert.

**Service industry** An industry that supplies services, such as banking, rather than producing manufactured goods.

**Shanty town** An area in or around a city where people live in temporary shacks, usually without basic facilities such as running water.

**Silt** Small particles, finer than sand, often carried by water and deposited on riverbanks, at river mouths, and harbors.

**Soil** A thin layer of rock particles mixed with the remains of dead organisms. Soil occurs naturally on the surface of the Earth and provides a medium for plants to grow.

**Soil erosion** The wearing away of soil more quickly than it is replaced by natural processes. Over-grazing and the clearing of land for farming, speeds up the process.

**Sorghum** A type of grass found in South America, similar to sugarcane.

**Spit** A narrow bank of pebbles or sand extending out from the seashore. Spits are made out of material transported along the coast by currents, wind, and waves.

**Staple crop** The main food crop grown in a region, for example, rice in Southeast Asia.

**Steppe** Large areas of dry grassland in the Northern Hemisphere – particularly found in southeast Europe and central Asia.

**Subsistence farming** A method of farming in which enough food is produced to feed farmers and their families but not providing any extra to generate an income.

**Taiga** A Russian name given to the belt of coniferous forest found in Russia, that borders tundra in the north and mixed forests and grasslands in the south.

**Temperate** The mild, variable climate found in areas between the tropics and cold polar regions.

**Terrace** Steps cut into steep slopes to create flat surfaces for cultivating crops.

**Tropics** An area between the equator and the Tropic of Cancer and Tropic of Capricorn that has heavy rainfall, high temperatures, and lacks any clear seasonal variation.

**Tundra** The land area lying in the very cold northern regions of Europe, Asia, and Canada, where winters are long and cold and the ground beneath the surface is permanently frozen.

**U-shaped valley** A river valley that has been deepened and widened by a glacier. They are flat-bottomed and steep-sided, and usually much deeper than river valleys.

**V-shaped valley** A typical valley eroded by a river in its upper course.

**Volcano** An opening or vent in the Earth's crust where magma erupts. Volcanos are caused by the movement of the Earth's plates. When the plates collide or spread apart, magma is forced to the surface, at or near the place where the plates meet.

**Watershed** The dividing line between one drainage basin and another.

# INDEX

◇ Administrative region ◆ Country ● Country capital ◇ Dependent territory ◎ Dependent territory capital ▲ Mountain range ▲ Mountain ♨ Volcano ♒ River ◎ Lake ▣ Reservoir

141

ARKHANGEL'SK


**Arkhangel'sk** *see* Archangel
**Arles 73 E6** SE France
**Arlington 48 H3** Texas, USA
**Arlington 43 H1** Virginia, USA
**Arlon 68 E9** SE Belgium
**Armagh 71 B5** S Northern Ireland, UK
**Armagnac 73 C6** *Cultural region,* S France
**Armenia 115 B2** W Colombia
**Armenia 97 H2** ◆ *Republic,* SW Asia
**Armidale 133 H5** NSW, SE Australia
**Armstrong 35 B4** Ontario, S Canada
**Armyans'k 85 F6** S Ukraine
**Arnedo 75 E2** N Spain
**Arnhem 68 E4** SE Netherlands
**Arnhem Land 133 E1** *Physical region,* Northern Territory, N Australia
**Arno 79 C3** ≈ C Italy
**Arnold 53 C6** California, USA
**Arnold 47 G6** Missouri, USA
**Arorae 137 J1** *Atoll,* Tungaru, W Kiribati
**Arran, Isle of 71 C5** *Island,* SW Scotland, UK
**Ar Raqqah 99 B2** N Syria
**Arras 73 D1** N France
**Arriaga 57 G5** SE Mexico
**Ar Riyad** *see* Riyadh
**Ar Rub 'al Khali 99 D6** *Desert,* SW Asia
**Ar Rustaq 99 F4** N Oman
**Árta 83 D5** W Greece
**Artashat 97 H3** S Armenia
**Artemisa 61 B2** W Cuba
**Artesia 48 E3** New Mexico, USA
**Arthur's Pass 135 C6** *Pass,* South Island, NZ
**Artigas 117 C5** N Uruguay
**Art'ik 97 H2** W Armenia
**Artois 73 D1** *Cultural region,* N France
**Artsyz 85 D6** SW Ukraine
**Artvin 97 G2** NE Turkey
**Arua 127 C5** NW Uganda
**Aruba 61 G7** *Dutch* ◇ S West Indies
**Aru, Kepulauan 109 H7** *Island group,* E Indonesia
**Arunachal Pradesh 107 F2** *Cultural region,* NE India
**Arusha 127 D6** N Tanzania
**Arviat 33 H5** Nunavut, C Canada
**Arvidsjaur 67 D3** N Sweden
**Arys' 94 C6** S Kazakhstan
**Asadabad 101 G5** E Afghanistan
**Asahi-dake 103 G1** ▲ N Japan
**Asahikawa 103 F1** N Japan
**Asamankese 124 D5** SE Ghana
**Asansol 107 F4** NE India
**Ascension Island 26** *Saint Helena* ◇, C Atlantic Ocean
**Ascoli Piceno 79 D4** C Italy
**Aseb 127 E3** SE Eritrea
**A Serra de Outes 75 B1** NW Spain
**Aşgabat 101 C3** ● C Turkmenistan
**Ashburton 135 C6** South Island, NZ
**Ashburton River 133 B4** ≈ W Australia
**Ashdod 99 G6** W Israel
**Asheville 43 F3** North Carolina, USA
**Ashland 53 B4** Oregon, USA
**Ashland 44 B2** Wisconsin, USA
**Ash Sharah 99 H7** ⛰ W Jordan
**Ash Shihr 99 D7** SE Yemen
**Ashtabula 44 F5** Ohio, USA
**Asia 90** *Continent*
**Asinara 79 A5** *Island,* W Italy
**Asipovichy 85 D2** C Belarus
**Aşkale 97 F3** NE Turkey
**Askersund 67 C6** C Sweden
**Asmar 101 G5** E Afghanistan
**Asmara 127 D2** ● C Eritrea
**Aspermont 48 F3** Texas, USA
**Assad, Lake 97 E5** ▣ N Syria
**Assam 107 G3** *Cultural region,* NE India
**Assamakka 124 E2** NW Niger
**As Samawah 99 C3** S Iraq
**Assen 68 F2** NE Netherlands
**Assenede 68 B6** NW Belgium
**As Sulaymaniyah 99 C2** NE Iraq
**As Sulayyil 99 C5** S Saudi Arabia
**Astana 94 C5** ● E Kazakhstan
**Asti 79 B2** NW Italy
**Astorga 75 C2** N Spain
**Astrakhan' 87 B8** SW Russ. Fed.
**Asturias 75 C1** *Cultural region,* NW Spain
**Astypálaia 83 F6** *Island,* Cyclades, Greece
**Asunción 117 C4** ● S Paraguay
**Aswan 122 J4** SE Egypt
**Asyut 122 I3** C Egypt
**Atacama Desert 117 A3** *Desert,* N Chile
**Atamyrat 101 E4** E Turkmenistan
**Atâr 124 B2** W Mauritania
**Atas Bogd 105 D2** ▲ SW Mongolia
**Atascadero 53 B8** California, USA
**Atatürk Barajī 97 F4** ▣ S Turkey
**Atbara 127 C2** NE Sudan
**Atbara 127 D2** ≈ Eritrea/Sudan
**Atbasar 94 C5** N Kazakhstan
**Atchison 47 E6** Kansas, USA
**Ath 68 B7** SW Belgium
**Athabasca 33 G6** Alberta, SW Canada
**Athabasca 33 F6** ≈ Alberta, SW Canada
**Athabasca, Lake 33 G5** ◎ Alberta/Saskatchewan, SW Canada
**Athens 83 E5** ● C Greece
**Athens 43 F4** Georgia, USA
**Athens 44 F7** Ohio, USA
**Athens 48 H3** Texas, USA
**Atherton 133 G2** Queensland, NE Australia
**Athína** *see* Athens
**Athlone 71 B6** C Ireland
**Ati 124 H3** C Chad
**Atikokan 35 A4** Ontario, S Canada
**Atka 94 H3** E Russ. Fed.
**Atka 54 B2** Atka Island, Alaska, USA
**Atlanta 43 E4** Georgia, USA
**Atlanta 48 I3** Texas, USA
**Atlantic 43 I3** North Carolina, USA
**Atlantic City 41 D6** New Jersey, USA
**Atlantic Ocean 14** *Ocean*
**Atlas Mountains 122 C2** ⛰ NW Africa
**Atlasovo 94 I3** E Russ. Fed.
**Atlin 33 E5** British Columbia, W Canada
**At Ta'if 99 B5** W Saudi Arabia
**Attawapiskat 35 C3** Ontario, C Canada
**Attawapiskat 35 C3** ≈ Ontario, S Canada
**Attu Island 54 A1** *Island* Aleutian Islands, Alaska, USA
**Atyrau 94 B4** W Kazakhstan
**Aubagne 73 E7** SE France
**Aubange 68 E9** SE Belgium
**Auburn 41 D3** New York, USA
**Auburn 53 B2** Washington, USA
**Auch 73 C6** S France
**Auckland 135 D2** North Island, NZ
**Audincourt 73 F3** E France
**Augathella 133 G4** Queensland, E Australia
**Augsburg 77 C7** S Germany
**Augusta 133 B6** W Australia
**Augusta 43 F4** Georgia, USA
**Augusta 41 G3** Maine, USA
**Augustów 81 G2** NE Poland
**Auki 137 F3** Malaita, N Solomon Islands
**Aunu'u Island 55** *Island* W American Samoa
**Auob 128 C6** ≈ Namibia/South Africa
**Aurangabad 107 D5** C India
**Auray 73 B3** NW France
**Aurès, Massif de l' 88 D4** ⛰ NE Algeria
**Aurillac 73 D5** C France
**Aurora 51 F5** Colorado, USA
**Aurora 44 C5** Illinois, USA
**Aurora 47 E7** Missouri, USA
**Aus 128 B6** SW Namibia
**Austin 47 E4** Minnesota, USA
**Austin 51 B5** Nevada, USA
**Austin 48 G4** Texas, USA
**Australes, Îles 131** *Island group,* SW French Polynesia
**Australia 133 D3** ◆ *Commonwealth Republic*
**Australian Alps 133 G6** ⛰ SE Australia
**Australian Capital Territory 133 G6** *Territory,* SE Australia
**Austria 77 E8** ◆ *Republic,* C Europe
**Auvergne 73 D5** *Cultural region,* C France
**Auxerre 73 D3** C France
**Avarua 131** ○ Rarotonga, S Cook Islands
**Aveiro 75 B3** W Portugal
**Avellino 79 D6** S Italy
**Avesta 67 C5** C Sweden
**Aveyron 73 C6** ≈ S France
**Avezzano 79 D5** C Italy
**Aviemore 71 D3** N Scotland, UK
**Avignon 73 E6** SE France
**Ávila 75 D3** C Spain
**Avilés 75 C1** NW Spain
**Avranches 73 B2** N France
**Awaji-shima 103 E6** *Island,* SW Japan
**Awash 127 E3** C Ethiopia
**Awbari 122 F3** SW Libya
**Axel 68 B6** SW Netherlands
**Axel Heiberg Island 33 G1** *Island,* Nunavut, N Canada
**Ayacucho 115 C6** S Peru
**Ayagoz 94 D6** E Kazakhstan
**Ayamonte 75 B5** S Spain
**Aydarko'l Ko'li 101 F3** ◎ C Uzbekistan
**Aydın 97 A4** SW Turkey
**Ayers Rock** *see* Uluru
**Ayorou 124 D3** W Niger
**'Ayoûn el 'Atroûs 124 B3** SE Mauritania
**Ayr 71 C5** W Scotland, UK
**Aytos 83 F3** E Bulgaria
**Ayvalık 97 A3** W Turkey
**Azahar, Costa del 75 F4** *Coastal region,* E Spain
**Azaouâd 124 D2** *Desert,* C Mali
**Azerbaijan 97 I2** ◆ *Republic,* SW Asia
**Azoum, Bahr 124 H4** *Seasonal river,* SE Chad
**Azov 94 A4** SW Russ. Fed.
**Azov, Sea of 85 F6** *Sea,* NE Black Sea
**Aztec 48 C1** New Mexico, USA
**Azuaga 75 C5** W Spain
**Azuero, Península de 59 G7** *Peninsula,* S Panama
**Azul 117 C6** E Argentina
**Az Zarqa' 99 A2** NW Jordan
**Az Zawiyah 122 F2** NW Libya

## B

**Baardheere 127 E5** SW Somalia
**Baarle-Hertog 68 D5** N Belgium
**Baarn 68 D4** C Netherlands
**Babayevo 87 B4** NW Russ. Fed.
**Babeldaob 109 H5** *Island,* N Palau
**Bab el Mandeb 99 B7** *Strait,* Gulf of Aden/Red Sea
**Babruysk 85 D3** E Belarus
**Babuyan Channel 109 F3** *Channel,* N Philippines
**Babuyan Island 109 F3** *Island,* N Philippines
**Bacabal 115 G4** E Brazil
**Bacău 85 C6** NE Romania
**Bacheykava 85 D2** N Belarus
**Back 33 G4** ≈ Nunavut, N Canada
**Badajoz 75 B4** W Spain
**Baden-Baden 77 B6** SW Germany
**Bad Freienwalde 77 E3** NE Germany
**Badgastein 77 D8** NW Austria
**Bad Hersfeld 77 C5** C Germany
**Bad Homburg vor der Höhe 77 B5** W Germany
**Bad Ischl 77 E7** N Austria
**Bad Krozingen 77 B7** SW Germany
**Badlands 47 A4** *Physical region,* North Dakota, USA
**Badlands 47 A2** *Physical region,* South Dakota, USA
**Badu Island 133 F1** *Island,* Queensland, NE Australia
**Bad Vöslau 77 F7** NE Austria
**Badwater Basin 53 D7** *Depression,* California, USA
**Bafatá 124 A4** C Guinea-Bissau
**Baffin Bay 33 I2** *Bay,* Canada/Greenland
**Baffin Island 33 I3** *Island,* Nunavut, NE Canada
**Bafing 124 B4** ≈ W Africa
**Bafoussam 124 F5** W Cameroon
**Bafra 97 D2** N Turkey
**Bagaces 59 E5** NW Costa Rica
**Bagé 115 F9** S Brazil
**Baghdad 99 C2** ● C Iraq
**Baghlan 101 F4** NE Afghanistan
**Baghran 101 E5** S Afghanistan
**Bagoé 124 C4** ≈ Côte d'Ivoire/Mali
**Baguio 109 F3** Luzon, N Philippines
**Bagzane, Monts 124 F3** ▲ N Niger
**Bahamas 61 D2** ◆ *Commonwealth Republic,* N West Indies
**Baharly 101 C3** C Turkmenistan
**Bahawalpur 107 C2** E Pakistan
**Bahia 115 G5** ◈ *State,* E Brazil
**Bahía Blanca 117 B6** E Argentina
**Bahir Dar 127 D3** NW Ethiopia
**Bahraich 107 E3** N India
**Bahrain 99 D4** ◆ *Monarchy,* SW Asia
**Bahushewsk 85 D2** NE Belarus
**Baia Mare 85 B5** NW Romania
**Baïbokoum 124 G5** SW Chad
**Baie-Comeau 35 F4** Québec, SE Canada
**Baikal, Lake 94 F5** ◎ S Russ. Fed.
**Bailén 75 D5** S Spain
**Ba Illi 124 G4** SW Chad
**Bainbridge 43 E6** Georgia, USA
**Bairiki 131** ● Tarawa, NW Kiribati
**Bairnsdale 133 G6** Victoria, SE Australia
**Baishan 105 H2** NE China
**Baiyin 105 E3** N China
**Baja 81 E8** S Hungary
**Baja, Punta 137 C6** *Headland,* Easter Island, Chile
**Bajram Curri 83 D3** N Albania
**Bakala 124 H5** C CAR
**Baker 53 C3** Oregon, USA
**Baker & Howland Islands 131** *US* ◇ C Pacific Ocean
**Baker Lake 33 H4** Nunavut, N Canada
**Bakersfield 53 C8** California, USA
**Bakhtaran** *see* Kermanshah
**Baki** *see* Baku
**Bakony 81 D8** ⛰ W Hungary
**Baku 97 J2** ● E Azerbaijan
**Balabac Strait 109 E5** *Strait,* Malaysia/Philippines
**Balaguer 75 G2** NE Spain
**Balaïtous 73 B7** ▲ France/Spain
**Balakovo 87 C7** W Russ. Fed.
**Bala Morghab 101 E4** NW Afghanistan
**Balashov 87 B6** W Russ. Fed.
**Balaton, Lake 81 D8** ◎ Hungary
**Balbina, Represa 115 E3** ▣ NW Brazil
**Balboa 59 H6** C Panama
**Balcarce 117 C6** E Argentina
**Balclutha 135 B8** South Island, NZ
**Baldy Mountain 51 D1** ▲ Montana, USA
**Baldy Peak 48 C3** ▲ Arizona, USA
**Baleares, Islas** *see* Balearic Islands
**Balearic Islands 75 G4** *Island group,* Spain
**Baleine, Rivière à la 35 E2** ≈ Québec, E Canada
**Balen 68 D6** N Belgium
**Baleshwar 107 F4** E India
**Bali 109 E8** *Island,* C Indonesia
**Balıkesir 97 A3** W Turkey
**Balikpapan 109 E7** C Indonesia
**Balkanabat 101 B3** W Turkmenistan
**Balkan Mountains 83 E3** ⛰ Bulgaria/Serbia and Montenegro (Yugoslavia)
**Balkh 101 F4** N Afghanistan
**Balkhash 94 C6** SE Kazakhstan
**Balkhash, Lake 94 C6** ◎ SE Kazakhstan
**Balladonia 133 C5** W Australia
**Ballarat 133 F6** Victoria, SE Australia
**Ballinger 48 G4** Texas, USA
**Balsas 115 G4** E Brazil
**Balsas, Río 57 E5** ≈ S Mexico
**Bălţi 85 D5** N Moldova
**Baltic Sea 67 D7** *Sea,* N Europe
**Baltimore 43 H1** Maryland, USA
**Baluchistan 107 B3** *Cultural region,* SW Pakistan
**Balykchy 101 H2** NE Kyrgyzstan
**Bam 99 F3** SE Iran
**Bamako 124 C4** ● SW Mali
**Bambari 124 H5** C CAR
**Bamberg 77 C5** SE Germany
**Bamenda 124 F5** W Cameroon
**Banaba 137 H1** *Island,* W Kiribati
**Bananga 107 H6** Nicobar Islands, India
**Bandaaceh 109 A5** Sumatra, W Indonesia
**Bandama 124 C5** ≈ S Côte d'Ivoire
**Bandarbeyla 127 G3** NE Somalia
**Bandar-e 'Abbas 99 E4** S Iran
**Bandarlampung 109 B7** Sumatra, W Indonesia
**Bandar Seri Begawan 109 D5** ● N Brunei
**Banda Sea 109 G7** *Sea,* E Indonesia
**Bandırma 97 A2** NW Turkey
**Bandundu 128 B2** W Dem. Rep. Congo
**Bandung 109 C8** Java, C Indonesia
**Bangalore 107 D6** S India
**Bangassou 124 I5** SE CAR
**Banggai, Kepulauan 109 F6** *Island group,* C Indonesia
**Banghazi** *see* Benghazi
**Bangka, Pulau 109 C7** *Island,* W Indonesia
**Bangkok 109 B4** ● C Thailand
**Bangladesh 107 G3** ◆ *Republic,* S Asia
**Bangor 71 C5** E Northern Ireland, UK
**Bangor 71 D6** NW Wales, UK
**Bangor 41 G2** Maine, USA
**Bangui 124 H5** ● SW CAR
**Bangweulu, Lake 128 D3** ◎ N Zambia
**Bani 124 C4** ≈ S Mali
**Banja Luka 83 C2** NW Bosnia and Herzegovina
**Banjarmasin 109 E7** C Indonesia
**Banjul 124 A3** ● W Gambia
**Banks Island 33 F3** *Island,* NW Terr., NW Canada
**Banks Islands 137 G4** *Island group,* N Vanuatu
**Banks Lake 53 C2** ▣ Washington, USA
**Banks Peninsula 135 C6** *Peninsula,* South Island, NZ
**Banks Strait 133 G7** *Strait,* SW Tasman Sea
**Bankura 107 F4** NE India
**Banmauk 109 A2** N Myanmar
**Ban Nadou 109 C3** S Laos
**Banská Bystrica 81 E6** C Slovakia
**Bantry Bay 71 A7** *Bay,* SW Ireland
**Banyak, Kepulauan 109 A6** *Island group,* NW Indonesia
**Banyo 124 F5** NW Cameroon
**Banyoles 75 H2** NE Spain
**Baoji 105 E4** C China
**Baoro 124 G5** W CAR
**Baoshan 105 D5** SW China
**Baotou 105 F3** N China
**Ba'qubah 99 C2** C Iraq
**Baraawe 127 E5** S Somalia
**Baranavichy 85 C3** SW Belarus
**Barbados 61 K6** ◆ *Commonwealth Republic,* SE West Indies
**Barbastro 75 F2** NE Spain
**Barbate de Franco 75 C6** S Spain
**Barbuda 61 J4** *Island,* N Antigua and Barbuda
**Barcaldine 133 G3** Queensland, E Australia
**Barcelona 75 G2** E Spain
**Barcelona 115 D1** NE Venezuela
**Barcs 81 D9** SW Hungary
**Bardaï 124 G2** N Chad
**Bardejov 81 F6** NE Slovakia
**Bareilly 107 E3** N India
**Barendrecht 68 C4** SW Netherlands
**Barentin 73 C2** N France
**Barents Sea 87 C2** *Sea,* Arctic Ocean
**Bar Harbor 41 G2** Mount Desert Island, Maine, USA
**Bari 79 E6** SE Italy
**Barikowt 101 G4** NE Afghanistan
**Barillas 59 A2** NW Guatemala
**Barinas 115 C2** W Venezuela
**Barisal 107 G4** S Bangladesh
**Barisan, Pegunungan 109 B7** ⛰ Sumatra, W Indonesia
**Barito, Sungai 109 E7** ≈ Borneo, C Indonesia
**Barkly Tableland 133 E2** *Plateau,* Northern Territory/Queensland, N Australia
**Bârlad 85 C6** E Romania
**Bar-le-Duc 73 E2** NE France
**Barlee, Lake 133 B5** ◎ W Australia
**Barlee Range 133 B4** ⛰ W Australia
**Barletta 79 E5** SE Italy
**Barlinek 81 C3** W Poland
**Barmouth 71 D7** NW Wales, UK
**Barnaul 94 D5** C Russ. Fed.
**Barnstaple 71 D8** SW England, UK
**Baroghil Pass 101 G4** *Pass,* Afghanistan/Pakistan
**Barquisimeto 115 C1** NW Venezuela
**Barra de Río Grande 59 E4** E Nicaragua
**Barranca 115 B5** W Peru
**Barrancabermeja 115 B2** N Colombia
**Barranquilla 115 B1** N Colombia
**Barreiro 75 A4** W Portugal
**Barrier Range 133 F5** *Hill range,* NSW, SE Australia
**Barrier Reef 59 C1** *Reef,* E Belize
**Barrow 54 E1** Alaska, USA
**Barrow 71 B7** ≈ SE Ireland
**Barrow-in-Furness 71 D6** NW England, UK
**Barrow Island 133 A3** *Island,* W Australia
**Barstow 53 D8** California, USA
**Bartang 101 G4** ≈ SE Tajikistan
**Bartın 97 C2** N Turkey
**Bartlesville 47 D7** Oklahoma, USA
**Bartoszyce 81 E2** N Poland
**Baruun-Urt 105 F2** E Mongolia
**Barú, Volcán 59 F6** 🌋 W Panama
**Barva, Volcán 59 E6** 🌋 NW Costa Rica
**Barwon River 133 G5** ≈ NSW, SE Australia
**Barysaw 85 D2** NE Belarus
**Basarabeasca 85 D6** SE Moldova
**Basel 77 B7** NW Switzerland
**Basilan 109 F5** *Island,* SW Philippines
**Basingstoke 71 E8** S England, UK
**Basque Country, The 75 E1** *Cultural region,* N Spain
**Basra 99 D3** SE Iraq
**Bassano del Grappa 79 C2** NE Italy
**Bassein 109 A3** SW Myanmar
**Basse-Terre 61 J5** ○ Basse Terre, SW Guadeloupe
**Basseterre 61 J4** ● Saint Kitts, Saint Kitts and Nevis
**Bassett 47 C4** Nebraska, USA
**Bassikounou 124 C3** SE Mauritania
**Bass Strait 133 F7** *Strait,* SE Australia
**Bassum 77 B3** NW Germany
**Bastia 73 G5** Corsica, France
**Bastogne 68 E8** SE Belgium
**Bata 124 F6** NW Equatorial Guinea
**Batangas 109 F4** Luzon, N Philippines
**Batdambang 109 C4** NW Cambodia
**Batéké, Plateaux 128 B2** *Plateau,* S Congo
**Bath 71 D8** SW England, UK
**Bath 41 G3** Maine, USA
**Bathinda 107 D2** NW India
**Bathurst 133 G6** NSW, SE Australia
**Bathurst 35 F4** New Brunswick, SE Canada
**Bathurst Island 133 C1** *Island,* Northern Territory, N Australia
**Bathurst Island 33 G2** *Island,* Parry Islands, Nunavut, N Canada
**Batin, Wadi al 99 C3** *Dry watercourse,* SW Asia
**Batman 97 G4** SE Turkey
**Batna 122 E1** NE Algeria
**Baton Rouge 43 C6** Louisiana, USA
**Batticaloa 107 E8** E Sri Lanka
**Battipaglia 79 D6** S Italy
**Battle Mountain 51 B5** Nevada, USA
**Bat'umi 97 G2** W Georgia
**Batu Pahat 109 C6** Peninsular Malaysia
**Bauchi 124 F4** NE Nigeria
**Bautzen 77 E4** E Germany
**Bavaria 77 C7** *Cultural region,* SE Germany
**Bavarian Alps 77 C7** ⛰ Austria/Germany
**Bavispe, Río 57 C2** ≈ NW Mexico
**Bawiti 122 I3** N Egypt
**Bawku 124 D4** N Ghana
**Bayamo 61 D3** E Cuba
**Bayamón 55** E Puerto Rico
**Bayan Har Shan 105 D4** ⛰ C China
**Bayanhongor 105 D2** C Mongolia
**Bayano, Lago 59 H6** ◎ E Panama
**Bayard 48 C3** New Mexico, USA
**Bay City 44 D4** Michigan, USA
**Bay City 48 H5** Texas, USA
**Baydhabo 127 E5** SW Somalia
**Bayern** *see* Bavaria
**Bayeux 73 C2** N France
**Bay Islands 59 D2** *Island group,* N Honduras
**Baymak 87 D7** W Russ. Fed.
**Bayonne 73 B6** SW France
**Baýramaly 101 D4** S Turkmenistan
**Bayreuth 77 C5** SE Germany
**Baytown 48 I4** Texas, USA
**Baza 75 E5** S Spain
**Beacon 41 E4** New York, USA
**Beagle Channel 117 B9** *Channel,* Argentina/Chile
**Bear Lake 51 D4** ◎ NW USA
**Beas de Segura 75 E5** S Spain
**Beata, Isla 61 F5** *Island,* SW Dominican Republic
**Beatrice 47 D5** Nebraska, USA
**Beatty 51 B6** Nevada, USA
**Beaufort Sea 54 F1** *Sea* Arctic Ocean
**Beaufort West 128 C7** SW South Africa
**Beaumont 48 I4** Texas, USA
**Beaune 73 E4** C France
**Beauvais 73 D2** N France
**Beaver Falls 41 A5** Pennsylvania, USA
**Beaver Island 44 C3** *Island,* Michigan, USA
**Beaver River 47 B7** ≈ Oklahoma, USA
**Beaverton 53 B3** Oregon, USA
**Beawar 107 D3** N India
**Béchar 122 D2** W Algeria
**Beckley 43 G2** West Virginia, USA
**Bedford 71 E7** E England, UK
**Bedford 47 D7** Indiana, USA
**Bedum 68 F2** NE Netherlands
**Be'er Menuha 99 H7** S Israel
**Beernem 68 B6** NW Belgium
**Be'ér Sheva' 99 G6** S Israel
**Beesel 68 E6** SE Netherlands
**Beeville 48 G5** Texas, USA
**Bega 133 G6** NSW, SE Australia
**Beihai 105 F6** S China
**Beijing 105 F3** ● E China
**Beilen 68 E3** NE Netherlands
**Beira 128 E5** C Mozambique
**Beirut 99 A2** ● W Lebanon
**Beja 75 B5** SE Portugal
**Béjar 75 C3** N Spain
**Békéscsaba 81 F8** SE Hungary
**Bekobod 101 F3** E Uzbekistan
**Belarus 85 C2** ◆ *Republic,* E Europe
**Bełchatów 81 E4** C Poland
**Belcher Islands 35 C2** *Island group,* Nunavut, SE Canada
**Beledweyne 127 F4** C Somalia
**Belém 115 G3** N Brazil
**Belén 59 D5** SW Nicaragua
**Belen 48 D2** New Mexico, USA
**Belep, Îles 137 F6** *Island group,* W New Caledonia
**Belfast 71 C5** *Political division capital,* E Northern Ireland, UK
**Belfield 47 A2** North Dakota, USA
**Belfort 73 F3** E France
**Belgaum 107 D6** W India
**Belgium 68 B7** ◆ *Monarchy,* NW Europe
**Belgorod 87 A6** W Russ. Fed.
**Belgrade 83 D2** ● N Serbia and Montenegro (Yugoslavia)
**Belgrano II 138 B4** *Argentinian research station,* Antarctica
**Belitung, Pulau 109 C7** *Island,* W Indonesia
**Belize 59 B2** ◆ *Commonwealth Republic,* Central America
**Belize 59 B1** ≈ Belize/Guatemala
**Belize City 59 C1** NE Belize
**Belkofski 54 C3** Alaska, USA
**Belle Île 73 A3** *Island,* NW France
**Belle Isle, Strait of 35 G3** *Strait,* Newfoundland, E Canada
**Belleville 44 B7** Illinois, USA
**Bellevue 47 D5** Nebraska, USA
**Bellevue 53 B2** Washington, USA
**Bellingham 53 B1** Washington, USA
**Bellingshausen Sea 138 A4** *Sea,* Antarctica
**Bellinzona 77 B8** S Switzerland
**Bello 115 B2** W Colombia
**Bellona 137 E3** *Island,* S Solomon Islands
**Bellville 128 C7** SW South Africa
**Belmopan 59 B2** ● C Belize
**Belo Horizonte 115 G7** SE Brazil
**Belomorsk 87 B3** NW Russ. Fed.
**Beloretsk 87 D6** W Russ. Fed.
**Belorussia** *see* Belarus
**Belozersk 87 B4** NW Russ. Fed.
**Belton 48 H4** Texas, USA
**Belukha, Gora 94 D5** ▲ Kazakhstan/Russ. Fed.
**Belyy, Ostrov 94 D2** *Island,* N Russ. Fed.
**Bemaraha 128 G5** ⛰ W Madagascar
**Bemidji 47 E2** Minnesota, USA
**Bemmel 68 E4** SE Netherlands
**Benavente 75 C2** N Spain
**Bend 53 B4** Oregon, USA
**Bendery** *see* Tighina
**Bendigo 133 F6** Victoria, SE Australia
**Benešov 81 B5** W Czech Republic
**Benevento 79 D6** S Italy
**Bengbu 105 G4** E China
**Benghazi 122 G2** NE Libya
**Bengkulu 109 B7** Sumatra, W Indonesia
**Benguela 128 B4** W Angola
**Ben Hope 71 C3** ▲ N Scotland, UK
**Beni 128 D1** NE Dem. Rep. Congo
**Benidorm 75 F4** SE Spain
**Beni-Mellal 122 C2** C Morocco
**Benin 124 D4** ◆ *Republic,* W Africa
**Benin, Bight of 124 E5** *Gulf,* W Africa




◈ Administrative region ◆ Country ● Country capital ◇ Dependent territory ○ Dependent territory capital ⛰ Mountain range ▲ Mountain 🌋 Volcano ≈ River ◎ Lake ▣ Reservoir

CALTANISSETTA

Benin City 124 E5 SW Nigeria
Beni, Río 117 A2 ⇝ N Bolivia
Beni Suef 122 I3 N Egypt
Ben Nevis 71 C4 ▲ N Scotland, UK
Benson 48 C3 Arizona, USA
Benton 43 B4 Arkansas, USA
Benton Harbor 44 D5 Michigan, USA
Benue 124 F5 ⇝ Cameroon/Nigeria
Beograd see Belgrade
Berat 83 D4 C Albania
Berau, Teluk 109 H7 Bay, E Indonesia
Berbera 127 F3 NW Somalia
Berbérati 124 G5 SW CAR
Berck-Plage 73 D1 N France
Berdyans'k 85 G6 SE Ukraine
Bereket 101 C3 W Turkmenistan
Berettyó 81 F8 ⇝ Hungary/Romania
Berettyóújfalu 81 F7 E Hungary
Berezniki 87 D5 NW Russ. Fed.
Berga 75 G2 NE Spain
Bergamo 79 B2 N Italy
Bergen 77 D2 NE Germany
Bergen 68 C3 NW Netherlands
Bergen 67 A5 S Norway
Bergerac 73 C5 SW France
Bergeyk 68 D6 S Netherlands
Bergse Maas 68 D5 ⇝ S Netherlands
Beringen 68 D6 NE Belgium
Bering Sea 54 B1 Sea N Pacific Ocean
Bering Strait 54 D1 Strait Bering Sea/Chukchi Sea
Berja 75 E6 S Spain
Berkeley 53 B7 California, USA
Berkner Island 138 B4 Island, Antarctica
Berlin 77 D3 ● NE Germany
Berlin 41 F3 New Hampshire, USA
Bermejo, Río 117 B3 ⇝ N Argentina
Bermuda 26 UK ◇ N Atlantic Ocean
Bermeo 75 E1 N Spain
Bern 77 A8 ● W Switzerland
Bernau 77 D3 NE Germany
Bernburg 77 D4 C Germany
Berner Alpen 77 A8 ⛰ SW Switzerland
Bernier Island 133 A4 Island, W Australia
Berry 73 D3 Cultural region, C France
Berry Islands 61 C1 Island group, N Bahamas
Bertoua 124 G5 E Cameroon
Berwick-upon-Tweed 71 D4 N England, UK
Besançon 73 E4 E France
Betafo 128 G5 C Madagascar
Betanzos 75 B1 NW Spain
Bethlehem 128 D6 C South Africa
Bethlehem 41 D5 Pennsylvania, USA
Bethlehem 99 H6 C West Bank
Béticos, Sistemas 75 D5 ⛰ S Spain
Bétou 128 C1 N Congo
Bette, Pic 122 G4 ▲ S Libya
Beulah 44 D3 Michigan, USA
Beveren 68 C6 N Belgium
Beverley 71 E6 E England, UK
Beyla 124 C4 SE Guinea
Beyrouth see Beirut
Beyşehir Gölü 97 B4 ◎ C Turkey
Béziers 73 D6 S France
Bhadravati 107 D6 SW India
Bhagalpur 107 F3 NE India
Bhaktapur 107 F3 C Nepal
Bharuch 107 C4 W India
Bhavnagar 107 C4 W India
Bhopal 107 D4 C India
Bhubaneshwar 107 F4 E India
Bhusawal 107 D4 C India
Bhutan 107 G3 ◆ Monarchy, S Asia
Biak, Pulau 109 H6 Island, E Indonesia
Biała Podlaska 81 G3 E Poland
Białogard 81 C2 NW Poland
Białystok 81 G2 E Poland
Biarritz 73 B6 SW France
Biddeford 41 F3 Maine, USA
Bideford 71 D8 SW England, UK
Biel 77 A8 W Switzerland
Bielefeld 77 B4 NW Germany
Bielsko-Biała 81 E5 S Poland
Bielsk Podlaski 81 G3 E Poland
Biên Hoa 109 C4 S Vietnam
Bienville, Lac 35 D3 ◎ Québec, C Canada
Bié Plateau 128 C4 Plateau, C Angola
Big Bend National Park 48 E5 National park, Texas, USA
Big Cypress Swamp 43 G8 Wetland, SE USA
Bighorn Mountains 51 E3 ⛰ Wyoming, USA
Bighorn River 51 E3 ⇝ NW USA
Big Sioux River 47 D4 ⇝ N USA
Big Smoky Valley 51 B6 Valley, Nevada, USA
Big Spring 48 F3 Texas, USA
Bihać 83 B2 NW Bosnia and Herzegovina
Bihar 107 F3 Cultural region, N India
Biharamulo 127 C6 NW Tanzania
Bihosava 85 C1 NW Belarus
Bijelo Polje 83 D3 SW Serbia and Montenegro (Yugoslavia)
Bikaner 107 D3 NW India
Bikin 94 H5 SE Russ. Fed.
Bilaspur 107 E4 C India
Biläsuvar 97 I3 SE Azerbaijan
Bila Tserkva 85 D4 N Ukraine
Bilauktaung Range 109 B4 ⛰ Myanmar/Thailand
Bilbao 75 E1 N Spain
Bilecik 97 B3 NW Turkey
Billings 51 E2 Montana, USA
Bilma, Grand Erg de 124 G2 Desert, NE Niger
Biloela 133 H4 Queensland, E Australia
Biloxi 43 C6 Mississippi, USA
Biltine 124 H3 E Chad
Bilzen 68 D6 NE Belgium
Bimini Islands 61 C1 Island group, W Bahamas
Binche 68 C7 S Belgium
Binghamton 41 D4 New York, USA
Bingöl 97 F3 E Turkey
Bintulu 109 D6 East Malaysia
Binzhou 105 G3 E China
Bío Bío, Río 117 A6 ⇝ C Chile
Bioco, Isla de 124 F6 Island, NW Equatorial Guinea
Birak 122 F3 C Libya
Birao 124 I4 NE CAR
Biratnagar 107 F3 SE Nepal
Birhar Sharif 107 F3 N India
Birjand 99 F2 E Iran
Birkenfeld 77 A6 SW Germany
Birkenhead 71 D6 NW England, UK
Birmingham 71 E7 C England, UK
Birmingham 43 D4 Alabama, USA
Bîr Mogreïn 122 A3 N Mauritania
Birnin Kebbi 124 E4 NW Nigeria
Birnin Konni 124 E3 SW Niger
Birobidzhan 94 H5 SE Russ. Fed.
Birsk 87 D6 W Russ. Fed.
Birżebbuġa 88 B6 SE Malta
Bisbee 48 C4 Arizona, USA
Biscay, Bay of 73 B4 Bay, France/Spain
Bishah, Wadi 99 B5 Dry watercourse, C Saudi Arabia
Bishkek 101 H2 ● N Kyrgyzstan
Bishop 53 C7 California, USA
Biskra 122 E1 NE Algeria
Biskupiec 81 F2 N Poland
Bislig 109 G5 S Philippines
Bismarck 47 B2 North Dakota, USA
Bismarck Archipelago 137 B1 Island group, NE PNG
Bismarck Sea 137 B1 Sea, W Pacific Ocean
Bissau 124 A4 ● W Guinea-Bissau
Bistrița 85 B6 N Romania
Bitam 128 A1 N Gabon
Bitburg 77 A5 SW Germany
Bitlis 97 G4 SE Turkey
Bitola 83 D4 S FYR Macedonia
Bitonto 79 E6 SE Italy
Bitterfeld 77 D4 E Germany
Bitterroot Range 51 C2 ⛰ NW USA
Biu 124 G4 E Nigeria
Biwa-ko 103 E6 ◎ Honshu, SW Japan
Bizerte 122 F1 N Tunisia
Bjørnøya 139 D5 Island, N Norway
Blackall 133 G4 Queensland, E Australia
Black Drin 83 D3 ⇝ Albania/FYR Macedonia
Blackfoot 51 D4 Idaho, USA
Black Forest 77 B7 ⛰ SW Germany
Black Hills 47 A4 ⛰ N USA
Black Mountain 51 D5 ▲ Colorado, USA
Blackpool 71 D6 NW England, UK
Black Range 48 D3 ⛰ New Mexico, USA
Black River 109 B2 ⇝ China/Vietnam
Black Rock Desert 51 A4 Desert, Nevada, USA
Black Sea 62 Sea, Asia/Europe
Black Sea Lowland 85 E6 Depression, SE Europe
Black Volta 124 D4 ⇝ W Africa
Blackwater 71 B7 ⇝ S Ireland
Blagoevgrad 83 E3 W Bulgaria
Blagoveshchensk 94 H5 SE Russ. Fed.
Blanca, Bahía 117 B6 Bay, E Argentina
Blanca, Costa 75 F5 Physical region, SE Spain
Blanche, Lake 133 F4 ◎ S Australia
Blanc, Mont 73 F5 ▲ France/Italy
Blanco, Cape 53 A4 Headland, Oregon, USA
Blanes 75 H2 NE Spain
Blankenberge 68 B5 NW Belgium
Blankenheim 77 A5 W Germany
Blanquilla, Isla 61 I7 Island, N Venezuela
Blantyre 128 E4 S Malawi
Blaricum 68 D4 C Netherlands
Blenheim 135 C5 South Island, NZ
Blida 122 D1 N Algeria
Bloemfontein 128 D6 ● C South Africa
Blois 73 C3 C France
Bloomfield 48 C1 New Mexico, USA
Bloomington 44 B6 Illinois, USA
Bloomington 44 D7 Indiana, USA
Bloomington 47 E3 Minnesota, USA
Bloomsburg 41 D5 Pennsylvania, USA
Bloomsbury 133 G3 Queensland, NE Australia
Bluefield 43 G2 West Virginia, USA
Bluefields 59 E4 SE Nicaragua
Blue Mountains 133 G6 ⛰ NSW, SE Australia
Blue Mountains 53 C3 ⛰ NW USA
Blue Nile 127 C3 ⇝ Ethiopia/Sudan
Bluff 51 D6 Utah, USA
Blumenau 115 F8 S Brazil
Blythe 53 E9 California, USA
Blytheville 43 C3 Arkansas, USA
Bo 124 B5 S Sierra Leone
Boaco 59 D4 S Nicaragua
Boa Vista 115 E3 NW Brazil
Bobaomby, Tanjona 128 G4 Headland, N Madagascar
Bobo-Dioulasso 124 C4 SW Burkina Faso
Boca Raton 43 G8 Florida, USA
Bocay 59 D3 N Nicaragua
Bocholt 77 A4 W Germany
Bochum 77 A4 W Germany
Bodaybo 94 F4 E Russ. Fed.
Boden 67 D3 N Sweden
Bodmin 71 C8 SW England, UK
Bodø 67 C2 C Norway
Bodrum 97 A4 SW Turkey
Boende 128 C2 C Dem. Rep. Congo
Bogalusa 43 C6 Louisiana, USA
Bogatynia 81 B4 SW Poland
Boğazlıyan 97 D3 C Turkey
Bogia 137 B1 N PNG
Bogor 109 C8 Java, C Indonesia
Bogotá 115 B2 ● C Colombia
Bo Hai 105 G3 Gulf, NE China
Bohemia 81 B6 Cultural region, W Czech Republic
Bohemian Forest 77 D6 ⛰ C Europe
Bohol Sea 109 F5 Sea, S Philippines
Bohoro Shan 105 B2 ⛰ NW China
Boise 51 B3 Idaho, USA
Boise City 47 A7 Oklahoma, USA
Boizenburg 77 C3 N Germany
Bojnūrd 99 E1 N Iran
Boké 124 A4 W Guinea
Boknafjorden 67 A5 Fjord, S Norway
Bol 124 G3 W Chad
Bolesławiec 81 C4 SW Poland
Bolgatanga 124 D4 N Ghana
Bolivia 117 A2 ◆ Republic, W South America
Bollene 73 E6 SE France
Bollnäs 67 C5 C Sweden
Bollon 133 G4 Queensland, C Australia
Bologna 79 C3 N Italy
Bol'shevik, Ostrov 94 F2 Island, Severnaya Zemlya, N Russ. Fed.
Bol'shezemel'skaya Tundra 87 E3 Physical region, NW Russ. Fed.
Bol'shoy Lyakhovskiy, Ostrov 94 G2 Island, NE Russ. Fed.
Bolton 71 D6 NW England, UK
Bolu 97 C2 NW Turkey
Bolungarvík 67 A1 NW Iceland
Bolzano 79 C1 N Italy
Boma 128 B3 W Dem. Rep. Congo
Bombay see Mumbai
Bomu 128 C1 ⇝ CAR/Dem. Rep. Congo
Bonaire 61 H7 Island, E Netherlands Antilles
Bonanza 59 E3 NE Nicaragua
Bonaparte Archipelago 133 B2 Island group, W Australia
Bon, Cap 88 E4 Headland, N Tunisia
Bondo 128 C1 N Dem. Rep. Congo
Bondoukou 124 D5 E Côte d'Ivoire
Bone, Teluk 109 F7 Bay, Celebes, C Indonesia
Bongaigaon 107 G3 NE India
Bongo, Massif des 124 H4 ⛰ NE CAR
Bongor 124 G4 SW Chad
Bonifacio 73 G6 Corsica, France
Bonifacio, Strait of 79 A5 Strait, C Mediterranean Sea
Bonin Trench 15 Undersea feature, NW Pacific Ocean
Bonn 77 A5 W Germany
Boonville 41 D3 New York, USA
Boosaaso 127 F3 N Somalia
Boothia, Gulf of 33 H3 Gulf, Nunavut, NE Canada
Boothia Peninsula 33 H3 Peninsula, Nunavut, NE Canada
Boppard 77 B5 W Germany
Boquete 59 F6 W Panama
Boquillas 57 D2 NE Mexico
Bor 127 C4 S Sudan
Bor 83 D2 E Serbia and Montenegro (Yugoslavia)
Borah Peak 51 B3 ▲ Idaho, USA
Borås 67 C6 S Sweden
Bordeaux 73 B5 SW France
Bordj Omar Driss 122 E3 E Algeria
Børgefjelt 67 C3 ⛰ C Norway
Borger 68 F2 NE Netherlands
Borger 48 F2 Texas, USA
Borgholm 67 C6 S Sweden
Borisoglebsk 87 B6 W Russ. Fed.
Borlänge 67 C5 C Sweden
Borne 68 F4 E Netherlands
Borneo 109 D7 Island, Brunei/Indonesia/Malaysia
Bornholm 67 C7 Island, E Denmark
Borovichi 87 A4 W Russ. Fed.
Bosanski Novi 83 B1 NW Bosnia and Herzegovina
Boskovice 81 C6 SE Czech Republic
Bosna 83 C2 ⇝ N Bosnia and Herzegovina
Bosna i Hercegovina, Federacija 65 ⬖ Republic, Bosnia and Herzegovina
Bosnia and Herzegovina 83 C2 ◆ Republic, SE Europe
Boso-hanto 103 G6 Peninsula, Honshu, S Japan
Bosporus 96 B2 Strait, NW Turkey
Bossangoa 124 H5 C CAR
Bossembélé 124 H5 C CAR
Bossier City 43 B5 Louisiana, USA
Bosten Hu 105 C3 ◎ NW China
Boston 71 E6 E England, UK
Boston 41 F4 Massachusetts, USA
Boston Mountains 43 B3 ⛰ Arkansas, USA
Botany Bay 133 H6 Inlet, NSW, SE Australia
Boteti 128 C5 ⇝ N Botswana
Bothnia, Gulf of 67 D4 Gulf, N Baltic Sea
Botoșani 85 C5 NE Romania
Botrange 68 E7 ▲ E Belgium
Botswana 128 C5 ◆ Republic, S Africa
Bouar 124 G5 W CAR
Bou Craa 122 B3 NW Western Sahara
Bougainville Island 137 D2 Island, NE PNG
Bougaroun, Cap 88 D4 Headland, NE Algeria
Bougouni 124 C4 SW Mali
Boujdour 122 A3 W Western Sahara
Boulder 51 F5 Colorado, USA
Boulder 51 D2 Montana, USA
Boulogne-sur-Mer 73 D1 N France
Boûmdeïd 124 B3 S Mauritania
Boundiali 124 C4 N Côte d'Ivoire
Bountiful 51 D5 Utah, USA
Bourail 137 G6 C New Caledonia
Bourbonnais 73 D4 Cultural region, C France
Bourg-en-Bresse 73 E4 E France
Bourges 73 D4 C France
Bourgogne see Burgundy
Bourke 133 G5 NSW, SE Australia
Bournemouth 71 E8 S England, UK
Boutilimit 124 A3 SW Mauritania
Bowen 133 G3 Queensland, NE Australia
Bowling Green 43 E3 Kentucky, USA
Bowling Green 44 E5 Ohio, USA
Bowman 47 A2 North Dakota, USA
Boxmeer 68 E5 SE Netherlands
Boysun 101 F3 S Uzbekistan
Bozeman 51 D3 Montana, USA
Bozüyük 97 B3 NW Turkey
Brač 83 B3 Island, S Croatia
Bradford 71 E6 N England, UK
Bradford 41 B4 Pennsylvania, USA
Brady 48 G4 Texas, USA
Braga 75 B2 NW Portugal
Bragança 75 C2 NE Portugal
Brahmanbaria 107 G3 E Bangladesh
Brahmapur 107 F5 E India
Brahmaputra 107 H3 ⇝ S Asia
Brăila 85 D7 E Romania
Braine-le-Comte 68 C7 SW Belgium
Brainerd 47 E2 Minnesota, USA
Brampton 35 D6 Ontario, S Canada
Brandberg 128 B5 ▲ NW Namibia
Brandenburg 77 D3 NE Germany
Brandon 33 H7 Manitoba, S Canada
Braniewo 81 E2 N Poland
Brasília 115 G6 ● C Brazil
Brașov 85 C6 C Romania
Bratislava 81 D7 ● SW Slovakia
Bratsk 94 F5 C Russ. Fed.
Braunschweig 77 C4 N Germany
Brava, Costa 75 H2 Coastal region, NE Spain
Bravo, Río 57 D2 ⇝ Mexico/USA
Brawley 53 D9 California, USA
Brazil 115 C4 ◆ Federal Republic, South America
Brazil Basin 13 Undersea feature, W Atlantic Ocean
Brazilian Highlands 115 G6 ⛰ E Brazil
Brazos River 48 H4 ⇝ Texas, USA
Brazzaville 128 B2 ● S Congo
Brecht 68 C5 N Belgium
Breda 68 D5 S Netherlands
Bree 68 D6 NE Belgium
Bregalnica 83 E3 ⇝ E FYR Macedonia
Bremen 77 B3 NW Germany
Bremerhaven 77 B3 NW Germany
Bremerton 53 B2 Washington, USA
Brenham 48 H4 Texas, USA
Brenner Pass 77 C8 Pass, Austria/Italy
Brescia 79 C2 N Italy
Bressanone 79 C1 N Italy
Brest 85 B3 SW Belarus
Brest 73 A2 NW France
Bretagne see Brittany
Brewton 43 D6 Alabama, USA
Bria 124 H5 C CAR
Briançon 73 F5 SE France
Bridgeport 53 C6 California, USA
Bridgeport 41 E5 Connecticut, USA
Bridgetown 61 K6 ● SW Barbados
Bridlington 71 E6 E England, UK
Bridport 71 D8 S England, UK
Brig 77 B8 SW Switzerland
Brigham City 51 D4 Utah, USA
Brighton 71 E8 SE England, UK
Brighton 51 F5 Colorado, USA
Brindisi 79 F6 SE Italy
Brisbane 133 H4 Queensland, E Australia
Bristol 71 D7 SW England, UK
Bristol 41 E4 Connecticut, USA
Bristol 43 F3 Virginia, USA
Bristol Bay 54 C2 Bay, Alaska, USA
Bristol Channel 71 D8 Inlet, England/Wales, UK
British Columbia 33 E5 ⬖ Province, SW Canada
British Indian Ocean Territory 27 UK ◇ C Indian Ocean
British Isles 62 Island group, Ireland/United Kingdom
British Virgin Islands 61 I4 UK ◇ E West Indies
Brittany 73 B2 Cultural region, NW France
Brive-la-Gaillarde 73 C5 C France
Brno 81 C6 SE Czech Republic
Brockton 41 F4 Massachusetts, USA
Brodeur Peninsula 33 H3 Peninsula, Baffin Island, Nunavut, NE Canada
Brodnica 81 E2 N Poland
Broek-in-Waterland 68 D3 C Netherlands
Broken Hill 133 F5 NSW, SE Australia
Brookhaven 43 C5 Mississippi, USA
Brookings 47 D3 South Dakota, USA
Brooks Range 54 E2 Mountain range Alaska, USA
Brookton 133 B5 W Australia
Broome 133 C2 W Australia
Broomfield 51 F5 Colorado, USA
Brownfield 48 F3 Texas, USA
Brownsville 48 H6 Texas, USA
Brownwood 48 G4 Texas, USA
Bruges 68 B6 NW Belgium
Brugge see Bruges
Brummen 68 E4 E Netherlands
Brunei 109 D5 ◆ Monarchy, SE Asia
Brunner, Lake 135 C6 ◎ South Island, NZ
Brunswick 43 G6 Georgia, USA
Brunswick 41 G3 Maine, USA
Brus Laguna 59 E2 E Honduras
Brussel see Brussels
Brussels 68 C6 ● C Belgium
Bruxelles see Brussels
Bryan 48 H4 Texas, USA
Bryansk 87 A6 W Russ. Fed.
Brzeg 81 D4 SW Poland
Buala 137 E2 E Solomon Islands
Bucaramanga 115 C2 N Colombia
Buchanan 124 B5 SW Liberia
Buchanan, Lake 48 G4 ▣ Texas, USA
Bucharest 85 C7 ● S Romania
București see Bucharest
Bucyrus 44 E6 Ohio, USA
Budapest 81 E7 ● N Hungary
Budaun 107 E3 N India
Buenaventura 115 B3 W Colombia
Buena Vista 117 B2 C Bolivia
Buenos Aires 117 C5 ● E Argentina
Buenos Aires 59 F6 SE Costa Rica
Buenos Aires, Lago 117 A8 ◎ Argentina/Chile
Buffalo 41 B3 New York, USA
Buffalo 47 A3 South Dakota, USA
Buffalo 48 H4 Texas, USA
Buffalo Narrows 33 G6 Saskatchewan, C Canada
Bug 85 B3 ⇝ E Europe
Buguruslan 87 D6 W Russ. Fed.
Bujalance 75 D5 S Spain
Bujanovac 83 D3 SE Serbia and Montenegro (Yugoslavia)
Bujumbura 127 B6 ● W Burundi
Buka Island 137 D2 Island, NE PNG
Bukavu 128 D2 E Dem. Rep. Congo
Bukoba 127 C5 NW Tanzania
Bülach 77 B7 NW Switzerland
Bulawayo 128 D5 SW Zimbabwe
Bulgaria 83 E3 ◆ Republic, SE Europe
Bullhead City 48 A2 Arizona, USA
Bull Shoals Lake 47 F7 ▣ C USA
Bulukumba 109 E7 Celebes, C Indonesia
Bumba 128 C1 N Dem. Rep. Congo
Bunbury 133 B6 W Australia
Bundaberg 133 H4 Queensland, E Australia
Bungo-suido 103 D7 Strait, SW Japan
Bünyan 97 D3 C Turkey
Buon Ma Thuot 109 C4 S Vietnam
Buraydah 99 C4 N Saudi Arabia
Burco 127 F3 NW Somalia
Burdur 97 B4 SW Turkey
Burdur Gölü 97 B4 Salt lake, SW Turkey
Bure 127 D3 NW Ethiopia
Burgas 83 G3 E Bulgaria
Burgaski Zaliv 97 A1 Gulf, E Bulgaria
Burgos 75 D2 N Spain
Burgundy 73 E4 Cultural region, E France
Burhan Budai Shan 105 D4 ⛰ C China
Burjassot 75 F4 E Spain
Burkburnett 48 G2 Texas, USA
Burketown 133 F2 Queensland, NE Australia
Burkina Faso 124 C4 ◆ Republic, W Africa
Burkina see Burkina Faso
Burley 51 C4 Idaho, USA
Burlington 51 G5 Colorado, USA
Burlington 47 F5 Iowa, USA
Burlington 41 E3 Vermont, USA
Burma see Myanmar
Burnie 133 F7 Tasmania, SE Australia
Burns 53 C4 Oregon, USA
Burnside 33 G4 ⇝ Nunavut, NW Canada
Burns Junction 53 C4 Oregon, USA
Burnsville 47 E3 Minnesota, USA
Burriana 75 F3 E Spain
Bursa 97 B3 NW Turkey
Burundi 127 B6 ◆ Republic, C Africa
Buru, Pulau 109 F7 Island, E Indonesia
Bushire 99 D3 S Iran
Busselton 133 B6 W Australia
Buta 128 D1 N Dem. Rep. Congo
Butler 41 B5 Pennsylvania, USA
Buton, Pulau 109 F7 Island, C Indonesia
Butte 51 C2 Montana, USA
Button Islands 35 E1 Island group, Québec, NE Canada
Butuan 109 F5 S Philippines
Buulobarde 127 F4 C Somalia
Buur Gaabo 127 E5 S Somalia
Buxoro 101 E3 C Uzbekistan
Buynaksk 87 B9 SW Russ. Fed.
Büyükmenderes Nehri 97 A4 ⇝ SW Turkey
Buzău 85 C7 SE Romania
Büzmeýin 101 C3 C Turkmenistan
Buzuluk 87 C6 W Russ. Fed.
Bydgoszcz 81 D3 W Poland
Byelaruskaya Hrada 85 C3 Ridge, N Belarus
Byerezino 85 D2 ⇝ C Belarus
Bytča 81 D6 NW Slovakia
Bytów 81 D2 NW Poland

## C

Caazapá 117 C4 S Paraguay
Caballo Reservoir 48 D3 ▣ New Mexico, USA
Cabañaquinta 75 C1 N Spain
Cabanatuan 109 F3 N Philippines
Cabinda 128 B2 NW Angola
Cabinda 128 B3 Province, NW Angola
Cabora Bassa, Lake 128 E4 ▣ NW Mozambique
Caborca 57 B2 NW Mexico
Cabo Rojo 55 Puerto Rico, North America
Cabot Strait 35 G4 Strait, E Canada
Cabras Island 55 Island W Guam
Cabrera 75 G4 Island, Balearic Islands, Spain
Cáceres 75 C4 W Spain
Cachimbo, Serra do 115 E4 ⛰ C Brazil
Caconda 128 B4 C Angola
Čadca 81 D6 N Slovakia
Cadillac 44 D4 Michigan, USA
Cadiz 109 F4 C Philippines
Cádiz 75 C6 SW Spain
Cádiz, Golfo de see Cadiz, Gulf of
Cadiz, Gulf of 75 B6 Gulf, Portugal/Spain
Caen 73 C2 N France
Cafayate 117 B4 N Argentina
Cagayan de Oro 109 F5 Mindanao, S Philippines
Cagliari 79 A6 Sardinia, Italy
Caguas 61 I4 E Puerto Rico
Cahors 73 C6 S France
Cahul 85 D6 S Moldova
Caicos Passage 61 F3 Strait, Bahamas/Turks and Caicos Islands
Cairns 133 G2 Queensland, NE Australia
Cairo 122 I2 ● N Egypt
Cajamarca 115 B5 NW Peru
Calabar 124 F5 S Nigeria
Calahorra 75 E2 N Spain
Calais 73 D1 N France
Calais 41 H2 Maine, USA
Calama 117 A3 N Chile
Călărași 85 C7 SE Romania
Calatayud 75 E3 NE Spain
Calbayog 109 F4 Samar, C Philippines
Calcasieu Lake 43 B6 ◎ Louisiana, USA
Calcutta see Kolkata
Caldas da Rainha 75 A4 W Portugal
Caldera 117 A4 N Chile
Caldwell 51 B3 Idaho, USA
Caledonia 59 C1 N Belize
Caleta Olivia 117 B8 SE Argentina
Calgary 33 G7 Alberta, SW Canada
Cali 115 B3 W Colombia
Calicut 107 D7 SW India
Caliente 51 C6 Nevada, USA
California 53 C8 ⬖ State, W USA
California, Gulf of 57 B2 Gulf, NE Mexico
Callabonna, Lake 133 F5 ◎ S Australia
Callao 115 B5 W Peru
Callosa de Segura 75 F5 E Spain
Caloundra 133 H4 Queensland, E Australia
Caltanissetta 79 D8 Sicily, Italy

CAR Central African Republic FYR Former Yugoslavian Rebublic NSW New South Wales NZ New Zealand PNG Papua New Guinea Russ. Fed. Russian Federation UAE United Arab Emirates UK United Kingdom USA United States of America

◆ Administrative region  ◆ Country  ● Country capital  ◇ Dependent territory  ○ Dependent territory capital  ▲ Mountain range  ▲ Mountain  ⌀ Volcano  ⌀ River  ● Lake  ▢ Reservo

◆ Administrative region    ◆ Country    ● Country capital    ◊ Dependent territory    ○ Dependent territory capital    ▲ Mountain range    ▲ Mountain    ☒ Volcano    ↔ River    ☉ Lake    ▣ Reservo

KOKSOAK


**Koksoak** 35 D2 ≈ Québec, E Canada
**Kokstad** 128 D7 E South Africa
**Kola Peninsula** 87 C3 *Peninsula,* NW Russ. Fed.
**Kolari** 67 E2 NW Finland
**Kolárovo** 81 D7 SW Slovakia
**Kolda** 124 A3 S Senegal
**Kolding** 67 B7 C Denmark
**Kolguyev, Ostrov** 87 C2 *Island,* NW Russ. Fed.
**Kolhapur** 107 D5 SW India
**Kolín** 81 B5 C Czech Republic
**Kolka** 67 E6 NW Latvia
**Kolkata** 107 G4 NE India
**Köln** *see* Cologne
**Koło** 81 D3 C Poland
**Kołobrzeg** 81 C2 NW Poland
**Kolokani** 124 C3 W Mali
**Kolomna** 87 B5 W Russ. Fed.
**Kolpa** 83 B1 ≈ Croatia/Slovenia
**Kolpino** 87 A4 NW Russ. Fed.
**Kol'skiy Poluostrov** *see* Kola Peninsula
**Kolwezi** 128 D3 S Dem. Rep. Congo
**Kolyma** 94 H2 ≈ NE Russ. Fed.
**Kolyma Range** 94 H3 ⛰ E Russ. Fed.
**Komatsu** 103 F5 SW Japan
**Komoé** 124 C4 ≈ E Côte d'Ivoire
**Komotiní** 83 F4 NE Greece
**Komsomolets, Ostrov** 94 E1 *Island,* N Russ. Fed.
**Komsomol'sk-na-Amure** 94 H5 SE Russ. Fed.
**Kondopoga** 87 B4 NW Russ. Fed.
**Koné** 137 G6 W New Caledonia
**Köneürgenç** 101 D2 N Turkmenistan
**Kong Frederik VIII Land** 139 B5 *Physical region,* NE Greenland
**Kongolo** 128 D2 E Dem. Rep. Congo
**Kongor** 127 C4 SE Sudan
**Kongsberg** 67 B5 S Norway
**Konin** 81 D3 C Poland
**Kónitsa** 83 D4 W Greece
**Konosha** 87 B4 NW Russ. Fed.
**Konotop** 85 E3 NE Ukraine
**Konstanz** 77 B7 S Germany
**Konya** 97 C4 C Turkey
**Kopaonik** 83 D3 ⛰ S Serbia and Montenegro (Yugoslavia)
**Koper** 77 E9 SW Slovenia
**Köpetdag Gershi** 101 C3 ⛰ Iran/Turkmenistan
**Koppeh Dagh** 99 E1 ⛰ Iran/Turkmenistan
**Korat Plateau** 109 B3 *Plateau,* E Thailand
**Korçë** 83 D4 SE Albania
**Korčula** 83 B3 *Island,* S Croatia
**Korea Bay** 105 G3 *Bay,* China/N Korea
**Korea Strait** 103 C7 *Channel,* Japan/South Korea
**Korhogo** 124 C4 N Côte d'Ivoire
**Korinthos** *see* Corinth
**Koriyama** 103 G4 C Japan
**Korla** 105 C2 NW China
**Körmend** 81 C8 W Hungary
**Koro** 137 J5 *Island,* C Fiji
**Koróni** 83 E6 S Greece
**Koror** 130 ● N Palau
**Koro Sea** 137 J5 *Sea,* C Fiji
**Korosten'** 85 D4 NW Ukraine
**Koro Toro** 124 H3 N Chad
**Kortrijk** 68 B6 W Belgium
**Koryak Range** 94 I2 ⛰ NE Russ. Fed.
**Koryazhma** 87 C4 NW Russ. Fed.
**Kos** 83 G6 *Island,* Dodecanese, Greece
**Ko-saki** 103 C7 *Headland,* Tsushima, SW Japan
**Kościerzyna** 81 D2 NW Poland
**Kosciuszko, Mount** 133 G6 ▲ NSW, SE Australia
**Koshikijima-retto** 103 C8 *Island group,* SW Japan
**Košice** 81 F6 E Slovakia
**Koson** 101 E3 S Uzbekistan
**Kosong** 103 B5 SE North Korea
**Kosovo** 83 D3 *Cultural region,* S Serbia and Montenegro (Yugoslavia)
**Kosovska Mitrovica** 83 D3 S Serbia and Montenegro (Yugoslavia)
**Kossou, Lac de** 124 C5 ◎ C Côte d'Ivoire
**Kostanay** 94 C4 N Kazakhstan
**Kostroma** 87 B5 NW Russ. Fed.
**Kostyantynivka** 85 G5 SE Ukraine
**Koszalin** 81 C2 NW Poland
**Kota** 107 D3 N India
**Kota Bharu** 109 B5 Peninsular Malaysia
**Kota Kinabalu** 109 D5 East Malaysia
**Kotel'nyy, Ostrov** 94 F2 *Island,* N Russ. Fed.
**Kotka** 67 F5 S Finland
**Kotlas** 87 C4 NW Russ. Fed.
**Kotovs'k** 85 D5 SW Ukraine
**Kotto** 124 I5 ≈ CAR/Dem. Rep. Congo
**Kotuy** 94 F3 ≈ N Russ. Fed.
**Koudougou** 124 D4 C Burkina Faso
**Koulamoutou** 128 B2 C Gabon
**Koulikoro** 124 C4 SW Mali
**Koumac** 137 G6 W New Caledonia
**Koumra** 124 H4 S Chad
**Kourou** 115 F2 N French Guiana
**Kousséri** 124 G4 NE Cameroon
**Koutiala** 124 C4 S Mali
**Kouvola** 67 F5 S Finland
**Kovel'** 85 B4 NW Ukraine
**Kozáni** 83 D4 N Greece
**Kozara** 83 B2 ⛰ NW Bosnia and Herzegovina
**Kozloduy** 83 E2 NW Bulgaria
**Kozu-shima** 103 F6 *Island,* E Japan
**Kpalimé** 124 D5 SW Togo
**Kragujevac** 83 D2 C Serbia and Montenegro (Yugoslavia)
**Kra, Isthmus of** 109 B5 *Isthmus,* Malaysia/Thailand
**Kraków** 81 E5 S Poland
**Kraljevo** 83 D2 C Serbia and Montenegro (Yugoslavia)
**Kramators'k** 85 G5 SE Ukraine
**Kramfors** 67 D4 C Sweden
**Kranj** 77 E8 NW Slovenia
**Krasnoarmeysk** 87 B7 W Russ. Fed.
**Krasnodar** 87 A8 SW Russ. Fed.
**Krasnokamensk** 94 G5 S Russ. Fed.
**Krasnokamsk** 87 D5 W Russ. Fed.
**Krasnoyarsk** 94 E5 S Russ. Fed.
**Krasnystaw** 81 G4 SE Poland
**Krasnyy Kut** 87 C7 W Russ. Fed.
**Krasnyy Luch** 85 G5 E Ukraine
**Krefeld** 77 A4 W Germany
**Kremenchuk** 85 E5 NE Ukraine
**Kremenchuk Reservoir** 85 D5 ⊟ C Ukraine
**Kreminna** 85 G4 E Ukraine
**Kremmling** 51 E5 Colorado, USA
**Krishna** 107 E5 ≈ C India
**Krishnagiri** 107 D6 SE India
**Kristiansand** 67 B6 S Norway
**Kristianstad** 67 C7 S Sweden
**Kristiansund** 67 B4 S Norway
**Kriti** *see* Crete
**Kritikó Pélagos** *see* Crete, Sea of
**Krk** 83 B1 *Island,* NW Croatia
**Kronach** 77 C5 E Germany
**Kroonstad** 128 D6 C South Africa
**Kropotkin** 87 A8 SW Russ. Fed.
**Krosno** 81 F5 SE Poland
**Krosno Odrzańskie** 81 B3 W Poland
**Krško** 77 F8 E Slovenia
**Krung Thep, Ao** 109 B4 *Bay,* S Thailand
**Kruševac** 83 D2 C Serbia and Montenegro (Yugoslavia)
**Kryms'ki Hory** 85 F7 ⛰ S Ukraine
**Kryvyy Rih** 85 E5 SE Ukraine
**Ksar-el-Kebir** 122 C1 NW Morocco
**Kuala Lumpur** 109 B6 ● Peninsular Malaysia
**Kuala Terengganu** 109 C5 Peninsular Malaysia
**Kuantan** 109 C6 Peninsular Malaysia
**Kuban'** 85 G6 ≈ SW Russ. Fed.
**Kuching** 109 D6 East Malaysia
**Kuchnay Darweyshan** 101 E6 S Afghanistan
**Kudus** 109 D8 Java, C Indonesia
**Kugluktuk** 33 G4 Nunavut, NW Canada
**Kuhmo** 67 F3 E Finland
**Kuito** 128 C3 C Angola
**Kuji** 103 G3 C Japan
**Kula Kangri** 107 G2 ▲ Bhutan/China
**Kulob** 101 F4 SW Tajikistan
**Kulu** 97 C3 W Turkey
**Kulunda** 94 D5 S Russ. Fed.
**Kulunda Steppe** 94 D5 *Grassland,* Kazakhstan/Russ. Fed.
**Kuma** 87 B8 ≈ SW Russ. Fed.
**Kumamoto** 103 D7 SW Japan
**Kumanovo** 83 D3 N FYR Macedonia
**Kumasi** 124 D5 C Ghana
**Kumba** 124 F5 W Cameroon
**Kumertau** 87 D7 W Russ. Fed.
**Kumo** 124 F4 E Nigeria
**Kumon Range** 109 B1 ⛰ N Myanmar
**Kumul** *see* Hami
**Kunda** 67 F5 NE Estonia
**Kunduz** 101 F4 NE Afghanistan
**Kungsbacka** 67 B6 S Sweden
**Kungur** 87 D5 NW Russ. Fed.
**Kunlun Mountains** 105 B3 ⛰ NW China
**Kunming** 105 E5 SW China
**Kunsan** 103 B6 W South Korea
**Kununurra** 133 D2 W Australia
**Kuopio** 67 F4 C Finland
**Kupang** 109 F8 C Indonesia
**Kupiano** 137 C3 S PNG
**Kup"yans'k** 85 G4 E Ukraine
**Kura** 97 H2 ≈ SW Asia
**Kurashiki** 103 E6 SW Japan
**Kurdistan** 97 H4 *Cultural region,* SW Asia
**Kurdzhali** 83 F3 S Bulgaria
**Kure** 103 D7 SW Japan
**Küre Dağları** 97 D2 ⛰ N Turkey
**Kurile Islands** 94 I4 *Island group,* Russ. Fed.
**Kurile Trench** 15 *Undersea feature,* NW Pacific Ocean
**Kuril'sk** 94 I5 Kurile Islands, SE Russ. Fed.
**Kuril'skiye Ostrova** *see* Kurile Islands
**Kurnool** 107 D6 S India
**Kursk** 87 A6 W Russ. Fed.
**Kuruktag** 105 C3 ⛰ NW China
**Kurume** 103 D7 SW Japan
**Kushiro** 103 G2 NE Japan
**Kuskokwim Mountains** 54 D2 ⛰ Alaska, USA
**Kütahya** 97 B3 W Turkey
**K'ut'aisi** 97 G1 W Georgia
**Kutno** 81 E3 C Poland
**Kuujjuaq** 35 E2 Québec, E Canada
**Kuusamo** 67 F3 E Finland
**Kuwait** 99 D3 ● E Kuwait
**Kuwait** 99 C3 ◆ *Monarchy,* SW Asia
**Kuybyshev Reservoir** 87 B6 ⊟ W Russ. Fed.
**Kuytun** 105 C2 NW China
**Kuznetsk** 87 B6 W Russ. Fed.
**Kvaløya** 67 D1 *Island,* N Norway
**Kvarnbergsvattnet** 67 B3 ◎ N Sweden
**Kvarner** 83 B2 *Gulf,* W Croatia
**Kwangju** 103 B7 SW South Korea
**Kwango** 128 B3 ≈ Angola/Dem. Rep. Congo
**Kwekwe** 128 D5 C Zimbabwe
**Kwidzyn** 81 D2 N Poland
**Kwigillingok** 54 D2 Alaska, USA
**Kwilu** 128 C3 ≈ W Dem. Rep. Congo
**Kyabé** 124 H4 S Chad
**Kyaikkami** 109 B3 S Myanmar
**Kyakhta** 94 F5 S Russ. Fed.
**Kyjov** 81 D6 SE Czech Republic
**Kyklades** *see* Cyclades
**Kymi** 83 E5 C Greece
**Kyoga, Lake** 127 C5 ◎ C Uganda
**Kyoto** 103 E6 SW Japan
**Kyrenia** 88 C6 N Cyprus
**Kyrgyzstan** 101 G2 ◆ *Republic,* C Asia
**Kythira** 83 E6 *Island,* S Greece
**Kythnos** 83 E6 *Island,* Cyclades, Greece
**Kythrea** 88 D6 N Cyprus
**Kyushu** 103 A7 *Island,* SW Japan
**Kyustendil** 83 E3 W Bulgaria
**Kyyiv** *see* Kiev
**Kyzyl** 94 E5 C Russ. Fed.
**Kyzyl Kum** 101 E2 *Desert,* Kazakhstan/Uzbekistan
**Kyzylorda** 94 C5 S Kazakhstan
**Kyzyl-Suu** 101 I2 NE Kyrgyzstan

## L

**La Algaba** 75 C5 S Spain
**Laarne** 68 B6 NW Belgium
**Laâyoune** 122 A3 ● NW Western Sahara
**Labasa** 137 J5 N Fiji
**la Baule-Escoublac** 73 B3 NW France
**Labé** 124 B4 NW Guinea
**Laborec** 81 F6 ≈ E Slovakia
**Labrador** 35 F2 *Cultural region,* Newfoundland, SW Canada
**Labrador City** 35 F3 Newfoundland, E Canada
**Labrador Sea** 35 F2 *Sea,* NW Atlantic Ocean
**La Carolina** 75 D5 S Spain
**Laccadive Islands** 107 C7 *Island group,* India, N Indian Ocean
**La Ceiba** 59 D2 N Honduras
**La Chaux-de-Fonds** 77 A8 W Switzerland
**Lachlan River** 133 G5 ≈ NSW, SE Australia
**la Ciotat** 73 E7 SE France
**La Concepción** 59 F7 W Panama
**Laconia** 41 F3 New Hampshire, USA
**La Coruña** *see* A Coruña
**La Crosse** 44 B4 Wisconsin, USA
**La Cruz** 59 D5 NW Costa Rica
**Ladoga, Lake** 87 A4 ◎ NW Russ. Fed.
**Ladysmith** 44 B3 Wisconsin, USA
**Lae** 137 B2 W PNG
**La Esperanza** 59 C3 SW Honduras
**Lafayette** 44 C6 Indiana, USA
**Lafayette** 43 B6 Louisiana, USA
**Lafia** 124 F4 C Nigeria
**la Flèche** 73 C3 NW France
**Lagdo, Lac de** 124 F4 ◎ N Cameroon
**Laghouat** 122 D2 N Algeria
**Lagos** 124 E5 SW Nigeria
**Lagos** 75 A5 S Portugal
**Lagos de Moreno** 57 E4 SW Mexico
**Lagouira** 122 A4 SW Western Sahara
**La Grande** 53 C3 Oregon, USA
**La Grange** 43 E5 Georgia, USA
**Lagunas** 117 A3 N Chile
**Lagunillas** 117 B3 SE Bolivia
**La Habana** *see* Havana
**Lahat** 109 C7 Sumatra, W Indonesia
**Laholm** 67 C6 S Sweden
**Lahore** 107 D2 NE Pakistan
**Lahr** 77 B7 S Germany
**Lahti** 67 E5 S Finland
**Laï** 124 G4 S Chad
**La Junta** 51 G6 Colorado, USA
**Lake Charles** 43 B6 Louisiana, USA
**Lake Havasu City** 48 A2 Arizona, USA
**Lake Jackson** 48 H5 Texas, USA
**Lake King** 133 B5 W Australia
**Lakeland** 43 G7 Florida, USA
**Lake of the Woods** 35 A4 Minnesota, USA
**Lakeside** 53 D9 California, USA
**Lakeview** 53 C5 Oregon, USA
**Lakewood** 51 F5 Colorado, USA
**Lakonikós Kólpos** 83 E6 *Gulf,* S Greece
**Lakselv** 67 E1 N Norway
**Lakshadweep** *see* Laccadive Islands
**La Libertad** 59 B2 N Guatemala
**La Ligua** 117 A5 C Chile
**Lalín** 75 B2 NW Spain
**Lalitpur** 107 F3 C Nepal
**La Louvière** 68 C7 S Belgium
**La Maddalena** 79 B5 Sardinia, Italy
**Lamar** 51 G6 Colorado, USA
**La Marmora, Punta** 79 A6 ▲ Sardinia, Italy
**Lambaréné** 128 A2 W Gabon
**Lambert Glacier** 138 D4 *Glacier,* Antarctica
**Lamego** 75 B3 N Portugal
**Lamesa** 48 F3 Texas, USA
**Lamezia Terme** 79 E7 SE Italy
**Lamía** 83 E5 C Greece
**Lamiti** 137 J5 C Fiji
**Lamlam, Mount** 55 ▲ SW Guam
**Lamoni** 47 E5 Iowa, USA
**Lamy** 48 D2 New Mexico, USA
**Lana'i** 55 C2 *Island* Hawai'i, USA
**Lana'i City** 55 C2 Lana'i, Hawai'i, USA
**Lanbi Kyun** 109 A4 *Island,* Mergui Archipelago, S Myanmar
**Lancaster** 71 D6 NW England, UK
**Lancaster** 53 C8 California, USA
**Lancaster** 41 D5 Pennsylvania, USA
**Lancaster Sound** 33 H2 *Sound,* Nunavut, N Canada
**Landen** 68 D7 C Belgium
**Lander** 51 E4 Wyoming, USA
**Landerneau** 73 A2 NW France
**Landes** 73 B5 *Cultural region,* SW France Europe
**Land's End** 71 C8 *Headland,* SW England, UK
**Landshut** 77 D7 SE Germany
**Langar** 101 E3 C Uzbekistan
**Langres** 73 E3 N France
**Langsa** 109 B5 Sumatra, W Indonesia
**Languedoc** 73 D6 *Cultural region,* S France
**Länkäran** 97 J3 S Azerbaijan
**Lansing** 44 D5 Michigan, USA
**Lanta, Ko** 109 B5 *Island,* S Thailand
**Lanzhou** 105 E4 C China
**Laon** 73 E2 N France
**La Orchila, Isla** 61 I7 *Island,* N Venezuela
**Laos** 109 C3 ◆ *Republic,* SE Asia
**La Palma** 59 I6 SE Panama
**La Paz** 117 A2 ● W Bolivia
**La Paz** 57 C4 NW Mexico
**La Paz, Bahía de** 57 B3 *Bay,* W Mexico
**La Perouse Strait** 103 F1 *Strait,* Japan/Russ. Fed.
**Lápithos** 88 C6 NW Cyprus
**Lapland** 67 D2 *Cultural region,* N Europe
**La Plata** 117 C5 E Argentina
**Lappeenranta** 67 F5 SE Finland
**Lapta** *see* Lapithos
**Laptev Sea** 94 F2 *Sea,* Arctic Ocean
**Lapua** 67 E4 W Finland
**Łapy** 81 G3 E Poland
**La Quiaca** 117 B3 N Argentina
**L'Aquila** 79 D5 C Italy
**Laramie** 51 F4 Wyoming, USA
**Laramie Mountains** 51 F4 ⛰ Wyoming, USA
**Laredo** 75 D1 N Spain
**Laredo** 48 G6 Texas, USA
**Largo** 43 F7 Florida, USA
**Largo, Cayo** 61 B3 *Island,* W Cuba
**La Rioja** 117 B4 NW Argentina
**La Rioja** 75 E2 *Cultural region,* N Spain
**Lárisa** 83 E5 C Greece
**Larkana** 107 B3 SE Pakistan
**Larnaca** 88 D6 SE Cyprus
**Lárnaka** *see* Larnaca
**la Rochelle** 73 B4 W France
**la Roche-sur-Yon** 73 B4 NW France
**La Roda** 75 E4 C Spain
**La Romana** 61 G4 E Dominican Republic
**Las Cabezas de San Juan** 75 C5 S Spain
**Las Cruces** 48 D3 New Mexico, USA
**La See d'Urgel** 75 G2 NE Spain
**La Serena** 117 A5 C Chile
**la Seyne-sur-Mer** 73 E7 SE France
**Lashio** 109 B2 E Myanmar
**Lashkar Gah** 101 E6 S Afghanistan
**La Sila** 79 E7 ⛰ SW Italy
**La Sirena** 59 E4 E Nicaragua
**Łask** 81 E4 C Poland
**Las Lomitas** 117 C4 N Argentina
**La Solana** 75 D4 C Spain
**La Spezia** 79 B3 NW Italy
**Las Tablas** 59 G7 S Panama
**Las Tunas** 61 D3 Las Tunas, E Cuba
**Las Vegas** 51 B7 Nevada, USA
**Lata** 137 G3 Nendö, Solomon Islands
**Latacunga** 115 B3 C Ecuador
**la Teste** 73 B5 SW France
**Latina** 79 C5 C Italy
**La Tortuga, Isla** 61 I7 *Island,* N Venezuela
**La Tuque** 35 E5 Québec, SE Canada
**Latvia** 67 E6 ◆ *Republic,* NE Europe
**Lau Group** 137 K5 *Island group,* E Fiji
**Launceston** 133 G7 Tasmania, SE Australia
**La Unión** 59 D3 C Honduras
**La Unión** 75 F5 SE Spain
**Laurel** 41 D6 Delaware, USA
**Laurel** 43 C5 Mississippi, USA
**Laurel** 51 E3 Montana, USA
**Laurentian Mountains** 35 E4 *Plateau,* E Canada
**Lauria** 79 E6 S Italy
**Laurinburg** 43 G4 North Carolina, USA
**Lausanne** 77 A8 SW Switzerland
**Laut, Pulau** 109 E7 *Island,* C Indonesia
**Laval** 35 E5 Québec, SE Canada
**Laval** 73 C3 NW France
**Lavanggu** 137 F3 Rennell, S Solomon Islands
**La Vega** 61 F4 C Dominican Republic
**La Vila Joíosa** *see* Villajoyosa
**Lawrenceburg** 43 D3 Tennessee, USA
**Lawrence** 41 F4 Massachusetts, USA
**Lawton** 47 C8 Oklahoma, USA
**Layla** 99 C5 C Saudi Arabia
**Laytonville** 53 B6 California, USA
**Lazarev Sea** 138 B2 *Sea,* Antarctica
**Lázaro Cárdenas** 57 E5 SW Mexico
**Læsø** 67 B6 *Island,* N Denmark
**Leamington** 35 C6 Ontario, S Canada
**Lebak** 109 F5 Mindanao, S Philippines
**Lebanon** 47 F7 Missouri, USA
**Lebanon** 41 F3 New Hampshire, USA
**Lebanon** 53 B3 Oregon, USA
**Lebanon** 99 A2 ◆ *Republic,* SW Asia
**Lebap** 101 D2 NE Turkmenistan
**Lębork** 81 D1 NW Poland
**Lebrija** 75 C6 S Spain
**Lebu** 117 A6 C Chile
**le Cannet** 73 F6 SE France
**Lecce** 79 F6 SE Italy
**Lechainá** 83 D5 S Greece
**Leduc** 33 G6 Alberta, SW Canada
**Leech Lake** 47 E2 ◎ Minnesota, USA
**Leeds** 71 E6 N England, UK
**Leek** 68 E2 NE Netherlands
**Leer** 77 B3 NW Germany
**Leeuwarden** 68 E2 N Netherlands
**Leeward Islands** 61 K4 *Island group,* E West Indies
**Lefkáda** 83 D5 *Island,* Ionian Islands, Greece
**Lefká Óri** 83 E7 ⛰ Crete, Greece
**Legaspi** 109 F4 N Philippines
**Legnica** 81 C4 W Poland
**le Havre** 73 C2 N France
**Leicester** 71 E7 C England, UK
**Leiden** 68 C4 W Netherlands
**Leie** 68 B6 ≈ Belgium/France
**Leinster** 71 B6 *Cultural region,* E Ireland
**Leipzig** 77 D4 E Germany
**Leiria** 75 A4 C Portugal
**Leirvik** 67 A5 S Norway
**Lek** 68 D4 ≈ SW Netherlands
**Leksand** 67 C5 C Sweden
**Lelystad** 68 D3 C Netherlands
**le Mans** 73 C3 NW France
**Lemesós** *see* Limassol
**Lemhi Range** 51 C3 ⛰ Idaho, USA
**Lena** 94 G3 ≈ NE Russ. Fed.
**Leningradskaya** 138 D6 SW Russ. Fed.
**Leninogorsk** 94 D5 E Kazakhstan
**Lenti** 81 C8 SW Hungary
**Leoben** 77 E7 C Austria
**León** 57 E4 C Mexico
**León** 59 D4 NW Nicaragua
**León** 75 C2 NW Spain
**Leone** 55 W American Samoa
**Leonídio** 83 E6 S Greece
**Lepe** 75 B5 S Spain
**le Portel** 73 D1 N France
**le Puy** 73 D5 C France
**Léré** 124 G4 SW Chad
**Lérida** *see* Lleida
**Lerma** 75 D2 N Spain
**Léros** 83 G6 *Island,* Dodecanese, Greece
**Lerwick** 71 E1 NE Scotland, UK
**Lesbos** 83 F5 *Island,* E Greece
**Leshan** 105 E5 C China
**les Herbiers** 73 B4 NW France
**Leskovac** 83 D3 SE Serbia and Montenegro (Yugoslavia)
**Lesotho** 128 D6 ◆ *Monarchy,* S Africa
**les Sables-d'Olonne** 73 B4 NW France
**Lesser Antarctica** 138 B5 *Physical region,* Antarctica
**Lesser Antilles** 61 I5 *Island group,* E West Indies
**Lesser Caucasus** 97 G2 ⛰ SW Asia
**Lesser Sunda Islands** 109 F8 *Island group,* C Indonesia
**Leszno** 81 C4 W Poland
**Lethbridge** 33 G7 Alberta, SW Canada
**Leti, Kepulauan** 109 G8 *Island group,* E Indonesia
**Letsôk-aw Kyun** 109 A4 *Island,* Mergui Archipelago, S Myanmar
**Leuven** 68 C6 C Belgium
**Leuze-en-Hainaut** 68 B7 SW Belgium
**Levanger** 67 B4 C Norway
**Levelland** 48 F3 Texas, USA
**Leverkusen** 77 A5 W Germany
**Levice** 81 D7 SW Slovakia
**Levin** 135 D4 North Island, NZ
**Lewes** 41 D6 Delaware, USA
**Lewis, Isle of** 71 B3 *Island,* NW Scotland, UK
**Lewis Range** 51 C1 ⛰ Montana, USA
**Lewiston** 51 B2 Idaho, USA
**Lewiston** 41 F3 Maine, USA
**Lewistown** 51 D2 Montana, USA
**Lexington** 43 E2 Kentucky, USA
**Lexington** 47 C5 Nebraska, USA
**Leyte** 109 F4 *Island,* C Philippines
**Leżajsk** 81 F5 SE Poland
**Lhasa** 105 C4 W China
**Lhazê** 105 B4 W China
**L'Hospitalet de Llobregat** 75 G2 NE Spain
**Liancourt Rocks** 103 C5 *Island group,* Japan/South Korea
**Lianyungang** 105 G4 E China
**Liaoyuan** 105 G2 NE China
**Libby** 51 C1 Montana, USA
**Liberal** 47 B7 Kansas, USA
**Liberec** 81 B5 N Czech Republic
**Liberia** 59 D5 NW Costa Rica
**Liberia** 124 B5 ◆ *Republic,* W Africa
**Libourne** 73 C5 SW France
**Libreville** 128 A2 ● NW Gabon
**Libya** 122 F3 ◆ *Islamic state,* N Africa
**Libyan Desert** 122 H4 *Desert,* N Africa
**Lichtenfels** 77 C5 SE Germany
**Lichtenvoorde** 68 F4 E Netherlands
**Lichuan** 105 F4 C China
**Lida** 85 C2 W Belarus
**Lidköping** 67 C6 S Sweden
**Lidzbark Warmiński** 81 E2 N Poland
**Liechtenstein** 77 C8 ◆ *Principality,* C Europe
**Liège** 68 D7 E Belgium
**Lienz** 77 D8 W Austria
**Liepāja** 67 E6 W Latvia
**Liezen** 77 E7 C Austria
**Liffey** 71 B6 ≈ E Ireland
**Lifou** 137 G6 *Island,* Îles Loyauté, E New Caledonia
**Lighthouse Reef** 59 C1 *Reef,* E Belize
**Ligure, Appennino** 79 B2 ⛰ NW Italy
**Ligurian Sea** 79 A3 *Sea,* N Mediterranean Sea
**Lihir Group** 137 D1 *Island group,* NE PNG
**Lihu'e** 55 B1 Kaua'i, Hawai'i, USA
**Likasi** 128 D3 SE Dem. Rep. Congo
**Liknes** 67 A6 S Norway
**Lille** 73 D1 N France
**Lillehammer** 67 B5 S Norway
**Lillestrøm** 67 B5 S Norway
**Lilongwe** 128 E4 ● W Malawi
**Lima** 115 B5 ● W Peru
**Limanowa** 81 E5 S Poland
**Limassol** 88 C6 SW Cyprus
**Limerick** 71 B7 SW Ireland
**Límnos** 83 F4 *Island,* E Greece
**Limoges** 73 C4 C France
**Limón** 59 F6 E Costa Rica
**Limón** 59 D2 NE Honduras
**Limon** 51 F5 Colorado, USA
**Limousin** 73 C5 *Cultural region,* C France
**Limoux** 73 D7 S France
**Limpopo** 128 E5 ≈ S Africa
**Linares** 117 A6 C Chile
**Linares** 57 E3 NE Mexico
**Linares** 75 D5 S Spain
**Lincoln** 71 E6 E England, UK
**Lincoln** 41 G2 Maine, USA
**Lincoln** 47 D5 Nebraska, USA
**Lincoln Sea** 139 B4 *Sea,* Arctic Ocean
**Linden** 115 E2 E Guyana
**Lindi** 127 E7 SE Tanzania
**Líndos** 83 G6 Rhodes, Dodecanese, Greece
**Line Islands** 131 *Island group,* E Kiribati
**Lingen** 77 B3 NW Germany
**Lingga, Kepulauan** 109 C6 *Island group,* W Indonesia
**Linköping** 67 C6 S Sweden
**Linton** 47 C2 North Dakota, USA
**Linz** 77 E7 N Austria
**Lion, Golfe du** 73 D7 *Gulf,* S France
**Lipari** 79 D7 *Island,* Aeolian Islands, S Italy
**Lipetsk** 87 B6 W Russ. Fed.
**Lira** 127 C5 N Uganda
**Lisala** 128 C1 N Dem. Rep. Congo
**Lisboa** *see* Lisbon
**Lisbon** 75 A4 ● W Portugal
**Lisieux** 73 C2 N France
**Liski** 87 A6 W Russ. Fed.
**Lisse** 68 C4 W Netherlands
**Litang** 105 D5 C China
**Lithgow** 133 G6 NSW, SE Australia
**Lithuania** 67 E7 ◆ *Republic,* NE Europe
**Little Alföld** 81 D7 *Plain,* Hungary/Slovakia
**Little Andaman** 107 H5 *Island,* Andaman Islands, India
**Little Barrier Island** 135 D2 *Island,* N NZ
**Little Cayman** 61 C4 *Island,* E Cayman Islands
**Little Colorado River** 51 D7 ≈ Arizona, USA
**Little Falls** 47 E3 Minnesota, USA
**Littlefield** 48 F3 Texas, USA
**Little Inagua** 61 E3 *Island,* S Bahamas
**Little Minch, The** 71 B3 *Strait,* NW Scotland, UK
**Little Missouri River** 47 A3 ≈ NW USA




❖ Administrative region ◆ Country ● Country capital ◇ Dependent territory ○ Dependent territory capital ⛰ Mountain range ▲ Mountain ⚶ Volcano ≈ River ◎ Lake ⊟ Reservoir

◈ Administrative region ◆ Country ● Country capital ◇ Dependent territory ○ Dependent territory capital ▲ Mountain range ▲ Mountain ☒ Volcano ☾ River ☺ Lake ☐ Reservoir

# S

SUKAGAWA

Schwyz 77 B8 C Switzerland
Scilly, Isles of 71 C9 *Island group,* SW England, UK
Scioto River 44 E7 Ohio, USA
Scotia Sea 138 A2 *Sea,* SW Atlantic Ocean
Scotland 71 C4 *National region,* UK
Scott Base 138 C6 *NZ research station,* Antarctica
Scottsbluff 47 A5 Nebraska, USA
Scottsboro 43 E4 Alabama, USA
Scottsdale 48 B3 Arizona, USA
Scranton 41 D4 Pennsylvania, USA
Scutari, Lake 83 C3 Albania/Serbia and Montenegro (Yugoslavia)
Searcy 43 B3 Arkansas, USA
Seattle 53 B2 Washington, USA
Sébaco 59 D4 W Nicaragua
Sebastían Vizcaín, Bahía 57 A2 *Bay,* NW Mexico
Secunderabad 107 E5 C India
Sedan 73 E2 N France
Seddon 135 D5 South Island, NZ
Seddonville 135 C5 South Island, NZ
Sédhiou 124 B4 SW Senegal
Sedona 48 B2 Arizona, USA
Seesen 77 C4 C Germany
Segezha 87 B3 NW Russ. Fed.
Ségou 124 C3 C Mali
Segovia 75 D3 C Spain
Séguédine 124 G2 NE Niger
Seguin 48 G5 Texas, USA
Segura 75 E5 S Spain
Seinäjoki 67 E4 W Finland
Seine 73 D2 N France
Seine, Baie de la 73 C2 *Bay,* N France
Sekondi-Takoradi 124 D5 S Ghana
Selenga 105 E2 Mongolia/Russ. Fed.
Sélestat 73 F3 NE France
Selfoss 67 A1 SW Iceland
Sélibabi 124 B3 S Mauritania
Selma 53 C7 California, USA
Semarang 109 D8 Java, C Indonesia
Sembé 128 B1 NW Congo
Seminole 48 E3 Texas, USA
Seminole, Lake 43 E6 SE USA
Semipalatinsk 94 D5 E Kazakhstan
Semnān 99 E2 N Iran
Semois 68 D8 SE Belgium
Senachwine Lake 44 B6 Illinois, USA
Sendai 103 G4 C Japan
Sendai 103 D8 SW Japan
Sendai-wan 103 G4 *Bay,* E Japan
Senec 81 D7 W Slovakia
Senegal 124 A3 ◆ *Republic,* W Africa
Senegal 124 A3 W Africa
Seney Marsh 44 D2 *Wetland,* Michigan, USA
Senftenberg 77 E4 E Germany
Sênggê Zangbo 105 B4 W China
Senica 81 D6 W Slovakia
Senja 67 C1 *Island,* N Norway
Senkaku-shoto 103 A8 *Island group,* SW Japan
Senlis 73 D2 N France
Sennar 127 C3 C Sudan
Sens 73 D3 C France
Seoul 103 B6 ● NW South Korea
Sepik 137 A2 Indonesia/PNG
Sept-Îles 35 F4 Québec, SE Canada
Seraing 68 D7 E Belgium
Seram, Pulau 109 G7 *Island,* Maluku, E Indonesia
Serang 109 C7 Java, C Indonesia
Serasan, Selat 109 D6 *Strait,* Indonesia/Malaysia
Serbia 83 D2 *Republic,* Serbia and Montenegro (Yugoslavia)
Serbia and Montenegro (Yugoslavia) 83 C3 ◆ *Federal Republic,* SE Europe
Serdar 101 C3 W Turkmenistan
Serengeti Plain 127 C6 *Plain,* N Tanzania
Serenje 128 D4 E Zambia
Serhetabat 101 D4 S Turkmenistan
Sérifos 83 E6 *Island,* Cyclades, Greece
Serov 94 C4 C Russ. Fed.
Serowe 128 D5 SE Botswana
Serpukhov 87 A5 W Russ. Fed.
Sesto San Giovanni 79 B2 N Italy
Sète 73 D6 S France
Setesdal 67 B5 *Valley,* S Norway
Sétif 122 E1 N Algeria
Setté Cama 128 A2 SW Gabon
Setúbal 75 A4 W Portugal
Setúbal, Baía de 75 A5 *Bay,* W Portugal
Seul, Lac 35 A4 Ontario, S Canada
Sevan 97 H2 C Armenia
Sevan, Lake 97 H2 E Armenia
Sevastopol' 85 F7 S Ukraine
Severn 35 B3 Ontario, S Canada
Severn 71 D7 England/Wales, UK
Severnaya Zemlya 94 E2 *Island group,* N Russ. Fed.
Severnyy 87 E3 NW Russ. Fed.
Severodvinsk 87 C3 NW Russ. Fed.
Severomorsk 87 C2 NW Russ. Fed.
Sevier Lake 51 C6 Utah, USA
Sevilla *see* Seville
Seville 75 B5 S Spain
Seychelles 118 ◆ *Republic,* W Indian Ocean
Seydhisfjördhur 67 B1 E Iceland
Seýdi 101 E3 E Turkmenistan
Seymour 48 G3 Texas, USA
Sfântu Gheorghe 85 C6 C Romania
Sfax 122 F2 E Tunisia
's-Gravenhage *see* The Hague
's-Gravenzande 68 C4 W Netherlands
Shache 105 A3 NW China
Shackleton Ice Shelf 138 E5 *Ice shelf,* Antarctica
Shahany, Ozero 85 D6 SW Ukraine
Shahrak 101 E5 C Afghanistan
Shahr-e Kord 99 D2 C Iran
Shahrud 99 E1 N Iran
Shalkar 95 B5 W Kazakhstan
Shamrock 48 F2 Texas, USA
Shanghai 105 G4 E China
Shangrao 105 G5 S China
Shannon 71 B6 W Ireland
Shan Plateau 109 B2 *Plateau,* E Myanmar
Shantou 105 G5 S China
Shaoguan 105 F5 S China
Shar 94 D5 E Kazakhstan
Sharjah 99 E4 NE UAE
Shark Bay 133 A4 *Bay,* E Indian Ocean
Sharon 41 B4 Pennsylvania, USA
Shashe 128 D5 Botswana/Zimbabwe
Shasta Lake 53 B5 California, USA
Shawnee 47 D8 Oklahoma, USA
Shchëkino 87 A6 W Russ. Fed.
Shchors 85 E3 N Ukraine
Shchuchinsk 94 C5 N Kazakhstan
Shchuchyn 85 B2 W Belarus
Shebekino 87 A6 W Russ. Fed.
Shebeli 127 E4 Ethiopia/Somalia
Sheberghan 101 E4 N Afghanistan
Sheboygan 44 C4 Wisconsin, USA
Shebshi Mountains 124 F4 E Nigeria
Sheffield 71 E6 N England, UK
Shelby 51 D1 Montana, USA
Sheldon 47 D4 Iowa, USA
Shelekhov Gulf 94 H3 *Gulf,* E Russ. Fed.
Shendi 127 C2 NE Sudan
Shenyang 105 G2 NE China
Shepherd Islands 137 H5 *Island group,* C Vanuatu
Shepparton 133 F6 Victoria, SE Australia
Sherbrooke 35 E5 Québec, SE Canada
Shereik 127 C1 N Sudan
Sheridan 51 E3 Wyoming, USA
Sherman 48 H3 Texas, USA
's-Hertogenbosch 68 D5 S Netherlands
Shetland Islands 71 D1 *Island group,* NE Scotland, UK
Shevchenko *see* Aktau
Shibetsu 103 G1 NE Japan
Shibushi-wan 103 D8 *Bay,* SW Japan
Shihezi 105 C2 NW China
Shijiazhuang 105 F3 E China
Shikarpur 107 C3 S Pakistan
Shikoku 103 E7 *Island,* SW Japan
Shilabo 127 F4 SE Ethiopia
Shiliguri 107 G3 NE India
Shilka 94 G5 S Russ. Fed.
Shillong 107 G3 NE India
Shimbiris 127 F3 ▲ N Somalia
Shimoga 107 D6 W India
Shimonoseki 103 D7 Honshu, SW Japan
Shinano-gawa 103 F5 Honshi, C Japan
Shindand 101 D5 W Afghanistan
Shingu 103 F7 Honshu, SW Japan
Shinjo 103 G4 Honshu, C Japan
Shinyanga 127 C6 NW Tanzania
Shiprock 48 C1 New Mexico, USA
Shiraz 99 D3 S Iran
Shivpuri 107 D3 C India
Shizugawa 103 G4 NE Japan
Shizuoka 103 F6 Honshu, S Japan
Shkodër 83 D3 NW Albania
Shoshoni 51 E4 Wyoming, USA
Shostka 85 E3 NE Ukraine
Show Low 48 C2 Arizona, USA
Shreveport 43 A5 Louisiana, USA
Shrewsbury 71 D7 W England, UK
Shu 94 C6 SE Kazakhstan
Shumagin Islands 54 C3 *Island group* Alaska, USA
Shumen 83 F2 NE Bulgaria
Shuqrah 99 C7 SW Yemen
Shymkent 94 B6 S Kazakhstan
Sialum 137 B2 C PNG
Šiauliai 67 E7 N Lithuania
Sibay 87 D7 W Russ. Fed.
Siberia 94 E4 *Physical region,* Russ. Fed.
Siberut, Pulau 109 A6 *Island,* Kepulauan Mentawai, W Indonesia
Sibi 107 B2 SW Pakistan
Sibiti 128 B2 S Congo
Sibiu 85 B6 C Romania
Sibolga 109 B6 Sumatra, W Indonesia
Sibu 109 D6 East Malaysia
Sibut 124 H5 S CAR
Sibuyan Sea 109 F4 *Sea,* W Pacific Ocean
Sichon 109 B5 SW Thailand
Sichuan Pendi 105 E4 *Basin,* C China
Sicilia *see* Sicily
Sicily 79 C8 *Island,* Italy
Sicily, Strait of 79 B8 *Strait,* C Mediterranean Sea
Siderno 79 E8 SW Italy
Sîdi Barrâni 122 H2 NW Egypt
Sidi Bel Abbès 122 D1 NW Algeria
Sidley, Mount 138 B5 ▲ Antarctica
Sidney 51 F2 Montana, USA
Sidney 47 A5 Nebraska, USA
Sidney 44 E6 Ohio, USA
Siedlce 81 F3 E Poland
Siegen 77 B5 W Germany
Siemiatycze 81 G3 E Poland
Siena 79 C4 C Italy
Sieradz 81 D4 C Poland
Sierpc 81 E3 C Poland
Sierra Leone 124 A5 ◆ *Republic,* W Africa
Sierra Madre 59 A3 Guatemala/Mexico
Sierra Madre Occidental 57 C3 C Mexico
Sierra Madre Oriental 57 E4 C Mexico
Sierra Morena 88 B4 SW Spain, Europe
Sierra Nevada 75 D6 S Spain
Sierra Nevada 53 B6 W USA
Sierra Vieja 48 E4 Texas, USA
Sierra Vista 48 C4 Arizona, USA
Sífnos 83 E6 *Island,* Cyclades, Greece
Sigli 109 A5 Sumatra, W Indonesia, Asia
Siglufjördhur 67 A1 N Iceland
Signal Peak 48 A3 ▲ Arizona, USA
Signy 138 A3 *UK research station,* South Orkney Islands, Antarctica
Siguatepeque 59 C3 W Honduras
Siguiri 124 B4 NE Guinea
Siilinjärvi 67 F4 C Finland
Siirt 97 G4 SE Turkey
Sikasso 124 C4 S Mali
Sikeston 47 G7 Missouri, USA
Siklós 81 D9 SW Hungary
Silchar 107 H3 NE India
Silesia 81 D4 *Physical region,* SW Poland
Silicon Valley 53 B7 *Industrial and business region,* California, USA
Silifke 97 D5 S Turkey
Siling Co 105 C4 W China
Silisili 137 A4 ▲ C Samoa
Silistra 83 F2 NE Bulgaria
Šilutė 67 E7 W Lithuania
Silvan 97 F4 SE Turkey
Silverek 97 F4 SE Turkey
Simav 97 B3 W Turkey
Simav Çayı 97 A3 NW Turkey
Simcoe, Lake 41 B2 Ontario, S Canada
Simeto 79 D8 Sicily, Italy
Simeulue, Pulau 109 A6 *Island,* NW Indonesia
Simferopol' 85 F7 S Ukraine
Simpelveld 68 E6 SE Netherlands
Simplon Pass 77 B8 *Pass,* S Switzerland
Simpson Desert 133 E4 *Desert,* Northern Territory/S Australia
Sinai 122 J2 *Physical region,* NE Egypt
Sincelejo 115 B2 NW Colombia
Sinclair, Lake 43 E4 Georgia, USA
Sind 107 B3 *Cultural region,* SE Pakistan
Sindelfingen 77 B6 SW Germany
Sines 75 A5 S Portugal
Singapore 109 C6 ● SE Asia
Singapore 109 C6 ◆ *Republic,* SE Asia
Singen 77 B7 S Germany
Singida 127 D6 C Tanzania
Singkawang 109 D6 C Indonesia
Siniscola 79 B5 Sardinia, Italy
Sinmi-do 103 A5 *Island,* NW North Korea
Sinoie, Lacul 85 D7 *Lagoon,* SE Romania
Sinop 97 D2 N Turkey
Sinp'o 103 B4 E North Korea
Sinsheim 77 B6 SW Germany
Sint-Michielsgestel 68 D5 S Netherlands
Sint-Niklaas 68 C6 N Belgium
Sint-Pieters-Leeuw 68 B7 C Belgium
Sintra 75 A4 W Portugal
Sinuiju 103 A4 W North Korea
Sinujiif 127 F3 NE Somalia
Sion 77 A8 SW Switzerland
Sioux City 47 D4 Iowa, USA
Sioux Falls 47 D4 South Dakota, USA
Siping 105 G2 NE China
Siple, Mount 138 A5 ▲ Siple Island, Antarctica
Siquirres 59 F6 E Costa Rica
Siracusa 79 D8 Sicily, Italy
Sir Edward Pellew Group 133 E2 *Island group,* Northern Territory, NE Australia
Siret 85 C6 Romania/Ukraine
Sirikit Reservoir 109 B3 N Thailand
Sirjan 99 E3 S Iran
Şırnak 97 G4 SE Turkey
Sirte, Gulf of 122 G2 *Gulf,* N Libya
Sisimiut 139 A5 S Greenland
Sitges 75 G3 NE Spain
Sittang 109 A3 S Myanmar
Sittard 68 E6 SE Netherlands
Sittwe 109 A2 W Myanmar
Siuna 59 E3 NE Nicaragua
Sivas 97 E3 C Turkey
Sivers'kyy Donets' 85 F4 Russian Federation/Ukraine
Siwa 122 H3 NW Egypt
Six-Fours-les-Plages 73 E7 SE France
Siyäzän 97 J2 NE Azerbaijan
Sjælland 67 B7 *Island,* E Denmark
Skagerrak 67 B6 *Channel,* N Europe
Skagit River 53 B1 Washington, USA
Skalka 67 D2 N Sweden
Skegness 71 F6 E England, UK
Skellefteå 67 D3 N Sweden
Skellefteälven 67 D3 N Sweden
Ski 67 B5 S Norway
Skikda 122 E1 NE Algeria
Skopje 83 D3 ● N FYR Macedonia
Skovorodino 94 G5 SE Russ. Fed.
Skrīveri 67 E6 S Latvia
Skye, Isle of 71 B3 *Island,* NW Scotland, UK
Skýros 83 F5 *Island,* Vóreioi Sporádes, Greece
Slagelse 67 B7 E Denmark
Slatina 85 B7 S Romania
Slavonski Brod 83 C1 NE Croatia
Sławno 81 C2 NW Poland
Sliema 88 B6 N Malta
Sligo 71 B5 NW Ireland
Sliven 83 F3 E Bulgaria
Slovakia 81 E6 ◆ *Republic,* C Europe
Slovenia 77 E8 ◆ *Republic,* SE Europe
Slovenské rudohorie 81 E6 C Slovakia
Slov"yans'k 85 G4 E Ukraine
Słubice 81 B3 W Poland
Sluch 85 C4 NW Ukraine
Słupsk 81 D1 NW Poland
Slutsk 85 C3 S Belarus
Smallwood Reservoir 35 F3 Newfoundland, S Canada
Smara 122 B3 N Western Sahara
Smederevo 83 D2 N Serbia and Montenegro (Yugoslavia)
Smederevska Palanka 83 E2 C Serbia and Montenegro (Yugoslavia)
Smoky Hill River 51 H5 Kansas, USA
Smøla 67 B4 *Island,* W Norway
Smolensk 87 A5 W Russ. Fed.
Snake River 53 C2 NW USA
Snake River Plain 51 C4 *Plain,* Idaho, USA
Sneek 68 E2 N Netherlands
Sněžka 81 C5 ▲ N Czech Republic
Snina 81 F6 E Slovakia
Snowdon 71 C6 ▲ NW Wales, UK
Snyder 48 F3 Texas, USA
Sobradinho, Represa de 115 G5 E Brazil
Sochi 87 A8 SW Russ. Fed.
Society Islands 131 *Island group,* W French Polynesia
Socorro 48 D2 New Mexico, USA
Socorro, Isla 57 B5 *Island,* W Mexico
Socotra 99 D7 *Island,* SE Yemen
Socuéllamos 75 E4 C Spain
Sodankylä 67 E2 N Finland
Söderhamn 67 D5 C Sweden
Södertälje 67 D5 C Sweden
Sodiri 127 B2 C Sudan
Sofia 83 E3 ● W Bulgaria
Sofiya *see* Sofia
Sogamoso 115 C2 C Colombia
Sognefjorden 67 A5 *Fjord,* NE North Sea
Sohag 122 I3 C Egypt
Sokch'o 103 B5 N South Korea
Söke 97 A4 SW Turkey
Sokhumi 97 F1 NW Georgia
Sokodé 124 D4 C Togo
Sokol 87 B4 NW Russ. Fed.
Sokolov 81 A5 W Czech Republic
Sokone 124 A3 W Senegal
Sokoto 124 E4 NW Nigeria
Sokoto 124 E4 NW Nigeria
Solapur 107 D5 W India
Sol, Costa del 75 D6 *Coastal region,* S Spain
Solec Kujawski 81 D3 W Poland
Solikamsk 87 D5 NW Russ. Fed.
Sol'-Iletsk 87 D7 W Russ. Fed.
Solingen 77 A4 W Germany
Sollentuna 67 D5 C Sweden
Solomon Islands 137 F2 ◆ *Commonwealth Republic,* W Pacific Ocean
Solomon Sea 137 C2 *Sea,* W Pacific Ocean
Soltau 77 C3 NW Germany
Sol'tsy 87 A4 W Russ. Fed.
Solwezi 128 D4 NW Zambia
Soma 103 G4 C Japan
Somalia 127 F4 ◆ *Republic,* E Africa
Somaliland 127 F3 *Cultural region,* E Africa
Somali Plain 15 *Undersea feature,* W Indian Ocean
Sombrero 61 J4 *Island,* N Anguilla
Someren 68 E5 SE Netherlands
Somerset 43 E3 Kentucky, USA
Somerset Island 33 H2 *Island,* Queen Elizabeth Islands, Nunavut, NW Canada
Somerton 48 A3 Arizona, USA
Somme 73 D1 N France
Somotillo 59 D4 NW Nicaragua
Somoto 59 D4 NW Nicaragua
Songea 127 D7 S Tanzania
Songkhla 109 B5 SW Thailand
Sonora 48 F4 Texas, USA
Sonoran Desert 53 D9 *Desert,* Mexico/USA
Sonsonate 59 B4 W El Salvador
Sopot 81 D2 N Poland
Sopron 81 C7 NW Hungary
Sorgues 73 E6 SE France
Sorgun 97 D3 C Turkey
Soria 75 E2 N Spain
Sorong 109 G6 E Indonesia
Sørøya 67 D1 *Island,* N Norway
Sortavala 87 A3 NW Russ. Fed.
Sotkamo 67 F3 C Finland
Sŏul *see* Seoul
Soúrpi 83 E5 C Greece
Sousse 122 F1 NE Tunisia
South Africa 128 C7 ◆ *Republic,* S Africa
South America 117 *Continent*
Southampton 71 E8 S England, UK
Southampton Island 33 I4 *Island,* Nunavut, NE Canada
South Andaman 107 H5 *Island,* Andaman Islands, India
South Australia 133 D4 *State,* S Australia
South Bend 44 D5 Indiana, USA
South Bruny Island 133 G7 *Island,* Tasmania, SE Australia
South Carolina 43 F4 *State,* SE USA
South China Sea 109 E3 *Sea,* SE Asia
South Dakota 47 B3 *State,* N USA
Southeast Indian Ridge 15 *Undersea feature,* Indian Ocean/Pacific Ocean
South East Point 133 F7 *Headland,* Victoria, S Australia
Southend-on-Sea 71 F7 E England, UK
Southern Alps 135 B6 South Island, NZ
Southern Cook Islands 131 *Island group,* S Cook Islands
Southern Cross 133 B5 W Australia
Southern Indian Lake 33 H5 Manitoba, C Canada
Southern Ocean 14 *Ocean,* Atlantic Ocean/Indian Ocean/Pacific Ocean
South Geomagnetic Pole 138 C5 *Pole,* Antarctica
South Georgia 138 A2 *Island,* South Georgia and the South Sandwich Islands, SW Atlantic Ocean
South Goulburn Island 133 E1 *Island,* Northern Territory, N Australia
South Indian Basin 15 *Undersea basin,* S Indian Ocean
South Island 135 C6 *Island,* S NZ
South Korea 103 A6 ◆ *Republic,* E Asia
South Lake Tahoe 53 C6 California, USA
South Orkney Islands 138 A3 *Island group,* Antarctica
South Platte River 51 G5 C USA
South Pole 138 C5 *Pole,* Antarctica
South Sandwich Islands 138 A2 *Island group,* SE South Georgia and South Sandwich Islands
South Sandwich Trench 138 B2 *Undersea feature,* SW Atlantic Ocean
South Shetland Islands 138 A3 *Island group,* Antarctica
South Shields 71 E5 NE England, UK
South Sioux City 47 D4 Nebraska, USA
South Taranaki Bight 135 C4 *Bight,* SE Tasman Sea
South Uist 71 B3 *Island,* NW Scotland, UK
South West Cape 135 A8 *Headland,* Stewart Island, NZ
Southwest Indian Ridge 15 *Undersea feature,* SW Indian Ocean
Southwest Pacific Basin 14 *Undersea feature,* SE Pacific Ocean
Soweto 128 D6 NE South Africa
Spain 75 C3 ◆ *Monarchy,* SW Europe
Spanish Town 61 D4 C Jamaica
Sparks 51 A5 Nevada, USA
Spartanburg 43 F4 South Carolina, USA
Spárti 83 E6 S Greece
Spearfish 47 A3 South Dakota, USA
Spencer 47 E4 Iowa, USA
Spencer Gulf 133 E6 *Gulf,* S Australia
Spey 71 D3 NE Scotland, UK
Spijkenisse 68 C4 SW Netherlands
Spin Buldak 101 E6 S Afghanistan
Spitsbergen 139 C5 *Island,* NW Svalbard
Split 83 B2 S Croatia
Spokane 53 D2 Washington, USA
Spratly Islands 109 D4 *Disputed* ◇ SE Asia
Spree 77 E4 E Germany
Spring City 51 D5 Utah, USA
Springer 48 E1 New Mexico, USA
Springfield 51 G6 Colorado, USA
Springfield 44 B6 Illinois, USA
Springfield 41 E4 Massachusetts, USA
Springfield 47 E7 Missouri, USA
Springfield 44 E6 Ohio, USA
Springfield 53 B4 Oregon, USA
Spring Hill 43 F7 Florida, USA
Springs Junction 135 C5 South Island, NZ
Springsure 133 G4 Queensland, E Australia
Springville 51 D5 Utah, USA
Spruce Knob 43 G2 ▲ West Virginia, USA
Sri Aman 109 D6 East Malaysia
Sri Jayawardanapura 107 E8 W Sri Lanka
Srikakulam 107 F5 E India
Sri Lanka 107 B8 ◆ *Republic,* S Asia
Srinagar 107 D1 N India
Srpska, Republika 83 C2 *Republic,* Bosnia and Herzegovina
Stabroek 68 C5 N Belgium
Stade 77 C3 NW Germany
Stadskanaal 68 F2 NE Netherlands
Stafford 71 E7 C England, UK
Stakhanov 85 G4 E Ukraine
Stalingrad *see* Volgograd
Stalowa Wola 81 F5 SE Poland
Stamford 41 E5 Connecticut, USA
Stanley 117 C9 ○ Falkland Islands
Stanthorpe 133 H5 Queensland, E Australia
Staphorst 68 E3 E Netherlands
Starachowice 81 F4 SE Poland
Stara Zagora 83 F3 C Bulgaria
Starbuck Island 131 *Island,* E Kiribati
Stargard Szczeciński 81 B2 NW Poland
Starkville 43 D4 Mississippi, USA
Starobil's'k 85 G4 E Ukraine
Starogard Gdański 81 D2 N Poland
Starominskaya 87 A7 SW Russ. Fed.
Staryy Oskol 87 A6 W Russ. Fed.
State College 41 C5 Pennsylvania, USA
Statesboro 43 G5 Georgia, USA
Staunton 43 G2 Virginia, USA
Stavanger 67 A5 S Norway
Stavropol' 87 A8 SW Russ. Fed.
Steamboat Springs 51 E5 Colorado, USA
Steenwijk 68 E3 N Netherlands
Steinkjer 67 C4 C Norway
Stendal 77 D3 C Germany
Stephenville 48 G3 Texas, USA
Steps Point 55 *Headland* W American Samoa
Sterling 51 G5 Colorado, USA
Sterling 44 B5 Illinois, USA
Sterlitamak 87 D6 W Russ. Fed.
Steubenville 44 F6 Ohio, USA
Stevenage 71 E7 E England, UK
Stevens Point 44 B3 Wisconsin, USA
Stewart Island 135 A8 *Island,* S NZ
Steyr 77 E7 N Austria
Stillwater 47 D7 Oklahoma, USA
Stirling 71 D4 C Scotland, UK
Stjørdalshalsen 67 B4 C Norway
Stockach 77 B7 S Germany
Stockdale 48 G5 Texas, USA
Stockholm 67 D5 ● C Sweden
Stockton 53 B7 California, USA
Stockton Plateau 48 E4 *Plain,* Texas, USA
Stoke-on-Trent 71 D6 C England, UK
Støren 67 B4 S Norway
Stornoway 71 C3 NW Scotland, UK
Storsjön 67 C4 C Sweden
Storuman 67 D3 N Sweden
Storuman 67 C3 N Sweden
Strabane 71 B5 W Northern Ireland, UK
Strakonice 81 B6 SW Czech Republic
Stralsund 77 D2 NE Germany
Stranraer 71 C5 S Scotland, UK
Strasbourg 73 F3 NE France
Stratford 135 D4 North Island, NZ
Stratford 48 F1 Texas, USA
Straubing 77 D6 SE Germany
Strehaia 85 B7 SW Romania
Strelka 94 E4 C Russ. Fed.
Strickland 137 A2 SW PNG
Stromboli 79 D7 ▲ Isola Stromboli, SW Italy
Stromeferry 71 C3 N Scotland, UK
Strömstad 67 B6 S Sweden
Strömsund 67 C4 C Sweden
Strymónas 83 E4 Bulgaria/Greece
Stryy 85 B5 NW Ukraine
Studholme 135 B7 South Island, NZ
Sturgis 47 A3 South Dakota, USA
Stuttgart 77 B6 SW Germany
Stykkishólmur 67 A1 W Iceland
Styr 85 C4 Belarus/Ukraine
Suakin 127 D1 NE Sudan
Subotica 83 D1 N Serbia and Montenegro (Yugoslavia)
Suceava 85 C5 NE Romania
Suckling, Mount 137 C3 ▲ S PNG
Sucre 117 B3 ● S Bolivia
Sudan 127 B3 ◆ *Republic,* N Africa
Sudbury 35 C5 Ontario, S Canada
Sudd 127 B4 *Swamp region,* S Sudan
Sudeten 81 C5 Czech Republic/Poland
Sue 127 B4 S Sudan
Sueca 75 F4 E Spain
Suez 122 I2 NE Egypt
Suez Canal 122 I2 *Canal,* NE Egypt
Suez, Gulf of 88 J6 *Gulf,* NE Egypt
Suğla Gölü 97 B4 SW Turkey
Suhar 99 E4 N Oman
Sühbaatar 105 E1 N Mongolia
Suhl 77 C5 C Germany
Sujawal 107 B3 SE Pakistan
Sukabumi 109 C8 Java, C Indonesia
Sukagawa 103 G5 C Japan

CAR Central African Republic FYR Former Yugoslavian Rebublic NSW New South Wales NZ New Zealand PNG Papua New Guinea Russ. Fed. Russian Federation UAE United Arab Emirates UK United Kingdom USA United States of America 157

◆ *Administrative region* ◆ *Country* ● *Country capital* ◇ *Dependent territory* ○ *Dependent territory capital* ▲ *Mountain range* ▲ *Mountain* ☒ *Volcano* ∿ *River* ⊚ *Lake* ⊠ *Reservoir*

## NORTH AMERICA

CANADA · UNITED STATES OF AMERICA · MEXICO · BELIZE · COSTA RICA · EL SALVADOR · GUATEMALA · HONDURAS

GRENADA · HAITI · JAMAICA · ST KITTS & NEVIS · ST LUCIA · ST VINCENT & THE GRENADINES · TRINIDAD & TOBAGO

## SOUTH AMERICA

COLOMBIA

URUGUAY · CHILE · PARAGUAY

## AFRICA

ALGERIA · EGYPT · LIBYA · MOROCCO · TUNISIA

LIBERIA · MALI · MAURITANIA · NIGER · NIGERIA · SENEGAL · SIERRA LEONE · TOGO

BURUNDI · DJIBOUTI · ERITREA · ETHIOPIA · KENYA · RWANDA · SOMALIA · SUDAN

SOUTH AFRICA · SWAZILAND · ZAMBIA · ZIMBABWE

## EUROPE

DENMARK · FINLAND · ICELAND · NORWAY

MONACO · ANDORRA · PORTUGAL · SPAIN · ITALY · SAN MARINO · VATICAN CITY · AUSTRIA

BOSNIA & HERZEGOVINA · CROATIA · MACEDONIA · SERBIA & MONTENEGRO (YUGOSLAVIA) · BULGARIA · GREECE · MOLDOVA · ROMANIA

## ASIA

ARMENIA · AZERBAIJAN · GEORGIA · TURKEY · IRAQ · ISRAEL · JORDAN · LEBANON

IRAN · KAZAKHSTAN · KYRGYZSTAN · TAJIKISTAN · TURKMENISTAN · UZBEKISTAN · AFGHANISTAN · PAKISTAN

TAIWAN · JAPAN · BRUNEI · INDONESIA · EAST TIMOR · MALAYSIA · SINGAPORE · MYANMAR

## AUSTRALASIA & OCEANIA

MAURITIUS · SEYCHELLES · AUSTRALIA · NEW ZEALAND · PAPUA NEW GUINEA · SOLOMON ISLANDS · MARSHALL ISLANDS · MICRONESIA